José Saramago
History, Utopia, and the Necessity of Error

LEGENDA

LEGENDA is the Modern Humanities Research Association's book imprint for new research in the Humanities. Founded in 1995 by Malcolm Bowie and others within the University of Oxford, Legenda has always been a collaborative publishing enterprise, directly governed by scholars. The Modern Humanities Research Association (MHRA) joined this collaboration in 1998, became half-owner in 2004, in partnership with Maney Publishing and then Routledge, and has since 2016 been sole owner. Titles range from medieval texts to contemporary cinema and form a widely comparative view of the modern humanities, including works on Arabic, Catalan, English, French, German, Greek, Italian, Portuguese, Russian, Spanish, and Yiddish literature. Editorial boards and committees of more than 60 leading academic specialists work in collaboration with bodies such as the Society for French Studies, the British Comparative Literature Association and the Association of Hispanists of Great Britain & Ireland.

The MHRA encourages and promotes advanced study and research in the field of the modern humanities, especially modern European languages and literature, including English, and also cinema. It aims to break down the barriers between scholars working in different disciplines and to maintain the unity of humanistic scholarship. The Association fulfils this purpose through the publication of journals, bibliographies, monographs, critical editions, and the MHRA Style Guide, and by making grants in support of research. Membership is open to all who work in the Humanities, whether independent or in a University post, and the participation of younger colleagues entering the field is especially welcomed.

ALSO PUBLISHED BY THE ASSOCIATION

Critical Texts
Tudor and Stuart Translations • *New Translations* • *European Translations*
MHRA Library of Medieval Welsh Literature

MHRA Bibliographies
Publications of the Modern Humanities Research Association

The Annual Bibliography of English Language & Literature
Austrian Studies
Modern Language Review
Portuguese Studies
The Slavonic and East European Review
Working Papers in the Humanities
The Yearbook of English Studies

www.mhra.org.uk
www.legendabooks.com

STUDIES IN HISPANIC AND LUSOPHONE CULTURES

Studies in Hispanic and Lusophone Cultures are selected and edited by the Association of Hispanists of Great Britain & Ireland. The series seeks to publish the best new research in all areas of the literature, thought, history, culture, film, and languages of Spain, Spanish America, and the Portuguese-speaking world.

The Association of Hispanists of Great Britain & Ireland is a professional association which represents a very diverse discipline, in terms of both geographical coverage and objects of study. Its website showcases new work by members, and publicises jobs, conferences and grants in the field.

Editorial Committee
Chair: Professor Trevor Dadson (Queen Mary, University of London)
Professor Catherine Davies (University of Nottingham)
Professor Andrew Ginger (University of Bristol)
Professor Hilary Owen (University of Manchester)
Professor Christopher Perriam (University of Manchester)
Professor Alison Sinclair (Clare College, Cambridge)
Professor Philip Swanson (University of Sheffield)

Managing Editor
Dr Graham Nelson
41 Wellington Square, Oxford OX1 2JF, UK

www.legendabooks.com/series/shlc

STUDIES IN HISPANIC AND LUSOPHONE CULTURES

1. *Unamuno's Theory of the Novel*, by C. A. Longhurst
2. *Pessoa's Geometry of the Abyss: Modernity and the Book of Disquiet*, by Paulo de Medeiros
3. *Artifice and Invention in the Spanish Golden Age*, edited by Stephen Boyd and Terence O'Reilly
4. *The Latin American Short Story at its Limits: Fragmentation, Hybridity and Intermediality*, by Lucy Bell
5. *Spanish New York Narratives 1898–1936: Modernisation, Otherness and Nation*, by David Miranda-Barreiro
6. *The Art of Ana Clavel: Ghosts, Urinals, Dolls, Shadows and Outlaw Desires*, by Jane Elizabeth Lavery
7. *Alejo Carpentier and the Musical Text*, by Katia Chornik
8. *Britain, Spain and the Treaty of Utrecht 1713-2013*, edited by Trevor J. Dadson and J. H. Elliott
9. *Books and Periodicals in Brazil 1768-1930: A Transatlantic Perspective*, edited by Ana Cláudia Suriani da Silva and Sandra Guardini Vasconcelos
10. *Lisbon Revisited: Urban Masculinities in Twentieth-Century Portuguese Fiction*, by Rhian Atkin
11. *Urban Space, Identity and Postmodernity in 1980s Spain: Rethinking the Movida*, by Maite Usoz de la Fuente
12. *Santería, Vodou and Resistance in Caribbean Literature: Daughters of the Spirits*, by Paul Humphrey
13. *Reprojecting the City: Urban Space and Dissident Sexualities in Recent Latin American Cinema*, by Benedict Hoff
14. *Rethinking Juan Rulfo's Creative World: Prose, Photography, Film*, edited by Dylan Brennan and Nuala Finnegan
15. *The Last Days of Humanism: A Reappraisal of Quevedo's Thought*, by Alfonso Rey
16. *Catalan Narrative 1875-2015*, edited by Jordi Larios and Montserrat Lunati
17. *Islamic Culture in Spain to 1614: Essays and Studies*, by L. P. Harvey
18. *Film Festivals: Cinema and Cultural Exchange*, by Mar Diestro-Dópido
19. *St Teresa of Avila: Her Writings and Life*, edited by Terence O'Reilly, Colin Thompson and Lesley Twomey
20. *(Un)veiling Bodies: A Trajectory of Chilean Post-Dictatorship Documentary*, by Elizabeth Ramírez Soto

José Saramago

History, Utopia, and the Necessity of Error

❖

Mark Sabine

LEGENDA

Studies in Hispanic and Lusophone Culture 23
Modern Humanities Research Association
2016

Published by Legenda
an imprint of the Modern Humanities Research Association
Salisbury House, Station Road, Cambridge CB1 2LA

ISBN 978-1-78188-453-9 (HB)
ISBN 978-1-78188-454-6 (PB)

First published 2016

All rights reserved. No part of this publication may be reproduced or disseminated or transmitted in any form or by any means, electronic, mechanical, photocopying, recording or otherwise, or stored in any retrieval system, or otherwise used in any manner whatsoever without written permission of the copyright owner, except in accordance with the provisions of the Copyright, Designs and Patents Act 1988, or under the terms of a licence permitting restricted copying issued in the UK by the Copyright Licensing Agency Ltd, Saffron House, 6–10 Kirby Street, London EC1N 8TS, England, or in the USA by the Copyright Clearance Center, 222 Rosewood Drive, Danvers MA 01923. Application for the written permission of the copyright owner to reproduce any part of this publication must be made by email to legenda@mhra.org.uk.

Disclaimer: Statements of fact and opinion contained in this book are those of the author and not of the editors or the Modern Humanities Research Association. The publisher makes no representation, express or implied, in respect of the accuracy of the material in this book and cannot accept any legal responsibility or liability for any errors or omissions that may be made.

Trademark notice: Product or corporate names may be trademarks or registered trademarks, and are used only for identification and explanation without intent to infringe.

© Modern Humanities Research Association 2016

Copy-Editor: Richard Correll

CONTENTS

	Acknowledgements	ix
	Notes on the Text	xi
	Introduction	1
1	Levantado do Chão	29
2	Memorial do Convento	71
3	O Ano da Morte de Ricardo Reis	118
4	A Jangada de Pedra	160
5	História do Cerco de Lisboa	205
	Afterword	243
	Bibliography	251
	Index	271

Untuk Arnab, daripada Beruang.
Terima kasih kerana menunggu.

ACKNOWLEDGEMENTS

First of all, I gratefully acknowledge the support provided to me by the UK Arts and Humanities Research Council, and by the School of Cultures, Languages, and Area Studies at the University of Nottingham, for my work on this volume. Without their generous support and the periods of research leave that it funded, it would not have been possible to bring this project to completion.

On a personal level, my most heartfelt thanks are due first of all to my colleagues in the Department of Spanish, Portuguese, and Latin American Studies at Nottingham. In the increasingly impersonal and authoritarian world of neo-liberalized higher education, their loyalty, generosity, and commitment to the highest critical and moral standards are themselves a worthy subject for a novel by Saramago. I am particularly indebted to Rui Gonçalves Miranda, for his brilliant review of several draft chapters, and to the insight and expert advice offered by Alexandra Campos, Jeremy Lawrance, Bernard McGuirk, Stephen Roberts, and Alvaro Vidal Bouzón.

I am also deeply grateful to my colleagues at the University of Nottingham Malaysia Campus, in particular to Tessa J. Houghton, Sumit Mandal, Sergio Camacho, and to Sean Matthews and his family, who provided me with encouragement, practical support, and a comfortable space for uninterrupted study during several extended academic visits. Terima kasih sekali lagi, kawan-kawanku.

I would also like to extend similar thanks to colleagues at the Universities of Bristol, Cambridge, Harvard, Leeds, and Minho, for so generously hosting me at their institutions to present working versions of this material, and, likewise, to the Associação Brasileira de Professores de Literatura Portuguesa for the honour of inviting me to their biennial congresses in 2013 and 2015, as a plenary speaker on Saramago.

A particular satisfaction of studying Saramago's writing is that it has afforded me the inspirational company, and, often, the treasured friendship, of so many brilliant, generous, and supportive scholars of his work. Amongst many friends in the community of Saramago studies, I am indebted most of all to David Frier, Anna M. Klobucka, Adriana Martins, Paulo de Medeiros, and especially Rhian Atkin, not only for the singular insights of their ground-breaking studies of Saramago's work, but also for helping me tease viable arguments out of inchoate impressions, in discussions over endless coffees and glasses of *bagaço* in cafés from Lisbon to Leeds, Dublin, Kraków, and beyond. I am also deeply grateful to Richard Zenith and to Margaret Jull Costa for dispensing advice on translating the texts of Fernando Pessoa and Saramago respectively, in a similarly generous, selfless, and companionable spirit. Especial thanks are owed to Hilary Owen, who has provided unstinting encouragement, brilliant critical insight, and good counsel ever since her supervision of my earliest doctoral work nearly two decades ago. In guiding my early research efforts, she followed in the footsteps of her late colleagues, Giovanni Pontiero and R. Clive Willis. These two irreplaceable scholars guided my first efforts in interpreting Saramago's work, and engineered my first, star-struck, encounters with the writer himself, who with genuine kindness supplied good-humoured yet cryptic answers to my sometimes clumsy questions. I am eternally grateful to all three of them for the privilege of their inspiring teaching, and for the treasured memories of our discussions.

Especial thanks are also due to Richard Correll and Graham Nelson at Legenda, for their consummate professionalism and patience, and for their expert and painstakingly thorough editing and typesetting of the text.

Parts of this study have had such a lengthy gestation that attempting to list all of the friends, family, and colleagues who provided encouragement and practical help would turn this acknowledgment note into a mini autobiography. I would, however, like to single out the invariably supportive and patient role played by my parents, John and Jenny Sabine, and by the long-suffering and heroically equanimous Arfizan Arshad, in helping me see this study to completion.

M.S., Nottingham, March 2016

NOTES ON THE TEXT

The following abbreviated titles are used in references to Saramago's novels:

Manual	=	*Manual de Pintura e Caligrafia*
Levantado	=	*Levantado do Chão*
Memorial	=	*Memorial do Convento*
Ricardo Reis	=	*O Ano da Morte de Ricardo Reis*
Jangada	=	*A Jangada de Pedra*
História	=	*História do Cerco de Lisboa*
Cegueira	=	*Ensaio sobre a Cegueira*

All translations into English, unless otherwise indicated, are my own. In order to expedite a focus on certain textual nuances and literary borrowings, this includes my own translation of quoted passages from Saramago's work. I am, however, greatly indebted to the much-acclaimed published translations by Giovanni Pontiero and Margaret Jull Costa, which I have consulted for their suggestions of elegant solutions to numerous problems of rendering Saramago's prose in English.

Passages of this study revise and expand upon material originally presented in the items listed in the Bibliography as Sabine (2001a), (2001b), (2002), (2006), (2011), and (2012), and Sabine and Martins (2006).

INTRODUCTION

Widely acclaimed today as one of the late twentieth century's most distinguished novelists and as a deserving winner of the 1998 Nobel Prize for Literature, José Saramago is a literary superstar for whom recognition came late, but swiftly reached global dimensions. Having published steadily and to modest critical praise since the mid 1960s, it was in 1980, and aged 57, that Saramago received rave reviews, and the City of Lisbon literary prize, for his novel *Levantado do Chão* [*Raised from the Ground*], a saga of agricultural labour, politics, and family life on the *latifundia* of Portugal's Alentejo province. This was followed two years later by the runaway critical and commercial success of the satirical eighteenth-century fable *Memorial do Convento* [*Baltasar and Blimunda*], whose sales — over 400,000 by 2004 — broke Portuguese records for a literary novel.[1] The appearance of a further three novels focusing on Portuguese history — *O Ano da Morte de Ricardo Reis* [*The Year of the Death of Ricardo Reis*] (1984), *A Jangada de Pedra* [*The Stone Raft*] (1986) and *História do Cerco de Lisboa* [*History of the Siege of Lisbon*] (1989) — confirmed Saramago's achievement of a new stylistic maturity, and the emergence of a corpus of texts that would establish him as a key contributor to debates about literary representation, historiography, cultural identity, subjectivity, popular protest, and initiatives for radical social and economic reform, all themes that remain global preoccupations in the early twenty-first century. Between them, these five novels would win nine major awards, and be translated into more than thirty languages, while collectively running into 120 editions in Portugal by 2014.[2]

Subsequently, Saramago's fame spread worldwide. Even an English-speaking world ever less attentive to literature in translation has concurred with the Swedish Academy's endorsement: no less powerful a critical guru than Harold Bloom proclaimed Saramago in 2002 to be 'the most impressive living novelist', and successful feature film adaptations have been made of three of his novels.[3] Critical attention to Saramago's texts in English, however, has focused predominantly on his more explicitly allegorical novels of the late 1990s and early 2000s, and, in particular, on *Ensaio sobre a Cegueira* [*Blindness*] (1995). This focus could be explained by the sparer prose and pared-down cultural references that make these later fictions more amenable to translation, and more universally accessible to a diverse readership. This study, however, aims to prove that the preceding 'historical' novels — all now available in acclaimed translations — have at least as much to offer to the non-Portuguese-speaking reader. It attempts this through closely linked readings that, while illuminating the Portuguese cultural and historical contexts of the five 1980s novels, also explore intertextual resonances of, or explicit references to, a wide range of literary, philosophical, and theoretical texts that articulate many of the preoccupations of the postmodern era. The volume aims thus to develop a creative dialogue between the potential insights that Saramago's historical novels offer into their original context — that of a national 'imagined community' struggling, in the aftermath of dictatorship, for stability and a workable consensus about identity, values, and political priorities — and those that they offer, as major components of Saramago's overall literary project, to a present-day readership facing comparably destabilizing challenges to principles of social justice and national sovereignty, and to the accountability of increasingly vast and globalized corporations.[4]

Saramago's use of 'national history' as a basis for literary and philosophical creativity means that this dialogue must commence by addressing both the ethical and epistemological questions raised by any representation of the past, and the methodology and purpose of historical enquiry in a world that has grown wary of the claims made for empiricism. Many of the first critical studies of Saramago's fiction — notably those of Carlos Reis and Teresa Cristina Cerdeira da Silva — focus on how such questions underpin Saramago's intervention in a process of national redefinition and repositioning in post-dictatorship Portugal, and of (often painful) rediscovery of the national past. The discussion initiated by Maurice Halbwachs's *On Collective Memory* (1952), and subsequently guided by, amongst others, Pierre Nora, Benedict Anderson, and David Lowenthal, has examined how collective memory, as a prerequisite of communal or national identity, is perpetually reconstructed in accordance with preoccupations of the present time, thereby steering belief in what is desirable or permissible for the future.[5] Long before such studies appeared, the *Estado Novo* had invested heavily in this idea; its educational and cultural policies focused with ruthless single-mindedness on inculcating recognition of Portugal's Catholic traditions, its conservative rural customs, and its imperial legacy. The regime's sudden overthrow on 25 April 1974, and the spectacular emergence of radical left parties in the ensuing 'Revolution of the Carnations', turned historical memory into an arena of fierce political contention. These events were, of course, contemporaneous with the appearance of seminal works by, amongst others, Jean-François Lyotard, Jacques Le Goff, and Hayden White that established the idea of a 'postmodern' era that had overcome credulity in both positivist and messianic 'metanarratives'.[6] However, political upheaval, whether in Portugal or elsewhere, did not presage any widespread defeat of the false consciousness of the past as being something that historiography could apprehend objectively and encapsulate in a single, integrated narrative. To date, outside the doors of academe, most discussion of politics and ethics remains predicated on the pursuit and expectation of demonstrable truth. The warnings of post-structuralists, and the cautious methodologies of both 'nouvelle histoire' and 'new historicism', have not yet reformed the historical generalizations and oversights of a globalized mass-media news industry. Jean Baudrillard and his followers have celebrated the potential of modern communications technology to condition societies to live ever more distanced from the historical 'real', and more absorbed in a constantly updated 'present', a temporal concept whose validity Saramago forcefully refuted.[7] Yet even in the most 'modernized' and media-savvy societies, the values or agendas of that 'present' are often affirmed by piecemeal and reductive appeals to communal historical experience or 'heritage'. A brief review of the output of political leaders or current affairs broadcasters at the time of the 2003 invasion of Iraq, or of the 1990s wars in the former Yugoslavia, confirms how, at worst, historical grand narratives are still regularly co-opted to legitimize authoritarianism, neo-imperialism, and genocide. The projection of the discussion of the uses of history beyond academe and beyond the domain of the professional historian therefore remains a political and ethical imperative. Saramago's denunciation of how simplistic narratives of the past furnish 'evidence' for false certainties about the future, and his insistence that debates of present-day political options be predicated on more nuanced and thorough processes of historicization, place him in exalted company amongst contemporary novelists.

However, while this focus on historiography and its vicissitudes makes it instructive to assess Saramago's work alongside that of Salman Rushdie, Günter Grass, Margaret Attwood, or Umberto Eco, to name but few, it also compels us to consider a seeming paradox. Right up to his death in June 2010, Saramago consistently and quite candidly used his rising mass-media exposure as a political platform. With equal regularity, he insisted that his literary output was integral to his political and social activism.[8] Yet while his literary interrogation of empiricist epistemologies became if anything increasingly fundamental and explicit, he continued to affirm his Marxist convictions, and remained an active, if sometimes maverick, member of Western Europe's most steadfastly Leninist Communist Party. While this study is not the first to ponder this paradox, it grounds its analysis in a wider-ranging investigation than previously attempted of how the ostensibly 'postmodern' probing of ethical, intellectual and practical dilemmas articulated by Saramago's novelistic project responds to (or, at times, anticipates) the propositions of Marxist and Marxist-influenced social and cultural theorists. As this introductory chapter outlines, Saramago's literary project emerged, in the last days of Portugal's forty year long *Estado Novo* dictatorship, out of a culture of resistance writing profoundly influenced by Marxist literary and aesthetic theories. Particularly in his fiction of the late seventies and early eighties, principles and devices inherited from mid-twentieth century Marxist-influenced 'neo-realist' writers are adapted to the transformed conditions for publication and reception in a freer, but much more unstable and fractious, polity. Such innovations, departing radically from the stated neo-realist principle of mimetic representation of historical conditions, can be related to alternative Marxist theories of politically engaged, or didactic, literature. Moreover, while following the lead of Bertolt Brecht, and other creative artists, who compel their audience or reader to engage in a 'dialectical' analysis of real life conditions, Saramago's critique of late capitalism — and of its continuities with earlier systems of socio-economic exploitation — evokes insights and conceptual models associated with a broad range of Marxist and post-structuralist Marxist thinkers. As this study argues, the ideas of Gramsci, Adorno, Marcuse, and Amílcar Cabral, not to mention Marxist feminism, are all critical points of reference in Saramago's contribution to current debates about political psychology, identity politics, and the organization of revolutionary movements. Simultaneously, however, his fiction after 1980, with its self-reflexive, anti-mimetic narrative form, makes no attempt to disregard or dodge the post-structuralist critique of classical Marxism's materialist premise and empiricist method.

I — Marxism, Culture, and Resistance in Portugal: The Matrix of Saramago's fiction

In an interview with Carlos Reis published in 1998, Saramago justified his habitual description of himself as a Marxist as follows:

> o marxismo serve-me para compreender o mundo de um modo que faz todo o sentido [...] estou nele e nem sequer posso conceber outro modo de tentar entender o funcionamento das sociedades humanas. (Reis 1998: 78)
>
> [Marxism enables me to understand the world in a way that makes perfect sense [...] I am a part of it and I cannot even conceive of another way of trying to understand the workings of human societies.]

As the phrases 'compreender [...] de um modo' and 'tentar entender' suggest, Marxism provides what Saramago considered to be the least inadequate of many inadequate interpretative tools: it 'há-de continuar a ser útil' [is bound to continue being useful], on condition that we refrain from misrecognizing it as 'um sistema de raiz universal, que também nunca chegou a ser' [an all-encompassing system, which it has also never been] (Reis 1998: 77). If this rejection of the notion of a 'sistema [...] universal' makes it appropriate or useful to label Saramago's world-view as postmodernist, then his is, as Mark Sabine and Adriana Martins summarize, an 'emphatically politically committed postmodernism'; one that constantly reasserts that 'admitting to the limitations of potential knowledge must never entail surrender to tyrannies sustained by cultivated ignorance' (2006: 1).[9] After living half of his life under the yoke of just such a tyranny, Saramago steadfastly refused to abandon the struggle for universal emancipation, or to despair of the capacity of memory, historical inquiry, and literature to contribute to that struggle. His recourse to historical materialism and other Marxist theories as contingently useful tools for socio-economic critique, agitation, and reconstruction is the fulfilment of his conviction that both utopian political thinking — and the moral and intellectual growth of citizens — remain not only viable, but indeed essential, even within the confines of an epistemological labyrinth.

Understanding Saramago's focus on historical enquiry in his earlier novels, and their seismic impact on Portuguese culture in the first decades of full parliamentary democracy, becomes easier through a basic knowledge of the ideology, culture, and historical practice of the *Estado Novo* regime of 1933 to 1974. The *Estado Novo*'s promulgation in 1933 had been the formal process by which António de Oliveira Salazar, the economics lecturer appointed by General Carmona's military regime in 1928 to balance the heavily indebted nation's budget, had ensconced himself as Portugal's de facto dictator.[10] Legislating a regime of stringent wage restraint, fiscal austerity, and corporatist authoritarianism, Salazar steadily reduced the national debt, and secured the political hegemony of a small elite composed of the haute bourgeoisie, landowners, and their allies within the Church and military.[11] These successes, plus Salazar's ruthless suppression of dissent, his adept political brinkmanship, and close alliance with a conservative Catholic hierarchy, allowed him to maintain Portuguese neutrality throughout the Second World War. Thereafter, Salazar exploited Portugal's accession to NATO, and the Communist threat to US hegemony in the Mediterranean and Atlantic, to deflect mounting criticism of Portugal's colonial presence in Africa, which from the early 1930s had constituted an increasingly crucial element in his highly centralized and isolationist corporatist system.[12] As in much of mid-twentieth-century Europe, a cult of 'national' — here, essentially, conservative Catholic — values and traditions formed a populist veneer on this brutally imposed corporatist project. The Portuguese state of the late Middle Ages and Renaissance, and its spectacular expansion, aggressive evangelization, and global dissemination of 'Catholic values' under strict and centralized government, became the subject of a pervasive official cult.[13] At times, indeed, the examples of the alleged Golden Age of 'Discoveries' appeared to dictate political policy in the present: George Ball, US Under-Secretary of State tasked by Kennedy with pressing for Portuguese decolonization in Africa, reported with exasperation in 1963 that the country was run not by a single dictator but by 'a triumvirate consisting of Vasco da Gama, Prince Henry the Navigator, and Salazar' (1982: 277). Under the pressures of the dictatorship's censor, its patronage of politically obedient historians, and its populist manipulation of historical references in school text books, political rhetoric, and public artworks, historical discourse in Portugal became particularly monolithic, insular, and overtly ideological.[14] The harassment and marginalization of dissident historians — even of foreign scholars as well-established as Prof. Charles Boxer — and the narrow syllabus of state education, sheltered from critique or contradiction the official narrative of national history and destiny that was employed to vindicate Salazar's corporatist, imperialist agenda.[15] The State's historiographical discourse affirmed the timeless alliance of great patriots and Christianity. The aims, deeds, and values of the kings, poets, warriors, and martyrs of a distant golden age were presented not merely as reason for patriotic pride, but also as precursors and justifications of fiscal austerity and authoritarian governance in the present-day metropole, and of continuing colonial domination in Africa.

Following the *Estado Novo*'s overthrow in 1974, Portugal achieved twenty-five years of remarkable progress in educational achievement, living standards, and public health, and saw the consolidation of parliamentary rule and other democratic institutions. Nevertheless, the dictatorship's stifling of critical enquiry and democratic participation has had a lasting impact. Even before the economic crisis of the early twenty-first century brought an alarming 'deconvergence' from average European Union standards of development, the ambitions of the radical Left for the empowerment of the common people remained unrealized.[16] Notwithstanding either the efforts of left-wing intellectuals and post-revolutionary governments to redirect literature and culture towards popular education and politicization, or the substantial contribution of the country's historians and cultural critics to discussions precipitated by the 'postmodern turn' of the 1960s and 1970s, it is worth asking how much has changed in *popular* conceptions of a national past, or in what is commonly understood by the study of history, either in post-dictatorship Portugal, or, indeed, wherever else 'historical fiction' is read. Saramago repeatedly made clear that his primary concern, in his venture into this literary genre, was to contest the simplistic and spuriously teleological representation of the past that is still all too commonly encountered not just in Portuguese popular journalism and political oratory, but also in the public dissemination of historiographical scholarship. A salient example is provided by the remarkably popular flagship documentaries produced for Portuguese state television by the doyen of *Estado Novo*-era Portuguese historians, and one-time Minister of Education, José Hermano Saraiva. Series such as *O Tempo e a Alma* ['Time and the Soul'] (1971–72) and *Horizontes da Memória* ['Horizons of Memory'] (1996–97) made few departures from either Salazarism's apologia for the Church militant and imperialist expansion, or the narrative format of matter-of-fact historical 'reconstruction', that together constitute what Saramago denounces as '*História Pátria*' (a phrase that can only problematically be translated as 'nationalist history').[17] Citing Georges Duby, Jacques le Goff, and the *Nouvelle Histoire* movement as the theoretical foundation of his critique, Saramago complains that 'a história é parcial e é parcelar' [history is partial, and it is parcelled]:

> A História que se escreve e que depois vamos ler, aquela em que vamos aprender aquilo que aconteceu, tem necessariamente que ser parcelar, porque não pode narrar tudo, não pode explicar tudo, não pode falar de toda a gente; mas ela é parcial no outro sentido, em que sempre se apresentou como uma espécie de 'lição', aquilo a que chamávamos a História Pátria.
> A questão é que a mim não me preocupa tanto que ela seja parcial, quer dizer, orientada e ideológica, porque isso eu posso mais ou menos verificar, perceber e encontrar os antídotos para essas visões mais ou menos deformadas daquilo que aconteceu ou da sua interpretação. Talvez a mim me preocupe muito mais o facto de a História ser parcelar. (Reis 1998: 81)
>
> [The History that is written and that we subsequently read, that in which we learn of what has happened, must of necessity be parcelled, because it cannot narrate everything, it cannot explain everything, it cannot talk to everyone; but it is also partial in another sense, insofar as it has always been packaged as a kind of 'lesson', namely that which we might call *História Pátria*.
> The point is that it doesn't worry me so much that it is partial — that is, tendentious and ideological — because I can, more or less, identify and understand this, and can find the antidote to such more or less distorted images of that which happened, or of its interpretation. What perhaps worries me much more is the fact of History being parcelled.]

Saramago's expansion of this basic critique makes his five novels of the 1980s characteristic of the two foremost preoccupations of Portuguese literature in the aftermath of the dictatorship's demise: the (re)definition of a national identity and purpose, and the reanimation of historical consciousness that had become ossified under the dictatorship. The debate about the representation of history, always highly politicized, had become both more viable and more urgent. As Mark Sabine and Claire Williams note,

> [by] the early 1980s, [...] there was a growing emphasis on the identification of long-term tropes and tendencies in Portuguese society and culture, and with it an implication that artists might assist social regeneration as much through

the analysis of such past continuities as through a focus on current turbulence. (2010: 187–88)

One can argue that, by this means, Saramago's work aimed to capitalize not simply on 'the discursive innovations and didactic initiatives of the revolutionary period' (Sabine and Williams 2010: 187), but also on the legacy of Marxist-influenced 'neo-realist' writers of the dictatorship era. His five 1980s novels expand on both the neo-realists' deft socio-economic critique, and their reinsertion of the experience of the poor and oppressed into the national imaginary (in the case of *História do Cerco de Lisboa*, taking this 'reinsertion' right back to the nation's 'birth' in the twelfth century). At the same time, in a radical departure from Communist Party orthodoxy on how literary fiction can represent reality, and politically engage its reader, these novels attempt something to which the neo-realists, contesting Salazarism's pervasive censorship and propaganda under the threat of persecution and imprisonment, could rarely aspire. They aim first to make the reader recognize the complexity of historical processes in all his/her imagining of the past, and secondly to encourage him/her to pursue strategies for enhanced social justice in his/her imagining of the future.

The 'neo-realist' movement had dominated left-wing resistance writing in the early decades of the dictatorship, spurred by the work of novelists such as Aquilino Ribeiro (1885–1963), José Maria Ferreira de Castro (1898–1974) and Alves Redol (1911–1969), and galvanized by leftist literary journals such as *Seara Nova* (founded 1921) and *Sol Nascente* (1937–40). Neo-realism responded with bold and effective single-mindedness to the increasing saturation of popular memory by Salazarism's monolithic and substantially mythologized inscriptions of 'national' origins, cultural characteristics, and values. The neo-realists' declared aim was the maximum approximation of literature to a comprehensive and objective representation of contemporary reality. Semi-clandestinely, they debated how contemporary literature might lay bare the historical determination of working people's socio-economic suffering, thereby informing and abetting popular resistance to dictatorship. Like its 'social realist' counterparts both elsewhere in southern Europe and in the Americas, Portuguese neo-realism responded to György Lukács's notion of ideal literary 'form' (first presented in works like his *Theory of the Novel* in 1916, but summarized in his monumental study of nineteenth-century realism, *The Historical Novel* of 1955). Lukács's work was endorsed by the International Communist Party in 1934; albeit, critically, as 'more a set of prescriptive rules [...] and a set of yardsticks for criticizing "decadent" literature than a literary theory as such', as David Forgacs summarizes (1986: 166).[18] Lukács's 'literary form' denotes not the poetic and narratological devices comprising the text's signifying fabric, but rather 'the aesthetic shape given to a content, a shape manifested through technical features such as narrative time and the interrelationship of characters and situations in a work' (Forgacs 1986: 171–72). 'Correct' literary form is thus the configuration of content in a manner that objectively represents the socio-economic laws and relations held by Marxism to determine historical development. Lukács famously eulogizes the politically conservative Balzac for revealing, particularly in *Les Paysans*, 'social beings as the basis of social consciousness, precisely through and in the contradictions between social being and social consciousness which must necessarily manifest themselves in every class of society' (Lukács 1950: 42). Effectively, Lukács argues that literature can constitute a form of knowledge, to the extent that its synthesis of the general movement of history, and its selection of unique, individual traits and types into a formal specificity (or *Besonderheit*, a dialectical sublation of both generality and particularity within a single 'notion') exposes historical conditions with a neatness and precision rarely encountered in life. Lukács, following in the footsteps of Engels, distinguishes Balzac's work — which he claims objectively presents the entire structure of reality — from those of Zola or Proust, in which an external totality is not correctly 'mediated' (Engels 2001: 167). Echoing Engels's definition of the realist literary ideal as 'the truth in reproduction of typical characters under typical circumstances' (ibid.), Lukács argues that the novelist must aim for 'typicality', since

> the central category and criterion of realist literature is the type, a peculiar synthesis which organically binds together the general and the particular both in characters and situations. (1950: 6)

'Typicality' is not, Lukács insists, synonymous with statistical 'average', but arises from the 'peculiar synthesis' of the general movement of history and a number of unique, individual traits into a particularity that gives the 'correct' literary work its distinctive 'three-dimensionality' (ibid). As literary historian António Pedro Pita identifies, Lukács's principle of 'particularity' was a presiding influence on early neo-realism, informing its claim to be 'insusceptível de se tornar [...] ideológico e mistificador' [not susceptible to ideological deformity or mystification] and its aim of creating a 'perspectiva *totalizante* dos problemas e das soluções' [totalizing perspective on problems and solutions] (1983: 21–22).

The narrative voice in each of Saramago's 1980s novels famously advertises the work's failure to 'se constituir em *imagem de totalidade*' [constitute an all-encompassing image] (ibid.). Yet even if the pursuit of this totalizing image is, as Pita claims, the 'traço mais característico da ideologia neo-realista' [defining characteristic of neo-realist ideology], Saramago's fiction is not, in fact, an absolute departure from the *practice* of neo-realist writing. As Pita, Carlos Reis, and Ana Paula Ferreira have all explored, from the outset, prominent neo-realists were questioning exactly how Lukács's theory might guide writers to the construction of a 'particular' image of 'totality'.[19] One shortcoming of Lukács's analysis is his reliance on notions of 'the great writer's thirst for truth, his fanatic striving for reality' (1950: 11) and of his 'genius', which (inexplicably) transcends any political allegiances and personal foibles to guarantee the objectivity of his delineation of 'typical' characters and data.[20] Lukács's insistence on the 'reflective' duty and capacity of literature was also challenged by writers such as Mário Dionísio, who insisted that a commitment to 'realism' presupposed the 'estrutura realista' honed by Balzac and his followers, but must also admit that 'o real [...] não é [...] unicamente o palpável mas o que ainda não é, mas será'.[21] As Pita concludes, in response to the debate stimulated by Dionísio here, 'a recorrente afirmação do primado do conteúdo e da arte como espelho deve ser considerada desde o início em polémica tensão com a valorização da forma e da arte como construção' [the recurrent insistence on the primacy of the content, and on the artwork as a mirror, should be assessed from the outset as having been held in a polemical tension with the appreciation of form, and of the artwork as a construction] (2002: 241). As will be explored below, just such a focus on literature as construction pervades the first novel Saramago produced after the relaxation of censorship in 1974, *Manual de Pintura e Caligrafia* (1978).

From the outset, the neo-realists also faced the challenges of pursuing 'objectivity' in spite of censorship, and of fostering — by means other than the doctrinaire critical guidance imposed by Stalin and Zhdanov in the Soviet Union — a 'correct' practice of reading. Leading neo-realists such as Alves Redol and Carlos de Oliveira increasingly conceived of the intended *perspectiva totalizante* as an overview constructed through the dialogic, and dialectical, interplay of individually partial and subjective perspectives on historical reality. Ana Paula Ferreira notes such writers' increasing reliance on symbolism and encryption, often effected through the manipulation of popular discursive material such as folksong, and examines Redol's experiments in narrative strategy in his 1962 novel *Barranco de Cegos*.[22] Other figures such as José Cardoso Pires, while committed to the struggle of the Marxist-dominated opposition movement, were using similar literary devices in a manner that evinced scepticism about the epistemological foundations of the social critique implicit in their texts. As Ana Paula Arnaut argues, both the discussion of historical analysis, and the representation of subjectivity and alienation, in Cardoso Pires's *O Delfim* portend the 'terramoto futuro da literatura nova do Post-Modernismo' [the coming earthquake of the new literature of postmodernism] (2002b: 100). Other Saramago scholars, such as Teresa Cristina Cerdeira da Silva and Víctor Viçoso, have pointed to such narrative innovations, to symbolic manipulation, and to Cardoso Pires's recourse to parody and irony, as precursors of Saramago's experiments in narrative voicing and 'neo-baroque' poetics.[23]

Such later 'neo-realist' fiction was, of course, responding not only to the discussions of Portuguese theorists, but also to the literary practice championed by Bertolt Brecht, who as early as 1938 had complained that Lukács's concepts of literary reflection and typicality were flawed, and his investment in the author or critic as arbiters of objective truth deleterious to Communist attempts to revolutionize society.[24] Brecht's 'theatre of calm contemplation and detachment, [...] of critical thoughtfulness' (Esslin 1984: 114), though banned by the *Estado Novo*, was by the early 1960s widely discussed and imitated in Portugal. New plays (also routinely banned from performance) such as Luís de Sttau Monteiro's *Felizmente há luar!*, and Bernardo Santareno's *O Judeu* and *A Traição do Padre Martinho*, emulated Brecht's practice of disrupting theatrical verisimilitude so as to preclude empathy with represented characters and events, and divert attention to the conditions in which they operate.[25] As Walter Benjamin summarizes, '[t]he task of the epic theatre [...] is not so much the development of actions as the representation of conditions' (1973a: 152).[26] Brecht inverts the Aristotelian principles of drama, repeatedly creating an experience of dramatic 'alienation' (*Verfremdung*) that reminds the audience that it is viewing an artificial representation, not a microcosm or facsimile of truth.[27] This discovery of conditions is effected through 'alienation effects' (*Verfremdungseffekte*): devices that interrupt the plot, expose it as artifice, and invite the audience to debate dialectically the reality to which it alludes. As Elin Diamond explains, *Verfremdungseffekte* can take the form of an anti-mimetic style of acting, when in performance the actor ' "quotes" or demonstrates the character's behavior instead of identifying with it' (1997: 45). The audience, in turn, does not empathize with the character so much as being 'astonished' (Benjamin 1973a: 152) at the circumstances in which that behaviour develops. The presentation of social circumstances not as mere background to emotional turmoil, but as remarkable in themselves, is also achieved through the most radical contravention of the Aristotelian precepts of realism. Devices in the written text and visual presentation of the play, such as the use of placards and captions and interpolated songs, purge historical incidents of sensation. According to Benjamin, this makes 'epic theatre [move] in spurts', punctuated by 'intervals which, if anything, impair the illusion of the audience and paralyse its readiness for empathy' (1973a: 155). It is surely no coincidence that Saramago's narratives move with a similarly intermittent or 'spurting' rhythm, discouraging the reader from relying on the author's presiding 'genius' and instead urging a self-consciously active role in interpreting the world to which the text alludes.

The *Estado Novo*'s wholesale prohibition of Brecht's work and of the emerging home-grown Brechtian theatre betrays their recognition of the power of Brecht's reconception of the dramatic text as, in Linda Hutcheon's words, 'not a closed and fetishized object, but an open process with an enunciative situation that changes with each receiver' (1988: 220). This 'receiver''s promotion, from passive spectator to critical and creative agent, offended the regime's view of culture and education, and threatened its propagandist mobilization of the national past. When the 1974 revolution transformed the 'enunciative situation' of literature, however, the previously suppressed Brechtian drama, and other overtly politicized genres, boomed.[28] The relaxation of censorship also enabled the appearance of hundreds of independent micro-publishers, disseminating formerly banned political texts, and remedying Portugal's long cultural and ideological isolation. Translations of both political theory and politically engaged fiction — from Europe, Latin America and, by the late 1970s, Africa — proliferated.[29] New, leftist publishing houses such as Caminho also, however, sponsored the experimental Portuguese literature inspired both by bolder, broader critical debate, and by the realization that many representational strategies crucial to oppositionist writing under censorship were now obsolete. Such developments went hand in hand with writers' and cultural activists' endeavours to engage the labouring classes culturally, through travelling theatres and libraries, poetry readings, and music festivals. Saramago himself served on the first executive of the Portuguese Writers' Association, and lead the 'dinamização cultural' [cultural animation] team of the state Youth Organization Support Fund in the mid-1970s.[30] His engagement during this period with political thinking in southern Europe and post-colonial Africa and Latin America was compounded by his work as a translator for Caminho Editora and other left-leaning publishers, translating political studies by Nicos Poulantzas and Todor Zhivkov, and novels by, amongst others, Sembène Ousmane, François Oyono, Jacques Roumain, and Mongo Beti, between 1974 and 1985.

In the late 1970s, the revolutionary effervescence of 1974–75 subsided, and Portugal's reintegration into a post-colonial North Atlantic capitalist order became assured. Saramago was ousted as *Diário de Lisboa* editor in November 1975 (Lopes 2010: 61–64), and responded to his own and his party's marginalization by dedicating himself to translation and to creative writing. While still soliciting the critical and political engagement of his reader, Saramago had to address more than the stalling of the revolutionary left agenda in Portugal. New challenges to the Portuguese Communist Party's Leninist doctrine emerging at this time ranged from the 'psychoanalytic' Marxisms of Althusser and the Frankfurt School to new paradigms developed in anti-colonialist revolutionary campaigns, and the critique of materialist epistemology inherent to the post-structuralist thinking of Derrida, Lyotard, Kristeva, and others.[31] From 1980 onwards, his fiction integrates a response to this critique into an intervention in a national landscape of now predominantly revisionist, rather than revolutionary, cultural politics. As Kaufman and Klobucka (1997: 20) have summarized, amid the economic stabilization and political retrenchment of the early 1980s, Portuguese cultural production became dominated by debate about national characteristics, values, and social and political objectives. The impact of Saramago's contribution to this particular debate is clear, both from the journalistic outpourings that greeted each best-selling novel, and from the proportion of early critical studies of his work that focus on the 'national' question. For a global readership thirty years later, what makes these works of greater interest than their putative 'rebalancing' of the portrayal of the Portuguese past and present are their abiding application of both Marxist and post-structuralist critique to the notion and practice of *História Pátria*, and their strategies for reanimating historical consciousness, and revising and reconciling identities, as the foundation for a revised internationalist, socialist project of socio-economic transformation.

To begin to examine these new strategies, one must return to the question of literary form and Marxist ideology, and to how Saramago's mature fiction style grows out of the challenges, in late neo-realism and in Brechtian drama, to the Lukácsian 'reflection model' stipulated by the Communist Party. It is helpful here to relate Brecht's revelation of textual construction in drama to the conception of the novel elaborated in the 1920s and 1930s by his contemporary, Mikhail M. Bakhtin. Bakhtin's key observation regards how language, as the raw material of the text, is stratified and hierarchized in relation to the social and ideological formations of the population(s) that use(s) it. Bakhtin exposes Lukács's 'universal' representation of real social conditions through a 'correct' novelistic 'form' as the 'artistic organization', into a deceptively seamless unity, of a 'diversity of social speech types (sometimes even diversity of languages) and a diversity of individual voices' (1981: 262). For Bakhtin, this 'internal stratification present in every language at any given moment of its historical existence is the indispensable prerequisite for the novel as a genre' (1981: 262–63). The novelist, Bakhtin argues, reworks and organizes these speech types 'into a structured stylistic system' (1981: 263), so as to achieve 'the refracted (indirect) expression of his intentions and values' (1981: 292). Such heteroglossia, Bakhtin claims, never slavishly transmit the author's ideology, even in the classic realist novel: indeed, it is precisely because '[t]he prose writer does not purge words of intentions and tones that are alien to him' (1981: 298) that (as Lukács argues but does not adequately explain) Balzac's novels can be interpreted as reflecting a Marxist world-view.

Realist fiction does, however, render the 'internal stratification' of language less conspicuous, disguising, or rather, seamlessly manipulating the tension between the socio-political and ideological positions expressed through different strata.[32] However, Bakhtin identifies a different practice to this dissimulation of discursive hybridity in the early European novel, from Rabelais to Cervantes, to the latter's British admirers Fielding, Smollett and Sterne, and to the German Romantic comic novelists Hippel and Jean Paul (1981: 309; 361–62). To varying (and ideologically determined) degrees, these writers' texts hybridize a panoply of discourses self-consciously or self-evidently, and in so doing upset both their hierarchized status and their ideological stability. This 'carnivalization', like Brechtian drama's 'quotation' of both text and gesture, makes apparent the manipulation of language.[33] Benjamin's claim that 'epic theatre' diverts attention from isolated events towards historical conditions and ideological coordinates is echoed by Bakhtin's claim that 'carnival, with its pathos of change and renewal, [permits us] to penetrate into the deepest strata of man and of human relations' (1973: 139).

Horácio Costa's 1997 study of Saramago's output up to 1979, while not applying Bakhtinian concepts to his prose fiction, has emphasized its demonstration (and exploitation) of the plasticity and, hence, the ideological volatility of language. This is exemplified with particular success in the short story collection *Objecto Quase* (1978). As Costa argues, Saramago's development through this collection of '[uma] estratégia de desconstrução e reconstrução textual, e semântica' [a strategy of textual and semantic deconstruction and reconstruction] (1997: 321) is already implicit in the pseudo-Baroque inversion of noun and adverb in the collection's title. This title simultaneously links the notion of the literary word or image as a de-/re-construction in progress to that of a concomitant de-/re-construction of a dehumanized society, its members reduced by a venal tyranny to the status of 'quasi-objects' (Costa 1997: 320).[34] In the stories that follow, a panoply of speech forms, jargons, literary references, narrative formats (from the mock epic to the fairy tale and science fiction), and representational modes (from the comic grotesque to neo-realist parable) is mixed and manipulated to forge highly politicized allegories of the dictatorship's death-throes and their aftermath.[35] The reader is compelled to reflect on the historical and ideological location of language and aesthetics, and is offered an example of how, in a context where relaxed censorship permits both more direct and more complex discursive strategies, a politically committed writer can stake a fresh claim to old rhetorical devices, and refashion them in order to deal with formerly proscribed subjects and deliver a more incisive denunciation of the dehumanizing logic and legacy of Salazarism.

A number of existing studies of Saramago — notably, those of António A. Lourenço (1991), Odil de Oliveira Filho (1993: 46–58; 79–82), and Ana Paula Arnaut (1996: 67–70; 96–102) — have already analysed his narrative style using Bakhtinian models and argued for its congruence with Brechtian principles. In all of Saramago's novels from 1980 onwards, punctuation is famously restricted to paragraphing, initializing capital letters, and deploying commas and, less frequently, full stops; in passages of dialogue, a change of speaker is marked with just a comma and an initial capital letter. According to Benjamin, erratic or 'spurting' progression in Brechtian theatre 'loosens the joints' of the dramatic plot' (1973a: 150). In Saramago's fiction, as Paulo Becker (1991: 130) enumerates, this minimalist punctuation, together with the interpolation of laundry lists of data and decontextualized jargon, and frequent literary quotation, paraphrase, and parody, directs the reader's attention both to the text's modulations among different quoted language strata, and to her/his own participation in interpreting reported utterances.

The most significant technical innovation is, however, that which Becker (ibid.) terms the 'narrador intruso' [interrupting narrator], a device more adequately described as an inconsistent and auto-interruptive narrative voicing, which radically undermines the concept of narrator as the fictional construct of a consistent enunciating subject. Saramago himself asserted that 'a figura do narrador não existe [...] só o Autor exerce função narrativa real na obra de ficção' [the figure of the narrator does not exist [...] only the Author holds a genuine narrative role in the work of fiction].[36] The (predominantly) extradiegetic narrative voice of his novels after 1980 lacks a recognizably consistent gender, age, or ethnic/class location, and is positioned inconsistently relative to events narrated. Sometimes, it digresses into hair-splitting critical analyses or jargon-laden displays of erudition; at other times, it professes ignorance of plot developments and character's thoughts. It speaks, at some times, from within the diegesis, and, at others, from outside it. The voice and its indeterminate subject position thus substantiate Bakhtin's claim that

> [a]s a living, socio-ideological concrete thing, as heteroglot opinion, language, for the individual consciousness, lies on the borderline between oneself and the other. The word in language is half someone else's. It becomes 'one's own' only when the speaker populates it with his own intention, his own accent, when he appropriates the word, adapting it to his own semantic and expressive intention. (1981: 293)

Bakhtin's concept of the 'carnivalization' of discourse in the pre-realist novel has received a mixed reception from Marxist literary critics such as Terry Eagleton. While Eagleton accepts that 'carnivalization', like Brechtian *Verfremdung*, effects parodic engagement with discourse, in order to direct criticism beyond the discourse itself and towards the ideology that it articulates (Eagleton 1981: 145–46), he questions what political efficacy can be attributed to such anarchic subversion. If the text executes a 'ceaseless practice of travesty and inversion [...] deconstructing images, misreading texts, and collapsing binary oppositions' then the obvious political limitation of such writing is that it, like the original Carnival, is 'a *licensed* affair in every sense, a permissible rupture of hegemony' (1981: 148). Yet, in Saramago's case, one can argue that, rather than presenting a 'ceaseless [...] groundswell of ambiguity' (1981: 145), his novels allow a dissident or critical voice to emerge or prevail in a position of privilege at key moments, thereby directing a consistent and constructive ideological opposition to the hegemonic ideology through 'the illumination of one language by means of another, the carving-out of a living image of another language' (Bakhtin 1981: 361). This practice is most prevalent in

Levantado do Chão, in passages such as that describing the charity handout organized by landowner's wife, Dona Clemência (*Levantado*: 187–88).[37] Here, the incongruous juxtaposition of — or slippage between — the rarefied discourse of prayer and pulpit (here, in italics) and demotic speech serves to reify the former, revealing how it falsely sanctifies the tight-fisted, calculating Clemência's actions:

> Dona Clemência [...] preside à composição das esmolinhas, *guiando e vigiando* a espessura da fatia do toucinho [...] *passando por escrúpulos de pura justiça* a rasoira na medidinha do feijão, *tudo pela caridade* de evitar as guerras da inveja infantil, Tens mais do que eu, Tenho menos do que tu. (*Levantado*: 187)

> [Dona Clemência [...] presides over the assembling of the handouts, *guiding and watching over* the thickness of each slice of bacon [...] *wielding* the strickle *with scruples of pure justice* in doling out the beans, *all in the charitable spirit* of preventing outbreaks of childish envy, You've got more than me, I've got less than you.]

On the following page, a shift in the narrative voice's position relative both to clerical discourse and to the reader is used to hit out at Clemência's moral hypocrisy. Addressing the reader as 'vós' (the second person plural form used only in oratory or to address the deity), the narrative mounts the rhetorical high ground, using bitter humour to denounce the systemic poverty and suffering, which Clemência's charity mitigates only once a week:

> *Vede como padecem*, e descalcinhos, doridos, *olhai* como as meninas levantam um pezinho e logo o outro a fugir do chão gelado, poriam os dois no ar se lhes crescessem em vida *as asas que se diz teriam depois de mortas*[.] (*Levantado*: 188)

> [*See how they suffer*, and bare-foot, in pain, *behold* how the little girls raise first one foot then the other, shrinking from the frozen earth, they would raise both in the air at once if only they could sprout, in life, *the wings people say they will gain once they're dead*.]

For all their rich conceptual humour and wordplay, such tableaux do not simply illustrate how all representation is inhabited by ideology. They also consistently confront the hegemonic ideology with an alternative that is presented as more socially progressive or humane. Yet their discursive discontinuities effectively constitute a disclaimer, reminding that neither is the text's representation of the world comprehensive, nor is the author's analysis infallible. Such a warning also poses the question of whether the political message that should be extrapolated from these texts is a pessimistic one of the futility (or worse, the danger) of predicating political action on historical analysis, or whether transformative or 'utopian' political projects — rather than essentially deconstructive ones — remain relevant in the 'postmodern' era, and, if so, whether or not the historiographical fiction emergent in that era might contribute to such projects.

II — Fiction, Historical Consciousness, and Utopian Politics in Postmodernity

Saramago's complaint that 'a história é parcial e é parcelar' provides an equally neat starting point for contextualizing his work relative to the development of the historical novel worldwide after the post-structuralist or 'linguistic' turn of the 1960s. While historiographical partiality arises in large part from the ideological manipulation of language itself, the 'packaging' of history relates to the phenomenon whose discussion is particularly associated with Hayden White's *Metahistory* (1973). White's immense work amplified discussion of the fundamental problem of emplotment in the writing of history. According to White, as Kuisma Korhonen summarizes, 'not only historiographical discourse was predetermined by literary styles, but historical consciousness in general was predetermined by certain linguistic structures' (2006: 11). If historians could not help but enfabulate the past, it would be essential to explore the hermeneutic and tropic conventions of the culturally and historically specific narrative paradigms, such as the four that White (1973: 5) identifies as having been widely employed in nineteenth-century historiography to create a realistic 'explanatory effect' (romance, comedy, tragedy, and satire). While White's contribution, in placing the problematic of narratology irrefutably at the centre of historiographical practice, is widely acknowledged, many historians have also complained that his critique of their profession in the contemporary era has at times been reductive or even simplistic. However, in the realm of collective memory and of popular conceptions of the past, it is hard to deny that ideologically 'packaged' narrative histories still hold sway. In the specific case of 1980s Portugal, the political and psycho-social impact of this was deftly characterized by cultural theorist and critic Eduardo Lourenço. His *O Labirinto da Saudade* (1978) identified a disturbing continuity of narrative paradigm and 'motific characterization' imposed upon the nation's imperial and evangelical past, from the late nineteenth century, through the dictatorship to the early years of democracy. Such continuity extended to a remarkable degree across the political spectrum, with the Socialist Party governments (1976–78 and 1983–85) and presidency of Mário Soares (1986–96) aiming to configure a modernized and democratized model of national identity without either disturbing an established teleology of national exceptionalism, or denouncing the enterprise of 'Discoveries' and empire upon which it was predicated. Public discussion of the national past was preponderantly led by the TV series and pictorial histories of J. H. Saraiva and his peers, by the superficially sanitized cult of Camões and his *Lusíadas*, and by the re-branding of the 1974 Revolution as precursor of Portugal's 'reintegration' into a now post-imperial, capitalist Western Europe. Hence, it was primarily in the realm of literary fiction that White's basic proposal for historiography to turn its 'ironic consciousness against itself' was brought into public consciousness. As Kaufman and Ornelas (1997), Sapega (1997), and Sabine and Williams (2010: 188), amongst others, have surveyed, a more nuanced and probing reassessment of the national past emerged in the 1980s fiction of not only Saramago, but also contemporaries such as Augusto Abelaira and José Cardoso Pires, and younger figures including António

Lobo Antunes, Lídia Jorge, Teolinda Gersão, and Mário Cláudio. A substantial critical bibliography has traced the proliferation — and the remarkable commercial successes — of this Portuguese emanation of the literary turn frequently referred to using Linda Hutcheon's coinage of 'historiographical metafiction'.

Hutcheon's influential — though not unproblematic — analysis in *A Poetics of Postmodernism* traces the move from the traditional historical novel, 'modelled on historiography to the extent that it is motivated and made operative by a notion of history as a shaping force', to the archetypal postmodernist literary genre of 'historiographical metafiction', which 'acknowledges the paradox of the *reality* of the past but its *textualized accessibility* to us today' (Hutcheon 1988: 114). In so doing, Hutcheon aims to counter the charge laid against this literary turn by Fredric Jameson in *Post-Modernism, or The Cultural Logic Of Late Capitalism*, of conceiving of historical enquiry as doomed to confinement with a structuralist 'prison-house' of language. For Jameson, postmodernist art and literature reduces its engagement with the past to a frivolous practice of quotation or ornamentation, fatefully lending itself to the celebration of an amnesiac presentism that reinforces the late capitalist status quo and all of its iniquities. In response to Jameson's critique, Hutcheon, citing Barbara Foley's earlier study of the postmodern novel, counters that historiographical metafiction partakes of a postmodernist aesthetic that is 'fundamentally contradictory, resolutely historical, and inescapably political' (1988: 4) in its attempts not

> 'to tell the truth' [(Foley 1986: 26)] [...] so much as to question *whose* truth gets told. It does not so much associate this truth with claims to empirical validation as contest the ground of any claim to such validation. (1988: 123)

Hutcheon's study, with its wide-ranging survey of the output of 'historiographical fiction' in a number of languages and regions, offers a useful introduction to the development of late-twentieth-century historically referenced fiction. Its substantial dialogue with Jameson and his antecedents in Marxist literary theory is particularly significant for its discussion of the 'many parallels' between the representational strategies of 'historiographical metafiction' and Brechtian epic theatre. Hutcheon notes that both

> place the receiver in a paradoxical position, both inside and outside, participatory and critical: we are to be thoughtful and analytic, rather than either passive or unthinkingly empathetic. (1988: 219–20)

However, while both direct attention to the '"particular historical field of human relations" in which art is written [and] received [...] in Brecht's work there is more of a sense that these relations are open to change *by art itself*' (ibid).

Exploring how we access past and present realities in the textualized forms imposed by the dominant ideology, Brecht's work identifies how ideology (as a superstructural product of the material, economic 'base' that Marxism presupposes as the primary determinant of history) can itself become a historically shaping force. Where it occludes or justifies the inherent contradictions of the prevailing socio-economic configuration, it impedes what, in a Marxist analysis, is that configuration's terminal crisis, and its transcendence through revolution. For

Hutcheon, however, the key question is that of what literature can claim to achieve, in a political sense. Her comparison of Brecht and a politically engaged practice of 'historiographical metafiction' is anticipated by Catherine Belsey's concept of the 'interrogative text', which raises questions for the reader by '[disrupting] the unity of the reader by discouraging identification with a unified subject of the enunciation' (2002: 84). By such means, the 'interrogative text' makes a robust political intervention as it 'invites an answer or answers to the questions it poses' (Belsey 2002: 85). Hutcheon is sceptical about Belsey's 'wishful projection' (1988: 221) that any such 'invitation to produce answers' might indeed effect what, as Althusser details, was Brecht's intention, namely a dialectical synthesis of literature and life that makes 'the spectator into an actor who would complete the finished play' (1969: 146). Yet even if one concludes, with Hutcheon, that such literature's capacity to '[reveal] the contradictions within [...] the prevailing ideology, may be all we have' (1988: 221), it is impossible to ignore Elisabeth Wesseling's pithy riposte that in politics, 'one has to make decisions and choose sides [...] [o]ne cannot remain within the realm of the undecidable' (1991: 8).

Wesseling alludes to the literary praxis endorsed by Belsey when arguing for the political efficacy of *some* of the postmodern literary engagements with history that Hutcheon surveys. In so doing, Wesseling takes issue first with Hutcheon's conflation of what she identifies as several distinct postmodern literary approaches to the writing of the past, and secondly with what she considers Hutcheon's exclusively deconstructionist methodology. For Wesseling, the politics that Hutcheon identifies is never more than

> an aborted politics, for it only allows for the subversion of the status quo, while it rules out the invention of alternatives. Hutcheon's explication of the political implications of postmodernism, then, negates what is probably the most important strategy by means of which twentieth-century artists have sought to acquire political significance, namely the utopian anticipation of the future. (1991: 12)[38]

Wesseling looks at how literature might articulate an effective challenge to the dominant ideological formations of the present by foregrounding and countering 'the ways in which versions of history function as instruments of *power* in the present' (1991: 118). Her study proposes to 'obtain a view of those aspects of postmodernism that do not overlap with deconstruction' through a diversified analysis, and diversified typology, of postmodern fiction. It analyses those postmodernist texts — 'most notably works by Reed, Grass, Rushdie, Fuentes and Pynchon' — that 'still partake of the utopian, without naively perpetuating either the illusion of the autonomous creative subject' or — by extension — the fantasy of a comprehensively empirical appraisal of historical truth (Wesseling 1991: 13). Questioning Hutcheon's clear distinction between 'classical' historical fiction and postmodern 'historiographical metafiction', Wesseling traces the origins of her corpus back to the work of modernists such as Woolf, Mann, and Henry James, and proposes the label of 'ucronian fantasy' or 'ucronian fiction'. Crucially, the utopian thinking that these works propose is not a simple projection of ideology, but proceeds from a 'counter-factual' engagement with documented history:

> The imaginative anticipation of the future which these novels figure forth proceeds along a somewhat more circuitous route than traditional utopian thought. Postmodernist novelists do not straightforwardly project inspiring alternatives for the status quo into the future. Rather, they turn to the past in order to look for unrealized possibilities that inhered in historical situations, and subsequently imagine what history would have looked like if unrealized sequences of events and courses of action had come about.' (ibid.)

As will be explored below, Saramago's engagement with Portuguese history over the course of his five novels of the 1980s partakes of both of these models of 'historiographical metafiction' and 'ucronian fiction', maintaining a critical perspective on all narrative reconstructions of the past (and political extrapolations thereof) and making no rebuttal of post-structuralist refutations of dialectical materialism's capacity to achieve a comprehensive synthesis of true historical conditions. It does, however, heed accusations such as that of Bryan Palmer, that a post-structuralist historiography based on the 'rather uncritical adoption of what has come to be known as critical theory' has resulted in

> the wholesale jettisoning of historical materialist assumptions and understandings, to the detriment of historical sensitivities and the denigration of the actual experience of historically situated men, women and children. (Palmer 1997: 104)

Saramago's novels, while reminding of our textually mediated relationship with past reality, nevertheless present what Wesseling terms 'enclaves of authenticity [...] signs that point toward the possibility of valid, authentic, historical knowledge, however hesitantly' (1991: 134). If such fictional signs can thus foster 'a sustained interest in the interpretative dimension of historiography', in Saramago's work such interest is solicited particularly with regard to the material reality of disregarded past suffering, injustice, and oppression, as if insisting on the ethical and political imperative of continued historical enquiry. Bryan Palmer makes an analogy between his own attack on post-structuralism (or more precisely, on the complacent acceptance of e.g. Lyotard's (1988) refutation of rational consensus) and Marx and Engels's attack, in *The German Ideology*, on 'what was inadequate and *ideological* in the philosophical conventions of their time', namely 'the idealism that refused acknowledgment of the primacy of actual humanity, the determining power of social relations over the consciousness of those relations' (1997: 106). Saramago's work eschews naïve insistence on the untrammelled legibility of those relations as historical determinants. Rather, it defies the reader to behold the revealed social injustice and violence of such relations, and still content herself/himself with the ludic, or pessimistic, response of deconstruction (in Hutcheon and Wesseling's arguably imprecise use of this term). Instead his work suggests maintaining the materiality of relations at the heart of socio-economic analysis, as the surest basis for a politics focused on basic human needs and rights, and observing a principle of collective responsibility. His work also makes clear, however, that such analysis, and such a politics, can only progress as a catalogue of errors.

III — De-harmonizing the Siren Song of History: On the Necessity of Error

This book's title derives from an episode in *Memorial do Convento* that allegorizes how heavily our perceptions of history are influenced by aesthetics, narratology, and their translation of ideology into art. This episode thereby also illuminates the motivations for Saramago's aesthetics of 'alienation', of dissonance, dissent, and unresolved dialectical oppositions. *Memorial*, set in the reign of Portugal's absolutist King João V, 'the Magnanimous' (1706–50), focuses on the vast monastery of Mafra, raised — at punitive financial and human cost — in fulfilment of the King's vow to thank God for the granting of an heir. In the *Estado Novo*'s narrative of national history, the Mafra monastery was made an icon of the power of prayer and miracles, and the might and benevolence of an imperial Portugal under God. Characteristically, Saramago's emphasis on the cruelty, waste, and arrogance of João V's administration seeks not to 'set the record straight' so much as to warn of 'the presentness of the past'; in this case, the monarch and monastery's contributions to a Catholic-corporatist ideological tradition spanning two hundred and fifty years. In a playful scene punctuating an often bleak and indignant narrative, Saramago imagines the first meeting between two luminaries of the Joanine court. Bartolomeu de Gusmão (1685–1724), the Brazilian-born Jesuit orator, theologian, mathematician, engineer, and pioneering aviator, strikes up conversation with the Neapolitan composer and harpsichord virtuoso, Domenico Scarlatti (1685–1757), as the latter exercises the skills with which he won his reputation as the greatest keyboard improviser of his day. This encounter prepares the ground for an intricate neo-baroque allegory of the epistemological and ethical dilemmas of the historian, which — as this book's second chapter explores more fully — is developed by comparison of Scarlatti's music-making to the search for historical truth. For the purposes of this Introductory chapter, however, it is sufficient to consider one (admittedly lengthy) fragment of the two men's dialogue:

> Terminou a lição, desfez-se a companhia, [...] e no salão de música apenas ficaram Domenico Scarlatti e o padre Bartolomeu de Gusmão. O italiano dedilhou o cravo, primeiro sem destino, depois como se estivesse à procura de um tema ou quisesse emendar os ecos [...] Senhor Scarlatti, disse o padre quando o improviso terminou e todos os ecos ficaram corrigidos, senhor Scarlatti, não me gabo de saber dessa arte, mas estou que até um índio da minha terra, que dela sabe ainda menos do que eu, haveria de sentir-se arrebatado por essas harmonias celestes, Porventura não, respondeu o músico, porque bem sabido é que há-de o ouvido ser educado se quer estimar os sons musicais, como os olhos têm de aprender a orientar-se no valor das letras e a sua conjunção de leitura, e os próprios ouvidos no entendimento da fala, São palavras ponderadas, essas, que emendam as levianas minhas, é um defeito comum nos homens, mais facilmente dizerem o que julgam querer ser ouvido por outrem do que cingirem-se à verdade, Porém, para que os homens possam cingir-se à verdade, terão primeiramente de conhecer os erros, E practicá-los, Não saberei responder à pergunta com um simples sim ou um simples não, mas acredito na necessidade do erro. (*Memorial*: 161–62)

[The lesson ended, the assembly was dismissed, [...] and in the music room there remained only Domenico Scarlatti and Padre Bartolomeu de Gusmão. The Italian ran his fingers over the keyboard, at first idly, then as if he were searching for a theme or wanted to tune its echoes [...] Senhor Scarlatti, I make no claims to knowledge of this art, but you make me feel like an Indian from my native land, who knows even less of it than I do, one can only feel enraptured by such celestial harmonies, Perhaps not, the musician replied, for it is well known that the ear must be educated if it wishes to appreciate musical sounds, just as the eye must learn to recognize the meaning of letters and their combination in writing, and as the same ear must learn to understand speech, These are well-chosen words, which temper my frivolous remarks, for it is a common fault in men, that they say what they believe others wish to hear more readily than they cleave to the truth, However, in order that men might cleave to the truth, they first must recognize their errors, And carry them out, Well I could not answer that question with a mere yes or a mere no, but I do believe in the necessity of error.]

Harking back to the Pythagorean theory of a primordial celestial harmony, and the Humanist concept of the musician's task as imitating or replicating that harmony on Earth, Gusmão and Scarlatti concur that humans' attempts to 'cingirem-se à verdade' proceed through acts of (musical or verbal) composition. *Memorial* invites us to read Scarlatti's music-making as metaphor. The descriptions of his playing (161; 164; 171) stress a need for painstaking motific exploration and experimentation in pursuit of a finished musical composition. The progression from the 'procura de um tema' [pursuit of a musical theme] to the 'emendar [d]os [seus] ecos' [the harmonization of its echoes] is, moreover, reflected in the taut wit of the dialogue that is inspired by his playing. In this context, Scarlatti's notion of the 'necessity of error' within attempts at such composition, offers insight into at least three crucial aspects of Saramago's deconstruction — and tentative, nuanced recomposition — of hegemonic historical narratives.

First, in a context where 'error' entails the sounding of 'wrong' notes, the idea of the *necessity* of error affirms the need to break the laws and harmony of accepted aesthetic codes (as does Brechtian drama) in order to venture beyond what is already known and accepted as correct. In considering the analogy between this and Saramago's 'alienating' use of inconsistent narrative voicing, of minimal punctuation, and of discursive disjunction and hybridization, it is worth recalling that Scarlatti's most acclaimed compositions, his 550-odd binary sonatas, served an expressly didactic purpose. Conceived as keyboard exercises for his royal pupils, each sonata develops two motifs, in contrasting harmonic keys, through a sometimes fiendishly complex sequence of melodic and rhythmic variations and key changes. Repeatedly threatening to wrong-foot the player, Scarlatti's sonatas compel her/him to recognize, and respond to, the changing relationship between notes written on a stave in the score, and keys and intervals on the keyboard, and thereupon alter her/his fingering accordingly. Saramago's Scarlatti, insisting upon the importance of error, implies that the music pupil's education should not be confined to learning and respecting a conventional musical language, but needs to explore that which is excluded or prohibited, to identify how rules and conventions mould the raw material of simple musical motifs, in order to appreciate the nature and potential of the task of composition. There is at least a basic analogy that can be traced between this analysis of 'dos and don'ts' of harmony, form, and motific development in an art form conceived of as the pursuit of a primordial truth, and the narratological assessment of historiography proposed by Hayden White and others, with its exploration of narrative emplotment, and especially of the 'motific characterization' of data drawn from the 'archive' of the past. The task of the 'composer' of history who wishes to advance knowledge is, obviously, not imitation of the existing account, but a critical interrogation of its potential narrative, factual, and hermeneutic rules and/as 'errors'.

At the same time, however, the composer of history must acknowledge both the inevitability of analogous factual and hermeneutic errors in an alternative account of the past, and the consequent 'necessity' of *aesthetic* error — dissonance — as a warning of that new composition's distortions. Saramago's aesthetics of alienation is thus not purely deconstructive or satirical. Rather, it can be related to proposals of Theodor Adorno concerning both musical aesthetics and philosophical method. Scarlatti's insistence on 'the necessity of error' recalls Adorno's endorsement of the harmonic and structural 'rule-breaking' in Schoenberg or late Beethoven, which trounces the listener's expectations by stalling the dialectic of nineteenth-century positivist aesthetics.[39] It also recalls Adorno's proposal of an analytical 'negative dialectics', which progresses by identifying *flaws* in the received knowledge or framework from within which it undertakes its analysis, and by seeking to identify and rehabilitate what has been omitted. Hence, *Memorial* concludes with the contrasting worlds of João V and his court and of lowly religious dissidents wholly 'unreconciled' by its emplotment, and the aspirations of the latter group still brutally suppressed.

Wesseling's concept of 'ucronian fiction' as a medium for an affirmative political engagement with the past in the era of postmodernity enables us to consider a third category of 'necessary error'. Saramago's interpolation of apocrypha, or even fantasy, into historical narratives is an ontological error. However, it is one that Wesseling, citing historian Alexander Demandt, argues has validity, insofar as counter-factual conjecture can effect a 'hypothetical, tentative correction of the distortions which necessarily result from the retrospective position of the historian' (1991: 104). Some postmodern historiographical fiction may 'haphazardly transform history' in a 'negational parody' (Wesseling 1991: 157) conducive to the presentism that Jameson decries. Yet where counter-factual conjecture exposes hegemonic history's 'teleological delusion', it may also reveal 'differing options and possibilities which prevailed at the time' (Wesseling 1991: 104). A simple case in point is *Memorial*'s imagining of outlawed scientific and rationalist thinking, which illuminates the opportunities for socio-economic progress lost to Portuguese society while its 'magnanimous' monarch squandered the Brazilian gold bonanza on monumental and ceremonial affirmations of his divine right. Its emphasis on the persistence, and even growth, of political and religious dissidence in the heyday of Portuguese absolutism counters the 'teleological delusion' that inclines historians in the present to 'interpret every event as tending toward the eventual outcome of the process under study' (Wesseling 1991: 104).

By means of these 'errors', Saramago's fiction simultaneously effects five operations with significant political implications. First, it foregrounds as much as it can recuperate of the experience and culture of the marginalized and oppressed. While warning the reader of the imperfect legitimacy of this (or any other) act of historiographical reconstruction, it asserts the centrality to any *telos* of human development of the agency of the labouring classes, the defeated, and the dissident. Secondly, it uses deconstructive and satirical devices to delegitimize historical narratives that by corroborating elements of an oppressive ideology (or 'ideologemes') serve as 'instruments of power'. The interpolation into historical narratives of blatantly fantastical or anachronistic tropes is a third operation. Blimunda's X-ray vision in *Memorial*, and the movement of the Iberian peninsula in *Jangada*, serve to expose the false certainties of the dominant ideology and, in accordance with Wesseling's concept of 'confirmational' parodic counter-factual fiction (1991: 164), to posit utopian alternatives to, for example, the dedication of scientific and technological innovation to military and authoritarian pursuits, or the opening of Spanish and Portuguese borders for essentially corporate, capitalist interests. At the same time, of course, Saramago's fiction, with its constant meta-narrative self-interrogation, and disclaimers to the reader, reminds of the inevitable shaping of such traces of the past into narratives, and the inevitably problematic role of hermeneutics and 'motific characterization' in fixing the meaning of historical events and agents. Such interventions ensure that the fifth operation of Saramago's novels on the popular discourse on history is the assertion of dialectical materialism as provisionally instructive, or inspirational, method of conjecture, rather than as a simple formula for calculating a comprehensive historical truth.

It is upon this hypothesis, and with particular reference to the human body, desires, and emotions, and the transformations wrought thereupon by material conditions, that Saramago offers speculative visions of a revised, radically egalitarian socialism. Despite his ever-increasing pessimism regarding both the ruthlessness of established powers, and late capitalism's increasingly insidious systems of coercion and co-optation, Saramago always remained committed to the rehabilitation of revolutionary socialist politics. As will be explored in the following chapters, his five novels of the 1980s convey an increasingly comprehensive updating of Marxist definitions of the human, of both individual and collective identity, and of social and political organization, in response to (amongst other things) the propositions of psychoanalysis and identity politics, and the threats and opportunities deriving from globalization and from mass-media and communications technology.

Levantado's historical rewriting is the one most self-evidently based on dialectical materialist methodology. The novel's 'polyphonic' narrative style translates the diversity of a subaltern population which, while united by economic deprivation and political exclusion, is riven by gender, age, ethnicity, and differing relationships to systems of production. Initially in thrall to a conception of rural society as a perpetually semi-feudal order attuned to the sometimes violent cycles of nature, the protagonists achieve an effective understanding of their socio-economic situation only through the integration of the 'falas mil' [thousand voices] (*Levantado*: 332) of smallholders and landless labourers, of urban proletariat and intellectuals, of emigrants, soldiers, women, children, and others. The workers' progressive synthesis of their disparate perspectives into a common vision (which, in a manner recalling the ideas of the Guinean revolutionary Amílcar Cabral, reinterprets popular lore and customs through the prism of historical materialism) progresses in tandem with the fruits of political solidarity. Yet the novel's conclusion, while allegorizing a triumph of essentially Marxist analysis and organization over Salazarism, also reiterates earlier metanarrative questions about the limitations of the dialectical materialist method. As Chapter 1 explores, the narration of *Levantado*'s final scene switches between the view-points of an airborne *milhano* [red kite] and the more circumscribed vision of the human protagonists celebrating below. Thereby it implies that, while the workers' victory may derive from collective consciousness achieved through a dialectical scrutiny of socio-economic conditions, that dialectic has not yet been resolved, and they have not yet achieved the comprehensive perspective attributed to the *milhano*. As for *Levantado*'s reader, if he/she is thus invited to 'produce answers' (as Belsey claims), or (as Althusser claims of Brechtian drama's spectator) become an actor who would complete the work (Althusser 1969: 146), his/her political work might focus first on the novel's implicit questions about a deficit of genuinely collective decision-making, and the persistence of patriarchal structures and values, even in the revolutionary movements of its time (and, arguably, of our own).

This fanciful device of narration from the perspective of birds of prey and ants pioneers Saramago's use of apocrypha, speculation, and counter-factual hypothesis to 'compensate' for suppressed historical data, and to expose the workings of the dominant ideology. Yet *Memorial*'s 'confirmational' parodic counter-factual does not claim supreme heuristic authority, or assert an alternative theory of historical causation with certainty. While the reader can easily extrapolate a utopian socialist message, the apocryphal, and in places wholly fantastical, plot elements from which this message emerges are subtly contained, such that they may not 'contaminate' the novel's carefully researched presentation of documented historical fact. The fantasy of Blimunda's vision, and of the radical egalitarian ideas and technological advances that it permits, allows Saramago to expand on the rethinking of socialist strategy and principles commenced in *Levantado*. Blimunda's apprehension of collective popular will as the motor of economic and political developments may be anachronistic in eighteenth-century Portugal. However, it is an understanding more widely shared in the present day; and the technical understanding required to turn aviation from dream to reality is at hand. *Memorial*'s fantasy of Bartolomeu de Gusmão's flying machine can thus be read as an allegory of the arguments of Herbert Marcuse for the emancipatory potential of both modern technology and an as-yet unrealized feminist Marxism, and for the pursuit of a socialist integration or 'organon' of labour, love, and art.

Thus, while *Memorial*'s fantasy, and its tragic denouement, might seem to evoke the impossibility of dreams of egalitarian utopia, one should also recognize how it alerts the reader to the deceptive notion, peddled in cruder emanations of postmodernism, of the futility, or even danger, of utopian thinking. Frequently applied in a reductive sense, as Jameson (2007: xi–xii) observes, to label intolerantly totalizing (and ultimately totalitarian) philosophies of social transformation, the term 'utopian' can also connote a practice of imagining radical alternatives to present conditions; a practice that, whether or not it is predicated on a consistent theory of history, is essential to any progressive political programme. *Memorial* reminds its reader of the historical roles of technology and economic reorganization in moving certain utopian aspirations from the realm of the fanciful to that of the attainable, with the inference that further progress may remain achievable, even without a totalizing law of historical causation.

On a formal level, *Memorial* combines more persistent metanarrative interruption with a more critical scrutiny of narrative histories' formal limitations. As Cerdeira da Silva (1989: esp.193–94) has explored, although *Levantado*'s narrative asides increasingly mock the use of messianic and heroic symbols and tropes from the New Testament, and from Camões's *Os Lusíadas*, to exalt the protagonists' struggle, the novel's conclusion completes an essentially epic narrative structure. *Memorial*, while affirming the importance of the poor and oppressed as agents of, and witnesses to, history, affords their story no triumphant resolution, instead concluding the apocryphal aspect of its plot in a tender account of private tragedy. The inconclusive end of its *historical* plot aspect, meanwhile, forcefully redoubles *Levantado*'s warning that, while materialist analytical methodology can uncover hidden truths, the full picture always remains inaccessible. In this way, *Memorial* establishes a pattern of contradictory or 'negated' narrative form in Saramago's novels. *Ricardo Reis* reads as both a 'failed' comedy — in which Ricardo Reis dodges responsibility for the biological 'regeneration' that his philandering sets in train, leaving his unborn son destined for martyrdom in Salazar's colonial wars — and as an 'ignoble' tragedy, in which Reis refuses to revise his egocentric world-view, even as its ethical and existential inadequacy becomes intolerably evident. *Ricardo Reis*'s fantastical conceit of bringing to life both the recently deceased Fernando Pessoa (1888–1935) and his 'heteronymous' creation Ricardo Reis does not open up any 'utopian space' akin to that of the Quinta da Pedreira in *Memorial*; rather, it serves both to examine the role of intellectuals and artists in popular resistance to modern authoritarian dystopia, and also to examine the inevitable politicization of canonical authors and their texts. The reader is invited to condemn Reis not only for using literature as a space of retreat from the material repercussions of his socio-economic location and relationships, but moreover for repudiating the 'socially useful' implications of his (that is, Fernando Pessoa's) understanding of the complexity and mutability of human identity.

Ricardo Reis's radical reinterpretation of Pessoa's thinking also exemplifies Saramago's technique of appropriating a politically problematic literary 'heritage' in the form of aesthetic codes, literary devices, and canonical narratives, and of redeploying them against the ideologies and political institutions he seeks to disempower. *Memorial*'s deployment of the wordplay, *conceptismo*, and allegorical structures associated with the art and oratory of the eighteenth century is socially levelling not only in the manner of baroque satire; it becomes central to the novel's demonstration that Marxism's historical materialist thesis might still inspire and inform the struggle for justice, and to its suggestion that a synthesized, materialist popular consciousness might yet trump the hegemony of an exploitative oligarchy. *Jangada* demonstrates the full implications of this 'recuperation' of artistic traditions, since it is made fundamental to Saramago's riposte to the project of European Economic Community (later, European Union) expansion, which he condemned as the neo-colonization of the post-dictatorship Iberian nations. In a fantastically counter-factual future, where the Peninsula separates physically from Europe and sails away across the Atlantic, the protagonists 'excavate' forgotten local history, and late nineteenth-century discussions of Iberian identity and socio-political organization. This recovered intellectual inheritance informs an attitude of 'rooted cosmopolitanism' (Cohen 1992) that reconciles loyalties to local culture and community to an internationalist solidarity with the subaltern populations of other or 'enemy' nations. *Jangada* repeats *Memorial*'s device of an 'affective microcommunity' — here, three men, two women, and a dog, from diverse regions of Iberia — living beyond the jurisdiction of the state. Here, the device serves for an exploration of the possibility of community with gendered or ethnic Others through the very process of 'becoming other' that *Ricardo Reis*'s Ricardo Reis refuses. Yet not only does *Jangada* acknowledge the material — and biological — manifestations of inequality that impede any embryonic new utopia; it also emphasizes the role of ideology, and of its reification through the increasingly pervasive technology of mass-media simulation, in containing, dissipating, or misdirecting popular discontent and rebellion. As shown by the post-2008 malaise of the Euro currency and of European Union institutions, capitalist hegemony is so thoroughly embedded in international law and media that even the most profound geopolitical and economic crisis can have a limited destabilizing impact. Achieving the more nuanced and broad-based radical coalition needed to oppose it depends in part, *Jangada* implies, on the exposure of established historical narratives as ideologically partial projections.

This point is writ large by *História*, but here the plot features neither a crisis of the hegemonic powers, nor any mass popular mobilization, and instead focuses on the experience and agency of two individuals. The story of Raimundo Silva's acts of historiographical iconoclasm and counter-factual speculation, inspired by his line manager, Dr Maria Sara, render explicit the previous four novels' implicit agenda of using speculation to destabilize the verisimilitude and hegemony of *História Pátria*, while alerting the reader to the ideological distortions of any account of the past that replaces it. What is also more explicit in *História* is how Saramago's reconfiguration of building blocks of Portuguese national identity possesses a political relevance for almost any 'imagined community' of the postmodern era. Raimundo's rewriting of the siege of Lisbon reveals the supposed foundation of Portuguese identity to consist substantially of the imagining of a sequence of hostile ethnic Others. While exploring this — ironically, in the streets of Lisbon's most multi-ethnic *bairros históricos* or 'historical quarters' — Raimundo must also come to terms with his personal investment in an antagonistic hierarchy of gender, as he yields to the romantic attraction between himself and the formidably self-possessed Maria Sara. Building on *Ricardo Reis*'s appropriation of Pessoa's concept of 'heteronymous' creativity, *História* presents Raimundo's re-writing of the 1147 Lisbon siege as an experimental rewriting of his own identity, on the basis of which he dares to break the self-constraining habits of a lifetime and embrace the love and self-knowledge that he formerly feared.

In this way, *História* offers suggestions for a revised political praxis that are at once much more pessimistic than those affirmed in *Levantado*, yet which open up another, cautiously utopian front in pursuit of a radically socialist transformation. Unlike *Levantado*, *História* ends with no new dawn or resurrection, but only a darkened, windowless room in which two lovers ponder the uncertain future of their relationship, and their equal lack of certainty regarding the impressions of the material world that they receive from the confinement of their latter-day Platonic cave. Raimundo may have challenged the omissions and distortions of an ideological history, but in so doing he discovers the limits of any alternative historiography, and the new history that he constructs serves not to state truth about the past, so much as to suggest possibilities for the future, or specifically, his own future, in the form of a new sense of identity, or 'inter-identity', negotiated with his new lover. At the same time as it reviews Saramago's preceding novels and amplifies their interrogation of historical materialism, *História* also presages his subsequent fiction's focus on complexities of the individual psyche and how these trouble conceptions of consistent, class-based subjectivity. In particular, it anticipates the most acclaimed of Saramago's later 'allegorical' novels, *Ensaio sobre a Cegueira* (1995): here, a ray of hope illuminates the grimmest apprehension both of epistemological uncertainty and of humankind's capacity for 'inhumanity', through the proposal of reconceiving of both individual and group identities. The exploration of becoming both 'other' and multiple — as a precondition for new practices of cooperation and solidarity not galvanized by exclusory or antagonistic conceptions of collectivity — emerges in these works as new starting point for a revised socialist 'micropolitics'. As *História* and *Cegueira* both also suggest, however, a second precondition for such a micropolitics is the courage to live with incomplete knowledge and unreliable perceptions, heeding the postmodern era's critique of political thought-systems that admit of no aporetic or ethical impediment to a totalizing vision and agenda. In other words, to conceive of and pursue utopia, while accepting the inevitability — indeed, the necessity — of error.

Notes to the Introduction

1. See Lopes (2010: 134).
2. A comprehensive catalogue of Saramago's publications, including all works in translation, and of the honours bestowed upon him (including 24 literary awards, honorific decorations from five states, and no fewer than 34 doctorates *honoris causa*), is found at the website of his Portuguese publisher, Caminho, at <http://www.caminho.leya.com/pt/autores/biografia.php?id=22659> [accessed 14 November 2014]. For data about successive editions, and all translations, see the Fundação José Saramago's bibliography, at <http://www.josesaramago.org/bibliografia-ativa-de-jose-saramago/> [accessed 3 April 2015].
3. See Bloom (2002a: 203), and Bloom's thought-provoking (if not always meticulously researched) lecture in (2002b). Fernando Meirelles's film *Blindness* (2008), and Denis Villeneuve's *Enemy* (2013), were adapted respectively from *Ensaio sobre a Cegueira* (1995) and *O Homem Duplicado* (2002), and followed George Sluizer's 2002 film adaptation of *A Jangada de Pedra*.

4. I borrow the term 'imagined community' from Anderson (1991).
5. See, amongst other landmark studies, Halbwachs (1992); Nora (1996); Anderson (1991), and Lowenthal (1985).
6. See, in particular, Lyotard (1984); Le Goff and Nora (1985), and White (1973).
7. See Baudrillard's (1983b) exploration of the 'implosion' of reality and simulation in the culture and media of the postmodern era, and the consequent phenomenon of 'hyperreality', and Saramago (1989c: 45).
8. For a survey of Saramago's political activism, see Lopes (2010: 139–42) on his relationship with the Portuguese Communist Party, (2010: 143–48) on his media-based campaigning in the wake of the Nobel award, and (2010: 153–54) on the establishment of the Fundação José Saramago, and also see the blog that Saramago ran on its website from 2007 until his death.
9. The applicability of the term 'postmodernist' to Saramago's thinking is discussed at length in Lima (1998) and Arnaut (2002).
10. For a brief history of Portugal under the *Estado Novo*, see Gallagher (1983: 51–183), and Birmingham (2003: 161–84). On Salazar and his political philosophy, see Meneses (2010); Pinto (ed.) (1998), and Pinto (1995).
11. On Salazar's economic policy, see Madureira (2007).
12. On Salazar's colonial policy, see, further to the studies above, Newitt (1981: 175–200), and Cann (1997).
13. On the *Estado Novo*'s cult of Portugal's expansion and evangelism, see, especially, João (2002); Torgal (2009: II, 119–216); Trindade (2008); Ó (2008); Holton (2005: 23–38), and Sapega (2002).
14. For an overview of *Estado Novo* education policy, see Gallagher (1983: 98–101). More comprehensive accounts include Mónica (1978), and Rosas et al. (1992: 496–501) on the treatment of teachers and academics, and (1992: 456–61) on the development of education policy and curricula.
15. See Cummins and Rebelo (2001).
16. On Portugal's European integration and deconvergence, see Soares (2012).
17. *O Tempo e a Alma* (1971–72) was Saraiva's first series produced for RTP; he continued to make historical documentaries for RTP up to *A Alma e a Gente* [The Soul and the Nation] (1997–98) (sources: 'Morreu o historiador José Hermano Saraiva', <http://www.jn.pt/PaginaInicial/Cultura/Interior.aspx?content_id=2677400&page=-1> [accessed 20 November 2012], and 'José Hermano Saraiva', <http://pt.wikipedia.org/wiki/Jos%C3%A9_Hermano_Saraiva> [accessed 20 November 2012]. The case against both Saraiva's 'dangerous' and 'revisionist' brand of TV history, and its context of an academic establishment that debates national history only 'na exclusividade dos congressos e suas actas' [in the cloistered realm of academic conferences and their proceedings] is set out forcefully by João José Cardoso (2012).
18. For a full account of International Communist Party policy on literary aesthetics, see Bernard (1972).
19. See Pita's account (1989: 46) of the 1930s neo-realists' debates between the 'historicist' Marxism propounded by, amongst others, Bento de Jesus Caraça and Mário Dionísio, and the 'scientist' Marxism affirmed by Bukharin and Stalin. See also Pita's (2002: 37–79) full account of this polemic, as well as Ferreira (1992); Reis (1983: 34–76), and Silva (1990).
20. As Lukács claims, '[a] great realist such as Balzac, if the intrinsic artistic development of situations and characters he has created comes into conflict with his most cherished prejudices or even his most sacred convictions, will, without an instant's hesitation, set aside these his own prejudices and convictions and describe what he really sees, not what he would prefer to see' (1950: 11). See also Lukács (1962: 39; 59ff.) on the use of 'typical' characterization.
21. Dionísio, 'A propósito de Jorge Amado', *O Diabo*, 164 (14 November 1937); cited without page reference by Pita (2002: 236).
22. See Redol (1970), and Ferreira (1992: 152–64). On neo-realist symbolic encryption, see also Pires (1972), and Sabine (2011).
23. See Viçoso (1999: esp. 242), and Silva (1996). Also see Wittmann (1997) and Arnaut (2002).
24. See Brecht (1974).
25. For a concise history of the reception of Brecht's dramatic theory in Portugal, see Delille (1991).

26. See also Brecht (1990: 187).
27. See Aristotle (94 (English translation, 95), and also 34–37; 54–57).
28. On the prominence of Brechtian texts and staging practices from the mid-1970s to the early 1980s, see Sabine and Williams (2010: 184–85), and Barata (1997: esp. p. 114; p. 118, and pp. 120–22).
29. More than twenty African titles were published in translation in Edições 70's *Vozes de África* series in 1979 and 1980; Caminho commenced its *Uma Terra Sem Amos* series of world literature in 1979, including translations of Sembène Ousmane, Oyono, and Ngũgĩ wa Thiong'o.
30. See Lopes (2010: 55–56).
31. As Maria Teresa Patrício and Alan Stoleroff summarize, while, in the period 1974–91, 'the PCP energetically resisted the trend to Communist breakup' and 'unapologetically maintained its dedication to orthodox Leninism', nevertheless 'the party's electoral results suffered a continuous gradual decline after 1979' (1993: 69).
32. Crucially, however, Bakhtin (1981: 349) distinguishes between the 'smoothing over' of ideological disparity among heteroglossia in the realism of e.g. Turgenev, and the looser control over conflicting ideologies exercised in Dostoevsky's novelistic prose.
33. See Bakhtin (1973: 131–49) for his full definition of literary 'carnival', and outline of its history.
34. The theme of the restitution of a brutalized humanity is made explicit by *Objecto Quase*'s opening epigraphic quotation of Marx and Engels's assertion, in *The Holy Family*, that 'se o homem é formado pelas circunstâncias, é necessário formar as circunstâncias humanamente' [if mankind is formed by his circumstances, it is necessary to form those circumstances humanely] (Saramago 1986: 11). See also Neves (1999: esp.124–32) for further observations on this denunciation of the 'coisificação do ser humano ou a sua redução à dependência de uma infinidade de objectos' [objectification of the human being, or his/her reduction to dependence on an infinity of objects] (1999: 125).
35. On *Objecto Quase* and its reflection on the *Estado Novo*'s demise, see also Costa (1997: 319–49), Frier (2007b), and Sabine (2011: 43–51).
36. Saramago's full disquisition on this topic, delivered to the closing session of a literary summer school convened by the Universidad Complutense de Madrid at El Escorial in July–August 1996, is reproduced in his *Cadernos* entry for 9 August (1997: 191–96).
37. On discursive hybridity in this scene, see also Silva (1989: 207).
38. Wesseling notes Hutcheon's explicit indication (1988: 47; 215; 218; 230) that the postmodern and the utopian are at odds with one another.
39. See Adorno (2006: esp.96) and also (1998) on modern music and revolutionary consciousness.

CHAPTER 1

Levantado do Chão

In Portugal in 1980, the dust was settling on what for social democrats was a successful transition to parliamentary democracy, but for much of the left was a popular revolution aborted by the machinations of NATO, the Catholic Church, and international capital. While a liberalized, capitalist Portuguese state was inching towards economic and institutional stability with the aid of EEC structural funding, debates about social justice and the country's long-term direction and values remained heated. The passion of contemporary Portuguese politics was reflected in the critical and popular reception of Saramago's novel. Notwithstanding its convoluted syntax and sometimes disorienting multi-voiced narrative, *Levantado do Chão* has frequently elicited an impassioned response to its depiction, by turns raw, lyrical, and sardonic, of the violence and hardship of life on the agricultural estates — or *latifundia* — of Portugal's Alentejo region. Reviewing the novel in 1981, Maria Lúcia Lepecki warned her reader of its 'mágico encanto' [magic spell], and compared reading and re-reading it to falling in love (1988: 83). The novel was informed by Saramago's two-month residence, in Spring 1976, on the newly established 'Boa Esperança' agricultural cooperative in Lavre, near Montemor-o-Novo. Saramago befriended and interviewed many of the Cooperative's 400 workers, filling two hundred pages of notebooks with testimonies, local history, and lore (Lopes 2010: 67). Its plot, tracing the political struggle of four generations of agricultural workers to its apogee, as they occupy and collectivize the *latifundium*, suggests a now unfashionable faith in class politics, not to mention in social-realist aesthetics.[1] Noting Saramago's own claim that '*Levantado do Chão* é o último romance do neo-realismo, fora já do tempo neo-realista' [*Levantado do Chão* is the last neo-realist novel, outside the neo-realist period] (Reis 1998: 118) might only deepen suspicions that the novel is provincial and anachronistic. Closer investigation, however, reveals that Saramago's comment alludes not simply to the novel's appearance after the end of the political tyranny that the neo-realists confronted, but also to the radically different handling of fictional time in this compared to his subsequent novels. *Levantado* is, moreover, critically important to any understanding of Saramago's wider artistic and political project for ideological reasons as much as formal ones. It places the stock locations, topics, and poetic devices of the neo-realist novel of resistance to Salazarism within the framework of revised conceptions of historical or 'documentary' fiction, and of radically different conditions for the reception of politically engaged writing. Finally free from censorship, writers on the left could address the new conditions and challenges, and propose a revised revolutionary agenda. While perpetuating neo-realism's didactic and agitational aims, *Levantado* overturns Lukács's notions of formal unity, 'reflection', and typicality. Uniquely among Saramago's novels, it does this through gradually transforming its narrative voicing, in tandem with the socio-economic and ideological transformations that its plot represents. As Saramago's Alentejan labourers move away from alienation in pursuit of a shared materialist *perspectiva totalizante*, the treatment both of narrative authority, and of the historical and literary raw material that the novel processes, constantly shifts, compelling the reader to remain alert, and concurrently to adapt her/his mode of reading the text. With increasing frequency, the extradiegetic voice that dominates the narrative at the outset interrupts itself, effecting a Brechtian 'alienation' of the text that destabilizes the idea of an authoritative 'narrator'. The extradiegetic voice is, moreover, increasingly usurped by interpolated character narration and extended dialogue. This movement towards what Bakhtin would term a 'polyphonic' narrative form corresponds both to the novel's theme of subaltern protagonists finding their voices and asserting their own testimony to oppression and revolt, and to an implicit rethinking of how political consciousness and revolutionary mobilization might operate.[2] This gradual devolution of narrative authority affects particularly those narrative sequences that re-work neo-realist symbolism, or that revise the didactic tableaux that serve to reveal the 'true' socio-economic relations in classic neo-realist novels. The increasingly arch, self-parodic, and ultimately fantastical treatment of neo-realist derived tropes is key to the novel's strategy of privileging a Marxist interpretation of history, yet simultaneously using the disruption of mimesis to ensure the reader's critical detachment both from the diegesis and from the ideologies it articulates. However, the novel's innovations also recall contemporary international literary trends departing from socialist realism, particularly in Latin America. Its structural and symbolic allusions to *Cien años de soledad* (1967) signal Saramago's glossing both of Gabriel García Márquez's reconciliation of 'fantastical' elements with a Marxist literary project, and of that novel's warning about dehistoricizing 'grand narratives'.[3] *Levantado*'s plot, however, inverts the tragic course by which Márquez's Macondo succumbs to its own faith in a world-view that values pure blood-lines and kinship. The Alentejan workers' assumption of command of their destiny relates clearly to how they replace superstition and ahistorical supposition with dialectical materialist analysis, even as the text intimates that such analysis yields at best a very imprecise knowledge.

Levantado's innovatory narrative form thus celebrates the workers' struggle while challenging Marxist orthodoxies about aesthetics, historiography, and indeed even political mobilization. It illustrates the diversity of experience and identity of the oppressed, and emphasizes the need for grass-roots level dialogue and empathy in forging a collective consciousness and revolutionary will. In these aspects, the novel breaks with the Stalinist tenet of 'democratic centralism' in the revolutionary party. This and the novel's implicit critique of socialist programmes that accommodate the oppressive apparatus of patriarchy, pick up on debates within the clandestine Portuguese Communist leadership of the mid-twentieth century. It brings them into alignment with Gramscian notions of a radicalized 'historical bloc' in less-developed capitalist economies, and with Marxist-feminist demands (dating back to the writings of Alexandra Kollontai in the 1920s) for the revolution's extension to the domestic sphere, and to familial and sexual relations. The scrutiny that this entails of the minutiae of day-to-day social, economic, and emotional transactions prefigures the emphasis in Saramago's later novels on a micropolitical analysis of subjectivity and intersubjectivities. One might well consider how this relates to those novels' decreasing focus on the constitution of a mass political movement, and one must also acknowledge how *Levantado* ultimately questions the possibility of a totalizing synthesis of dialectically counterposed perspectives. This question of whether and how story-telling can give way to — or come to constitute — truth-telling is articulated through one of Saramago's most brilliant deployments of his recurrent, and increasingly central, metaphoric trope of vision.

I — Beyond Neo-Realism: Framing Representation, Training the Reader

Both *Levantado*'s concern with the Marxist pursuit of historical truth and its relationship with the neo-realist novel are established even before the reader opens its covers. This is due to Saramago's claim, in his dust-jacket epigraph, that

> Um escritor é um homem como os outros: sonha. E o meu sonho foi o de poder dizer deste livro, quando o terminasse: 'Isto é o Alentejo'. Dos sonhos, porém, acordamos todos, e agora eis-me não diante do sonho realizado, mas da concreta e possível forma do sonho. Por isso me limitarei a escrever: 'Isto é um livro sobre o Alentejo.' Um livro [...] que quis aproximar-se da vida, e essa seria a sua mais merecida explicação. (*Levantado*: cover)
>
> [A writer is a man like all others: he dreams. And my dream was to be able to say of this book, once I had finished it, 'This is the Alentejo'. All of us, however, awake from our dreams, and now here I am facing not the accomplished dream, but the material and possible form of my dream. Hence I will restrict myself to saying 'This is a book about the Alentejo'. A book [...] that wanted to get up close to life, and this would be its best explanation.]

A reader well-versed in Portuguese fiction would recognize this disclaimer as modelled on Alves Redol's famous preface to *Gaibéus* (1940), claiming that that seminal neo-realist novel 'não pretende ficar na literatura como obra de arte. Quer ser, antes de tudo, um documentário humano fixado no Ribatejo' [does not aim to be recognized as a literary work of art. It aims to be, above all, a human documentary focused on the Ribatejo] (1945: 9).[4] This act of parody serves at least three purposes. First, it enables Saramago to affirm his solidarity with the social and political agenda of neo-realism, while stressing, in his dismissal of the 'sonho' of a literary microcosm of reality ('isto é o Alentejo'), his rejection of the movement's founding aesthetic premise (if not also its objective of contributing to the comprehension of a historical truth). Secondly it proposes to 'os homens [*sic*] a quem me dirijo' [the men whom I address] (ibid.) a politically engaged assessment not simply of 'muitos sacrifícios e grandes fomes, as vitórias e os desastres' [many sacrifices and great famines, the victories and calamities] of the Alentejo, but particularly of 'a aprendizagem e a transformação' [education and transformation]

(*Levantado*: cover). This is not simply the apprenticeship of the protagonists and the transformation of the socio-economic conditions in which they live, struggle and die. Rather, as will be made clear in the novel's first chapter, it is also the 'aprendizagem' of the reader, and the 'transformação' of the narrative strategies used to compel her/him to reflect critically upon the novel's representation of the past. These strategies reflect the principle, implicit throughout the plot, that historical perception and political power develop concurrently through active, dialectical analysis, whether undertaken by the rural proletariat that the novel represents, or by the reader that it addresses. The plot's conclusion, however, leaves unanswered the question of whether the *perspectiva totalizante* that the literary text cannot encapsulate can nonetheless be elaborated through the reader's dialectical engagement with the text's partial but 'unpackaged' representations of historical reality.[5] Thirdly, Saramago's paraphrase of Redol introduces the novel's tactic of reworking tropes and tableaux from iconic neo-realist texts. As the 'aprendizagem' of both reader and protagonists advances, the style of these reworkings evolves from being reverential to gently burlesque. Thus, the novel suggests how strategies for representing reality in politically engaged fiction can usefully be revised in response to different circumstances of reception, or how, in the much-quoted phrase that closes the novel's first chapter: 'tudo isto pode ser contado doutra maneira' [all of this can be told in a different way] (*Levantado*: 14).

The phrase 'contar doutra maneira' has multiple meanings: it can be translated variously as 'to relate in another manner'; 'to account for in another manner'; 'to tell the story differently'; 'to tell a different story'.[6] Manuel Simões has noted that the phrase is reworked numerous times throughout the novel, to draw attention to the 'arquitectura do romance [...] [e] os limites da escrita' [the architecture of the novel and the limits of language] (1996: 74). First and most obviously, *Levantado* shows how a novel can relate a (hi)story of the Alentejo in a manner different to that of neo-realism. As Simões puts it, the opening chapter serves from the outset to 'criar o contexto histórico-morfológico que servirá de pano de fundo à narração dos eventos' [create the historical and morphological context providing the backdrop to the narration of events] (Simões 1996: 73). The minimal use of punctuation prompts a reading practice that is more deliberate, and thus more attentive to the stylistic and discursive incongruity and oscillations between past and present tense narration. Meanwhile, premature revelations of plot outcomes and the deliberately two-dimensional construction of character disrupt the reader's emotional engagement, prompting her/him instead to consider the historical conditioning of both individual and group identities and behaviour.

At the same time, of course, the novel aims, just as much as the works of Redol and his peers, to contest (or *account for in a different manner*) the dominant narrative of Alentejan history. The first chapter's opening sentences first introduce, then progressively undermine, that narrative. Initially, the purported facts of the predetermined and immutable cycle of Alentejo life are set out in one consistent voice or register:

> O que mais há na terra, é paisagem. Por muito que do resto lhe falte, a paisagem sempre sobrou, abundância que só por milagre infatigável se explica, porquanto

a paisagem é sem dúvida anterior ao homem, e apesar disso, de tanto existir, não se acabou ainda. Será porque constantemente muda: tem épocas no ano em que o chão é verde, e outras em que é amarelo, castanho ou negro. (*Levantado*: 11)

[The thing that most abounds on Earth is the landscape. However much else may be lacking, the landscape has never been in short supply, an abundance only explained by a timeless miracle, since the landscape undoubtedly predates humankind, and despite this, having existed for so long, it has still not come to an end. It might be because it is constantly changing: there are times of year when the ground is green, and others when it is yellow, brown, or black.]

The conflation of the cycle of agricultural life with Biblical myths of origin and destiny here subordinates perceptions of change to a justification of a status quo 'decidido desde o princípio do mundo, quando tudo era paisagem, com alguns bichos grandes e poucos homens de longe em longe, e todos assustados' [decided since the beginning of the world, when everything was landscape with a few large beasts and the occasional man sparsely scattered here and there, and all of them frightened] (*Levantado*: 12). The claim that 'levou séculos para chegar a isto' [it took centuries to achieve the present situation] underpins the belief that 'assim vai ficar até à consumação dos séculos' [thus things will remain until the end of times] (*Levantado*: 14). This conception of the present as a divinely ordained 'end of history' is, however, soon disrupted. Enunciatory splitting and inconsistency of register — the discursive clashes that Bakhtin terms 'dialogism', but which could equally be called *telling the story differently* — convey dissent and satirical disdain, as when it is noted that the earth can be

também vermelho, em lugares, que é cor de barro ou sangue sangrado. Mas isso depende do que no chão se plantou e cultiva, ou ainda não, ou não já, ou do que por simples natureza nasceu, sem mão de gente, e só vem a morrer porque chegou o seu último fim. Não é tal o caso do trigo, que ainda com alguma vida é cortado. Nem do sobreiro, que vivíssimo, embora por sua gravidade o não pareça, se lhe arranca a pele. Aos gritos. (*Levantado*: 11)

[also red, in places, which is the colour of clay or spilt blood. But this depends on what is sown and cultivated in the soil, or on that which by nature alone was born there, without human intervention, and only happens to die because its last hour has come. This is not the case with wheat, which is cut when there is still some life left in it. Nor the case with the cork oak, which is full of life, however solemn its appearance, and cries out as its skin is ripped off it.]

This first of innumerable narrative digressions corrects the initial identification of 'constant change' as an inexplicable (indeed, miraculous) paradox, revealing the nature of the landscape's cycles to be contingent on human agency, which, as the images of spilt blood and excoriation suggest, is frequently violent and permanently transformative. Thus these sentences reprise Saramago's exploration in *Objecto Quase* of the theme of the polysemy and plasticity of language, and of its susceptibility to de-/re-construction.[7] Just as the seemingly 'grave' and static cork-oak is 'vivíssimo', and capable of crying out in distress, so too is the linguistic raw material seemingly stabilized in established representations of the Alentejo. So too, moreover, can this linguistic material be unyoked from verisimilitude and reworked, thereupon destabilizing established ideological constructions that it formerly galvanized; so too can it cry out.[8] So too can language be appropriated and remoulded into forms that convey suppressed truths of suffering, conflict, and resistance; that is, forms that *tell a different story*. The image of harvested wheat, recurrent throughout the novel, exemplifies how fiction can exploit the clash between its mimicked and quoted discourses to expose an ideological spin on history, and to formulate an alternative history. The image triggers allusions both to the gospel parables of the Sower and of the Wheat and the Tares, employed under the *Estado Novo* to preach workers' obedience to the Church and its laws, and to the reworking of these in neo-realism's symbolic code to denote the revolutionary party 'harvesting' the working class.[9]

The novel's first chapters thus alert the reader to the role of discursive transformation in sustaining the dialectical counterposition of perspectives, and analytical practice of reading, that must be brought to bear on narrative accounts of the past. As the novel progresses, such subversion and contestation of established discourses, and de-/re-construction of familiar and seemingly stable images and concepts, will be carried out by an ever more inconsistent and self-conscious extradiegetic narrative voice. Moreover, this voice will increasingly be interrupted by intradiegetic voices, at first unidentified, but later including principal characters. While this proliferation of subaltern testimonies 'unparcels' the dominant narrative of Alentejo history, however, it also raises a question: can the incongruent perspectives of different oppressed constituencies be synthesized into one *perspectiva totalizante*, or must projects of social transformation always remain alert to other 'maneiras de contar'?

Levantado's plot follows a family of agricultural labourers, the Mau-Tempos, in the village of Montelavre, north of Montemor-o-Novo in the Alto Alentejo, from the early twentieth century to the summer of 1974. While initially perceiving their physical and social environment in the terms of the stable, incessant cycle analysed above, the Montelavre workers' outlook is transformed by their intensifying exploitation. Increasingly conscious of their common economic interests, they organize to challenge the 'santíssima trindade' [most holy trinity] of institutions that collude in their subjugation: State, Church, and *latifundium* (*Levantado*: 223–24). The workers' political awareness is shown to germinate in the 1910s, when the First Republic's broken promises of land and labour reform lead to spontaneous strike action. Class consciousness develops apace as Salazar's *Estado Novo* seeks to reconcile the modernization of agricultural methods and labour relations with harsh wage-restraint and a revival of Catholic and corporatist values. The ruthless responses of landowners and the state to workers' organization and protest create a sometimes violent, but always instructive, clash of insider and outsider perspectives. The novel's main protagonist, João Mau-Tempo, survives a childhood of deprivation and domestic violence to become active in the Portuguese Communist Party (PCP), as this develops into the most effective force of popular resistance to the *Estado Novo*.[10] João witnesses and suffers the brutality first of the landowning elite, and later of Salazar's *Polícia Internacional e da Defesa do Estado* (*PIDE*), whose suspected torture and murder, in 1945, of strike organizer Germano Santos Vidigal is depicted in sickening detail.[11] João and his wife Faustina nevertheless secure both a better upbringing and a basic education for their children. Their daughter Gracinda becomes active in the underground Party, where she presses for recognition of working women's rights and needs. Their son António, who joins the army, represents the radicalization of Portugal's armed forces in the post-war era, as increasing numbers of men from lower-class backgrounds entered the officer corps.[12] The growth of working-class consciousness and activism, and gradually weakening grip of *Estado Novo* ideology, is conveyed through a series of tableaux of Joao's arrest, torture, and imprisonment in the 1950s, of the bloody riots in Montemor-o-Novo in 1958, of increasingly powerful strikes in the 1960s, and, finally, of the workers' occupation of the *latifundium* at harvest-tide 1974, in which Gracinda's teenage daughter, Maria Adelaide, plays a leading role. This last tableau dovetails an element of fantasy into a reconstruction of historical events, as the spirits of the martyred dead arise to join the occupation. This caps the novel's series of Biblical parodies with a revolutionary socialist resurrection, while also reworking the fundamental concept in Émile Zola's *Germinal* of the radicalized proletariat as an 'organic' social force rising from the earth, an 'armée noire, vengeresse, qui germait lentement dans les sillons, grandissants pour les récoltes du siècle futur' [black and avenging army of men, germinating in its furrows, growing upwards in readiness for harvests to come] (1979: 502; translation. 1993: 524).[13]

The gradual transformation of narrative form over *Levantado*'s plot-arc, and its effect of suggesting a democratization of discourse, concomitant with the historical movement towards workers' politicization and empowerment, was noted early on. Review essays by Lélia Parreira Duarte (1982), and by Renato Cordeiro Gomes (1989), stress the dialectical logic both of this burgeoning dialogism, and of the workers' 'aquisição da consciência e [...] conquista do espaço' [acquisition of consciousness and [...] conquest of space] (Duarte 1982 : 87). Duarte sees *Levantado* as a book of two halves, the first of which is narrated 'dentro de pressupostos' [in conformity with conventional wisdom], and discursively 'monológico, predeterminado [...] pelo poder' [monologic, predetermined by power]. It is in the second half that the acquisition of consciousness is marked by discursive 'sinais de mudança e diálogo, de intertextualidade e distanciamento' [signs of change and dialogue, intertextuality and [ironic] distancing] (Duarte 1982: 87). While Duarte's insight into the relationship between processes of narratological change and the protagonists' empowerment is a crucial one, however, her bipartite division underplays the complexity of those processes. As Gomes puts it, although the extradiegetic narrative voice 'não abra mão de seu lugar de mestre, nem da mensagem ideológica forte (a Revolução), nem de sua pedagogia' [does not relinquish either its status as master, or its concerted ideological message (the Revolution), or its pedagogy] (1989: 23), it accepts that the 'livro do latifúndio' [book of the *latifundium*] is not written 'por apenas um sujeito autoritário' [solely by an authoritarian subject], and agrees to '[ver] o avesso e [aprender] com o *outro*' [observe from the obverse angle and learn along with the Other] (1989: 20). Thus, 'vai-se estabelecendo a troca, o diálogo' [dialogue and interchange become established] and the erstwhile 'mandador de falas' [director of speech] permits a dialogue between

> outros falantes que se tornam sujeitos à medida que adquirem seu próprio

discurso com o despertar da consciência, quando não são mais repetidores passivos e submissos de discursos alheios. (ibid.)

[Other speakers who become subjects in proportion to their acquisition of their own particular discourse, as consciousness is awoken when they are no longer passive and submissive parroters of alien discourses.]

Developing these insights into a thorough review of narrative evolution is crucial to an understanding of the novel's aesthetic and political meanings. It confirms that the movement towards dialogism corresponds to the dialectical, and unfinished, progress towards a materialist *perspectiva totalizante*, which first ruptures, and eventually usurps, the hegemonic ideology of the 'santíssima trindade'.

The corresponding evolutions of narrative form and popular consciousness are evident from the start of the Mau-Tempos's story, in the novel's second chapter (*Levantado*: 15–22). Here and throughout most of the following ten chapters (*Levantado*: 23–97), the intervention of intradiegetic voices is strictly limited. The narrative voice imitates the discursive status quo, where labourers' suffering is taken for granted, and where popular wisdom circulates in the forms of proverbs, folk tales, local gossip, and superstition; in other words, the residue of pagan belief in humanity's subjection to the cycles and bounty of the Earth.[14] The ideology justifying the 'santíssima trindade''s dominion is all the while trumpeted by characters whose implausible names denote their status as stock representatives of the essentially unchanging subjectivities of the social groups that uphold those institutions: the *latifundium* owners Sigisberto, Lamberto, and Adalberto, the government and army officers such as Tenente Contente and Cabo Tacabo, and Padre Agamedes, first of a succession of like-named, and equally reactionary, parish priests.[15]

Even at this stage, however, *Levantado*'s narrative form apprises its reader of the illegitimacy of the novelist's status as both spokesperson for the disenfranchised, and convenor of a totalizing historical perspective. This can be seen in the presentation of Domingos, Sara, and João Mau-Tempo, journeying under torrential rain to their new home in São Cristóvão (*Levantado*: 15). This simple tableau effectively tells at least two familiar narratives 'in a different manner'. Both the Biblical flight into Egypt (as Maria Graciete Besse (2000: 33) has noted), and the opening of Fernando Namora's influential 1954 representation of Alentejo life, *O Trigo e o Joio* (1963: 17), are recalled by the Mau-Tempo's journey. Yet this episode constitutes a kind of 'serious parody', which does not ridicule the original narratives *per se*, but rather advertises both how neo-realism's social critique relies on contrived analogies with Biblical parables, and how authors of fiction more generally speak for, rather than truly enfranchise, the historical subject. Whereas Namora deploys the 1950s neo-realist conventions of omniscient narration, *Levantado*'s narrative voicing draws attention to the ethically problematic 'ventriloquism of the speaking subaltern' that Gayatri Spivak famously denounced as 'the left intellectual's stock-in-trade' (1995: 28), which threatens to compound the marginalization or silencing of real-life subalterns. Notwithstanding the origins of the novel in the notebooks of workers' testimony that Saramago collected in Lavre in 1976 (Lopes 2010: 67), the narrative voice claims no access to characters' thoughts. Instead it surmises, for example, that although Sara Mau-Tempo's first utterance, comparing the family's new home to their previous one, 'pareceu só um dizer de comparação, seria talvez saudade' [seemed to be only a statement of comparison, it might perhaps have been regret] (*Levantado*: 16). Reporting utterances using undescriptive verbs like 'perguntar' [enquire] and 'responder' [reply], the narrative voice replicates the role of a 'dispassionate observer or thinker' (Benjamin 1973a: 151) in Brechtian 'epic theatre', of sustaining the audience's detachment. This, significantly, does not prevent it from speaking up for those silenced by the discursive hegemony of the 'santíssima trindade', or by the tyranny of husbands such as Domingos, who threatens Sara after she interrupts his drink in São Cristóvão's tavern to remind him that the family's belongings, infant João, and she are getting soaked in the rain outside (*Levantado*: 21). Yet the narrator's interventions — here, '[boas] razões são as dela' [her reasoning is sound] (ibid.) — are marked as interpretation rather than fact, and often hedged by disclaimers: '[isto] é um dito do narrador, que bem se dispensava' [this is a comment by the narrator, which could well be done without] (*Levantado*: 18). Such comments, however, only begin to be dispensed with when the third and fourth chapters re-tell the Mau-Tempos' story 'doutra maneira', jumping forward to Domingos's suicide, then back to João's conception and birth, and allowing the first intromission of character narration, by Sara Mau-Tempo (*Levantado*: 25).

Sara's timid intervention — praying that her absent husband will keep away from drink — conveys how geography and a stagnant feudal socio-economic order perpetuate Monte Lavre's isolation. Meanwhile, the characterization of her shiftless husband, named, as Duarte (1982: 87) notes, after the Sabbath, and dedicated to the Catholic god and institutions, suggests the prevalence of a self-defeating allegiance to the dominant ideology and institutions of what Besse calls this 'tempo dos silêncios e da opressão alienante' [time of silence and alienating oppression] (2000: 35). At the promulgation of the First Republic in 1910, technological and political transformation elsewhere still make only the faintest impression:

> A república veio despachada de Lisboa, andou de terra em terra pelo telégrafo, se o havia, recomendou-se pela imprensa, se a sabiam ler, pelo passar de boca em boca, que sempre foi o mais fácil. O trono caíra, o altar dizia que por ora não era este reino o seu mundo, o latifúndio percebeu tudo e deixou-se estar, e um litro de azeite custava mais de dois mil réis, dez vezes a jorna de um homem. (*Levantado*: 33)

> [The Republic arrived by dispatch from Lisbon, travelling from one place to the next by telegraph line, where there was one, commended by the newspapers, to those who could read them, and relayed by word of mouth, which had always been the simplest method. The throne had toppled, the altar said that for the time-being this kingdom was not its world, the *latifundium* took it all in and let things be, and a litre of cooking oil cost more than two thousand *réis*, ten times a man's daily wage.]

While the *latifundium* 'lets things be', in the unsettled but optimistic wake of the Republican coup, workers — women included — may for the first time ask difficult questions and directly express dissatisfaction, even if worthwhile responses remain rare:

> Viva a república, Viva. Patrão, quanto é o jornal agora, Deixa ver, o que os

outros pagarem, pago eu também, fala com o feitor, Então quanto é o jornal, Mais um vintém, Não chega para a minha necessidade, Se não quiseres, mais fica, não falta quem queira, Ai minha santa mãe, que um homem vai rebentar de tanta fome, e os filhos, que dou eu aos filhos, Põe-nos a trabalhar, E se não há trabalho, Não faças tantos, Mulher, manda os filhos à lenha e as filhas ao rabisco da palha, e vem-te deitar[.] (ibid.)

[Long live the Republic, Long may it live. Boss, how much is a day's pay now, Wait and see, whatever the others pay, I'll pay as well, speak to the foreman, How much is a day's pay, then, A penny more, That's not enough to meet my needs, If you don't want it, then I'll keep it, there's plenty of others who'll want it, Oh Holy Mother of God, this hunger would do a man in, and my children, what will I give my children, Put them to work, And if there is no work for them, Then don't have so many, Wife, send the boys out for firewood and the girls for straw, and come here to bed.]

This chapter suggests the freedom briefly lent by political instability following the Republican coup, when soldiers and two groups of workers usurp the narrative, in the novel's first sustained passage of unmediated dialogue (*Levantado*: 36–38). Yet the dominant social class soon re-establishes its monopoly on discourse, and on political power: years will pass while Monte Lavre's workers still 'vive longe, não lhe chegam notícias, ou não as entende, só ele sabe o esforço que lhe custa manter-se vivo' [live far away, where the news doesn't reach, or is little understood, and nobody knows how much effort it takes them to keep themselves alive] (*Levantado*: 91). Thus the First World War, fought in the distant land of Europe, a 'sítio de que pouca gente no lugar tinha notícias e luzes' [a place from which few people in the area received news or enlightenment], seems barely relevant to those at home battling unemployment and hunger:

Guerras também as havia ali, e não pequenas, todo o dia a trabalhar, se trabalho havia, todo o dia a ganir de fome, houvesse ou não houvesse. Só as mortes não eram tantas, e no geral os corpos iam para a cova inteiros. (*Levantado*: 47)

[Wars aplenty there were at home as well, working all through the day, if there was work to be had, groaning of hunger all through the day, whether there was work or not. The only difference was that the deaths were fewer, and that by and large the bodies went to the grave intact.]

What the workers do not perceive is the direct link between their battle against hunger, and the catastrophic strain that Portuguese involvement in the war placed on the country's administrative, financial, and human resources.[16] However, the first decade of the Republic also brings the first of many instructive confrontations precipitated by capitalist changes to age-old institutional and industrial practice, and the first attempt to articulate an independent voice in political affairs. Emboldened by the new Republic's proclamations of a new era of social justice, Alentejan harvesters first take advantage of the opportunities that the (partial) and short-lived legalization of strike action, and a newly instituted wage-payment system, created for wage bargaining.[17] The petition that they address to the municipal authorities for higher pay, 'notando as novas alegrias portuguesas e esperanças populares filhas da república' [remarking the new Portuguese joys and popular hopes born of the

Republic], is however treated by the local administrator, landowner Lamberto Horques, as an act of sedition (*Levantado*: 34). The subsequent arrest of the petition's organizers leads only to militancy, and when the workers strike, the landowners bus in strike-breakers from the famine-struck Beira region to the north (*Levantado*: 37–38). Here, the manner in which industrial conflict engenders dissident thinking and instructive clashes of perspectives is highlighted in an unprecedentedly extensive passage of dialogue between four parties, namely the *Beirões*, destitute and willing to work for any wage; the Alentejan workers, who attempt by violence to prevent this; the sergeant who intervenes to impose order; and the callous foreman, who holds all workers and their welfare in equal contempt: 'tanto faz de norte como de sul, é o mijo do patrão' [northerners and southerners alike, they're not worth the boss's piss] (*Levantado*: 38). Following the principle of Brechtian theatre, the opposition of interests and arguments is thrown into greater relief by the narrative voice's framing of speech with the neutral verb 'dizer' — 'Dizem os do sul, [...] Dizem os do norte, [...], Diz o feitor' [Those from the South say [...] Those from the North say [...] the steward says] (ibid.) — divesting the confrontation of a 'realistic' dramatic charge and keeping the reader analytically, not emotionally, engaged. Although no agreement is achieved, the exchange of views is instructive: when the landowners can bend the law with their bribes to the trigger-happy police (ibid.), neither appeals to divine justice — '[c]ada um sabe de si e Deus de todos' [every man knows himself, and God knows every man] — nor to regional identity — '[e]sta terra é nossa' [this land is ours] (ibid.) — cut much ice. Only a common bargaining position — 'juntem-se a nós e o patrão terá de pagar melhor jorna' [unite with us and the boss will have to offer better pay] (ibid.) — can protect labourers' interests.

This and subsequent episodes corroborate the assessment, by historians of rural Alentejan society such as Hammond, of the rapid growth of workers' solidarity in this period:

> In the south [of Portugal], where the regime disciplined the labor force for the benefit of industrial and agricultural employers, the wage relationship made possible the clandestine organization of political opposition. The rural proletariat was receptive to the organization of opposition based on economic grievances but upon which the regime, through repression, forced a political definition. [...] Rural social structure thus predisposed southern agricultural workers to opposition to the fascist regime and contributed to the development of a radical political consciousness. (1979: 258–59)

Levantado's depiction of such dynamic change, exploding the pernicious myth of the Alentejo's purported timelessness, contrasts with the tendency that Albert-Alain Bourdon criticizes, in much mid-twentieth-century Portuguese neo-realism, towards an anachronistic depiction of rural society as a feudalism that is 'immobile, figée, [...] régressive' [static, fixed, [...] regressive] (1986: 192–93). The novel's response to Bourdon's demand for a literary treatment that accommodates such twentieth-century transformations as the growth of the day-wage system and *mercados de lavra*, the squeeze on tenant farmers and small landholders, and the massification and mechanization promoted (not always successfully) by the *Estado Novo* is consolidated in the episode describing the introduction of an oil-powered threshing machine, or *debulhadora* (*Levantado*: 99–109).¹⁸ This episode is, as Cerdeira da Silva observes, effectively a rewriting of a crucial didactic tableau in Redol's *Gaibéus*; a rewriting that transforms the relationship of a scene based on historical reality to the symbolic and hermeneutic structures of the novel as a whole. As Cerdeira da Silva argues, in *Gaibéus* the scene contributes to the 'circularidade fatal' [fatal circularity] of a plot trajectory justified 'pela consciência — dramática — de que a revolução ainda tardaria' [by the (dramatic) awareness that the revolution was still far off] and that 'o tempo era ainda o da alienação, da incapacidade de responder ao poder' [this was still a time of alienation, of an inability to answer back to power] (1996: 46). In *Levantado*, by contrast, the corresponding scene hails 'o primeiro grande momento de questionamento efetivo do poder' [the first great moment of an effective questioning of power] (Cerdeira da Silva 1996: 42).

The characters who undertake this questioning are the teenage Manuel Espada and his three friends operating the machine, who down tools when no longer able to tolerate the risk of injury, the noise, and suffocating hay dust that it throws out (*Levantado*: 101). The boys suffer dismissal without pay by the foreman, followed by arrest and interrogation by the paranoid, inept authorities, convinced that the boys are receiving instructions from Communist agents (*Levantado*: 107).

As in the novel's dust-jacket note, the parodying of *Gaibéus* is respectful, but transformative. The didactic purpose of depicting workers' radicalization, through analysis of their increasingly antagonistic relations with capital, is the same. Yet in *Levantado*, Manuel himself takes over the narrative, prompting the reader to dialectical analysis not only of industrial relations, but also of modes of literary representation and interpretation of history. Manuel sets out his incipient grasp of how capitalism processes his labour into a product that it will sell back to him at a profit, by comparing himself to the wheat itself, and protesting at having to

> servir uma debulhadora que tanto vai debulhando o trigo como me vai debulhando a mim, entro pela boca da máquina e saem-me os ossos esburgados, e feito eu palha, poalha, moinha, e o trigo hei-de o comprar por preço que não escolhi (*Levantado*: 106)
>
> [serve a thresher that threshes me as surely as it threshes the wheat, I'm swallowed up by the machine and out at the other end come my bare bones, with me reduced to straw, dust, chaff, and as for the wheat, I'm forced to buy it at a price I never chose]

Manuel's choice of metaphor here typifies the novel's 'recycling' of time worn neo-realist discourse: it develops the analogy of workers and wheat that was a recurrent trope in the neo-realist system of symbolic encryption of political reference, and that is first intimated in the novel's dust-jacket note.¹⁹ Manuel and his friends here are still 'de verdura' [green] (ibid.) and unaware of how to organize politically against dictatorship. Yet they are growing into the metaphorical wheat that will be harvested not by the *latifundium*, but by the forces broadcasting their revolutionary message in publications like *Seara Nova*. In due course, Manuel's unintended 'aventuras de grevista' [exploits as a strike leader] (*Levantado*: 124) will inspire others, including his future brother-in-law, António Mau-Tempo: the two youths' discussions, and the comparisons that António makes with his own experiences of mistreatment (*Levantado*: 123), exemplify the growth of a common consciousness despite the repressive legislation, surveillance, and censorship imposed by Salazar during the tense years of the Spanish Civil War (*Levantado*: 120–22). This consciousness, and the solidarity it engenders, enable the sustained strike action of harvest time in 1945 (*Levantado*: 137–64), which will precipitate Monte Lavre's workers' first contact with the nationwide resistance movement dominated by the PCP.[20] Here, burlesque allusions to the evangelizing journeys of Christ's apostles serve to cast the spread, from village to village, of the campaign for a daily wage of 33 escudos as the growth of a new religion.

While challenging its reader to interpret a widening range of discursive reference, *Levantado* also demands that she/he be alert to increasingly complex and shifting modes of representation. A particularly significant example of this is the novel's increasingly inconsistent application of the Brechtian principle of sustaining emotional detachment, a device by means of which Saramago alternates didacticism with outbursts of polemic that heighten the emotional charge identified by Lepecki. In the confrontation with the *Beirão* strike-breakers, the narrative voice keeps to the role of 'non-participating third party' as 'dispassionate observer or "thinker" that interrupts audience-protagonist identifications (Benjamin 1970a: 146), and thus 'refracts the spectrum of the "thrill" (*Erlebnis*) in order to derive from it the hues of experience (*Erfahrung*)' (1970a: 148), and elicit reflection upon the historical lesson. By contrast, in the *debulhador* scene, the initial description of the machine as a 'besta [...] ligada por uma correia a um motor que trepida, estrondeia, retumba e, com perdão, fede' [a wild beast connected by a belt to a motor that trembles, bellows, rumbles, and, begging your pardon, stinks] that '[vomita] palha e grãos' [vomits out straw and grain] (*Levantado*: 99–100) goads the reader to denounce the workers' exploitation. Only after Manuel dramatically downs tools — and as the episode's significance as a re-writing of Redol's *Gaibéus* emerges — is the *Erlebnis* 'refracted', as the use of pathetic fallacy that emphasizes the young workers' suffering is debunked by sardonic humour: '[q]uem dali olha em redor vê tremer o ar, é a tremulina do calor, mas parece que é o latifúndio que treme, e afinal são apenas quatro rapazes' [whoever looks around will see the air tremble, it's the vibration caused by the heat, but it seems as if it's the whole *latifundium* which is trembling, and in reality, it's just four boys] (*Levantado*: 101).

This anticipates later passages, where verisimilitude, and, with it, the *Erlebnis* of horror and pity, are disrupted by the intruding, polemical voice of the author. One such passage is that depicting the brutal police murder of Germano Santos Vidigal (*Levantado*: 177), which, as Parreira Duarte (1982: 88) argues, constitutes a decisive 'rito de passagem', or tipping point in the agricultural workers' radicalization. The episode is equally pivotal in terms of both character narration and the deployment of appropriative literary parody and fantastical elements. Hereafter, galvanized by a common political consciousness and dialogue with a nationwide network of clandestine resistance (*Levantado*: 203–13), the workers increasingly stake claims to independent discursive and geographical space. Their first emphatic success comes during the wedding celebrations of Gracinda Mau-Tempo and Manuel Espada. Here, António Mau-Tempo, taking the role of 'mandador de falas' [master of ceremonies], demands that 'diga cada um o que quiser, consoante as suas inclinações' [let everyone say whatever they like, according to their inclination] (*Levantado*: 224). He initiates the rural workers' first open and uncensored denunciation of their lot with his own tirade against government and *latifundium*, concluding with an account of the hunger strike that he and his fellow soldiers staged to protest at meagre food rations, and of its impact in politicizing the rank and file (*Levantado*: 224–27).

The subsequent opening up of the narrative connotes a proliferation of radicalizing dialogue and debate that, in Gramscian terms, is essential to the development of a truly 'organic' workers' hegemony. Awareness of the connections between social relations and the mechanics of economic production is refined through dialogue and debate between civilians and military, but equally between rural workers and urban intellectuals (*Levantado*: 277–78), between returning emigrants and workers who stayed put (*Levantado*: 287–90), and, belatedly, between male and female union activists (*Levantado*: 333–36). This formation of the kind of 'historical bloc' that Gramsci prescribed for the workers' struggle in pre-industrialized countries — and which, as will be explored below, was in many ways effectively pursued in PCP organizational policy of the 1940s — is accelerated as, despite Salazar's intentionally obscurantist education policies, more young people learn to read, and circulate the clandestine opposition's leaflets and newspapers.

The dominion of the external narrative voice is overturned comprehensively as the workers campaign for an eight-hour working day in 1962. Here, a multitude of voices emerges during less-than-wholly secret nocturnal meetings: 'em Abril, falas mil. Nos campos há grandes ajuntamentos nocturnos' [in April, a thousand voices. By night there are great gatherings in the fields] (*Levantado*: 332). Workers' testimonials push the principal voice out of the narrative almost entirely for four pages (*Levantado*: 333–36), airing grievances, share experiences, and openly denouncing the landowners and police.

II — Folklore, Fable, and the Revolution in Popular Discourse

> Os ditados, se quiserem ir dizendo o mesmo por ser preciso continuar a dizê-lo, têm de adaptar-se aos tempos.
>
> [Sayings, if they wish to go on saying the same thing when the same thing needs saying, need to change with the times]
>
> SARAMAGO, *Ensaio sobre a Cegueira*, 269

This transformation of historical consciousness is characterized not as the replacement of 'superstitious' vernacular law with a 'scientific' episteme from the modern city, but as a synthesis. While gaining a grasp of the 'linguagem citadina' [city vocabulary] (Gomes 1989: 23) of urban opposition, and of the political analysis that it conveys, the rural labourers do not forsake, but rather *refit*, their inherited conceptualization of the world. This facet of the synthesis of a revolutionary hegemony is traceable in the novel's quotation, reformulation, and outright fabrication of Alentejan proverbs and folk tales that, as Marie Francès-Dumas remarks, are consistently recognized as repositories of 'sagesse populaire' [folk wisdom] and as oral literature of 'caractère pédagogique et didactique' [a pedagogic and didactic nature] directed to 'un auditoire composé d'illettrés' [an audience of illiterates] (2001: 220). In a manner that recalls the ideas of Amílcar Cabral and others on the place of pre-modern popular culture relative to socialist transformation, this 'sagesse populaire' will be revisited dialectically in the light of new ideas and information, the resulting synthesis embedding materialist critique into everyday thought and praxis, and building a revolutionary hegemony.

Saramago's use of proverbs has been extensively examined. In his study of proverbs and other popular cultural references in the novel, Manuel Simões makes recourse to Bakhtin's identification of a dialectic tension between the 'epic' and 'comic' tendencies of linguistic tradition, with one tendency founded on the 'indiscutabilidade da palavra veiculada' [indisputability of the word put forward], and the other on the 'reutilização deformante satírica e paródica' [satiric and parodic deformatory recycling], in order to explain Saramago's 'recuperação de elementos da cultura popular [...] para as reorganizar em termos de discurso ou para as subverter através da simples contextualização ou de processos retóricos mais complexos' [recovery of elements of popular culture, reorganizing them in discursive terms or in order to subvert them through a mere [re-]contextualization or through more complex rhetorical processes] (Simões 1996: 77). Simões exemplifies a taxonomy of proverbial phrases in the novel, distinguishing between (1) 'a simples reapropriação das formas da cultura popular' [a simple reappropriation of forms of popular culture] without ironic or transformative contextualization, (2) an ironic or transformative contextualization of popular set phrases, and (3) a similarly transformative reworking or paraphrasing.[21] Significantly, the aphorisms with which Simões exemplifies the first category are all attributed to characters aligned to the ideology of the status quo (e.g. Padre Agamedes, the municipal administrator, landowner Alberto, or the strike-breaking *Beirões*). These contrast with the reworked or recontextualized proverbs that consistently denote or comment on the experiences and attitudes of characters at odds with that ideology, like 'onde não comem sete não comem oito' [where there's not food for seven, there's not food for eight] and 'quem dá o pão da a criação' [he who provides the bread gives the orders] (*Levantado*: 33; 252). Such innovations do more than simply 'confirmar a historicidade da linguagem' [corroborate the historicity of language] (Simões 1996: 80): they constitute a 'reflexão crítica da tradição' [a critical reflection on tradition] that deploys sarcasm and burlesque, as Bakhtin argues, as 'formas de defesa [...] das classes dependentes relativamente à prepotência das classes dominantes' [the subjugated classes' forms of [self-]defence against the preponderant power of the dominant class] (Simões 1996: 79). Further, they illustrate the process by which workers experiment with the discursive materials at their disposal, in conditions of censorship and mass illiteracy, to articulate an independent, critical world-view. This creative reworking of proverbs and popular wisdom in general, by both narrator and protagonists, pioneers one of the key practices of rethinking and reinvigorating tradition that Saramago's subsequent novels make fundamental to progressive social transformation.

The same process of synthesis accounts for the evolving logic of the fantastical yarns with which characters punctuate the narrative. Initially these are 'old wives' tales', presented by anonymous character narrators in subsidiary plot-lines, of men turned into monstrous 'werepigs' and 'werechickens' (*Levantado*: 42–43). Faithfully modelled on documented rural Portuguese lore, such fables simultaneously dramatize and sublimate the inadmissible fears of disempowered wives and daughters regarding husbands and fathers driven beyond the point of self-control by poverty, hunger, and brutal subordination.[22] However, burgeoning historical consciousness encourages rural workers to question, rather than faithfully reiterate, such time-honoured elements of their traditional episteme. Supernatural creatures become confined to the realm of conscious make-believe, and the protagonists evince a knowing and ironic engagement with popular lore, and particularly with the fantastical fable. This is most evident at the wedding of Gracinda Mau-Tempo and Manuel Espada (*Levantado*: 219–29), when, in response to António's stirring account of hunger strikers' solidarity winning through, PCP stalwart Sigismundo Canastro offers a tall story about Constante, his hunting dog, who went missing when sent to retrieve a partridge brought down by Sigismundo's gun. Two years after losing both dog and partridge, Sigismundo claims, while traversing the same area of dense forest, he came upon the skeleton of Constante, magically preserved 'de pé a marrar o esqueleto da perdiz [...] com o foucinho esticado, a pata levantada' [upright, poised to grab the skeleton of the partridge [...] with its muzzle stretched wide, its paw raised] (*Levantado*: 229). Sigismundo suggests that his audience consider a comparative interpretation of his tale with António's report, since, although his story

> não é parecida com a de António Mau-Tempo, [...] talvez seja igual, porque isto de histórias e casos, procurando bem, acabamos sempre por lhes encontrar igualdade (*Levantado*: 227)

> [doesn't seem much like António Mau-Tempo's story, [...] though it might perhaps be the same, because when it comes to stories and cases, if we search hard, we always end up finding common ground between them]

As Cerdeira da Silva and others note, Sigismundo's story, and the equally improbable one of the inquisitive hare told later by António (*Levantado*: 282–83) are 'novas parabolas [...] estórias exemplares que, se as quisermos entender, explicam por metáforas a história do latifúndio' [new parables [...] exemplary tales that, if we wish to interpret them, explain the history of the *latifundium* through metaphors] (Silva 1989: 253). What is most significant about this device, however, is that Sigismundo intimates, by his call for comparative interpretation, that he is *self-consciously* presenting a didactic political allegory, and one that relies on a use of the same symbolic encryption of resistance discourse that the extradiegetic narrative deploys in increasingly arch fashion. Furthermore, some at least among his audience are savvy enough to read his fable as a call for defiance. João Mau-Tempo, although initially bemused by Sigismundo's claim of common ground between the two narratives, 'sabe de ciência segura que aquele ponto tem seu nó, a questão será entendê-lo' [knows for certain that there is method in this madness, it's just a question of understanding it] (*Levantado*: 228). Much later, when João is imprisoned and subjected to police interrogation, remembering the story inspires him to remain loyal to his comrades, and he refuses to talk:

> João Mau-Tempo lembra-se da família e da liberdade, lembra-se da história do cão e da perdiz, contada por Sigismundo Canastro, e não responde, Vá, conta lá a história, [...] se contares a história vais-te embora já amanhã para Monte Lavre, para a companhia dos teus filhos, e João Mau-Tempo, esqueleto de cão marrado contra a perdiz, repete, Senhor, a minha história está contada, [...] Empurraram-no contra a parede, bateram-lhe, chamaram-lhe de nomes todos quantos de insulto em português se inventaram, e isto foi feito e repetido[.] (*Levantado*: 249)[23]

> [João Mau-Tempo remembers his family and his freedom, remembers the story of the dog and the partridge that Sigismundo Canastro told, and doesn't reply, Come on, spill the beans, [...] if you talk you'll go straight home to Monte Lavre tomorrow, to be with your children, and João Mau-Tempo, skeleton of a dog poised to retrieve the partridge, says again, I have told you the whole story, sir, [...] They pushed him up against the wall, beat him, called him every offensive name thought up in Portuguese, and this was done again and again.]

Thus the people of Monte Lavre learn to distinguish between fact and fable and between the rhetorical uses of each. Trusting to empirical observation and personal experience, rather than to the metaphysical or mythological assertions of the 'Holy Trinity', they adapt their traditional modes of argumentation and pedagogy as an effective vehicle for a revised episteme. This depiction of how elements of a premodern popular culture are not jettisoned as 'unscientific', but instead critically reappointed and synthesized with materialist insights, is timely as a response to contemporary debates across the developing world about Marxist socialism and its propagation through literature. The motif certainly suggests a Gramscian conception of the negotiation between erudite and popular cultures necessary to usher in a revolutionary workers' hegemony.[24] One might also, however, posit the influence of Amílcar Cabral's 'National Liberation and Culture' and other writings, with their emphasis on demotic culture as necessarily the foundation of the popular movement to overthrow imperialism, and on the need for its synthesis with, or adaptation to, a Marxist analysis of socio-economic organization. In the realm of politically engaged fiction, comparable attempts to redress Marxism's insufficient engagement with non-western cultures, and to adapt Marxist praxis for the liberation of pre-industrial societies, can be encountered in, for example, the Senegalese Ousmane Sembène's liberation epic *Les Bouts de bois de Dieu* (1966) and in the 'magical realist' aesthetic of the 1960s Spanish American literature published by Caminho during Saramago's stint there as translator from 1976 to 1980. Writers such as the Guatemalan Miguel Angel Asturias and Colombian Gabriel García Márquez confronted situations in which non-materialist indigenous epistemes not only were adhered to by substantial subaltern populations, but also frequently constituted a foundation for resistance to capitalist hegemony. Such writers' 'magical realist' innovations were initially decried by many Marxists as frivolous or decadent deformations of the social realist method. As Gerald Martin argues, however, a keener analysis recognizes two very different fictional modes problematically subsumed under the label 'magical realism'. While this term often denotes fiction that 'assumes that reality [...] may be fantastic, or that the imagination is autonomous', there is a distinct literary practice 'which takes seriously [...] the fantasies or illusions of the fictional characters, whether by reproducing them "anthropologically" or by critically demystifying them', with particular attention to their encounter with, and (mis)interpretations of, capitalist modernity (1978: 103). The exuberant fantasy of the single most influential novel of the 'Boom', Márquez's *Cien años de soledad*, is, as Edwin Williamson (1978) explores, reconcilable to the materialist premises and political aims of social realism if it is considered as the 'sampling' of an often deceptive and regressive world-view, which the reader is at first helped, but later increasingly challenged, to decode.

Levantado's referencing of symbolic and hermeneutic tropes and systems from *Cien años* is not just a metafictional prank, but advertises the manner in which the Mau-Tempo family's story follows an inverse trajectory to *Cien años*'s tragic saga of the Buendía clan, and optimistically glosses Márquez's tragi-comic analysis of a rural community's struggle to come to terms with rapidly modernizing and violently exploitative economic forces. *Levantado* imposes upon *Cien años* the Marxist interpretation later set out in full by Martin, Williamson, and others, which attributes the *criollo* Buendía clan's demise to their misrecognition both of their historical circumstances and of their economic interests' progressive realignment with those of their increasingly proletarian *mestizo* neighbours. The Monte Lavre workers' triumph arises from their contrasting understanding of their environment's socio-economic determination, of time as linear and open-ended, and of themselves as sovereign historical agents. This is achieved through the (dialectical) clash of perspectives that breaks their ideological isolation. Their journey of increasing connectedness and solidarity is the inverse of Macondo in *Cien años*, where the frustration, suppression, undervaluing or mis-remembrance of precisely the same type of clashes leads the Buendías, as Edwin Williamson explores, towards a catastrophically narcissistic view of history as recurrent cycle. The invitation to compare the trajectories of Macondo and Monte Lavre reiterates the prompt to the reader to read life and literature dialectically, thereby recognizing and challenging ideological distortions — such as a messianic belief in the certainty of social transformation — still not eliminated either from real life, or from the novel's text.

To appreciate the significance of *Levantado*'s references to *Cien años*, it is worth outlining how the latter's 'magical realism' represents a journey into alienation. As Williamson argues, *Cien años* presents the Buendías's 'hallucinatory' perspective to the reader as 'a wilfully specious discourse' at its very first chapter, with the description of José Arcadio Buendía's first glimpse of ice, at a travelling fair. His awed contemplation of an 'enorme bloque transparente, con infinitas agujas internas en las cuales se despedazaba en estrellas de colores la claridad del crepúsculo' [enormous, transparent block with infinite internal needles in which the light of the sunset was broken up into coloured stars] is interrupted by the showman's scientific explanation: 'Es hielo' [it's ice] (Márquez 1967: 22–23; trans. 1978: 22). As Williamson (1987: 46) claims, the reader's reaction is one of sympathy mixed with comic detachment, as the 'sense of the marvellous' is dispelled by the novelist's 'creating a complicity behind the backs of his characters' (1987: 47). Having thus established 'that the reader's world-view is at odds with that of the characters', *Cien años* elaborates a dialectic that opposes the protagonists' naïve perceptions to the reader's more informed perspective on their world, and on the discourses that define their interpretation of it. This dialectic reveals magical realism as 'a manifestation of the malaise that causes the decline of the Buendía family' (Williamson 1987: 46). As Martin (1987: 101) outlines, Macondo's world-view conflates religious superstition and the fantastic with the ostensibly positivist but 'mainly metaphysical' ideologies, dominant until after the Second World War, that saw Latin America as doomed to consistent historical failure. The narrator's ironical mimicking of these historically dominant ideologies establishes that the novel does not vindicate myth and folklore willy-nilly as sources of knowledge. Rather, it mimics the ahistorical, escapist, and post-colonial intellectual hangover of a self-absorbed and self-defeating *criollo* class, who are receptive to the pioneering, progressive mindset that spurred Latin America to independence, but increasingly 'unable to bring themselves into focus in a world they have not made' (Martin 1987: 104).

In other words, as José David Saldívar (1985: esp. 32–34) and Jack B. Jelinski (1984) argue, Macondo's 'solitude' relates to the Marxist concept of alienation: an isolation both from the outside perspectives on events and phenomena past and present that might reveal both the changing relations of material production in the town, and their significance as determining historical factors. Within this 'solitude', the Buendía patriarch, José Arcadio I's, positivist faith in science blinds subsequent generations to the manner in which technology is turned against them. Simultaneously the Buendías are trapped by a neurotic conflation of notions of original sin and biological determinism, cooked up by José Arcadio's wife, Ursula, who dreads that her marriage to her first cousin will lead to the birth of a child with a pig's tail. Ursula's injunction against further inbreeding cannot however restrain the incestuous passions of the clan she raises with the narcissistic image of itself as the far-flung vestige of a colonial elite.[25] In Macondo, narcissistic parochialism invariably pre-empts or perverts geographic, intellectual, or sexual exploration. Hence, the Buendías fail to recognize their increasing subservience to a new metropolitan elite, which is allied to the Banana Company that colonizes Macondo with such an 'intricado frangollo de verdades y espejismos' [intricate stew of truths and mirages] — projected by telegrams, cinema, electric lighting and gramophones — that 'nadie podía saber a ciencia cierta dónde estaban los límites de la realidad' [nobody knew for certain where the limits of reality lay] (Márquez 1967: 195; trans. 1978: 186). Hence, also, they fail to recognize the increasing alignment of their economic interests with the *mestizo* labouring classes, at least — as Saldívar argues — until the plantation workers stage a strike (a development by which the novel alludes to the strike by United Fruit Company workers in Ciénaga, Colombia, suppressed by the 'Banana Massacre' of 6 December 1928).[26] However, the government and Banana Company's stranglehold on media and communications allows them to efface all evidence of their savage suppression of the strike. This cover-up, and the Banana Company's abandonment of its plantations, are experienced by Macondo as a devastating plague of amnesia, and a five-year long rainstorm that isolates the town and ruins its economic vitality.

It is at this point that Úrsula's conflation of original sin and biological determinism is subsumed within a (mis)conception of time as cyclical. This view is but the logical conclusion of Úrsula's tendentious law that simple family traditions like 'la tenaz repetición de los nombres' [the insistent repetition of names] allow her to reach 'conclusiones que le parecían terminantes' [conclusions that seemed to be certain] about Buendía children's destinies (Márquez 1967: 159; trans. 1978: 152). As Jelinski (1984: 330–32) and Martin (1987: 104–06), among others, claim, this belief that time moves cyclically is the most pernicious of all the Buendías' illusions, condemning Macondo to irrevocable oblivion and tragedy. Úrsula's interpretation of the Banana Company's departure as heralding Macondo's return to a state of innocence nurtures a nostalgic view of history, wherein the cost of the comforting notion of revisiting one's beginnings is resignation to the repetition of all the mistakes of the past. As the divination of a recognizable historical cycle from the traces of a misremembered family past leads the Buendías to contort logic and to mistrust empirical observation, the reader must increasingly be alert to the narrative's ironic inflection in order to identify the reality beyond the Buendías' fanciful perceptions.

Thus, in *Cien años de soledad* and *Levantado do Chão* alike, a strike and its suppression are the catalysts of seismic shifts both in the world-view of the protagonists and in narrative strategy. Yet in *Levantado do Chão*, this change in the protagonists' perception constitutes the transcendence of precisely the same illusion of time and history as cyclical. Innovations in technology and labour relations disrupt the seeming synchrony of human relations, fortunes, and economics with the immutable cycles of the earth. The most striking evocation of this new workers' consciousness is the comparison, during the account of the 1945 strike, of the world, viewed from Monte Lavre, as 'um relogiozito que só pode aguentar um tanto de corda e nem uma volta mais' which 'se põe a tremer, a palpitar, se um dedo grosso se aproxima da roda balanceira' [a little watch that can only take so much winding and not a single turn more [...] begins to shake and palpitate if a clumsy finger goes near the balance wheel] (*Levantado*: 137).[27] A watch, ordinarily, is 'sólido dentro da sua caixa polida, inoxidável', but 'se lhe tiram a casca, se o vento, o sol e a humidade começam a girar e abater por dentro dele, [...] acabaram os dias venturosos' [solid inside its polished rust-proof case [...] if the cover is removed, if the air, sunlight, and damp begin to circulate and cause damage inside it then happy days are over] (ibid.). At this moment, the workers perceive the world as they would a watch 'aberto [...] com as tripas ao sol, à espera de que chegue a sua hora' [open [...] belly up in the sun, waiting for its hour to come] (*Levantado*: 138): they see not just the hands going endlessly and calmly round and round, but also the vulnerable mechanism that sustains that erroneous indication of a cyclical movement of time.

The Mau-Tempos' liberation from the narcissistic, ahistorical, and fatalistic conception of time that condemns the Buendías to extinction in an orgy of incestuous indulgence is, moreover, signalled by the trope of the Mau-Tempo family's genetic throw-back of blue eyes, which creates an ironic echo of the pig's-tail deformity whose memory, and threatened recurrence, haunts the Buendías. In João Mau-Tempo's youth, his blue eyes 'que ninguém na família tinha ou se lembrava de ter visto em parente chegado ou afastado, grande espanto causaram, senão suspeita' [which no-one in the family possessed or remembered seeing in either a close or distant relative, caused great alarm, if not suspicion] (*Levantado*: 24). Yet, as the narrative voice reveals, they provide corporeal testimony to the violent origins of *latifundium* society, when its thirteenth-century masters raped the women inhabiting their newly conquered land. The blue eyes also illustrate that seeming historical recurrences do not imply an immutable and biologically programmed destiny. The potential for misinterpretation or mythologization of the relationship of recurrent events relative to historical change and continuity is highlighted by the comparison of 'estes olhos azuis vindos da Germânia [que] apareceram e desapareceram' [these blue eyes from Germany [that] appeared and disappeared] to comets — symbolically harbingers of sudden and violent change — 'que se perderam no caminho e regressam quando com eles já não se conta, ou simplesmente porque ninguém cuidou de registar as passagens e descobrir a sua regularidade' [that lost their way and returned when people least expected them, or simply because no one took the trouble to chart their passage and discover their regularity] (*Levantado*: 24). So much is demonstrated when Maria Adelaide inherits her grandfather's blue eyes but is, happily, spared the poverty, paternal violence, and state brutality that mould, scar, and batter his short and scrawny frame. Conceived through an act of free and egalitarian love in the same spot where her forebear was violated (*Levantado*: 216), Maria Adelaide's destiny will be shaped by the political stance of her parents' generation, and the victories that they have won. Finally, as is indicated by Maria Adelaide's decision to forsake the Mau-Tempo name for her father's obviously symbolic surname, Espada [Sword], these victories derive from the replacement of clan-based identities and loyalties by class-based ones, and from the more general displacement of an historical and social teleology ordered by dynastic succession (and the determinant 'power' of inherited names) by one that asserts the inheritance of socio-economic power by successively bigger and more inclusive social constituencies.

As the Mau-Tempo's education progresses, so does that of the reader, who must keep abreast of the changing logic by which fantasy and absurd parody are incorporated into the narrative. Such elements increasingly signal the partial, and sometimes conjectural, nature of the novel's reconstruction of scantily documented historical events, as well as the construction of the novel's diegesis and historical representations in accordance with a socialist ideology. Significantly, the first supernatural passage is interpolated into the same pivotal scene of the 1945 strike prefaced by the 'watchface' analogy. Here, the focus moves to 'os altos céus' [the high heavens], where mischievous, inquisitive angels, 'debruçados dos parapeitos' [leaning out from the window sills] gawp at the strike's suppression below on Earth (*Levantado*: 145). The immediate 'alienation effect' of this heretical satire's irruption within a previously naturalistic account both dissolves the dramatic tension and apprises the reader of the scene's doubtful historiographical authority. At the same time, by introducing a new practice of alluding to past reality through fiction, the scene prepares the ground for the poetic and dramatic *tour de force* in which *Levantado* recreates the brutal murder of Communist Party activist Germano Santos Vidigal, as witnessed by a worker ant in a police torture cell (*Levantado*: 168–77).

This ant's-eye view of the atrocity and its subsequent cover-up brilliantly combines fantasy, allegory, and parody, to demonstrate the importance of historical memory, even when only a partial and distorted version of the truth of the matter can now be achieved:

> sobre estes casos hão-de passar os anos e há-de pesar o silêncio até que as formigas tomem o dom da palavra e digam a verdade, toda a verdade e só a verdade[.] (*Levantado*: 176)
>
> [over these events the years must pass and silence must weigh, until the day that the ants gain the power of speech and tell the truth, the whole truth and nothing but the truth.]

Beyond its significance as self-evidently counter-factual conjecture that illuminates a suppressed history, the ant's testimony both sustains, and satirically undercuts, the novel's previously established analogy of the strikers' campaign and Vidigal's murder to the evangelism of Christ's apostles, and to his Passion. Just as the ants drink Vidigal's blood where it drips onto the prison floor (*Levantado*: 174), so the workers will follow the martyr's path and continue his works. At the same time, the presence of ants in the plot triggers an intertextual dialogue both with the neo-realist novel's use of worker insects as a cipher for the oppressed proletariat in neo-realist novels such as Carlos de Oliveira's *Uma abelha na chuva* (1960), and, of course, with *Cien años de soledad*.[28] Yet whereas in Márquez's novel the ants that gnaw away at the Buendía's home and carry away the last, pig-tailed, Buendía child are the harbingers of the annihilation of a dynasty that has lost contact with historical reality, in *Levantado do Chão* the preternaturally observant ant strikes a (purely symbolic) blow for the proletariat on a mission to inform itself about the reality of historical processes, by revealing the truth of the *Estado Novo*'s brutal suppression of workers' organizations. At the same time, the unconfirmed truth-value of Saramago's account of Vidigal's death is advertised by the conspicuously fanciful analogy between ants and workers.

Subsequently to this scene, the logic according to which symbols drawn from neo-realist fiction are deployed shifts again. This demonstrates the historicity of language as the reader gains interpretative skills and as the protagonists achieve access to historical knowledge, greater freedom of expression, and the understanding of rhetoric that informs Sigismundo's telling of the fable of his dog, Constante (*Levantado*: 227–29). As the protagonists effect a subtly political refashioning of popular lore, the narrative voice increasingly uses parody (including self-parody) to warn the alert reader against seduction by glib metaphoric equations. For example, the presentation of the birth of Maria Adelaide Mau-Tempo as a latter-day Nativity, while creating a companion piece to Vidigal's horrific 'Passion', deploys both Biblical reference and other stock encrypting symbols in a contrastingly comic manner. 'Virgin mother' Gracinda wears a halo of mosquitoes (*Levantado*: 295), while 'wise man' João Mau-Tempo arrives at his grand-daughter's birthplace dripping with sweat and so exhausted that he has hallucinatory visions of himself riding a camel (*Levantado*: 297). Such comic touches break the emotional and rhetorical spell of a narrative loaded with intimations of the birth of a new social order — wherein workers know their rights and pursue them with confidence.

Once again, such intimations are contrived by interweaving Biblical allusions with images of insects and the contrast between (dictatorial) darkness and (revolutionary) illumination. The radiant dawn with which the account of Maria Adelaide's birth concludes is still a while away when the first kindly light is provided by 'dois vagalumes' [two glow-worms], whose lights shine so brightly 'que as sentinelas dos formigueiros gritaram para dentro que estava o sol nascendo' [that the guards on the ants' nests called to within to say that dawn was breaking] (*Levantado*: 300–01). The symbolic code of neo-realism is redeployed in burlesque mode to urge continued reflection, warning against credulity in specious messianic and/or millenarian *grands récits* as the guarantors of the impending triumph of the workers' cause. Such burlesque scenes prepare the reader for the novel's finale, where a heady mix of fantasy and symbolism imbues a historically referenced account of the occupation of the *latifundium* with allegorical meaning. Only by exploring this allegorical structure does the reader perceive that this scene is not the conclusion of a messianic narrative. Even at the seeming dawn of revolution, the protagonists and reader alike must persist with their dialectical method, striving to view reality *doutra maneira*. Before that dawn, moreover, the dialectic must embrace the perspectives from the most disempowered subaltern positions, including those of women and children.

III — Polyphony and Unity in Difference: Towards a New Revolutionary Hegemony

Levantado do Chão presents the growth of Alentejan workers' political consciousness as entailing the recognition and synthesis of the 'falas mil' of a diverse subaltern population. Its 'polyphonic' account of a history of struggle thus implicitly challenges 1970s Portuguese Communist Party (PCP) orthodoxy, not only regarding how the past can be known and analysed, but also regarding the constitution of a revolutionary hegemony, and organization of a revolutionary party. However, this challenge recognizes, and celebrates, a tendency in PCP policy of the 1940s that recalled Gramscian approaches to revolutionary organization in a largely pre-industrial society. As this section explores, this representation of a Gramscian model of 'democratic centralism' in action, and likewise, that of a movement towards an effectively feminist Marxism, raises a question about the novel's self-consciously imperfect presentation of past reality. The plot's organization not around the *héros moyens* or 'mediocre [men] of the people' stipulated by Lukács (1962: 65), but around somewhat marginal, atypically visionary, figures, and its counter-factual and allegorical accretions, allow for *Levantado*'s recuperation of subaltern histories to be balanced with a utopian vision of how revolutionary organization might become more fully democratic, less paternalistic, and less androcentric.

The shortcoming in orthodox models of party democracy that *Levantado* confronts is summed up by Michael Waller, in his study of Western European Communism in the Cold War era:

> It is essential for a communist party that history should speak. The question is how is it to do so. Orthodox democratic centralism cannot accept that history should speak through a clamour of discordant voices; but nor can the party

leadership accept that, by drowning out all voices but its own, it is doing anything other than speaking for history. (1988: 14)

The PCP of the post-dictatorship period has received particular censure from historians and Marxist activists for allowing its commitment to what Ronald Tiersky terms 'monolithism as the political ideal' to deviate from the spirit of democratic organization (1985: 95). Saramago himself was prominent among the signatories of the 'Third Way' document presented to the PCP executive in 1987, calling for 'uma maior democratização da vida interna do PCP' [greater democratization of the internal life of the PCP] (Lopes (2010): 140). The careful line that Saramago trod between loyalty to his Party, and opposition to its intolerance of dissent and doctrinal innovation (Lopes (2010): 142), manifests itself in *Levantado*'s depiction of Communist agitation in the Alentejo from the 1940s to the 1970s. The novel's first representation of the workers' party in action occurs when, following his participation in the 1945 strike, João Mau-Tempo is invited by Sigismundo Canastro to a clandestine meeting in the 'Terra Fria' (*Levantado*: 207–13). This episode presents a detailed dramatization of the PCP activism in rural areas that followed the Party reorganization masterminded by Álvaro Cunhal and Júlio Fogaça in 1940–41.[29] Under Cunhal and Fogaça's direction, the PCP central committee of the early 1940s produced a series of reports identifying the necessity of tactical alliances against the *Estado Novo*, and the consequent priority of outreach work not just amongst the proletariat, but also amongst the peasantry, as the first step towards Portuguese workers' liberation.[30] This adaptation of classical Marxist theory of revolutionary organization contributed significantly to the Party's exponential growth: by 1945,

> the PCP appeared to offer a real revolutionary alternative, dominating a popular movement which posed a serious threat to the survival of clerico-fascism; it was widely respected among middle-class and intellectual circles, as well as being clearly hegemonic in the labour market. (Raby 1988: 42)

Cunhal and Fogaça's 'popular alliance strategy' of the 1940s calculated that Portugal, as a pre-industrial society, was not ripe for revolution, and that workers could not defeat the *Estado Novo* without engaging effectively with the peasantry. Their subsequent adaption of PCP organizational structures to the realities of the society and working conditions of the peasantry and rural proletariat is accurately illustrated by *Levantado*'s account of a party cadre recruiting. As Raby summarizes, 'it was essential that existing cadres of urban origin should immerse themselves completely in peasant society. These cadres should be workers, not intellectuals' (1988: 86). The enigmatic Silva — or Manuel Dias da Costa, depending on which of his pseudonyms one knows him by (Saramago *Levantado*: 208) — travels from meeting to meeting by bicycle, and is revealed as an urban worker when João Mau-Tempo shakes his hand: 'não era a mão grossa do trabalhador do campo, mas forte sim, e sólido no apertar' [it was not the horny hand of a rural labourer, but it was strong, with a firm grip] (*Levantado*: 210).[31] More importantly, 'Silva' fulfils his remit of basing his activity 'on careful study of specific local conditions' (Raby 1988: 86) by asking each individual worker for his experiences and observations: 'agora digam-me o que se passa, conta tu' [now tell me, all of you, what's happening, you, my friend, tell me] (*Levantado*: 211). In line with the reorganized PCP's short-term priority not of creating clandestine unions, but of supporting workers' struggles to establish an effective bargaining position within the state-controlled labour syndicates, discussion focuses on how these and the new *Casas do povo* are customarily 'de combinação com os patrões' [in cahoots with the bosses] (ibid.).[32]

By focusing on this aspect of the PCP's activity, Saramago traces a commonality with Gramsci's theorization of democratic centralism. *Levantado*'s account of the PCP's emergence in Monte Lavre stresses organizational principles that militate against the subordination of the grass roots to the type of potentially regressive leadership that Gramsci terms 'bureaucratic centralism'. Gramsci stipulates the convergence within the workers' party of the 'mass element [...] whose participation takes the form of discipline and loyalty' and of the 'principal cohesive element [...] centralizing and disciplinary' of the leadership through 'an intermediate element, which articulates the first element with the second [...] not only physically but also morally and intellectually'.[33] He asserts that '[i]n reality, for every party there exist "fixed proportions" between these three elements, and the greatest effectiveness is achieved when these "fixed proportions" are realised' (1971b: 153). Not only genuine democratic centralism, but also a truly integrated and comprehensive workers' hegemony, stem from this 'organic unity between theory and practice, between intellectual strata and popular masses, between rulers and ruled' (Gramsci 1971a: 190). The notion of 'organic' organization is crucial here: democratic centralism must 'take account of movement' as well as of 'that which is relatively stable and permanent, or [...] moves in an easily predictable direction' (1971a: 189). In order not to 'solidify mechanically into bureaucracy', party leadership must permit the expression of intellectual input from the rank and file.[34] Gramsci stipulates

> [a] continual adaptation of the organization to the real movement, a matching of thrusts from below with orders from above, a continuous insertion of elements thrown up from the depths of the rank and file into the solid framework of the leadership apparatus which ensures continuity and the regular accumulation of experience. (1971a: 188–89)

The accommodation of such 'thrusts from below' is suggested when Sigismundo argues against the PCP's cautious strategy, saying that 'o que devíamos fazer era ocupar as terras [...] o camarada já tem dito, seria um suicídio, mas suicídio é isto que se passa' [what we ought to do is to occupy the land [...] our comrade has already said that it would be suicidal, but what we're going through now is suicide] (*Levantado*: 211). 'Silva' does not contradict or silence Sigismundo, and ensures that all — especially newcomer João — have their say: '[cada] um disse das suas razões' [each one said what he thought] (*Levantado*: 212).

As Frier (2007a: 155–60) remarks in his Gramscian reading of the end of *Memorial do Convento*, another reason Gramsci gives for devolving the duties of cohesion, centralization, discipline, and innovation in part to the 'intermediate element' of proletarian and peasant cadres is so that, if the leadership 'is destroyed it should leave as its heritage a ferment from which it may be recreated' (1971b: 153). Subsequent chapters of *Levantado* depict how this ferment is 'formed and subsist[s]' (ibid.) in the rank and file and in the 'intermediary elements' during the decade of crisis for the PCP that followed the apprehension and imprisonment of most of its central committee members between 1948 and 1951.³⁵ Scenes of the arrest, torture, and imprisonment of João Mau-Tempo, Sigismundo, and their comrades in the early 1950s bring home the horrific experience of this crisis, but also indicate how a Gramscian 'ferment' bubbles even in prison through the camaraderie of inmates, who organize political discussions and educational initiatives (*Levantado*: 252–54; 259). On the outside, meanwhile, the same 'ferment''s effect of converting rural workers' world-view and culture into a defiantly socialist hegemony is suggested through António's story of inquisitive hares (*Levantado*: 281–87). This, like Sigismundo's story of the dog Constante, disseminates dissent through an encrypted parable. While the story warns of the risks run by the likes of João Mau-Tempo, 'lebre curiosa, caçada pela polícia política' [inquisitive hare, hunted by the secret police], intellectual curiosity and courage will build a future when 'a curiosidade não será mais cobrada e punida' [curiosity will not be censured and punished], and 'lebres curiosas como Maria Adelaide Espada poderão ler em paz os seus jornais e gozarão do direito de saber, de pensar e de agir' [inquisitive hares like Maria Adelaide Espada will be able to read their newspapers in peace and enjoy the right to know, think, and act] (Silva: 254).³⁶

Even without the active presence of the PCP leadership, this 'ferment' can swiftly bubble over into concerted action on the arrival of a catalyst such as Humberto Delgado's anti-Salazarist presidential candidacy in 1958, when rural workers organized a mass protest to the local council in Montemor that led to a running battle with police (*Levantado*: 311–16) and to the GNR's killing of protestor José Adelino dos Santos, which contributed to the greatest crisis that the *Estado Novo* had faced.³⁷ *Levantado*'s account contrasts the coroner, Dr Corda's, refusal to cover up dos Santos's killing with the complicity, earlier, of Dr Romano in covering up Vidigal's. This contrast highlights the burgeoning cross-class support for protests in 1958, compared to a decade earlier: Raby notes that 'tradesmen [...] closed their shops in sympathy with the strikers, and quite a number of managers and factory owners [...] showed support or at least did not oppose the work stoppages' (1988: 194).

Hereafter, the proliferation both of discussion and protest becomes both unstoppable, and indispensable. Although the events of 25 April herald an opportunity for change,

> muito se engana [...] quem julgue que basta levantar uma bandeira e dizer, Vamos. É preciso que Abril seja um mês de palavras mil, porque mesmo os certos e convencidos têm seus momentos de dúvida (Silva 1989: 333)
>
> [whoever thinks that it's enough to raise a flag and cry, Let's go, is much mistaken. April must be a month of a thousand words, because even the most correct and convinced of people have their moments of uncertainty]

During the revolutionary tumult of Spring 1974, Monte Lavre's limited contact with developments in Lisbon does not prevent the critical decision to realize Sigismundo's dream of occupying the *latifundia*. This occupation is, of course, facilitated by the rapport between rural workers and the *Movimento das Forças Armadas* (MFA), which in Monte Lavre is pioneered by Maria Adelaide (*Levantado*: 353).

Maria Adelaide's leading role exposes at least one flagrant oversight that the

Gramscian model has. The revolutionary vanguard cannot develop an inclusive, 'totalizing' hegemony if its 'intermediate' policy-building corps does not represent the demands and experiences of working women. *Levantado*'s device of narrative 'democratization' also helps to articulate the slow advances towards a general recognition of women as equals in the eyes of employers, kinsmen, and comrades. Observing that 'afinal não é assim tão grande a diferença entre mulher e homem, a não ser no salário' [in the end the difference between men and women is not so great, except in terms of their salary] (*Levantado*: 215), the novel charts how the revolutionary movement profits from the progressive breakdown of restrictive distinctions between male and female roles in labour, protest, and family structures. Its focus on women's political agency and aspirations is the foundation of a revised political agenda that extends the logic of socialist revolution into the domestic, familial and sexual realms. *Levantado*'s response to certain specificities of women's oppression that it identifies can seem over-optimistic and presumptuous about their empowerment within contemporary workers' organizations, and about how the subaltern status allotted to females is embedded deeply in language and symbolic constructs. Nevertheless, its response to key demands of radical feminist groups that, by the 1970s, were distancing themselves from the Marxist left, is distinctive, and establishes the paramount importance of women's emancipation and conceptions of gender in the political vision projected by Saramago's fiction.[38] While developing ideas first propounded as early as the 1920s by the Bolshevik Alexandra Kollontai (who, belatedly, became a significant influence on Marxist-feminist thinking in 1970s Portugal), *Levantado* also evinces Saramago's early attempts to think beyond hegemonic notions of gender binaries in seeking an end to the subjugation of women and the deprecation of 'feminine' attitudes.[39]

IV — On Gender, Paternity, and the Micropolitics of Affect

From its opening, *Levantado* is sensitive to the sexual inflection of socio-economic power relations across history. The material effect of women's association with the land — that 'mãe de tetas grossas' [ample-bosomed mother] (*Levantado*: 14) — and of their fertility as a male possession ripe for exploitation, is illustrated in the story of the first Mau-Tempo mother, brutally raped at the Fonte do Amieiro by the warlord who claimed the land for Christendom, Lamberto Horques Alemão (*Levantado*: 24). Ever since, Alentejan women's subjugation as 'parideiras e animais de carga' [broodmares and beasts of burden] has been legitimized by Christian mythology. This much is exposed when the narrative voice exploits the double meaning of 'parir' — to give birth, or simply to produce — to subvert the story of Eve's sin and eternal punishment of labour pains:

> Jeová determinou, Parirás com dor, e assim tem acontecido todos os dias a todas as mulheres, mesmo àquelas que do dito Jeová não conhecem nem o nome. (*Levantado*: 293)
>
> [Jehovah decreed, Thou shalt give birth in pain, and so it has been every day to every woman, even to those who do not even know the name of that same Jehovah.]

The biblical myth of perpetual female punishment validates what, with the development of capitalist economics in the twentieth century, became what Alexandra Kollontai termed woman's 'triple load' as mother, housekeeper, and wage-worker contracted for half the rate paid to male counterparts.[40] Formerly, women in the rural Alentejo were largely isolated and disempowered by the traditional structure of female labour domesticated under husbands' control (or indeed tyranny). Such is the case of Domingos and Sara. Yet despite the *Estado Novo*'s attempts to discourage women from undertaking paid labour and to confine them to an unwaged and non-unionized domesticity, by the 1940s the dialectic of mid-twentieth-century economic and social transformations that saw women taking paid work outside the home precipitated their politicization and development of class struggle.[41] This is demonstrated when Sara's wage-earning grand-daughter Gracinda becomes the first woman in Monte Lavre to risk death demonstrating against low wages (*Levantado*: 311). Soon afterwards, women — even the unwaged — are active in the campaign for an eight-hour working day (*Levantado*: 333).

Sara's experience is the starting point from which Monte Lavre's women struggle for an autonomous voice, concurrently with their challenge to traditional familial relations and the restrictions on their social and economic agency. Cooped up labouring in the home, Sara's oppression by Domingos has a discursive aspect as well as financial, spatial, and corporeal ones. In their first appearance in the second chapter, the only utterances of Sara's that Domingos sanctions are indications of subservient agreement or functional observations (*Levantado*: 15), and her agency beyond the family is restricted to pleading with shopkeepers for extended credit (*Levantado*: 83), or with State authorities for leniency (*Levantado*: 150–51). The alcoholic Domingos's alternation between violent abuse of, and pathetic reliance on, his wife, 'como criança que provavelmente continuava a ser' [like the child that he would probably go on being] (*Levantado*: 28), illustrates the ill effect of arbitrary power differentials within the family. Domingos's freedom to blame, beat, and yet still depend on, Sara means that he never learns from his mistakes, and never looks beyond his marriage for an explanation of his economic hardship.

Sara ends her long and harsh life reduced to demented incoherence (*Levantado*: 112–13), but the generations of women that follow are more successful in making themselves heard, in a process facilitated both by their new status as (unequal) wage-earners alongside men, and by Saramago's recurrent trope of the marginal, low-status male protagonist who, disregarding convention, defers to women's opinions and wisdom. The relationship of João Mau-Tempo and his wife Faustina is one that begins from mutual respect, which, untrammelled by any urgent financial need of Faustina's to bag a husband, develops into deep and reciprocal affection. The initial attraction is signalled as not sexually driven: 'namoro, nenhum, fora coisa que nunca se lhes pegara. [...] Porém, [...] [f]osse daquela boa liberdade, fosse porque enfim chegara o tempo de se atar aquele nó, pôs-se João a gostar de Faustina e Faustina a gostar de João' [romance was something they had never known. [...] However [...] whether because of the freedom with which they treated each other, or whether because the time had come for the knot to be tied, João began to have feelings for Faustina, and Faustina for João] (*Levantado*: 66–67). The nature of their courtship anticipates the 'new relations between the sexes' that Alexandra Kollontai argued would be necessary in the worker's state: the replacement of 'the indissoluble marriage based on the servitude of women' by 'a free union of two equal members of the workers' state who are united by love and mutual respect' (1977: 259). The account of the couple's first encounters, meanwhile, plays down conventional gender oppositions: the couple first meet as co-workers in a mixed-sex gang of *invernadeiros* at the significantly named Pendão das Mulheres (*Levantado*: 66). Here, they soon become dancing partners and sing together *a desafio* (ibid.), in a contest of wit and invention that, in the Alentejo, was more often held between two men than between a man and woman.[42] In the context of *Levantado*'s 'democratizing' discursive evolution, it is significant that João and Faustina's courting rites give them each a public voice on equal footing.

Faustina's status is most apparent when she assumes the narrative thread to introduce the discussion of her sixteen year-old daughter Gracinda's determination to marry (*Levantado*: 182). While rural Alentejan mothers often had the final say on their daughters' marriages at this time, the narrative makes clear that this family discussion, and Gracinda's parents' willing acquiescence to her demands, mark a watershed both in the community's history and in the novel's narrative (which previously gave insufficient account of women's experiences):

> [m]uito de homens se tem falado, alguma coisa de mulheres, mas quando assim foi, como de passageiras sombras ou às vezes indispensáveis interlocutoras, coro feminino, de costume caladas por ser grande o peso da carga ou da barriga, ou então mães dolorosas por várias razões, [...] De homens se continuará a falar, mas também cada vez mais de mulheres, e não por causa deste namoro e futuro casamento, [...] as razões são outras, ainda se calhar imprecisas e é que os tempos vêm aí. (*Levantado*: 183–84)

> [There has been much talk about men, a bit about women, but in the latter case, like fleeting shades or sometimes necessary interlocutors, a female chorus, customarily silent under the great weight of their burden or of their belly, or else mothers grieving for sundry reasons [...] There will be more talk about men, but also ever more talk about women, and not because of this love affair and future marriage [...] the reasons are different, still perhaps indistinct, and the times are a-changing.]

Gracinda's story will consolidate this depiction of working women's progress towards autonomy within discursive, geographical, and even psychic spaces to which, formerly, they were admitted only on their menfolk's terms. Duarte remarks how the change in marital relationships over three generations is just as much one of sexual and emotional interaction as of economic and social status, as sexual relations gradually become the

> resposta a uma necessidade bilateral, ainda praticamente biológica em Domingos e Sara, já mais consciente em João e Faustina, e de escolha, amadurecimento, preocupação com o diálogo e com o crescimento do outro em Manuel Espada e Gracinda. (1982: 89)

> [answer to a bilateral need, still essentially a biological one for Domingos and Sara, but more self-conscious for João and Faustina, and, in the case of Manuel

Espada and Gracinda, a relationship of choice, maturity, and concern for dialogue and for the personal growth of the Other.]

The stages of this transformation are set in relief by contrasted instances of sexual congress, as first when what Duarte (ibid.) terms the 'impulso sexual individualista e unilateral' [individualistic and unilateral sexual impulse] of Lamberto Horques's rape of the first Mau Tempo mother is juxtaposed with the scene where Domingos and Sara secretly consummate their unsanctioned union in a wheatfield and conceive son João (*Levantado*: 23–24). Venturing beyond her community's moral and geographical boundaries in her rebellion against her father and his patriarchal entitlements, Sara's bid to control her own social, biological, and economic destiny concludes tragically in her humiliation and servitude under the rule of a brutal and negligent husband. Faustina similarly defies her family in making a free choice of husband: she and João must also transgress boundaries, eloping by night and making love for the first time in the wilderness (*Levantado*: 70). Nevertheless, their marriage, founded in mutual respect, fares better, and they, in turn, respect Gracinda's wishes when she announces her readiness to rebel if she cannot give herself to the man of her choice in marriage:

> Minha mãe, já me quero casar, disse Gracinda Mau-Tempo, aqui está o meu enxoval, é coisa de pobre, mas há-de chegar para que nos deitemos eu e Manuel Espada numa cama dele e minha, e nela sejamos mulher e marido, e ele entre em mim e eu seja nele, [...] Minha mãe, se não me casar irei deitar-me [...] e [...] esperarei por Manuel Espada para que ele venha romper este meu corpo, e depois levantarei o meu vestido e na ribeira me lavarei, sangue de mim que irá correndo até não se saber onde está, mas sabendo eu quem sou. (*Levantado*: 215–16)

> [Mother, it's time for me to marry, said Gracinda Mau-Tempo, here is my trousseau, it's nothing much but it will have to suffice in order for Manuel Espada and I to lie together in a bed that's his and mine, for us there to be man and wife, and for him to enter in me and I to be in him [...] Mother, if I can't marry, I will lay down and [...] wait for Manuel Espada to come and break open my body, and afterwards I'll lift up my dress and wash at the riverbank, with my blood running away who knows where, but with me knowing who I am.]

By contrasting one idea of sex as a state of equitable union, of physical and metaphysical reciprocity and immanence ('e ele entre em mim e eu seja nele'), with another of it as her own violent dissolution, Gracinda indicates how her parents' blessing will allow her to fulfil her egalitarian and loving relationship with Manuel without being cast out to the social wilderness (just as her blood might be carried into the distance by the river). In the event, the parents suppress their fears that Gracinda is too young, her dowry still too meagre and that her wedding party can only be 'modesto' [humble] and not 'uma coisa bonita' [something special] (*Levantado*: 216), and bless the family's first genuine love match. This romance, significantly, blossoms when Manuel respectfully 'pega na mão de Gracinda' [clasps Gracinda's hand] at the foot of 'aquela mesma fonte' [that same spring] where her forebear was raped (*Levantado*: 184). This symbolic rehabilitation of a site of sexual and economic oppression as a site of women's (partial) erotic and social emancipation will be completed (albeit not unproblematically) by the story of Maria Adelaide (*Levantado*: 356).

Prior to that, however, the connection between women's challenges to matrimonial and erotic norms and their assertion of an autonomous voice and political agency is made clear when Gracinda determines to participate in the 1958 workers' demonstration in Montemor. As Duarte observes, as women attain the 'direito a um espaço junto ao homem' [right to a position alongside men], this space is 'representado também no que lhe é reservado na narrativa' [also represented in terms of what is allotted to them in the narrative] (1982: 88). Manuel opposes this, concerned for her safety, but equally for his reputation with his 'mais velhos e antigos' [older and more conservative] neighbours who say nothing about Gracinda's plans but secretly complain that 'já não há quem segure as mulheres' [no-one keeps their women under control any more] (*Levantado*: 310):

> Manuel, eu vou contigo, e Manuel Espada, apesar de ser quem é, julgou que a mulher estava a brincar e respondeu, responderam pela boca dele sabe-se lá quantas vozes de manuéis, Isto não é coisa para mulheres, [...] Falaram do caso no resto do serão, falaram já deitados, a conversa adianta, A menina fica com a minha mãe e nós vamos juntos, não é só dormirmos na mesma cama, enfim rendeu-se Manuel Espada e ficou contente por se ter rendido. (*Levantado*: 310–11)
>
> [Manuel, I'm coming with you, and Manuel Espada, despite the man he is, thought his wife was kidding and replied, giving voice to the response of goodness knows how many other Manuels, This is no business for a woman [...] They discussed the issue for the rest of the evening, they were still discussing it in bed, conversation moves things forward, The kid can stay with my mother, and we'll go together, [marriage] isn't just about sleeping in the same bed, in the end Manuel Espada gave in, and was happy to have given in.]

This account of the couple's discussion stresses both the typicality of Manuel's macho anxiety not to 'fica em pouco e perde autoridade' [mean little and lose standing], but equally his willingness to discuss at length and on equal terms, and to concede that matrimony 'não é só dormirmos na mesma cama', but also an economic, political, and intellectual partnership.

Their daughter Maria Adelaide is declared equal with any man even prenatally, by the tongue-in-cheek echoes of Christ's nativity in the account of her birth, and she emerges from the womb so determined to speak that she doesn't need to be slapped: 'na sua garganta voluntariamente se estava já formando o primeiro grito da sua vida' [the first cry of her life was already gathering voluntarily in her throat] (*Levantado*: 295). The assertion that one day 'há-de gritar outros que hoje nem por sombra deles se imaginarão possíveis' [others, of whom today one could not imagine it possible, will also cry out] foreshadows women's successful demand for inclusion in political decision-making, with Maria Adelaide and her symbolically named contemporary Emília Profeta taking a leading role in the planning of the occupations (*Levantado*: 363). Correspondingly, the narrative stresses Maria Adelaide's unprecedented freedom of movement and expression, as she happily wanders the countryside conversing with her fellow revolutionaries, and, in the days following the *25 de Abril* coup, gathers daisies by the Fonte do Amieiro, dismissing 'um estranho quebranto' [a strange discomfort] that comes upon her there, and hence completing the Mau-Tempo women's recovery of a site of sexual (and economic) violence (*Levantado*: 356). Seated 'no murete da fonte' [on the little wall of the spring] (ibid.) with her lap full of orange blossom, traditionally a symbol of virginity in wedding celebrations, Maria Adelaide enjoys control over her body and her destiny, and, as Letízia notes, is contrasted powerfully with her raped medieval ancestor.[43] This scene, moreover, prefigures a comparison of the rash of workers' land occupations across the Alentejo to the springtime blooming of daisies: 'isto que aconteceu aqui, aconteceu além, é como na Primavera, abre-se um malmequer do campo e [...] milhares de seus iguais nascem em um dia só' [what happened here, happened elsewhere, just like in Spring, a daisy blooms in the field and [...] thousands more are born in a single day] (*Levantado*: 361). The association of daisies with love and the liberation struggle, made on the occasion of Maria Adelaide's birth, here serves to 'feminize' the April revolution, and to evoke contemporary discussions of the principles of free love and compassion in revolutionary politics that will come to the fore in *Memorial do Convento* and subsequent novels.

Maria Adelaide's story thus consistently celebrates how an incrementally 'feminized' revolutionary movement is calling time on the worst abuses of women (and children) in pre-industrial society. However, her story is problematic, insofar as a transformation of working women's status that has been glacially slow (and often won in the teeth of resistance from working men) is rendered symbolically as a swift, spontaneous, and unstoppable process.[44] Furthermore, *Levantado*'s women achieve only a minority representation both in the novel's 'polyphonic' narrative and (like their real-life 1970s counterparts) in the decision-making of revolutionary organizations (*Levantado*: 363). And while Maria Adelaide's characterization as standard-bearer of her generation of workers detaches the novel from sexist hermeneutic and symbolic conventions, her depiction at the Fonte do Amieiro as a 'bride of the Revolution' — at a point before she will be called upon to reinsert herself into as yet largely unreformed patriarchal structures — also exemplifies *Levantado*'s limitations in responding to radical feminism's critique of mainstream Marxist thinking on women's liberation. As Ana Paula Ferreira observes, *Levantado*'s women still lack

> the social, economic, and above all, cultural space in which to raise/emancipate themselves on their own, by their own means, and not merely as men's helpmates. Is woman irrevocably collapsed on the patriarchal ground of her reproductive physiology? Or, in becoming a revolutionary subject, like Adelaide Espada for example, will she be able or necessarily want to give up maternity? In what circumstances can maternity become a deliberate step in women's struggle? (2001: 226–27)

Levantado's exposure of the relations between desire and economics, and between male supremacism and capitalist exploitation, clearly implies the necessity of viewing women as historical subjects and not 'helpmates'. However, it is only in *Memorial* that Saramago's fiction starts to move effectively beyond the conception of women as 'workers with wombs', and engages with the discursive and institutional construction of gender paradigms, and the psychological entrenchment of patriarchal hegemony. As the following chapter argues, the counter-factual scenario of the love between the visionary Blimunda and the eccentric Baltasar offers glimpses of a non-sexist micropolitics that aims to reconcile liberated desire and identity with a socialist and egalitarian ethics. Yet even here, and, later, in *A Jangada de Pedra*, the sexual aspect of Saramago's depiction of a possible socialist utopia is constrained by a symbolic double bind. Using counter-factual projections to allegorize a potential revolution in reproductive sexual politics, these novels risk entanglement with a well-established sexist dogma of 'renewal through reproduction', which conventionally has relegated women to the role of incubators of a male-conceived future. The contrastingly dystopian depiction of 1930s Lisbon in *O Ano da Morte de Ricardo Reis* exemplifies the constrained circumstances in which Saramago's fiction can offer a worthy response to Ferreira's question about maternity as a 'deliberate step in women's struggle'. Similarly problematic is these novels' suggestion of the transcendental power of heterosexual romance, guided by an equally transcendental female capacity for moral courage, generosity, and compassion. As the next chapter will explore, one can relate Saramago's vision of the dissemination of this idealized 'femininity' into political praxis to the later writings of Frankfurt School Marxist Herbert Marcuse. Nevertheless, in the one novel — *A Jangada de Pedra* — that posits a biological regeneration of society in which women might be legislators, as well as the incubators, of a better future, what Marcuse admits would be the painful and intricate labour of disestablishing patriarchy is represented only light-heartedly.

Levantado does, however, clearly illustrate how hegemonic patriarchal hierarchies in the domestic sphere must be recognized as fitting out the family as (in Althusser's terms) an ideological state apparatus, and how successful social transformation depends on these hierarchies being dismantled. Elements of a micro-political praxis challenging the violence and oppression engendered by such hierarchies appear in the eccentric and innovative attitudes of the Mau-Tempos, as when João and Manuel both face down macho scorn and relinquish part of their 'patriarchal dividend' so as to respect Gracinda's wishes.[45] António Mau-Tempo, meanwhile, is the main mouthpiece for Saramago's assault on mutually reinforcing creeds and (mal)practices of paternalistic authoritarianism within the family, the Church, and State institutions (an assault more fully developed in *O Ano da Morte de Ricardo Reis* and *O Evangelho segundo Jesus Cristo*). António grows up enjoying the protections and freedoms that his father, João, was denied by his own violent, tyrannical father, whose suicide leaves his family in destitution. Consequently, António passes his army medical and thus gains an education and professional training. He also learns to distinguish between nurturing parenting and abusive parenting, and to identify the perfidy of those — such as Padre Agamedes — who allude to both Salazar and the State as father and mentor of the people, and who employ the example of the Old Testament as apologia for state brutality:

> [D]eveis dar atenção e obedecer aos que mais sabem da vida e do mundo, olhai a guarda como vosso anjo da guarda, não lhe guardeis rancor, que até o pai é às vezes obrigado a bater no filho a quem tanto quer e ama, e todos nós sabemos que mais tarde o filho dirá, Foi para meu bem (*Levantado*: 120)

[You should pay attention to and obey those who know more of life and of the world, look upon the guardsman as your guardian angel, and don't bear him ill will, for even the father is sometimes obliged to beat the child that he loves so much, and all of us know that in time the child will say, It was for my own good]

Having himself silenced Agamedes during Gracinda and Manuel's wedding feast (itself the pivotal scene in Monte Lavre's transition from a clan-based society to a class-based one), António himself spells out the stark contrast between the paternalistic *Estado Novo*, which claims to be both his 'mãe' [mother] and his 'pai' [father] (*Levantado*: 225), and the self-sacrificing parents who welcome him home to Monte Lavre with open arms:

> de meus verdadeiros pais sei eu, e todos sabem dos seus, que tiraram à boca para não faltar à nossa, e então a pátria deverá tirar à sua própria boca para não faltar à minha, e se eu tiver de comer cardos, coma-os a pátria comigo, ou então uns são filhos da pátria e os outros filhos da puta. (ibid.)

> [I know about my real parents, and everybody knows about theirs, who take the food from their own mouths so that ours may not be empty, and so the Fatherland should take food from its own mouth so that mine may not be empty, and if I have to eat thistles, then let the Fatherland eat thistles too, unless some people are sons of the Fatherland and others merely sons of bitches.]

Thus, António reiterates the depiction of the state as a usurping, false parent, switching at its own convenience between paternal and maternal posturing, and between denial of responsibility to its 'children', and frank abuse and intimidation:

> A pátria chama os seus filhos, [...] tu que até hoje nada mereceste, nem o pão para a fome que tens, nem o remédio para a doença que te tem, nem o saber para a ignorância, tu, filho desta mãe que tem estado à espera desde que nasceste, tu vês o teu papel à porta da junta de freguesia [...] A pátria olha-te fixamente, hipnotiza-te, [...] desde que vieste a este mundo te espero, meu filho, para que saibas que mãe estremosa sou, e se durante todos estes anos te não dei muita atenção, haverás de perdoar porque vocês são muitos e eu não posso olhar por todos, andei a preparar os meus oficiais que hão-de mandar em ti[.] (*Levantado*: 197–98)

> [The Fatherland calls to its children, [...] you who up until today deserved nothing, neither bread for your hunger, nor the cure for your sickness, nor instruction for your ignorance, you, sons of this mother who has been awaiting you since you were born, you can see your call-up papers at the parish council door [...] The Fatherland is staring at you, hypnotizing you [...] since you entered this world I've been waiting, my son, for you to know what a loving mother I am, and, if for all of these years I've not paid you much attention, you must pardon me, for there are many of you and I can't look out for you all, I've been busy training my officers whose task is to give you orders.]

The same abusive paternalism is attributed to the third member of Agamedes's 'santíssima trinidade' when the narrative voice evokes the suffering of 'real' parents who must 'fazer os filhos e os entregar ao latifúndio' [make babies and hand them over to the *latifundium*] that bays for the cheap labour of six- and seven-year-olds (*Levantado*: 118). If this exploitation is comparable to 'Hitler Horques Alemão''s co-opting of 'crianças de doze ou treze anos para fazer deles as últimas batalhões da derrota' [children of twelve or thirteen to make of them the last battalions of defeat] (ibid.), it also prefigures *Ricardo Reis*'s attacks on the *Estado Novo*'s hunger for working class cannon-fodder, through its metaphor of the infanticidal dog, Ugolina (Saramago 1988a: 29–31). Coincidentally or not, *Levantado* employs a similar play on a name from a literary classic — Pedro Calderón de la Barca's *La vida es sueño* (1635) — to stress the malevolence of a paternalistic State. Like his namesake in Calderón's drama, Sigismundo Canastro is imprisoned by a paternal figure fearful of usurpation, though not by his biological father, but rather his purported Fatherland. The *pátria*'s fears, however, are realized when Sigismundo appeals to his fellow workers as a class, not as a clan, to rise up to assert their collective interests. Sigismundo becomes the *canastra* [harvester's basket] that gathers together the radicalized workers like harvested wheat, reiterating the analogy first presented in the novel's dust-jacket note's enumeration of 'homens' and 'espiga[s] de trigo' as things which are 'levantado do chão'. He thereby helps to pioneer a class-based politics that will socialize (some) family responsibilities, and reform the State as a conscientious, libertarian, and enabling parent.

What is also made clear by *Levantado*'s critique of the sexist and paternalistic status quo, however, is that, unlike stalks of wheat, the subaltern population that activists like Sigismundo seek to unite is subjectively diverse. There remains, therefore, a question as to whether their disparate experiences and aspirations can all be integrated dialectically into a 'perspectiva totalizante', or whether any such all-encompassing vision, as the basis for a Gramscian revolutionary hegemony, can only ever be considered a 'work-in-progress' arising from an unending process of historiographical reappraisal that is communal and dialogic, a dialectic whose resolution is infinitely deferred. In pursuit of an answer, one can return to the novel's intertextual dialogue with *Cien años de soledad*, and to the implicit contrasting of the relationships of the Buendías and the Mau-Tempos to their societies' evolving systems of production, their consciousness (or lack thereof) of the motives for, and consequences of, class politics, and, most of all, their contrasting perceptions of historical time. In itself, this contrast attests to the importance attributed by Saramago (as by García Márquez before him) to a *dialectical* practice of reading, and to the question of what such a practice can ultimately achieve, in both historiological and political terms. A tentative answer emerges when one compares the two novels' conclusions, beginning with Macondo's last and fatally unreflexive act of reading the past, when Aureliano deciphers the history of his family as prophesied by the gypsy Melquíades. Williamson and others stress the critical role in Macondo's demise of Melquíades's text itself, and its presumedly occultist epistemology. Yet, as Williamson suggests, arguably more fatal consequences derive from Aureliano's manner of reading. Only a miscomprehension of Melquíades's text could produce the implausible description of its narrative strategy as ordering a century's events not 'en el tiempo convencional de los hombres' [in the conventional time of humans], but concentrated 'de modo que todos coexistieran en un instante' [in such a way that they all coexisted in a single instant] (Márquez 1967: 350; trans. 1978: 335). As Aureliano reads the gypsy's narrative, the gap between it and the history to which it refers narrows to the point at which they — and Márquez's account of both — coincide and disappear as Macondo is wiped out by a hurricane. As Gerald Martin summarizes, this moment ends the century of alienating 'solitude', turning the reader out of what has for an instant become an absolutely self-reflexive text, and back into the historical sphere from which it abstracted itself.[46]

Hence, according to Williamson, the apocalypse that snuffs out Aureliano is revealed as neither preordained nor necessarily predicted, but the inevitable product of the Buendía's ahistorical consciousness, 'devoid of objectivity, of reference to an external reality and to linear time' (1987: 59). Swallowing up the words of what he perceives as an 'espejo hablado' [speaking mirror] (Márquez 1967: 335; trans. 11978: 336), Aureliano reads in absolute accordance with this solipsistic and tendentious phenomenology. Just as his forefathers failed to comprehend the significance of the new technology that Melquíades introduced, so Aureliano fails to transcend an interpretation of the manuscript as the logical reduction of Macondo's apparently endless, pointless existential cycle, until ultimately 'the past is not simply left behind by future events but acquires a fatal fascination as it creeps up on and eventually devours the present like a cyclone' (Williamson 1987: 59).[47]

As Williamson concludes, however, *Cien años de soledad*'s ending also alludes both to an alternative narrative and to an alternative mode of reading. Both emulate the dialectical practice of Aureliano's last mentor, the old Catalan bookseller who reads his erudite texts with 'una urdimbre de respeto solemne e irreverencia comadrera' [an interweaving of solemn respect and gossipy irreverence], and whose own writings are also subject to this 'dualidad' [dualism] (Márquez 1967: 337; trans. 1978: 323). The Catalan's clearest lesson for Macondo is his critique of nostalgia and of its fatal symbiosis with narcissism. This is a danger that he himself only appreciates after returning to his homeland, when nostalgia for Macondo clashes with that which he has always harboured for his native village (Márquez 1967: 339; trans. 1978: 325). His advice, ignored by Aureliano, is heeded by a fellow protégé, his friend Gabriel Márquez, who departs for Paris to become a writer, and, thus, to morph metafictitiously into the author who will make a critical and informed review of his experience and rewrite the history of Macondo (Williamson 1987: 61). Gabriel's account, as we have seen, urges the dialectical strategy to leap over the trap set by the mimetic logic of the realist novel and of positivist historiography. Instead of following the Lukácsian 'reflection' model, Márquez 'holds up a mirror [...] to Melquíades's mirror' and thus 'imbues his novel with an ironical duality' (Williamson, ibid.), balancing a 'respeto solemne' for the Buendía's undeserved suffering with the 'irreverencia comadrera' with which — in complicity with the reader — he observes the folly of their egocentric and irrational outlook.

Bringing Saramago back into the picture, we can find, in his discussion of historical representation in his *Diálogos* with Carlos Reis, neat analogies both for Aureliano's erroneous approach to Melquíades's history, and for the alternative and productive strategy demonstrated by the Catalan and by Gabriel. Adopting the perspective of Walter Benjamin's 'Angel of History' (1971b: 259–60),[48] Saramago observes that

> A única coisa que efectivamente há é passado e o presente não existe, é qualquer coisa que se joga continuamente, que não pode ser captado, apreendido, que não pode ser detido no seu curso; e portanto, uma vez que não pode ser detido, em momento nenhum eu posso intersectá-lo. (Reis 1998: 80)
>
> [The only thing that is actually there is the past, and the present does not exist, it's something that is constantly shifting, that cannot be caught, pinned down, that cannot be detained on its way, and, since it cannot be detained, at no time can I intercept it.]

While Saramago's linear conception of time eliminates the fallacy of the 'present', the Buendía's presumption that time is cyclical turns the Angel of History's view on its head, subsuming past events ahistorically into a hyperextended 'present' time. Aureliano's reading of Melquíades's text as a microcosm of this all-embracing present petrifies the dynamic by which his present interpretation of the past might inform and redirect the future: thus does he misrecognize the future as already set in stone. An alternative interpretation of the historical panorama that Melquíades constructs is, however, suggested by Saramago when, in the same interview, he offers a conception of history as 'uma imensa tela' [a huge canvas] upon which

> tudo está ao lado de tudo, numa espécie de caos, como se o tempo fosse comprimido e além de comprimido espalmado, sobre essa superfície; e como se os acontecimentos, os factos, as pessoas, tudo isso aparecesse ali não diacronicamente arrumado, mas numa outra 'arrumação caótica' na qual depois seria preciso encontrar um sentido. (Reis 1998: 80)
>
> [everything is side by side with everything else, in a kind of chaos, as if time was stretched out and, in addition to this, squashed flat against that surface; and as if events, facts, people, all this appeared there not diachronically ordered, but in another 'chaotic order' in which one would afterwards have to find a meaning.]

This concept of history as an 'arrumação caótica' explodes the microcosmic model, demanding the input of the reader to consider the links between

> as coisas todas que não têm (ou não parecem ter) nada que ver ali: Auschwitz ao lado de Homero, por exemplo; ou o homem de Néanderthal ao lado da Capela Sistina. (ibid)
>
> [all the things that don't have, or don't appear to have, anything in common there: Auschwitz side by side with Homer, for example, or Neanderthal Man side by side with the Sistine Chapel.]

or, in other words, the alternative parities, contrasts, and relations that unsettle entrenched metanarratives of historical causation. The discursive disjunctions and juxtaposition of subjective and objective perspectives, of fact, apocrypha, and counter-factual fantasy that both Márquez's and Saramago's novels employ repeatedly force the reader to detach from the diegesis, and recognize the textual and ideological Frankenstein's monster (however neatly stitched) that is the novelist's recreation of the outside world.

If the value of historical fiction, then, is only equal to the dialectic of its reading and of the reader's dialectical analysis of the world beyond the text, the ultimate question to be asked is that of how far, according to *Levantado do Chão* and its interpretation of *Cien años de soledad*, can dialectical analysis take us towards the Marxist goal of comprehensive historical knowledge? Here we must focus, finally, on *Levantado do Chão*'s finale, where the narrator assumes the viewpoint of a *milhano* [red kite] circling the *latifundium* as the workers invade and take control of the land. Long before it became an established topos within the neo-realist symbolic code, the kite, as J. Chevalier and A. Gheerbrant note, was a bird to which the augurs of Roman civilization attributed particular significance, associated with the god Apollo, and symbolizing clear-sightedness and clairvoyance.[49] This panoramic and pinpoint accurate bird's-eye view constitutes an obvious metaphor for the accurate and universalizing perspective that neo-realist writers aspired to impart, which must supersede the ant's-eye view as the oppressed masses become *levantados do chão*. The purely metaphoric function of the *topos* of the kite's vision, indeed, is indicated by its supernatural properties, when in a final anti-mimetic flourish Saramago resurrects Monte Lavre's fallen working-class heroes to create an all-inclusive 'arrumação caótica' of the characters and events that contributed to the triumphs of Spring 1974:

> Vai o milhano passando e contando, um milheiro, sem falar nos invisíveis, que é sina a cegueira dos homens vivos não darem a conta certa de quantos fizeram o feito, mil vivos e cem mil mortos, ou dois milhões de suspiros que se ergueram do chão, qualquer número servirá[.] (*Levantado*: 364)

> [The kite passes, counting as it goes, a thousand people, not to mention the invisible ones, which goes to show the blindness of the living who don't take full account of how many people did this deed, one thousand living and one hundred thousand dead, or two million sighs that have risen from the ground, any number will do.]

While a momentary suspension of disbelief might allow the reader to share the kite's impossibly privileged perspective across both space and time, this fantasy does not obscure the fact that the workers of Monte Lavre — less the 'armée vengeresse' of Zola's imagining than an organized, beneficent occupying force — have nevertheless risen only a relatively short distance from the ground. Their knowledge and understanding still fall short of the comprehensive perspective to which Marxist historical materialism aspires. Dialectical analysis and materialist presumptions have helped the workers free themselves (even if events since the book's publication indicate the failure of attempts to build the kind of revolutionary hegemony that would do more than mitigate the worst abuses of *Estado Novo* agribusiness). However, the dialectical process of the narrative itself is not resolved, and the process of reassessing the past and the current socio-economic order is carried through into Saramago's subsequent fictions. The following four novels will greatly expand *Levantado*'s assault on the pervasive presence of authoritarian, nationalist, and theistic metanarratives and ideologemes in the historiography and aesthetics of post-1974 Portugal (and indeed of other polities absorbed into the international project of neo-liberal late capitalism in the post-Second World War era). At the same time, these novels will emphasize the idea that any future 'ascent' to successful socio-economic transformation on Marxist principles must be preceded by a transformation of individual and collective consciousness more radical than that conceived by Marx. Such a transformation must be informed by psychoanalytical and post-structuralist interrogations both of human subjectivity and perception of material and social conditions. While having little to say about the structure and organization of a revolutionary party, the plots of *Memorial* and its successors will propose the elaboration of a revolutionary 'micropolitics' of the everyday, which would depend as much on a revised understanding of gender relations, and of the politics of affect, and on individuals' willingness to question their own sense of identity, as it would on recognizing common socio-economic interests.

Notes to Chapter 1

1. It is significant that the novel appeared in English translation only in 2012; by contrast Russian and German translations appeared in the USSR and German Democratic Republic respectively as early as 1982.
2. Analysis of *Levantado*'s narrative form in relation to Bakhtin's conception of the post-Dostoevskian 'polyphonic novel' is made in Sabine (2001a: 56–59), and Frier (2007b: 102).
3. Márquez's *Cien años de soledad* was published in Portuguese by Europa-América press, Lisbon, in 1971, as *Cem anos de solidão*, trans. by Eliane Zagury. It is possible that Saramago knew of, and read, the novel earlier, in the original Spanish.
4. Redol partially rescinded this statement in 1965, in a revised preface to the novel's sixth edition, saying that *Gaibéus* 'seria um compromisso deliberado da reportagem com o romance' [aims to be a considered compromise between reportage and novel] (1965: 9). On *Gaibéus*'s importance in the development of Portuguese neo-realism, see Carlos Reis (1983: esp. 479–84), and Ferreira (1992: esp. 134–70). Studies of the novel's relationship with *Levantado* by Cerdeira da Silva (1996: 39) and Viçoso (1999: 240) concur in viewing *Gaibéus* as an inaugural work in Portuguese neo-realism.
5. See this volume's Introduction, pp. 8–9 for a discussion of the concept of a *perspectiva totalizante*.
6. On the significance of this sentence in relation to both the novel's narrative and hermeneutic strategies, and its approach to historiography, see Lanciani (1993) and Simões (1996).
7. See this volume's Introduction chapter, p. 12.
8. As Grossegesse has observed, in a number of other texts Saramago has exploited the image of excoriation not only to assert 'a poetics of conflict, imperfection, and screams born out of pain, against the art which aims at beauty and harmony even in the representation of cruelty and pain', but simultaneously 'related in the first place to the act of writing, and in the second to a kind of self-birth' in a manner that configures literary expression as a vehicle for 'an active ethics of self-liberation from social and discursive oppression (religion, politics, art) that separates the pain from the image' (Grossegesse 2006: 59).
9. See Mark 4. 1–20; Luke 8. 1–15, and Matthew 13. 1–23 for the Parable of the Sower, and Matthew 13. 24–30 for the Parable of the Tares. The neo-realist use of wheat and harvests as metaphor for workers' organization, deriving perhaps from the name of the journal *Seara Nova*, was taken up not only by novelists but equally by political songwriters such as José Afonso in songs such as 'Maio, maduro Maio' [May, ripe May] (1971).
10. For a brief synopsis of the PCP's growth and activism from the 1940s to the 1970s, see Rosas and Brandão de Brito (1996: I, 173–81). For fuller accounts, see Raby (1988) and Cunha (1992).
11. On Vidigal's death, see José Dias Coelho, *A Resistência em Portugal* (Porto: Inova, 1974), p. 50, and Ramiro da Costa, *Elementos para a História do Movimento Operário e das Ideias Socialistas em Portugal* (Lisbon: Assírio & Alvim, s.d. [1978]), cited by Raby (1988), p. 146, note 56.
12. For figures on the changing class backgrounds of the officer corps, see Maxwell (1995: 37).
13. The allusion, already implicit in the comparison made between men and wheat in *Levantado*'s dust-jacket note, is reinforced by the final chapter's description of the occupying workers as

'gente escura, um formigueiro que se espalha pelo latifúndio' [swarthy people, an ants' nest spreading out across the latifundium] (*Levantado*: 361).
14. On proverbs in *Levantado*, see Simões (1996: esp. 76–80), Aldeamil (2001), and Helena Vaz Duarte's (2006) meticulous study of Saramago's quotation, adaptation, and invention of proverbs. On the novel's folk tales, see Cerdeira da Silva (1989: 249; 251, and 253–56), and Sabine (2006: 151).
15. On *Levantado*'s comical and symbolic names, see also Cerdeira da Silva (1989: 205–07), and Duarte (1982: 86–87).
16. On the repercussions of Portugal's entry into the War, see Wheeler (1978: 126–28, and 182–83), and Birmingham (2003: 153–57).
17. On the Republic's reform of labour laws, and contrasting neglect of agrarian reform, see Birmingham (2003: 156–57), Wheeler (1978: 18–19, and 65–66) and Marques (1972b: II,120–22; 135–37).
18. On the *Estado Novo*'s agricultural policy and its mixed results, see Robinson (1979: 146–51).
19. 'Também do chão pode levantar-se um livro, como uma espiga de trigo ou uma flor brava. Ou uma ave. Ou uma bandeira' [from the ground there can also arise a book, like a stalk of wheat or a wild flower. Or a bird. Or a flag] (Levantado: cover). On symbolic encryption in resistance writing under the *Estado Novo*, see this volume's Introduction, p. 9.
20. On *Levantado*'s dovetailing of the apocryphal experiences of fictional characters with authenticated data relating to the latifundium strikes of 1945, see Letízia (1991), and especially Silva (1989: 195–229).
21. For more comprehensive attempts at a taxonomy of proverbial forms in Saramago's novels, see Duarte (2006).
22. The former abundance in rural Portugal of such fables of metamorphic affliction is attested in, for example, Carnarvon (1848: 268). I am indebted to the generous help of Professor Malyn Newitt in bringing this source to my attention.
23. Sigismundo's and João's manipulation of the discourses of anti-fascist resistance is consistent with their close involvement, at this point, with the PCP, and with Hammond's assertion that 'there is considerable impressionistic evidence that ideological thinking is widely diffused among ordinary and relatively unsophisticated Portuguese' (1979: 268). *Levantado*'s account of the PIDE's interrogation and torture of political detainees is also remarkably accurate. A comprehensive overview of these procedures, drawing on numerous survivor testimonies, is provided in Calderia et al. (2011: esp. 33–43, and 117–20).
24. See Gramsci (1971c: esp. 334–35).
25. For a full discussion of the theme of incest in the novel, see Williamson (1987) and Incledon (1986).
26. On the Ciénaga massacre, see Palacios (2006: 83–84), and Bushnell (1993: 179–80). Both authors note a lack of reliable data, even today, about the precise circumstances, and the extent, of the violence perpetrated: estimates at the time ranged as high as one thousand dead, though Bushnell claims that 'from sixty to seventy-five' is most probable.
27. This image may be adapted from Tolstoy's description of the workings of an army in Book 1 of *War and Peace* (1972: I, 298). On the 1944–45 wave of strikes in Ribatejo and Alentejo, and PCP involvement in this, see Raby (1988: 76–89).
28. See Oliveira (1987) and Fagundes (1980).
29. On this reorganization, see Raby (1988: esp. 47–55).
30. See Raby (1988: 64–72).
31. As asserted in the PCP pamphlet *Temas de Estudo* of May 1942, '[without] this general reorientation of the whole activity of Party cadres in rural centres towards the peasant sector, all the guiding slogans and all the activity of the Party's central cadres will be futile, will be no more than impotent gesturing' (p. 13; quoted in translation by Raby (1988: 86)).
32. On this significant policy change, and the subsequent exponential growth in the PCP's popular following, see Raby (1988: 45; 55–57, and 68–69).
33. Tiersky observes that, in his approach to democratic centralism, Gramsci 'as generally in his theory, insisted on adapting general ideas of Bolshevism and communism to local conditions' (1985: 109). While exasperatingly inexact, Gramsci's characterization of democratic or 'organic'

centralism is also 'practical and experimental' in stressing how this 'elastic formula [...] comes alive in so far as it is interpreted and continually adapted to necessity' (Gramsci 1971b: 189).

34. Distinguishing between 'democratic centralism' and 'bureaucratic centralism', Gramsci explains that '[t]he policing function of a party can [...] be either progressive or regressive. It is progressive when it tends to keep the dispossessed reactionary forces within the bounds of legality, and to raise the backward masses to the level of the new legality. It is regressive when it tends to hold back the vital forces of history and to maintain a legality which has been superseded, which is anti-historical, which has become extrinsic' (Gramsci 1971b: 155).
35. See Raby (1988: 107–09), for a detailed account of the arrests and subsequent crisis. As Raby details, the PCP 'was not destroyed, but the recovery was to be a long and difficult process' (1988: 108).
36. On these two stories, see also Frier (2007b: 100), and Francès-Dumas (2001: 222–23).
37. On the Montemor protests of 23 June 1958, and the broader political crisis surrounding the presidential election, see Raby (1988: 194–95). According to Raby, the PCP's 'failure to provide leadership in [this] frankly insurrectional climate' was trenchantly criticized by Cunhal in his 1961 attack on the 1950s Party leadership's pursuit of a 'peaceful solution' to Salazar's dictatorship (1988: 132).
38. On the emergence of radical feminist groups in Portugal's cities and universities, and their critique of Marxist organizations' reduction of women's oppression to simply a facet of class struggle, see Tavares (2000: 89–100).
39. Tavares (2000: 98) notes the publication of Portuguese translations of Kollontai's work by organizations like the Grupo de Mulheres da Associação Académica de Coimbra in the mid-1970s.
40. See Kollontai (1977: 252).
41. On the sexual politics of the *Estado Novo*, see Ferreira (1996), Pimentel (2002), and Rosas and Brandão de Brito (1996: II, 608–11, and 675–76).
42. An *invernadeiro* (lit. 'winterer') is a worker responsible for winter crops or for the wintering of livestock. The narrative voice playfully notes the contrivance of 'um monte que se chamava Pendão das Mulheres, vá lá saber porquê [a mountain called the Women's Banner, goodness knows why] (*Levantado*: 66). The employment together here of João, his siblings Anselmo and Maria da Conceição, and Faustina indicates how and when the strict sexual division of agricultural tasks, which Letízia (1991: 161) accurately notes is maintained in early twentieth-century Monte Lavre, becomes less absolute.
43. Letízia contrasts Maria Adelaide's 'núpcias com o futuro radiante' [wedding with the glowing future] with the likely fate of her raped ancestor, denied any 'direito a casamento' [right to marriage] and hence 'condenada a viver na desgraça' [condemned to live in penury] (1991: 175).
44. For a survey history of feminist thinking and activism in Portugal, and its reception by Marxist organizations there, see Virgínia Ferreira (1998), Magalhães (2007: esp. 10–14), and Tavares, Magalhães, and Mathee (2009).
45. On the notion of an unequally distributed 'patriarchal dividend' in male-dominated societies, see Connell (1995, esp. 79).
46. While accepting Martin's analysis of how the conclusion reconnects the reader with the historical realist narrative sphere, I disagree with his assertion that Aureliano is also 'negating the past dialectically' (1987: 111). Aureliano's only escape from the 'false circularities, meaningless repetitions' (ibid.) established by Úrsula is through the annihilation that he believes Melquíades's text to identify correctly as Macondo's predetermined and inevitable destiny.
47. Williamson's reading of the novel's conclusion expressly notes the manner in which 'the Buendía vice of nostalgia [is] figured forth as a gathering wind from the past' (1987: 58), in the passage 'Entonces empezó el viento, tibio, incipiente, lleno de voces del pasado, de murmullos de geranios antiguos, de suspiros de desengaños anteriores a las nostalgias más tenaces' [Then the wind started — warm, incipient, full of voices from the past, murmurings of ancient geraniums, sighs expressing disappointments that preceded the most tenacious nostalgia] (Márquez 1967: 350; trans. 1978: 335).
48. On the influence of Benjamin's 'Theses on the Nature of History' on Saramago's fiction, see also, in particular, Rebelo's (1993) pioneering study.

49. See Chevalier and Gheerbrant, *Dictionnaire des Symboles* (Paris: Laffont, 1982), p. 504, cited in Francès-Dumas (2001), pp. 225–26, n. 46.

CHAPTER 2

Memorial do Convento

Levantado do Chão reconstructs a recent, and still hotly debated, history of a community hauling itself up off its knees. *Memorial do Convento* looks back another two hundred years, to imagine an earlier attempt to raise the common people from the ground. Inserting fantasy alongside documented fact, it explores how the instructive potential of historical analysis can be enhanced by such counter-factual speculation. In its retelling of documented history, *Memorial* presents a disturbing continuity between the powers of Church and State in the age of absolutism and in that of Salazarism. The reliance of both on censorship, surveillance, and terror, conscription and bonded labour, religious mysticism, and propagandist spectacle to dominate a dispossessed populace suggests a trajectory of Portuguese history that Ellen Sapega has called 'desastrosamente cíclico' [disastrously cyclical] (1995: 35).[1] However, it is *Memorial*'s introduction of self-evidently fantastical elements, slotted into its historical account without 'contaminating' the factual data from which this is constructed, that most powerfully disrupts Salazarism's specious narrative of Portuguese 'values', and posits a radical alternative. The tale of a flying machine built in secret, and powered by captured human wills, allegorizes a materialist challenge to the notion of divine will, and to the constraint, exploitation, and corruption of the human body and spirit legitimized by that notion. Moreover, by opening up a discrete, fantastical, space in the narrative, this tale permits Saramago's utopian speculation on further revisions to revolutionary socialist politics.

Memorial, more than any of Saramago's novels, is a narrative that uses dualities and oppositions, symmetries and inversions, to interrogate, supplement, and reconfigure *História Pátria*. The novel opens in the year 1711, with King João V's vow to build a monastery if God will grant him an heir, and concludes in 1739, after the completion of his monumental monastery-palace complex at Mafra, until the late nineteenth century the largest building in Portugal.[2] In the account of national history that the *Estado Novo* propagated, this lavish tribute to divine benevolence was one of the crowning achievements of a second Portuguese 'Golden Age', funded by the mineral wealth and trade of a renascent empire. *Memorial* offers the reverse image of João V's reign and of his vow, highlighting how the monastery symbolized both the power of a tyrannous theocracy, and the wealth extracted from that theocracy's subjects, of whom up to 45,000 had been forced to toil in hellish conditions, over two decades, to build the monastery.[3] The 'partiality' of the established account is challenged by recovering the experiences and agency of these and other foot soldiers of history. *Memorial*'s apocryphal labourers, soldiers, and religious dissenters are foregrounded as heroic agents, in juxtaposition to the monarchs, courtiers, and clergy formerly afforded a monopoly in official memory, but characterized here with their complement of physical and moral frailties. The novel simultaneously counters the *Estado Novo*'s historiographical 'packaging' of Joanine Portugal through its unresolved discursive dualism, where opposed linguistic registers and generic conventions clash, to astonishing, bitingly satirical, effect. This enables Saramago both to critique the metaphysical elements embedded in many accounts of Dom João's reign, and to advertise the artifice of his own parable of a possible utopian alternative to its culture and ideology.

Focusing on life at Court only long enough to ridicule the King and to question the 'miracle' that prompted the Mafra monastery's construction, *Memorial* shifts its focus to the fortunes of Baltasar Sete-Sóis [Seven Suns], an infantryman demobbed after losing his hand in the War of the Spanish Succession. Through a seemingly magical intercession, Baltasar is united with the part-Jewish Blimunda, subsequently dubbed 'Sete-Luas' [Seven Moons] in reference to the clairvoyance with which she can see through, or inside, solid objects. The plot follows the progress of the couple's tender and egalitarian romance, between Mafra, where Baltasar works on the monastery's construction, and Lisbon, where they befriend the free-thinking Jesuit polymath and pioneer aviator Bartolomeu Lourenço de Gusmão (1685–1724). Bartolomeu confides in them regarding his heretical speculations about the nature of God, and his belief that God wills the continuing, incremental revelation of wisdom to humans through their scientific enquiry, claiming that 'o saber de Deus é como um rio de água que vai correndo para o mar, é Deus a fonte, os homens o oceano' [the wisdom of God is like a river that runs unto the sea, God is the source, and mankind the ocean] (*Memorial*: 122). He also confides that, in accordance with God's design that such enquiry should ultimately enable humans to fly (*Memorial*: 63–64), he is building a flying machine. Bartolomeu's *passarola* will be raised by the energy of *vontades* — human wills — which, he explains, dwell in people's bodies as a 'nuvem fechada' [dense cloud] (*Memorial*: 124), detaching themselves at death and in certain other circumstances. Baltasar and Blimunda help Bartolomeu to complete the *passarola*, exploiting Blimunda's X-ray vision to identify and collect a sufficiency of *vontades* from the dying bodies of victims of a plague. The three friends work in secret, remote from the Inquisition and Court intrigues, and visited by the Court composer, Domenico Scarlatti, whose sublime harpsichord playing cures Blimunda of a virulent sickness. When one day Bartolomeu learns that the Inquisition is approaching, intent on arresting him, he and the lovers escape in their newly completed *passarola*, but, after it makes landfall in the wilderness, he suffers a mental breakdown and disappears, fleeing to Spain and dying soon afterwards. Blimunda and Baltasar hide his *passarola*, but Baltasar's efforts to keep the machine sky-worthy end in tragedy: he accidentally lets the machine take flight, only to discover that, single-handed, he cannot control its course. Following his disappearance, Blimunda roams the country for nine years in search of her lover, only to find him at the moment of his execution as a heretic in a Lisbon auto-da-fé.

Saramago's elaboration in *Memorial* of a counter-factual narrative of resistance to

Church and State tyranny obviously entails a far more extensive use of the fantastic than *Levantado* employs. Nevertheless, his ideological agenda remains unchanged, albeit with an intensification of *Levantado*'s use of metanarrative interjections and other alienation devices to question the capabilities of historical materialism. *Memorial* develops its diegesis through a sequence of tableaux counterposing documented historical material with apocryphal elements. As in *Levantado*, this sequence implies a materialist thesis of historical progression, and the possibility of transcendental social change through a reorganization of labour and production. The key change of emphasis is that, in contrast to *Levantado*'s infrequent use of fantastical tropes to overcome self-evident historical lacunae and 'recuperate' lost data (from which an alternative historical narrative can be extrapolated), in *Memorial*, fantastical elements assume much greater prominence and create a more complex 'ucronian' dimension. Saramago builds the fantastic elements of his plot in the lacunae of history, making use of genuine eighteenth-century sources recording both Gusmão's experiments in aviation, and the inexplicable power of a local woman to see inside bodies and through solid objects.[4] Two fantastical tropes — Blimunda's X-ray vision, and the power of human wills, captured in a glass vessel, to power Gusmão's aerostat — are the motor of much of the plot, yet without 'contaminating' the novel's representations of past realities. Developed as a self-contained strand of the diegesis, the story of the *passarola*'s flight, and the fate of its builders, constitutes an allegory of popular emancipation attempted before its time. This allegory, while warning of the limitations of progressive projects developed without the support of a popular consensus, at the same time offers inspiration to a later society, armed with the capacity to overcome ignorance and tyranny. Further to its implicit call for the revolutionary mobilization of popular will, the *passarola* story enables Saramago to envisage a free and egalitarian social order, based on a revolution in industrial and libidinal attitudes and relations.

The prominence of counter-factual conjecture in *Memorial* corresponds to a shift of emphasis on two preoccupations of Saramago's previous works. First, where *Levantado* questions historical materialism's capacity to achieve a comprehensive synthesis of knowledge, *Memorial* attempts to affirm a Marxist agenda within the restricted parameters identified by the post-structuralist critique of historiography. To *Levantado*'s question of how we who suffer 'estas mazelas de miopia' [this handicap of short-sightedness] can aspire to the totalizing vision of the red kite in its conclusion, *Memorial* responds that '[u]sa cada qual os olhos que tem para ver o que pode ou lhe consentem, ou apenas parte pequena do que desejaria' [each man uses the eyes he has to see what he can, or what they permit him, or only a small part of what he would like to see] (*Memorial*: 84). In accordance with this observation, Saramago's subsequent 'historical' fiction does not simply investigate abuses of the traces of the past, of the concept of history, and of humankind's reliance on historical narratives. Rather, it assesses the political options remaining when historical enquiry cannot identify secure truths about historical causation. It conceives of new, 'recuperative', narratives of the past, which challenge the constraining conclusions offered by the hegemonic narratives, thereby altering political consciousness, vision, and agency. Furthermore, however, each novel focuses much more on a range of epistemological, psychological, and institutional obstacles to social transformation, obstacles that are often sidestepped or disregarded in *Levantado*. The *passarola*'s construction and flight constitutes a parable demonstrating that, in the eighteenth century, only anachronistic insights and consciousness such as those afforded by Blimunda's supernatural vision can enable the downtrodden to escape from the Church-State oligarchy and the alienating socio-economic order that it maintains, to change from being a 'bicho de terra' [earthworm, but, more literally, 'creature of the earth'] into a subject 'levantado do chão' [raised from the ground].[5] In the late twentieth century, however, the technological, social, and intellectual conditions for revolutionary change are at hand or practically realizable. What is required now is not a miracle, but a change of consciousness and a collective will to challenge the iniquities of the status quo.

This chapter's three sections attempt a full account of how *Memorial* connects a revised historical narrative content and form to a more cautious, yet more utopian, development of the revised Marxist socialist agenda privileged in *Levantado*. The first section explores how the novel debunks and displaces the dominant narrative in a self-critical manner. Applying Bakhtin's analysis of 'dialogism' in novelistic prose reveals how a system of topical and discursive symmetries and oppositions overturns the selective and hermeneutic operations through which *História Pátria* grants credibility to an elitist, authoritarian world-view. Yet this same system also makes a crucial contribution to *Memorial*'s 'alienation' of the reader from its text and from the ideology privileged therein. This section also reviews how similar tricks, entailing the appropriation of the baroque aesthetics of eighteenth-century Portugal, support — and simultaneously question — the novel's alternative inscription of national identity and values, and its correspondingly Marxist thesis of socio-economic development. Saramago expounds a materialist thesis through an effectively dialectical counterposition of a rewritten documentary history and of counter-factual speculation that centres on the fantasy of the *passarola*. The proposal of such a dialectics, as an analytical process that is effective only insofar as one concedes that no complete synthesis can ever be reached, is set out in a 'neo-baroque' allegory that uses Scarlatti's music-making as metaphor for contrasting models of historiography. While elements of the established history are forced into a sonata-like dialogue with Saramago's subversive and partly apocryphal account of the period, the novel refuses synthesis into a neat narrative, or resolution of the emergent tensions. Instead, following what Esther Leslie claims is Walter Benjamin's association of 'the allegorical method with the dialectical method' (2000: 199), *Memorial* uses both allegory and the counter-factual to incite its reader to think of the past in the metanarrative mode urged in Benjamin's 'Theses', identifying a fleeting image of the past 'as it flashes up at a moment of danger' (1973b: 257).

The second section develops the Bakhtinian approach further, in considering the centrality of the body and corporeal imagery to *Memorial*'s ideological agenda. It explores how the appropriated literary devices and styles both of baroque panegyric and of baroque satire subvert flattering images of the status quo, and assert many of the same materialist and egalitarian ideologemes privileged in *Levantado*. Humorous images of the body disrupt the discursive protocols sustaining an idealist world-view and a hierarchized society. Thereby, they expose the contradictions between the dissimulated corporeality of political and religious leaders, and the simultaneous use of a monumentalist, often unmistakeably phallic, aesthetics to assert power and will. Meanwhile, a less playful optic exposes the physically and psychologically perverting influence of the state ideology and social organization in Joanine Portugal. By these means, *Memorial* identifies corporeal and psycho-sexual malaise as symptomatic of the alienation due to eighteenth-century absolutism (and, implicitly, to modern capitalism as well). Hereupon, it rehabilitates somatic agency, erotic love, and pleasure as crucial components of the utopian, egalitarian vision that is carried forward in Saramago's subsequent fiction.

The final section explores *Memorial*'s broader vision of a revolutionary utopian politics. The fantasy of the *passarola* develops into a pseudo-Baroque allegory of power, resistance, and potential transformation. While the monastery's construction commandeers popular will for the glorification of an arrogant monarch and of his aloof or non-existent God, the *passarola* project, in defiance of the prohibitions of Church and State, channels the same will for the edification and empowerment of all humanity. While having a parabolic function, the *passarola* fantasy also provides a 'legitimate' (since hypothetical) forum in which to present a sympathetic treatment of (unproven) Marxist assumptions; assumptions, that is, about political and historical consciousness, about the role of conditions of production in dictating social development, and about the need for collective, cooperative actions, for democratization, and for sexual equality in order to secure socio-economic progress. These ideologemes are showcased through their association with the 'heroic' protagonists Blimunda and Baltasar, whose blissful and productive union contrasts with the unjust, perverse, and often wretched existence of rulers and their abject minions. Relations between the lovers — and their friends Padre Bartolomeu and Scarlatti — represent a socialist utopia in microcosm. The counter-factual scenario of the *passarola*'s construction, in the confines of a rural manor, suggests the possibility of an industrious idyll arising from the correct blend of ethics, economics, and technology, if the Church and State's oppressive hegemony (and the false consciousness it fosters) could be overthrown. This in significant ways recalls Herbert Marcuse's concept of a new and better humanity ascending through a 'revolutionary' deployment of technology, a rethinking of identity and self–Other relations, and rehabilitation of the body and sexuality through a harmonious integration of work, pleasure, art and love. Thus *Memorial* expands on *Levantado*'s engagement with feminist and Gramscian critiques of the operations of power in everyday life, and posits the integration into Marxist theory and praxis of a radical 'micro-politics' of day-to-day agency.

I — Productive Dissonances: Carnival, Memorialism, and the Open Materialist Dialectic

At the heart of *Memorial* is a lengthy account of the deadly struggle of an army of labourers to transport a gigantic marble block fifteen kilometres, from its quarry to the Mafra building site (*Memorial*: 239–64). En route, one labourer, Manuel Milho, tells his workmates a bizarre fairy tale, which, by disrupting the discursive unities and hermeneutics of conventional fairy tales, constitutes a kind of *mise-en-abîme* of *Memorial*'s strategies both for unpacking a 'partial and parcelled' representation of the past, and for advertising the inevitable partiality and imperfection of its revised account. Initially, Manuel's story of a queen, unfulfilled by her station, who elopes with a hermit (*Memorial*: 262) might seem to follow *Levantado*'s examples of how grass-roots resistance and dissent is disseminated through fables and folklore. Yet in the event, Manuel's friends express consternation with his unconventional treatment of themes in a story that 'não se parece nada com as histórias que se contam' [is nothing like the stories most people tell] (*Memorial*: 255). What exasperates Manuel's companions further is his disruption of the formal unity of his story, which he relates 'em bocadinhos' [in little bits] (ibid.) over four nights, breaking off in mid-flow each night, and which he refuses to bring to a clear and 'meaningful' ending (*Memorial*: 263). Manuel defends this lack of closure by asserting that 'foi o caso há tantos anos que já não podem estar vivos, nem um nem outro, e com a morte sempre se acabam as histórias' [it all happened so long ago that they can no longer be living, neither one nor the other, and death brings all stories to an end] (*Memorial*: 264). If the protagonists are dead and have left no trace, his implication seems to be, does it matter what *really happened*? Or does the real importance of the story that gets told lie in its relationship to the reality of the present? The response of Manuel's companions is to use conjecture — 'cada qual pensando [...] consoante as suas conhecidas inclinações' [each one thinking in accordance with his well-known inclinations] (*Memorial*: 252) — to try to make sense of the uncertainties revealed by the tale's narrative and discursive errors.

Manuel's transgression of recognized rules of emplotment, characterization, and linguistic register does more than simply make his audience recognize that 'cada dia é um bocado de história' [every day is a little bit of history] and that 'ninguém a pode contar toda' [no one can recount it in full] (*Memorial*: 262). His juxtaposition of certain lexical, hermeneutic, and narrative elements of fairy tales with others drawn from genres as incongruent as Socratic dialogue creates an embryonic model of the dialogic confrontation, throughout the novel, of 'two socio-linguistic consciousnesses, [...] that are not here unconsciously mixed [...], but that come together and consciously fight it out on the territory of the utterance' (Bakhtin 1981: 360). The collision between differing points of views on the world that are embedded in these genres (ibid.) invites the reader to consider afresh both the relationships between the social types in the story, and that between the storyteller and his material. Of course, *Memorial*'s accretions to the familiar historical narrative do not simply counterpose topics, hermeneutics, and discourses. They also level or, often, invert the hierarchies that govern them. This subverts the dominant narrative's articulation of the world-view — fundamental to the Christian ideology of eighteenth-century Portugal — that, as Bakhtin recalls, exalts 'all that is high, spiritual, ideal' over 'the material level [...] the sphere of the earth and the body' that is fundamental to Saramago's Marxist socialism (1984: 19–20). This is particularly noteworthy in the counterposed accounts of the 'great men' of *História Pátria*, and of the subaltern population. Dom João and his Queen's laboured, loveless attempts at procreation (*Memorial*: 15–18), contrast with the unabashed, tender love-making of Baltasar and Blimunda (e.g. *Memorial*: 56); the progress of Infanta Maria Bárbara's gilded wedding cortège from Lisbon to Elvas is recounted in alternation with the journey of penniless, hungry João Elvas along the same route on foot (*Memorial*: 297–318). Accounts of the opulent street processions affirming the might of God and King counterpose descriptions of press-ganged monastery labourers being marched overland to Mafra with shackles on their wrists and ankles, and of Franciscan novitiates forced to walk the six leagues to Mafra barefoot (*Memorial*: 295; 312; 323–24).

The intrusion of demotic discourse, subverting the authoritative tone in which the established historical account is couched, not only challenges that account's claims to comprehensiveness, but also redresses the preponderant focus on the ruling class without claiming comprehensivity for Saramago's retelling. What Carlos Reis calls the novel's 'memorialist' form of discourse (Reis 1986: 94) 'alienates' the reader from the text and its ideological baggage, thus amplifying *Levantado*'s admission of the ideological investment made in all attempts to represent the past *doutra maneira*. This use of 'memorialism' to reinsert the lowlier agents of history into historiographical calculations is movingly exemplified in the account of the transportation of the gigantic balcony stone, when a porter trips and has his foot crushed under a wheel of the giant cart. Within minutes, his personal tragedy is forgotten, with only a single bloodstained pebble remaining as evidence:

> Já não se vê sinal do sangue que ficou no chão, passaram as rodas do carro, pisaram os pés dos homens, as patas patudas dos bois, a terra sugou e confundiu o resto, só um calhau que foi arredado para o lado ainda conserva alguma cor. (*Memorial*: 247)

> [Already there's no sight of the blood spilt on the ground, the wheels of the cart have passed, the men's feet and the hulking hooves of the oxen have tramped over it, the earth has absorbed and mixed up what remained, only a pebble knocked to one side still retains a tinge of colour.]

As society marches on under the direction of an absent tyrant, traces of the history of the subaltern survive only where they happen to be 'arredado para o lado' for future generations to rediscover and reinterpret.

Memorial's switching of the heroic characterization of the rich, and contrastingly comic-grotesque characterization of the marginal poor, avoids the 'carnivalesque' practice of 'travesty and inversion' that Eagleton accuses of 'collapsing binary oppositions into a mounting groundswell of ambiguity' (1981: 145). Rather, as Arnaut points out, it invites the reader to consider 'some very obvious ideological conclusions' (1999: 191). It makes evident the Church and State oligarchy's contempt for notions of human equality, its disdain for the body and for labour, its obscurantist dogma, and its coercion of popular will. Moreover, it concludes that this oligarchy's misrule is stalling the motors of economic, social, and intellectual progress. The building of the monastery exposes the backward state of Portuguese manufacturing, engineering, and artistry, and diverts manpower from an already inadequate agricultural sector. A series of references intimates that socio-economic development is stuck in the mud, just like the processions weighed down by the Mafra balcony stone and by the royal wedding retinue (*Memorial*: 241–64; 297–318). The response of Portugal's rulers to the growing threat of Great British, French, and Dutch mercantile and military strength combines complacency with incompetence (*Memorial*: 60). The Portuguese empire is reliant on grain imports to feed its populace (*Memorial*: 59), its single university has no faculty of science (*Memorial*: 117), and its King commands an inadequate civil service on the basis of patronage, bribes, and tyranny. If the persons and status symbols of Crown and Church are weighty burdens that slow down human progress, the fantasy of the lighter-than-air *passarola* permits speculation on the forces and values that could exalt society if the dominion of Church and reactionary State were overcome.

In the course of inverting the established hierarchies of linguistic register, *Memorial* draws inspiration from the baroque aesthetic so typical of early eighteenth-century Portugal. Óscar Lopes has noted how *Memorial* parodies the baroque 'tendência [...] de aproximar, bruscamente, o prosaico do poético, o erudito ou solene do corriqueiro' [tendency rudely to bring together the prosaic and the poetic, the learned or solemn and the scurrilous] (1986: 207–08).[6] The observation of the great art critic Mario Praz that baroque taste admired 'out-of-the-way notions as [...] those which supplied the best means of arousing astonishment' (1964: 63) gives an insight into how amenable the baroque style is to adaptation for the literary practitioner of Brechtian 'alienation'. As will be explored below, the arousal of 'astonishment' and 'alienation' is also fundamental to the 'neo-baroque' aesthetic that Severo Sarduy identified in mid-twentieth century Latin American literature. Sarduy's concept of a contemporary aesthetic that 'refleja estructuralmente la inarmonía, la ruptura de la homogeneidad, del logos en tanto que absoluto [...] arte del destronamiento y la discusión' [structurally reflects disharmony, the disruption of sameness, of the *logos* as absolute [...] an art of usurpation and contention] (1974: 102–03) has great relevance when analysing Saramago's fiction, whether or not he was consciously influenced by the 'neo-baroque' innovations of García Márquez, Alejo Carpentier, and others.[7] Saramago's exploitation of jarring discursive mismatches is immediately evident in *Memorial*'s first chapter, depicting Dom João swearing his fateful vow. The chapter opens with a pastiche of the florid prose of baroque-era court and pulpit, which dissimulates the mechanics of dynastic coupling within a stately flow of aggrandizement and euphemism, but then deviates into emphatically vulgar corporeal reference that implies the monarchs' equality with the common herd:

> Dom João, quinto do nome na tabela real, irá esta noite ao quarto de sua mulher, Dona Maria Ana Josefa, que chegou há mais de dois anos da Áustria para dar infantes à coroa portuguesa e *até hoje ainda não emprenhou*. (*Memorial*: 11, my italics)[8]

[Dom João, the fifth king of that name in the royal list, will tonight visit the bedchamber of his queen, Dona Maria Ana Josefa, who arrived from Austria more than two years ago to furnish heirs to the Portuguese Crown, and *to this day has still not fallen pregnant*.]

The verb 'emprenhar' here does not simply lower the tone. It strips off the desexualizing veil lent by the courtly use of synecdoche ('dar infantes à coroa portuguesa'), redefining Her Majesty's status as that of a brood-mare, and revealing the dynastic system's vulnerability to the vagaries of human fertility.[9] The discursive mismatch also highlights the role of quasi-religious ritual in disguising how Catholic and absolutist power depends on the instrumentality not of an ineffable deity, but of sexual reproduction. As Ana Paula Arnaut observes, it recasts the Church's supplication for an heir, and the 'dever real e conjugal' [royal and conjugal duty] (*Memorial*: 11) of copulation, as throwbacks to pagan fertility rites.[10] The insincerity of the supposedly Christian motivation for the King's vow first starts to emerge with the intrusion both of the 'visionary' Frei António into the choreographed ceremony of royal coupling, and of the demotic register in which he is introduced. Frei António's intervention, to affirm that the King will secure an heir if he vows to build a monastery, lends the narrative a fairy-tale quality. This posits the idea that the Mafra 'miracle' was nothing more than a convenient fantasy, or — as the chapter's conclusion speculates — a put-up job by the Franciscans, who already knew, through 'segredos de confissão divulgados' [divulged secrets of the confessional], that the queen was pregnant (*Memorial*: 26). Subsequent scenes use the interpolation of 'low' register phrases into passages with theological reference to generate bawdy word-play, exposing the unholy pride and carnal appetites of the King, whose imagined musings, during the *Corpo de Deus* procession, assert his status as God's anointed on Earth so as to justify his affairs with nuns:

> bem sabeis como as monjas são esposas do Senhor, é uma verdade santa, pois a mim como a Senhor me recebem nas suas camas, e é por ser eu o Senhor que gozam e suspiram segurando na mão o rosário, carne mística, misturada, confundida [...] (*Memorial*: 156)
>
> [you all know how nuns are the brides of the Lord, it is a holy truth, for they receive me as Lord in their beds, and it is on account of my being the Lord that they sigh in ecstasy, clutching their rosary in one hand, mystical flesh, mixed up and entangled]

The king who exalts himself — and even his adultery with Prioress Paula of Odivelas (conveniently overlooked by *Estado Novo*-era historians) — to divine status by the *double entendre* of 'senhor' [lord], is brought low by the same device: transferred from an ecclesiastical context to a colloquial one, the terms 'gozar', 'segurar o rosário', and 'carne' acquire base, sexual meanings, rendering Dom João's statement heretical.

A further function of both *Memorial*'s plot and its discursive mixing is to reveal the unremarked — or falsely refuted — interrelations of the lives and agency of rulers and subalterns. As Oliveira Filho has noted, the description of Blimunda's home, a lean-to of 'telhado e três paredes inseguras' [a roof and three rickety walls] built up against the ramparts of the Castelo de São Jorge (*Memorial*: 87) exemplifies the 'interpenetração que o texto [...] opera entre o país oficial e o clandestino' [interpenetration that the text effects between the official and the clandestine nations] (1993: 59). When Blimunda abandons her hovel to be with Baltasar, a curious metanarrative intervention remarks on the historical oblivion that befalls the poor and marginalized:

> se ninguém por ali passar e disser, Olha uma casa vazia, e dizendo, nela não se instalar, um ano não tardará que as paredes abatam, e o telhado, e então ficarão apenas alguns adobes partidos e desfeitos em terra no lugar [...] onde abriu Blimunda pela primeira vez os olhos para o espectáculo do mundo[.] (*Memorial*: 87)

> [if no one should pass by and say, Look, an empty house, and so saying, move into it, it will take not a year for the walls to tumble, and the roof, and so there will be only a few broken and dissolving mud bricks left of the place where first Blimunda opened her eyes unto the spectacle of the world.]

Here, a colloquial register gives way to a grandly periphrastic phrasing ('onde abriu Blimunda pela primeira vez os olhos') and a quotation from the line by Ricardo Reis that serves as epigraph to *Ricardo Reis*. Together, these parody the language of memorial plaques such as rarely mark the birthplaces of the poor. The location of Blimunda's hovel is, however, also a reminder of the tendency of posterity to actively destroy or falsify the material traces of the past in order to corroborate its preferred historical narrative. Similar dwellings built onto Lisbon's castle walls stood until the late 1930s, when the *Estado Novo* undertook a 'restoration' of the Castelo that removed such accretions, in order to make of the Castelo a symbol of Portugal's unsullied and noble Christian origins.[11]

As in *Levantado*, discursive oppositions and incongruities also enable self-conscious allusions to canonical literary texts and tropes, and particularly to the Bible and Camões's *Lusíadas*. This exposes the commonplace use of revered literature to bolster a hegemonic narrative of national history, often turning the quoted texts against that same historical narrative. Yet *Memorial*'s allusions never intimate any inevitable workers' revolution, such as is suggested by the 'resurrection' scene that closes *Levantado* (365–66). *Memorial*'s protagonists are only compared sympathetically to those of Camões's epic when they are bullied by more powerful adversaries, as when an elderly *labrego* [peasant] borrows the words of Camões's *velho do Restelo*, from the fourth canto of *Os Lusíadas* (*Memorial*: 292–95), to denounce the 'vã cobiça' of a 'rei infame' and 'pátria sem justiça' that press-gangs every able-bodied man in his village into service on the Mafra construction site, and he is beaten senseless by the recruiting officers (*Memorial*: 293).[12] The comparison contributes to the novel's warning about the ideological and institutional continuity between Joanine absolutism and Salazarism. Such modern counterparts to Joanine forces and strategies of oppression form the background to the account of Ricardo Reis's existential and moral malaise in Saramago's subsequent novel: the *Estado Novo*'s manipulation of the 'miraculous' 1917 Fátima apparitions as Catholic-nationalist rallying point and anti-Communist propaganda, the draconian censorship, the mass conscription it introduced in the late 1960s to sustain the fight against pro-independence movements in Africa, and the bloody suppression of the naval mutiny of September 1936.

Through the positing of such analogies, *Memorial* opens up a critical perspective on the Salazarist inscription of Portuguese characteristics, values, and traditions. At the same time, its appropriation of icons of national identity into depictions of subaltern dissent and resistance, while not — as in *Levantado* — intimating an inevitable triumph of popular will, continues to suggest the possibility of alternative common values and, thereupon, the viability of a political agenda of radical reform. This affirmative utopianism is, of course, tempered by the novel's warnings regarding the uncertain epistemological and historiological basis for such an agenda. The novel's dialectical approach to historical analysis, and the inevitable shortfall of any pursuit of comprehensive historical knowledge, are set out in an elaborate allegory, a representational mode that, according to Walter Benjamin, itself serves to open up the dialectic within familiar images and thereby offers an opportunity for genuine 'historical materialist' analysis.[13] This allegory is based on an analogy between the search for harmony, and that for a flawless epistemology; an analogy that is suggested by Bartolomeu de Gusmão's first conversation with Domenico Scarlatti, part of which is discussed in this volume's Introduction. The analogy is subsequently reinforced through repeated emphasis on the transcendental, magical sense of harmony created by the Neapolitan composer:

> Domenico Scarlatti [...] senta-se ao cravo, que subtil música é esta que sai para a noite de Lisboa por frinchas e chaminés, ouvem-na os soldados da guarda portuguesa e da guarda alemã, e tanto a entendem uns como a entendem os outros, ouvem-na sonhando os marujos que dormem à fresca nos conveses e acordando a reconhecem, ouvem-na os vadios que se acoitam na Ribeira, debaixo dos barcos varados em terra, ouvem-na os frades e as freiras de mil conventos, e dizem, são os anjos do Senhor, terra esta para milagres ubérrima, ouvem-na os embuçados que vão a matar e os apunhalados que, ouvindo, não pedem mais confissão e morrem absolvidos, ouviu-a um preso do Santo Ofício, no seu fundo cárcere, e estando perto um guarda lhe jogou as mãos à garganta e o esganou, por este assassínio não terá pior morte, ouvem-na, tão longe daqui, Baltasar e Blimunda, que deitados perguntam, Que música é esta[.] (*Memorial*: 164)

> [Domenico Scarlatti sits down at the harpsichord, what subtle music is this that slips out into the Lisbon night through grates and chimneys, the Portuguese guardsmen and German guardsmen hear it, and the former understand it as well as the latter understand it, the old seadogs slumbering in the cool on deck hear it, and waking, recognize it, the vagrants dossing down at Ribeira hear it, beneath the fishing smacks dragged up onto the shore, the friars and nuns of a thousand abbeys hear it, and say, It's the angels of the Lord, this being a land above all others for miracles, the hooded assassins going about their killing hear it, and those they have stabbed, who, hearing it, ask for no further confession and die with absolution, a prisoner of the Inquisition hears it, sunk deep in his cell, and clasping his hands around the throat of a nearby guard, strangles him, for this murder his death sentence will be no worse, far away from here, Baltasar and Blimunda, lying in their bed, hear it and ask, What music is this]

Here, as earlier, Scarlatti's 'harmonias celestes' (*Memorial*: 161), and their universal, seemingly supernatural effect of 'arrebato' [rapture], evoke the Ptolemaic connection of the regulation of the universe to the perfect musical accord of the celestial spheres (a concept that lived on, long after the scientific acceptance of Copernicus's heliocentric model of the cosmos, as a literary metaphor).[14] The connection is made explicit through the repeated trope of Bartolomeu's contemplation of the night sky, first throwing his windows open after having listened to his new friend improvising, and having discussed with him the mysterious force that raises his *passarola*, and then, days later at the *quinta* of São Sebastião, picking out 'a estrada luminosa que atravessava a abóbada celeste de um lado a outro, caminho de Santiago' [the luminous path traversing the celestial vault from one side to the other, the Milky Way] (*Memorial*: 171). These images of the philosopher-priest hearing magical harmonies and pondering, through the dark night of unknowing, the powers that mobilize the universe recall the Spanish humanist poet Luis de León's evocation of the 'no perecedera | música, que es la fuente, y la primera' [undying music | which is the origin, and the first], and the *imitatio* of this achieved in the past by the poem's dedicatee, organist and composer Francisco Salinas, and now by Scarlatti.[15] Scarlatti's harmony is also depicted as heavenly, of course, insofar as it is redemptive. It offers resolution to discord between humans and gives the comfort of absolution to the dying, while also inspiring an act of violent resistance to the tyranny of the Inquisition (*Memorial*: 164). Its magical qualities are further suggested when Blimunda has succumbed to an undiagnosable malaise after collecting the wills of dying plague victims in Lisbon. Here, it is Scarlatti's music at her bedside that restores Blimunda to health:

> [Scarlatti] sentou-se e começou a tocar, branda, suave música que mal ousava desprender-se das cordas feridas de leve, vibrações subtis de insecto alado que, imóvel, paira, e de súbito passa de uma altura a outra, acima, abaixo, [...] Nessa noite, Domenico Scarlatti ficou na quinta, tocando horas e horas, até de madrugada, já Blimunda estava de olhos abertos, corriam-lhe devagar as lágrimas, se aqui estivesse um médico diria que ela purgava os humores do nervo óptico ofendido, talvez tivesse razão [...] (*Memorial*: 184–85)
>
> [Scarlatti sat down and began to play, gentle, sweet music that barely presumed to break free from the softly injured strings, the subtle vibrations of a winged insect that settles immobile then suddenly sweeps from one point to another, upwards, downwards [...] That night, Domenico Scarlatti stayed at the *quinta*, playing for hours at a stretch, until first light, when Blimunda was already wide-eyed and awake, her tears running slowly, if a doctor were here he would say that she was purging the humours from her injured optic nerve, and perhaps he would be right]

As explored in this study's Introduction, this notion of mortal music as *imitatio* of primordial harmony is the basis for Bartolomeu's analogy between the search for harmony and that for truth, and hence also for Scarlatti's rejoinder about the 'importância do erro' (*Memorial*: 162) and its implications for both historiography and historical fiction. This and later passages elaborate that analogy into a comparison between formal conventions of studying and representing the past, and the two musical genres in which Scarlatti famously excelled: free improvisation, and the binary-form sonata.[16] Improvisation explores the gamut of possible variations and harmonic modulations on a melodic motif in a process of trial and emendation that does not exclude either harmonic or formal 'errors'. The result of this exploration — variations developed from the initial theme — provides the raw material for the binary sonata, a form that Scarlatti pioneered. The binary sonata presents two musical motifs in different, but related, keys, and then develops each, transposing them through sequences of often distant keys. Their tonal and formal opposition is ultimately resolved in a concluding passage that incorporates both themes.[17] Scarlatti's development of raw musical fragments in the sonata, from experimentation through succinct argumentation to formal and harmonic resolution, is outlined in two of the four passages describing his playing. First, on the occasion of his first encounter with Gusmão, the Neapolitan musician sets to improvising, playing 'primeiro sem destino, depois como se estivesse à procura de um tema ou quisesse emendar os ecos' [first without any destination, then as if he were searching for a theme or was seeking to attune its echoes] (*Memorial*: 161). Later, the progression from improvisation to composition is described when he installs his harpsichord alongside the workshop in which Baltasar and Blimunda are at work on the *passarola*:

> Scarlatti pôs-se a tocar, primeiro deixando correr os dedos sobre as teclas, como se soltasse as notas das suas prisões, depois organizando os sons em pequenos segmentos, como se escolhesse entre o certo e o errado, entre a forma repetida e a forma perturbada, entre a frase e o seu corte, enfim articulando em discurso novo o que parecera antes fragmentário e contraditório. (*Memorial*: 177)

> [Scarlatti began to play, first letting his fingers run over the keys, as though freeing the notes from their prisons, then organizing the sounds into tiny segments, as if choosing between the correct and the faulty, between the consistent form and the distorted form, between a phrase and its cadence, eventually conveying in a new discourse that which had previously seemed fragmentary and contradictory.]

As already noted, however, this analogy has a critical flaw, relating to the ineradicable propensity to error, which confounds the most unimpeachably empirical efforts of the historian or philosopher to synthesize a comprehensive truth. The western concept of 'harmony' presumes a finite and (almost) stable ontology of the twelve semi-tones of the scale and underpins aesthetic conventions that, for many centuries before twentieth-century experiments in atonalism and serialism, conferred a relatively stable 'motific characterization' on given harmonic intervals, chords, and modulations. Hence Scarlatti's compositions, with their famously vertiginous harmonic flights and switchbacks resolved ultimately in the key of the first motif's exposition, assume a miraculously 'universal' quality, seeming 'tanto [...] brinquedo infantil como colérica objurgação, tanto [...] divertirem-se anjos como zangar-se Deus' [as much childish playfulness as furious denunciation, as much the merriment of angels as the fury of God] (*Memorial*: 177).[18] While the sonata's formula of exposition, counterposition, development, and reconciliation mirrors the basic dialectical structure of thesis, antithesis, and synthesis (or 'expor, contrapor e concluir' as Scarlatti puts it (*Memorial*: 162)), the sonata achieves its concluding 'synthesis' of two motifs by a transposition of its second subject, assimilating or 'subordinating' it harmonically to the first and thus permitting their unification in a single, final theme. In historical analysis, meanwhile, to eliminate discord by subordinating one source of evidence to the logic of another obviously entails ignoring or suppressing one or more aspects of a multifaceted truth. As Scarlatti speculates, 'talvez só o silêncio exista verdadeiramente' [perhaps only silence really exists] (*Memorial*: 162–63). At least, in the absence of an infallible episteme that is indicated by Pilate's unanswered question to Jesus of 'o que era a verdade' [what was truth] (ibid.), only by remaining silent does one eliminate the risk of cleaving to the error ('cingir-se ao erro') that can be 'composed' from the incomprehensible range of historical data. Attempts to represent the past in a fixed, integrated form make a false impression of comprehensiveness and objectivity. Yet to blench at the risk of error — to remain silent in the consciousness of history's tragedies and injustices, rather than seeking to use scrutiny of the past to characterize or account for the present, or issue warnings about dangerous precedents — is arguably no less a dereliction of moral duty than was Pilate's infamous act of hand-washing.

The use of Scarlatti's music-making to present a lesson on the search for historical truth is particularly significant for the manner in which it provides a fresh evocation of the Benjaminian conception of history that is intimated in *Levantado*'s finale, and does so while also following the 'allegorical' logic that Esther Leslie attributes to Walter Benjamin. For Leslie,

> [f]rom *Ursprung des deutschen Trauerspiels* (1923–25) through to the 'Baudelaire file' in the *Passagenwerk* Benjamin associates the allegorical method with the dialectical method. Allegory's fragmented and manifold articulation forces an active mode of reception on the audience. Allegory ties together disparate things in vivid images, shooting across a total picture, blasting meaning into significant parts. The totality appears to us, fetishistically, in fragments. (2000: 199)

As this chapter's third section explores, *Memorial*'s story of the *passarola* itself functions as an allegory to blast the 'total picture' of absolutist Portugal into 'significant parts'. Yet before the *passarola* gets airborne, Saramago's warning about the capacities and limits of historical investigation are twice allegorized, in an emphatically 'neo-baroque' manner. The first such allegorization is through the analogies between Scarlatti's musical composition and historical narratives that subordinate one perspective to another's dominance. The second is that between Scarlatti's improvised music and water, whose infinite and mutable nature cannot be comprehensively encapsulated. Hence, Scarlatti's hands are compared to a boat traversing shifting waters:

> Corriam-lhe as mãos sobre o teclado como uma barca florida na corrente, demorada aqui e além pelos ramos que das margens se inclinam, logo velocíssima, depois pairando nas águas dilatadas de um lago profundo, baía luminosa de Nápoles, secretos e sonoros canais de Veneza, luz refulgente e nova do Tejo[.] (*Memorial*: 161)

> [His hands ran over the keyboard like a boat flowing with the current, delayed here and there by branches hanging down from the riverbanks, then shooting ahead, before coming to rest on the spreading waters of a deep lake, luminous Bay of Naples, secretive and sonorous canals of Venice, sparkling, fresh light of the Tagus.]

This image of a mercurial flow of concordant sound, not yet marshalled into the neat harmonic and formal argument of a sonata, is reiterated a few pages later when Scarlatti's music escapes like liquid under the lintels and through the keyholes of closed windows and doors (*Memorial*: 164). In a symbolic context in which harmony is established as a metaphor for an unattainable whole truth, or epistemological certainty regarding past events, this fleeting, pervasive music corresponds not to a narrativized interpretation of past phenomena, but rather to their elusive traces, not yet gathered by historians into narrative vessels of varying shapes and sizes.

This watery allegory reappears in more explicit form later in the novel, when officers of the Inquisition approach the *quinta*, intent on investigating accusations of Bartolomeu's heresy. So desperate are he, Blimunda and Baltasar to destroy the evidence of their activities and flee in the recently completed *passarola*, that they forget to hide Scarlatti's harpsichord (*Memorial*: 195). Fortunately, Scarlatti returns and heaves it into the *quinta*'s deep well (*Memorial*: 198). From there, 'por baixo da terra' [under the Earth] there may emanate 'as músicas que a água estará dedilhando no cravo' [the music that the water is picking out on the harpsichord], and musical fragments may rise unexplained to the surface, offering enigmatic intimations of past events at the *quinta* (*Memorial*: 224). This fragmentary music may *suggest* a celestial harmony, or inspire the search for this, but it cannot be grasped and objectively comprehended in its totality. No composition of the traces of the past — dialectical or not — can ever yield a comprehensive encapsulation of the truth. The novel's narrative later asserts that

> a verdade caminha sempre por seu próprio pé na história, é só dar-lhe tempo, e um dia aparece e declara, Aqui estou, não temos outro remédio senão acreditar nela, vem nua e sai do poço como a música de Domenico Scarlatti. (*Memorial*: 281)

> [in history, truth always moves at its own pace, one must simply give it time, and one day it will appear and say, here I am, we have no choice but to believe it, it appears naked out of the well like the music of Domenico Scarlatti.]

With this last image, Saramago adds a twist to his allegory: the analogy between truth, harmony, and liquid is linked simultaneously to the emblem — frequently exploited in the literature and art of baroque Europe — of Truth the daughter of Time (*Veritas filia Temporis*), and to Benjamin's concept, in both his 'Theses on the Philosophy of History' and the 'Central Park' component of the *Arcades Project*, of the truth of the past as a flare or fleeting image.[19] Evoking the emblematic image of Time freeing his daughter, Truth, from her imprisonment in a cave or underground well suggests that only the action of time will prevail against obscurantism and oblivion to release truth. However, this emerging truth, albeit 'naked', will not assume the solidity and coherence of a young female body.[20] Rather, in Benjamin's words,

> [t]he true picture of the past flits by. The past can be seized only as an image which flashes up at the instant when it can be recognized and is never seen again.
> [...] To articulate the past historically does not mean to recognize it 'the way it really was'. It means to seize hold of a memory as it flashes up at a moment of danger. (Benjamin 1973b: 257)

The writer — or reader — of history can 'seize hold of' fragmentary echoes but can only glimpse the 'true picture' when these fragments are 'articulated' in a dialectical, comparative analysis, or, as Leslie puts it, by 'cracking open the idea of the pastness of the past [...] and [...] wresting the past away from the single ruling-class narrative of history' (2000: 201). Saramago's use of allegory, of course, summarizes both the strategy of composition deployed in his novel, and the strategy of reading that it solicits. At the same time, the novel's reader is reminded of the ideological significance of aesthetic systems and conventions of emplotment, and warned of the impression of coherence and objectivity that a parcelled narrative form bestows on a partial representation of the past. Although *Memorial* attempts to delve deeper into the well of Portuguese history, and excavate the hidden or disputed sources of this, it issues disclaimers about its attempts to re-harmonize the emerging sounds. It sets up a sonata-like dialogue between the ideological subject and countersubject it exposes. Yet it refuses to supply the neat resolution that characterizes sonata form, the archetypal musical expression of Enlightenment positivism. Saramago allows his history to disrupt the hegemony of the official one, but it remains recognizable as just the development of musical fragments rising from the well of history.

II — Carnival and Satire: Allegorizing the Degradation of the Body

As already emphasized, Saramago's approach to the 'problems of history' is simultaneously (and paradoxically) deconstructive and reconstructive. *Memorial* refuses simply to replace one historical narrative with another one that is predicated upon an alternative ideology. Nevertheless, beyond its deconstruction of the idealist, corporatist world-view that it imputes to Dom João's absolutism and to Salazarism, it conjecturally but consistently asserts an alternative, and emphatically materialist, logic. This materialism underpins its vision of human redemption as allegorized in the *passarola*'s construction, arising not from faith or self-abnegation, but from non-alienating labour, intellectual enquiry, comradeship, and emphatically physical love. *Memorial*'s satire on the contradictions and distortions of Joanine absolutism focuses on that ideology's attempts to subdue (and, in many instances, dissimulate) corporeality. It holds up the human body as evidence both of human equality, and of the material basis of social organization. Saramago adapts many of the stock devices of baroque satire, using them to disrupt the discursive protocols that disassociate Church and State leaders from the body and its functions, and subverting the monumentalist aesthetic that asserts the metaphysical power of monarch and deity in physical form. Scatological and sexual humour reconnects the potentates of Church and State to the body, to the Earth, and to its cycles of life and death, thereby demonstrating the biological commonality of all humans. Meanwhile, a grotesque use of perspectivism, recalling Jonathan Swift's use of disparities of scale in *Gulliver's Travels*, serves to belittle Dom João's self-aggrandizement. Countering the King's pseudo-Hobbesian absolutist conception of sovereignty with the Gramscian notion of hegemony, *Memorial* uses such perspectivist images to illustrate the contingency of royal and divine authority upon the harnessed will and strength of a coerced populace. Grotesque corporeal imagery is also, however, used to grimmer effect, to allegorize the degrading effect on the body's harmony and nobility of an exploitative economy and of extreme disparities of status, and also to illustrate how the Church's teaching on pleasure, suffering, desire, and discipline leads to psycho-sexual perversion. *Memorial* conceives of humanity in terms of a materialist, and emphatically sexual, ideal. Sexual desire, if redeemed from its association with shame, coercion, and violence, could play a crucial role in the building of a fairer and freer society, as is explored in this chapter's third section.

Memorial's satirical use of corporeal imagery can, just like its satirical use of discursive incongruence, be illuminated with reference to Bakhtinian theory. Like the literature and imagery of carnival celebrations that Bakhtin analyses, *Memorial* valorizes the material, the physical, and the telluric, exalting it through both literal and figurative inversions of the conventional vertical hierarchy, which associates the head with the life of the mind, and the belly, buttocks, and genitals with the Earth and matter (Bakhtin 1984: 20–21). Bakhtin's theory of the historical relationship between Judeo-Christian ideology and corporeal humour is, of course, amply exemplified in the discursive mis-matches, noted above, in the novel's opening scene. Courtly language, protocol, and ritual serve here to represent the monarch as transcending sexual urges and other 'base' corporeal drives and functions, and to associate his transcendental being with a conception of the divine as disembodied spirit. The invasion of courtly discourse by frank allusions to corporeality, however, exposes the dependence of royal power on the hereditary principle, hence on (strictly regulated) sexual activity, and ultimately on the libido. Prosaic corporeal references — to body parts, soiled undergarments, and 'cheiros e secreções' [smells and secretions] (*Memorial*: 15) — disturb the hyperbolic reverencing of the sacrament of royal marriage. With solemn ceremony, the King is robed in 'o trajo da função e do estilo' [the robes appropriate to the function and style] (*Memorial*: 13), or rather, his nightshirt. An absurd number of footmen passes his dirty clothes 'de mão e mão tão reverentemente como relíquias de santas que tivessem trespassado donzelas' [from hand to hand as reverently as if they were relics of saints that expired in maidenhood] (ibid.). More footmen, obediently waiting while the first group dresses the King in the manner of priests reverencing an altar, are enumerated in an ornate tripartite schema, which collapses into an admission of the superfluity of the 'dois que não se movem, dois que imitam estes, mais uns tantos que não se sabe o que fazem nem por que estão' [two who stand motionless, two more who imitate the first two, plus another few of whom no one knows what they're doing or why they're there] (ibid.). The first consequence of this scene's mismatch of elevated discourse and base referents is that the sexual act usurps the conventional position of religious observance or acts of statecraft. This is particularly so thanks to sexual double-entendres such as 'trespassado' [died], which can also mean 'penetrated', and 'transgressed', or precisely what Dom João had done to many *donzelas* within Lisbon's religious houses.[21] The exalted status conferred on the King's 'dever real e conjugal' [royal and conjugal duty] (*Memorial*: 12) belies the King's priorities, and reveals the vulnerability of his 'absolute' power to his human frailty (and not least, his crippling attacks of wind) (*Memorial*: 112–13). The discursive mismatch highlights the role of quasi-religious ritual in disguising how Catholic and absolutist power depends on the instrumentality not of an ineffable deity, but of sexual reproduction. The Christian ethic supposedly motivating the King's actions is as superficial and insincere as the rarefied discourse used to denote them. Religious observances are presented as a hindrance or 'dificultação canónica' (*Memorial*: 11) to royal intercourse.

The contradiction inherent in the alliance of a hereditary monarch and an idealist theology that disparages the body is intensified by Dom João's enthusiastic conception of his power in physical and often expressly phallic terms. Both canon and crown law proclaim the divine justice that enables and informs his rule on the basis of metaphysics. At the same time, the king's authority and might are symbolized in public ceremonies, in art, and, of course, in the architecture of the Mafra monastery, through what José Antonio Maravall and Fernando de la Flor characterize as a 'Barroco de Estado' [official baroque]: an aesthetics of primacy, unity, power, and domination that propagandized the ideology of 'una monarquía absolutista confesional y de sus aliados' [a confessional absolutist monarchy and its allies] (Flor 2002: 13).[22] *Memorial*'s subversion of this monumentalist aesthetic is closely entwined with its mockery of the monarch's logical, but heretical, view of his genitals as a site of power. Prior to disrobing for intercourse with his consort, the King is depicted toying with a huge scale model of St Peter's basilica:

> uma construção sem caboucos nem alicerces, [...] miniatura de basílica dispersa em pedaços de encaixar, segundo o antigo sistema de macho e fêmea, que à mão reverente, vão sendo colhidos pelos quatro camaristas de serviço. (*Memorial*: 12)

> [a construction without foundations or cornerstones [...] a miniature basilica disassembled in small blocks that interlock according to the established system of male and female [and] which are selected in turn by the respectful hands of the four chambermen.]

Further to its comic attack on Dom João's megalomaniac regalist fantasy of usurping the Pope, or even assuming the role of God, this scene also suggests that the King's monastery vow was substantially motivated by his enthusiasm for a more permanent architectural statement of royal might. At the same time, the toy St Peter's construction, from interlocking wooden blocks, symbolically prefigures how the Mafra monastery rises as a consequence of the more literally sexual coupling of male and female 'pedaços de encaixar' in the 'antigo sistema' of hereditary monarchy. The law of dynastic succession, so inconveniently integral to absolutist ideology, makes it nonsensical to associate the royal personage and power with 'all that is high, spiritual, ideal, abstract' and to repudiate their foundation in 'the material level [...] of the earth and the body' (Bakhtin 1984: 20). This is observed again when the King dreams that he sees

> erguer-se do seu sexo uma árvore de Jessé, frondosa e toda povoada dos ascendentes de Cristo, até ao mesmo Cristo, herdeiro de todas as coroas, e depois dissipar-se a árvore e em seu lugar levantar-se, poderosamente, com altas colunas, torres sineiras, cúpulas e torreões, um convento de franciscanos. (*Memorial*: 18)

> [arise out of his penis a spreading tree of Jesse, populated withal with the ancestors of Christ, down to Christ himself, heir of every Crown, and then

he sees the tree dissolve and in its place arise, magnificently, a Franciscan monastery with lofty columns, bell towers, cupolas and turrets]

These successive fantasies — first, of being the progenitor of Christ's line, then that of the Mafra monastery as penis extension — suggest the King's unconscious belief in the power not of God but of the material, sexual body. His monastery serves as a façade covering the sexual mechanics of the hereditary principle, as much as tribute to that principle's allegedly divine instigator.

Many of *Memorial do Convento*'s comic allusions to the male member serve not only to disrupt the Church-State discourse's dissimulation of corporeal agency, but also to render incongruous and ridiculous the phallic symbolism deployed in establishment art and discourse, which affirms the power of a unitary and aggressively domineering patriarchal authority. *Memorial*'s descriptions of the monastery dwell on the gargantuan scale both of the building itself and of such decorative elements as the statues on its façade, the largest of them 'quase cinco metros de altura, gigantões atléticos, hércules cristãos, campeões da fé' [almost five metres tall, athletic giants, Christian versions of Hercules, champions of the faith] (*Memorial*: 321). Thus the novel presents the Mafra monastery as partaking — like many state buildings of the age of absolutism — of a monumentalist language symbolizing the monopolistic power and cohesion of the newly centralized polity. Projects such as the palace of Versailles, or the new imperial Russian capital of St Petersburg, employed not just an unprecedented scale of ground-plan and elevation, but also a preponderance of massive forms, imposing or enclosing architectural rhythms and lines (e.g. in colonnades, windows, staircases etc.), and the false perspective created by pilasters and trompe l'oeil decoration, so as to overawe the visitor to official and religious buildings with a sense of size, solidity and power. The novel's accounts of royal and religious ritual conducted at Mafra also note the recourse to this aesthetic of monumentalism. In the ceremony of the laying of the cornerstone of the monastery (*Memorial*: 130–36), for example, the power of Church and State is represented through the transformation of material wealth and subservient humanity into imposing physical mass, centred on the King himself and demonstrating 'a suma grandeza deste monarca que vem entrando' [the exceeding grandeur of this monarch now making his entrance] (*Memorial*: 133). Art historian José Fernandes Pereira (quoting the contemporary account given by Frei Cláudio da Conceição) describes this ceremony as 'uma inequívoca "ostentação do real grandeza"' [an unmistakeable 'demonstration of royal greatness'] (Pereira 1994: 190) intended by Dom João to make Mafra 'um símbolo duradoiro do seu poder absoluta, a "teoria em pedra" do seu reinado' [an enduring symbol of his absolute power, a 'lesson in stone' for his reign] (1994: 191).[23] These artistic strategies to assert gigantic status and power by proxy are the nearest possible realization of the megalomaniac fantasy in which the King indulges as he towers over his model of St Peter's and the diminutive sculpted saints of its façades (*Memorial*: 12). When Dom João stipulates to his architect that the Mafra monastery must prove 'que também o homem é capaz de fazer o trabalho que gigantes fariam' [mankind too is capable of the work of giants] (*Memorial*: 328), he is thinking of asserting only his individual gigantism. The absolutist, rather than humanist, cast of his ambition becomes evident when he sets men to work on a construction whose bulk renders them ant-like by comparison (ibid.), ironically echoing *Levantado*'s symbolism. Not even when the King belatedly considers his own mortality — and thus the contingency of his power on universal material forces — does he heed the narrator's warning that 'todas as coisas têm de ser entendidas na sua justa proporção, os formigueiros e os conventos, a laje e a pargana' [each thing must be understood in accordance with its proportions, from anthills to monasteries, from a flagstone to a head of corn] (*Memorial*: 329).

Elsewhere, however, *Memorial*'s account makes the King's efforts to dwarf his subjects rebound spectacularly, by appropriating to Saramago's egalitarian and materialist ideology the Swiftian standby of grotesque images of disproportion. In Lemuel Gulliver's account of Lilliput, the Lilliputians' diminished stature satirizes the pride and pettiness of a British imperialist ascendancy by inverting the aesthetics of monumentalist bombast. Likewise, in *Memorial*, images of diminished human stature turn architectural and sculptural monumentalism against its creator, proving the King's ambition and arrogance to be disproportionate to his physical capabilities. In the account of the ceremony of dedication of the monastery foundations, Dom João is belittled by the outsized stage, implements, and religious artefacts created especially to demonstrate his 'suma grandeza' (*Memorial*: 133). His descent of the sweeping flight of thirty steps, two metres wide, to lay the cornerstone would seem like his 'despedida do mundo [...] descida aos infernos se não estivesse tão bem defendido por bênçãos, escapulários e orações' [farewell to the world [...] a descent into Hell, were he not so well defended by blessings, scapularies, and prayers] (*Memorial*: 135). He grapples with an absurdly huge 'balde de prata cheio de água benta' [silver bucket full of holy water] in order to moisten and affix the cornerstone (ibid.). Saramago's ridicule homes in again on the King's phallic conception of his own power, punning on the double-entendre of the word 'pau' ('wood' or 'staff', but also, colloquially, 'penis' or 'erection') when he presents the King dwarfed by the altar cross before which he bows, an 'enorme pau com cinco metros de altura, que daria para um gigante' [enormous shaft, five metres long, big enough for a giant] (*Memorial*: 133).

Beyond humiliating the bumptious monarch, this use of 'conceptualist' punning highlights how Church ceremonial emphasizes not Christian values of self-sacrifice and love so much as the established authorities' agenda of expressly patriarchal domination. At the same time, it indicates divisions and ideological contradictions within the absolutist establishment. Spectacles such as the dedication ceremony were conceived to propagandize Dom João's fundamentalist interpretation of absolutist monarchy, which, as Oliveira Marques argues, exceeded the traditional conception of absolutism, wherein the monarch was beholden to the established laws of the land. Joanine absolutism instead

> vinha proclamar que usos e costumes não desempenhavam qualquer papel; defender o princípio de que as leis naturais eram interpretadas pelo soberano e de que as leis de Deus estavam depositadas no próprio rei, incluindo a submissão da Igreja à sua vontade; e finalmente, negar que as leis do reino obrigassem o monarca.

[proclaimed that tradition and customs played no role whatsoever, asserted that natural law was to be interpreted by the sovereign and that the laws of God were embodied in the King himself, entailing the submission of the Church to his will, and finally denied that the laws of the land constrained the Monarch][24]

In the light of this, one might note that the recourse to gigantic representations of the royal personage and power that *Memorial* records is also made in the age of absolutism's most influential treatise on sovereignty, namely Thomas Hobbes's *Leviathan*. The famous engraving on the cover of Hobbes's work — depicting a gigantic sovereign, holding a sword and ecclesiastical crozier in place of orb and sceptre, his body composed of the figures of hundreds of individuals standing or kneeling to face his head in attitudes of willing obedience — fleshes out Hobbes's titular metaphor for a corporatist (but not necessarily absolutist) view of the state as a giant body made up of the united bodies of the whole populace.[25] The rhetoric of Joanine architecture and ceremony, however, works to suggest that the monarch alone embodies the will and agency of the 'leviathan' state. While *Memorial*'s suggestion of the King's hankering for a prosthetic giant phallus derides such self-aggrandizement, its accounts of the monastery's construction render visible the individual bodies of its ant-like builders. Moreover, as will be explored below, the *passarola* story presents a humanist riposte to Dom João's monument to the absolutist conception of sovereignty, by allegorizing the idea of popular will united and dedicated to a progressive, emancipatory agenda. The monastery rises, exalting God and King, through the enslavement of the wills of the populace: specifically, those of the labourers led to Mafra in chains, without whose bonded strength 'todo o poder de el-rei será vento, pó e coisa nenhuma' [all of His Majesty's power will be wind, dust, and nothingness] (*Memorial*: 244). The issue of the subjugated will of the monastery's labourers is expressly raised at this juncture, when the narrative voice asks 'se Blimunda tivesse vindo [...] que vontade veria em cada um' [if Blimunda should arrive [...] what will might she see in each [worker]] (*Memorial*: 243). The *passarola*, by contrast, is conceived by Bartolomeu as a means of exalting all humanity, and rises powered by the bonded wills only of the dead. The machine not only saves its creators from the clutches of the Inquisition (*Memorial*: 193), but also presents a symbolic challenge to divine, ecclesiastical, and royal power on its brief flight. This flight affords another Swiftian belittlement of the tyrannical monarch, whose half-built monastery appears from this aerial vantage point to be 'pouco maior que capela' (*Memorial*: 212). This shift of focus — employing the typically baroque rhetorical device of 'perspectivism' — raises the question of whether the power of oppressive ideologies might be diminished by present-day initiatives such as Saramago's literary project of redressing an unbalanced vision of the past. *Memorial*'s shrinking of Dom João and of his leviathan erection is the correlative of its magnification of the common people, whose suffering and historical contributions are too frequently backgrounded in accounts of the past that focus on the wealthy and powerful.

When exploring Saramago's borrowings from Swift's and his contemporaries' satiric texts, it is crucial to remark how similar models of corporeal reference — in particular, the grotesque — are employed to confront a hegemonic state ideology with a world-view radically different to those of the prominent dissident voices of early eighteenth-century Britain, Ireland, or Iberia. Bakhtin's theory of the changing relationship between comic conventions and ideology holds that whereas in medieval Europe the 'grotesque realism' of carnival attempts to chart 'the very act of becoming and growth' (Bakhtin 1984: 39), in the capitalist era (and most evidently, according to Bakhtin, in the culture of Romanticism), the grotesque expresses an 'alienated' view to which 'something frightening is revealed in that which was habitual and secure' (ibid.). There is a strong argument for expanding Bakhtin's period of reference in his extremely brief treatment of this 'alienated grotesque' to include the early modern period that witnessed the emergence of capitalist economics, and the struggle of the bourgeoisie and humanism — and later liberalism — against the feudal elite and against absolutism. Indeed, Maravall's discussion of the baroque image of the world, and of the human, poses questions about Bakhtin's sparse reference to the prominence in baroque culture of the topsy-turvy, the dissonant, and the grotesque (a topic that he may have explored in his lost study of the eighteenth-century German novel). For Maravall, this reflects baroque culture's expression of a 'sentimiento de desconcierto ante el mundo de los hombres' [feeling of discomfort on contemplating the human world] (1975: 313) and its generally pessimistic view of the human as 'un ser agónico, en lucha dentro de sí' [an agonistic being, at war with himself] (1975: 325). However, in discussing how such devices articulated not only a conservative reaction of dismay at the pressure for socio-economic change that threatened a habitual and secure world order, but equally could constitute 'una fórmula de protesta social' [a formula for social protest] (Maravall 1975: 315) through the conversion of 'la referencia a la "oposición" en la de "desconcierto"' [reference to opposition into that to disconcertedness] (p. 323), Maravall indicates a link between the baroque grotesque of Gracián or Quevedo, and a similarly dystopian vision to that identified by Bakhtin in the romantic grotesque and, indeed, in 'Swift's gloomy world' (Bakhtin 1984: 308). Saramago's corporeal humour draws on these writers' techniques for reinserting the human body and its functions into those eighteenth-century discourses — from Catholic idealism to a more secular transcendental rationalism — which sought at times to disregard them. It rejects, however, their characterization of human flesh as irredeemably messy, wayward, and corrupted, as a hazardous staging house for the soul. Alan D. Chalmers (1995) has discussed how, in *Gulliver's Travels*, the 'positive regenerating power' of 'images of bodily life such as eating, drinking, copulation, defecation' (Bakhtin 1984: 38) is reduced to a capacity to expose ideological contradictions, permitting no celebration of the body's connectedness to time and to the equalizing forces of life and death. Chalmers notes that 'Rabelais, according to Bakhtin, perceives the body as the basis of our vital connectedness to the larger sweeps of time, and as such it is to be revelled in and celebrated. In Swift's vision, the body and time form no such benign mutuality' (1995: 79). This is exemplified both in Gulliver's humiliations in Lilliput (where his faecal excretions must be cleared away daily by the cart-load) and in the gross physicality he describes in the gigantic Brobdingnagians (Chalmers 1995: 88–91). Even in his non-satirical writings, Chalmers claims, Swift presents the human body as 'a calamity of conflicting functions from which to retreat, not an organic synthesis in which to revel' (1995: 80). Saramago, conversely, offers images that celebrate the inherent dignity and value of the body, suggesting, thereby, that the faith and devotion dedicated in eighteenth-century Portugal to an ineffable deity might instead be invested in the material world, and in the body. Saramago's depictions of Blimunda and Baltasar's love-making suggest the body — even when mutilated or incomplete — to be a beautiful thing, to be venerated and enjoyed without a rigid agenda for procreation set by religious and dynastic diktats. These depictions, of course, contrast with those of the King and Queen's loveless couplings. Yet significantly, Saramago's satire never derides the royal flesh or libido *per se*, but rather the dissimulation (or phallic aggrandizement) of these, and the monarchs' imposition upon their bodies of the Church's injunctions. This latter is exemplified in the Queen's martyrdom to demands for women's asexual passivity and submission to male lusts. During sex the Queen 'sacrifica-se a uma imobilidade total' [submits herself to total motionlessness] (*Memorial*: 11) in order to prevent any loss of the monarch's seed, an act of self-abnegation that, ironically, minimizes her reproductive organs' response to the sovereign's attentions, which, far from translating his allegedly leviathan power, are poor, nasty, brutish, and — most unhelpfully — short (ibid.).

At other times, Dona Maria Ana attempts to preserve her chastity by smothering her unsated desires under a suffocating eiderdown, but her erotic urges rebound in feverish dreams about her brother-in-law, Dom Francisco (*Memorial*: 17). Her predicament is but a minor symptom of a universal social ill that confines *Memorial*'s positive vision of the desiring body to the utopian space of São Sebastião da Pedreira and to other hideaways in which Blimunda and Baltasar can develop their intimacy on terms of mutual respect, affection, and devotion. The novel repeatedly demonstrates that the socio-economic iniquity of Joanine Portugal brutalizes and malnourishes the body. Simultaneously, however, a religious ideology that strips sexual encounters of joy, egalitarianism and dignity fosters oppressive and coercive sexual practices. These sexual attitudes are presented as perverse; repressed desire resurfacing in oblique and malignant forms. It is in scenes that attest to the worst consequences of this that Saramago employs grotesque imagery satirically. Such imagery expresses alienation *not* from the body in what the novel implies is its 'natural' form, but from the corrupting effects on the body of the dominant ideology, and of the deprivation and oppression that it legitimates. In a curious echo of Bakhtin's terms of discussion, Saramago's use of grotesque imagery, first in the context of a 'redemptive', 'carnivalesque' humour, and secondly in that of an alienated, satiric humour, are most clearly contrasted in his descriptions of Joanine-era Lisbon's observations of Carnival and Lent (*Memorial*: 28–30). Indeed, while the licentious spirit of carnival does little to mitigate the filth, disease, and deprivation suffered by the urban poor, it is Lent that temporarily redresses inequalities, since 'a Quaresma [...] quando nasce, é para todos' [Lent [...] when it arrives, is for everyone] (*Memorial*: 27). This, however, only takes place in the sense that mortification of the flesh causes the wealthy to go hungry when fasting, and makes customarily dominant men the victims of psycho-sexual violence. The description of *entrudo* [carnival] offers images of the inversion, along the vertical plane, of the functions, relative locations, and status of body parts, in such fashion as Bakhtin claims articulates the subordination of social and ideological hierarchies to the egalitarian laws of the body and the natural world. Mouths and anuses (or faces and buttocks) swap places when 'esguichou-se água à cara com seringas de clisteres' [water is squirted into people's faces from enema pipes] (*Memorial*: 28). However, the freedom to '[espojar], de travessas, praças e becos, de barriga para o ar' [wallow, belly up, in alleyways, squares, and lanes], and the short-lived liberation from the dominant order that it entails, are curtailed by the prevailing squalor of a city which 'é imunda, alcatifada de excrementos, de lixo, de cães lazarentos e gatos vadios, e lama mesmo quando não chove' [filthy, carpeted with excrement and refuse, mangy dogs and stray cats, and thick mud even when there's no rain] (ibid.). This description offers no more than a gesture towards the 'regenerative' life of the body in this account of carnival inversions that are prematurely curtailed. Meanwhile, it introduces grotesque images of the body that exploit the opposition not of 'higher' and 'lower' body zones, but of body parts across a *horizontal* continuum. The physical deformities of rich and poor appear side by side on the same body, as a hideous vision of social inequality, when Lisbon is described as

> uma boca que mastiga de sobejo para um lado e de escasso para o outro, não havendo portanto mediano termo entre a papada pletórica e o pescoço engelhado, entre o nariz rubicundo e o outro héctico, entre a nádega dançarina e a escorrida, entre a pança repleta e a barriga agarrada às costas. (*Memorial*: 27)
>
> [a mouth that munches to excess on one side, and scarcely at all on the other, there being therefore no middle term between the bulging jowl and the scrawny neck, the rosy nostril and the pallid one, the bouncing buttock and the shrunken one, the swelling paunch and the empty belly clinging tight to the ribs]

This allegory of a divided civic body, each side grotesque in its morbidity rather than any 'life affirming' excess, is surely bitterly satirical, rather than merely 'irreverente' [irreverent], as Oliveira Filho suggests, in the manner it opposes one social class to another (1993: 54). It offers a further example of Saramago's employment, to satiric and polemical effect, of allusions to baroque iconography and rhetoric, with their frequent recourse to allegory and emblems. It is a contrastive reminder of the emblem of the conjoined twins that symbolized harmony between two individuals or entities.[26] It also, however, recalls the allegorical — and often satiric — use of the fantastical grotesque body by artists such as Arcimboldo, and also could be considered a re-working of the well-known allegory of Death found in Baltasar Gracián's *Criticón* (1651–1657):

> entró finalmente la tan temida reina, ostentando aquel su tan estraño aspecto a media cara; de tal suerte, que era de flores la una mitad y la otra de espinas, la una de carne blanda y la otra de huessos; muy colorada aquélla y fresca, que parecía de cosas entreveradas de jazmines, muy seca y muy marchita ésta [...]. (1980: 773)
>
> [finally there entered the Queen so greatly feared, showing forth that extraordinary aspect in profile, in such manner that one half of her face was made of flowers and the other half of thorns, one half of soft flesh and the other bare

bones, the one brightly hued and fresh, so that it seemed to be varicoloured as jasmine, the other parched and shrivelled.]

Gracián's image can be read as voicing either protest — through conversion of 'la referencia a la "oposición" en la de "desconcierto"' [reference to opposition into an expression of disharmony] (Maravall 1975 : 323) — or merely, as Santos Alonso suggests, a 'perspectivist' belief that 'el mundo lo ven los personajes con doble perspectiva tan sólo porque [...] [el] mundo es engañoso, tiene dos caras' [people see the world in double perspective simply because the world is deceptive, it has two faces] (Gracián 1980: 41).[27] Saramago's use of the same device, however, presents not the human being *per se*, but rather Joanine society, as 'un ser agónico, en lucha dentro de sí' [an agonic being, at war with itself] (Maravall 1975: 325). The two equally distorted halves of the body of Lisbon correspond to a social order seen not as timeless and natural, but as human-made and perverse. The horror that the image provokes arises not out of the innate characteristics of the body, but out of alienation from a perversion of that body's natural harmony. Furthermore, the image vindicates the principle of the equality of all human beings, by presenting the unequal status quo as an aberration, so disharmonious that not even the temporary inversion of carnival affords any significant relief.

The Lenten period, by contrast, creates a more substantial redistribution of privilege, through fasting, but also through relaxation of the surveillance of women's sexual conduct. The Lenten 'costume de deixar que as mulheres corram às igrejas sozinhas' [custom of letting women run off to church unchaperoned] suspends the normal habit of keeping women 'em casa presas' [imprisoned at home] (*Memorial*: 30). Upper-class women, 'livres de uma vez no ano' [freed once a year] (ibid.), can exploit these six weeks of relative liberty to seek excitement outside marriage; failing this, the custom of spectating at the frequent street processions of male penitents affords an opportunity for discreet masturbation (*Memorial*: 29). Despite Saramago's consistent privileging of feminist and sexual libertarian values, *Memorial* does not present these temporary freedoms as beneficial. On the contrary, images that stress the Lenten inversion of the gender hierarchy through the symbolic use of a vertical continuum suggest that such inversion constitutes the liberation of masochistic and sadistic urges, arising respectively in men and women who at other times submit to the sexual laws that reduce a woman's sexual role to that of a 'vaso de receber' [vessel to be filled] (*Memorial*: 11). When male penitents process through the streets, their lovers are presented overlooking them from the superior position of balconies, 'possessas, frenéticas' [possessed, frenzied], and inciting their consorts to ever more extreme self-flagellation:

> as mulheres reclamam força no braço, querem ouvir o estralejar dos rabos do chicote, [...] Está o penitente diante da janela da amada, em baixo na rua, e ela olha-o dominante. (*Memorial*: 29)
>
> [the women demand forceful strokes, they want to hear the whip-crack of the flails [...] The penitent, down in the street, has reached the window of his lover, and she contemplates him, dominant.]

Religious devotion is but a pretext for this sado-masochistic interplay of 'espasmos' [spasms] of self-mortification and orgasm, and guzzling of blood and semen, by which unhealthily antagonistic relationships — both with the body and with the gendered other — are satisfied:

> Deus não tem nada que ver com isto, é tudo coisa de fornicação, e provavelmente o espasmo de cima veio em tempo de responder ao espasmo de baixo, o homem de joelhos no chão, desferindo golpes furiosos, já frenéticos, enquanto geme de dor, a mulher arregalando os olhos para o macho derrubado, abrindo a boca para lhe beber o sangue e o resto. (*Memorial*: 29–30)
>
> [God has nothing to do with this, it's all pure fornication, and probably the spasms above come just in time to answer those from below, the man on his knees on the ground, raining down furious, frenzied blows, while he groans in pain, the woman training her gaze on the fallen male, opening her mouth to drink his blood and everything else.]

This account of Lenten observances and penitential processions not only justifies Óscar Lopes's contention that 'a religião oficial aparece [no romance] como reverso de uma luxúria incontida e indisfarçável' [official religion appears as the flip-side of an incontinent and undisguisable lubricity] (Lopes 1986: 205). It ties in with other references to the prominent role of horrific spectacles of 'la violencia [...] la muerte' [violence [and] death] (Maravall 1975: 333) in the official iconography and popular entertainment of a 'regimen integrador' [authoritarian regime] (ibid.), to exemplify what, as Maravall claims, is the prime objective of

> todo el planeamiento patético y pesimista del Barroco: la necesidad de poner en claro la condición humana, para dominarla, contenerla y dirigirla. (1975: 335)
>
> [the whole baroque logic of pathos and pessimism: the need to explicate the human condition, in order to dominate, contain, and direct it.]

The scene also suggests, however, that, under the pressure of such a merciless interpretation of the 'human condition', innate sexual urges do not re-emerge as a means of expressing love. Rather, they are twisted into a means of dissipating or transmitting feelings of hate, humiliation, aggression, and guilt, feelings that are fostered by subjugation to a hierarchical, repressive, and brutal ideology. *Memorial*'s fantasy of the *passarola* serves to suggest — again, by employing baroque devices of allegory and conceit — the socio-economic changes that could foster a contrastingly benign (and implicitly more 'natural') psychology.

III — Ucronian Fantasy: Allegorizing the Liberation of the Will

The *passarola* story opens up a space in the novel in which the hegemonic ideology can be opposed with cooperative egalitarianism, creativity, and a celebration of human corporeality and sexuality. The utopian vision that emerges here is not presented as wishful fantasy, but rather as an ideal that could become achievable in the present day, through a revolutionary movement entailing not simply civil equality between men and women, but even their 'sharing' of masculine and feminine roles and attributes in all areas of life. This vision is predicated on the power of human free will — *vontade* — and on how this might be lent not to the dictates of an ineffable deity but to securing social justice and material improvement of living conditions. In accordance with basic Marxist tenets, however, the *passarola* story suggests that an alternative, progressive hegemony — such as that synthesized by *Levantado*'s rural workers — cannot coalesce before certain necessary socio-economic conditions are established. Only Bartolomeu's esoteric learning, and Blimunda's clairvoyant powers, enable them and Baltasar to identify the primacy of human (rather than divine) will. These insights permit them to raise the *passarola*, and to replace oppressive Catholic dogma with the free and egalitarian values that order their existence at the Quinta de São Sebastião da Pedreira.

The clandestine nature of their project, however, taints this existence with moral ambiguity. While the three friends dedicate their labour, love, and creativity not to a remote deity and tyrannical monarch, but to each other and to their fellow humans, their efforts to exalt humanity through flight rely on the dubious practice of capturing the wills of the dead. Moreover, the curtailment of this idyll by the mortal threat of the Inquisition, and the tragedy that ensues when Baltasar tries to renovate, and pilot, the *passarola* single-handedly, prove that the time is not yet ripe for even this embryonic socialism. In this sense, the *passarola* story serves, as David Frier has argued, as a parable speculating on 'the ways in which popular advancement may — and may not — be achieved' (Frier 1994: 130). As such, it reiterates *Levantado*'s Gramscian insistence on the need for organic, grass-roots revolutionary consciousness and political consensus. It goes much further than its predecessor, however, in urging radical changes both to revolutionary organization, and to socialist restructuring. In a manner recalling the thinking of Herbert Marcuse, it looks to the emancipatory potential of modern technology, while calling not simply for an end to women's subjugation, but, further, for a 'feminine' sensibility to inform the negation of capitalist values.

The affirmation of humans' will as a prime determinant of their destiny is set out in Bartolomeu's explanation to Baltasar that the 'éter' required to raise the *passarola* consists not of the souls of the dead, but rather of the wills of the living (*Memorial*: 123–24). Initially Baltasar can conceive of an immaterial substance housed in the body only in the idealist terms of a soul. Bartolomeu's distinction between the soul and the will, and his greater concern with the properties of the latter (*Memorial*: 124) posits the existence of a motor for human agency more directly linked to the material world. While Bartolomeu's description of *vontades* and their purpose does not explain whether they originate in the material body or beyond, it suggests that, unlike souls, they are a form of energy, and subject to the laws of physics. They are akin to energy in their unfixed volume — 'onde couber uma, cabem milhões, o um é igual ao infinito' [where one fits, millions fit, a single one is equal to an infinity] (ibid.) — their motile power, and in their attraction to amber, a conductive material 'também chamado electro' [also called electrum] (ibid.) that is used in the *passarola*'s construction. The critical aspect of Bartolomeu's account, however, is his speculation on the fate of an individual's *vontade* after death. Here, Saramago exploits a fault-line in eighteenth-century Portuguese Catholic thinking in order to overturn the Christian conception of humankind's dependence on God. Into what kind of *céu* do the *vontades* ascend? Is it into the stratosphere — which was then being explored by Newton and by Bartolomeu's colleagues in Holland — or into the heavens that, according to pre-Copernican cosmology, lay above the Earth? Prior to making the ascent himself, Bartolomeu professes that

> A vontade, ou se separou do homem estando ele vivo, ou a separa dele a morte, é ela o éter, é portanto a vontade dos homens que segura as estrelas, é a vontade dos homens que Deus respira. (*Memorial* : 124)

> [A man's will either detaches itself from him while he's alive, or death detaches it from him, it's ether, therefore it's human will that holds the stars in place, it's human will that God breathes.]

As Teresa Cristina Cerdeira da Silva first argued, Saramago is 'invertendo o mistério da criação, segundo o qual o homem fora criado pelo sopro divino, se aqui é o sopro dos homens que dá vida ao Criador' [inverting the mystery of the Creation, according to which man was created by the divine breath, since here it is human breath that gives life to the Creator] (1991: 120). The insights provided by Blimunda's vision, and the subsequent flight of the *passarola*, will provide 'evidence' for an atheist revision of Bartolomeu's theories, suggesting that humans have willed God into (seeming) existence, and can just as easily will him out of existence. Divine will, far from being the *primum mobile* of the universe, is thereby never more than co-opted, or mis-recognized, human will.

Further to claiming that God depends on the tribute of will from humans, Bartolomeu affirms that the relationship existing between God and humankind at the Creation was revised by the ministry of Christ and the sacrament of communion, which affords humans the *choice* to allow God to enter them bodily. Since 'é preciso que o homem o tome, e assim Deus não fica no homem quando quer, mas quando o homem o deseja tomar' [man must [choose to] take [communion], and thus God does not dwell in man as and when He chooses, but when man wishes to partake of Him], the power differential between God and humanity has changed and 'de alguma maneira o criador se fez criatura do homem' [in a certain way the creator has made himself man's creature)] (*Memorial*: 172–73). Bartolomeu asserts that humankind, as a consequence of this new relationship, became more powerful and more perfect:

> Antes de Cristo se ter feito homem, Deus estava fora do homem e não podia estar nele, depois, pelo sacramento, passou a estar nele, assim o homem é quase Deus, ou será afinal o próprio Deus, sim, sim, se em mim está Deus, eu sou Deus, Deus nós, ele eu, eu ele, Durus est hic sermo, et quis potest eum audire. (*Memorial*: 173)

> [Before Christ was made man, God was outside of man and could not dwell within him, afterwards, by means of the sacrament, He came to dwell within him, thus, man is almost God, or will in the end become God himself, yes, yes, if God is within me, then I am God, God is us, He I, I He, Durus est hic sermo, et quis potest eum audire.]

Bartolomeu's ideas evoke the tension between Jesuit theology and Enlightenment thinking. The notion, crudely precursive of Hegelian positivism, that humanity is gradually evolving towards perfection through approximation to (or absorption of) a benevolent and libertarian God is Bartolomeu's justification for attempting to fly. Divine knowledge, he believes, is humankind's birthright:

> Todo o saber está em Deus [...] mas o saber de Deus é como um rio de água que vai correndo para o mar, é Deus a fonte, os homens o oceano, não valia a pena ter criado tanto universo se não fosse para ser assim (*Memorial*: 122)

> [All wisdom dwells in God [...] but God's wisdom is like a river that runs towards the sea, God is the source, humans are the ocean, it would not be worth the trouble of having created such a universe if it were not for things to end up that way.]

Thus, 'querendo nós e não o contrariando insuportavelmente Deus' [if we wish it and God does not oppose it irresistibly] (*Memorial*: 92), the *passarola* can fly. Attempts at flight — considered diabolic by many among the Church authorities — are not heretically presumptuous if, as Bartolomeu claims, '[o]s homens são anjos nascidos sem asas' [men are angels born without wings], and if God wills that humans should 'nascer sem asas e fazê-las crescer' [be born without wings and make their own wings grow] (*Memorial*: 137).

From a theistic perspective, the implications of Bartolomeu's argument are discomfiting. Given that the *passarola* is propelled by the sun's attraction of the same *vontades* upon which God depends for breath, if God did not 'contrariar' the *passarola*'s flight 'insuportavelmente', he would be sanctioning the possibility of his own obsolescence and demise. But although Bartolomeu's attempts to reconcile Catholic doctrine with humanist positivism eventually render him insane, Blimunda and Baltasar find the atheist route out of his theological cul-de-sac.[28] Guided by Blimunda's clairvoyance, they come to see God as a mere product of the human mind: a specious belief that the Church and State cultivate as a means of harnessing popular will.

This idea gains credence when Blimunda attends mass and, looking into the communion wafer, sees not God but merely 'uma nuvem fechada' [a dense cloud] (*Memorial*: 129). The mystery of whether or not God is sitting in heaven breathing *vontades* is never resolved. However, Blimunda's discovery reveals that what enters the body during Holy Communion is not the body of Christ, but instead an alien will. Directed by the clergy, Christians are voluntarily subordinating their own will to that of an apparently human Other, or allowing their own wills to drift away, as Bartolomeu suggests, 'por as não merecerem as almas, ou os corpos as não merecerem' [because the souls, or the bodies, do not deserve them] (*Memorial*: 143) in circumstances such as religious processions (*Memorial*: 144). Hence, as Eduardo Lourenço identifies, far from the physical world being a pale and imperfect reflection of the kingdom of God, there is only one world, powered by human endeavour: 'o mundo é ele uma nora e são os homens que, andando em cima dele, o puxam e fazem andar' [the world is a waterwheel and it is the human beings who, by walking in circles above it, pull it round and make it turn] (*Memorial*: 66).[29]

As an attempt to channel popular will into a project that defies the omnipotence of the eighteenth-century monarch and Church, and that affirms humans' potential to free themselves through the application of learning, the *passarola* soon gets grounded. Its significance (like that of Saramago's counter-factual fantasy in general) lies in demonstrating to the present-day reader the *possibility* of liberation, and of becoming *levantado do chão*. In this demonstration, *Memorial* is much bolder than *Levantado*, both in terms of the utopian transformation it envisages, and in its exploration of the complexities of (inter-)identity and desire, and of their impact upon revolutionary initiatives. Key elements of the *passarola* plotline suggest that Saramago is responding to the utopian 'libertarian socialism' of Herbert Marcuse, which gained a high profile in 'new Left' debates from the late 1960s, as a response both to the new challenges of late capitalism and to the contemporary diversification of radical protest. In Portugal, although Marcuse's ideas were rejected by the PCP leadership, they were circulating widely among left-wing activists even before the 1974 revolution.[30] In a series of works from *Eros and Civilization* (1955) to his *Essay on Liberation* (1969), Marcuse radically reassessed the emancipatory potential of technology while integrating psychoanalytical theory into a dialectical materialist sociology.[31] The Marcusean focus that emerges here first on the integration of work and pleasure, technology and art, and secondly on the central role of both sex equality and sexual liberation in the negation of capitalist alienation, retains significance throughout Saramago's subsequent fiction.

In his writings from 1969 onwards, Marcuse sets out his calculation that 'the material and intellectual forces for the transformation [of society] are technically at hand', but that the actions of the ruling class ensure that 'their rational application is prevented by the existing organization of the forces of production' (Marcuse 1970a). Such forces have long focused technology towards goals that perpetuate suffering rather than eliminating it, such as the development of ever more sophisticated weapons of mass destruction to sustain imperial domination. A more recent and alarming development, as Marcuse argues in *One Dimensional Man* (1964), is the use of technology by the ruling class to 'institute new, more effective, and more pleasant forms of social control and social cohesion' (Marcuse 1991: xlvi). In advanced capitalist societies, the use of technology to 'change [...] the character of the basic productive forces' (Marcuse 1991: 38–39) has, as Douglas Kellner summarizes, left the labouring classes 'immunised against political action, indoctrinated with the dominant ideology, and integrated into the consumer society' (1984: 269). To Marcuse, the greatest tragedy of this increased coercion is that freeing the technological resources of the late twentieth century from the 'framework of domination' (Marcuse 1991: xlvii) could 'make possible even more radical and emancipatory social transformation than Marx envisaged' (Kellner 1984: 324). The grounds for this envisaged transformation are first set out in *Eros and Civilisation*, in which Marcuse essays the integration of the insights of Freudian psychoanalysis into a dialectical materialist framework that is essential to his later writings.[32]

Marcuse's late writings, notably *An Essay on Liberation*, revise this, considering social and technological change as opportunities to circumvent the obstacles to liberation that are identified in *One-Dimensional Man*. Drawing on Freud, Marcuse proposes the reconciliation of the false ontological dualities of *necessity and freedom*, and *work and play*, to articulate a theory of 'surplus repression', and to stress the liberating power of sexual/libidinal energy.[33] This theory breaks with Marx's insistence on humanity as an animal whose natural occupation is non-alienating production. Extrapolating arguments from Marx's introduction to his early work *Grundrisse*, and working against Marx's later position (in *Capital* III) that '[h]uman freedom in a true form is possible only beyond the realm of necessity', Marcuse formulates a model of production which integrates joy and creativity into the processes of necessary work.[34] This model is based on the principles of collective control over the entire apparatus of labour; the gearing of production to need, not profit; the use of technology to increase leisure time, and of education to promote creativity, autonomy, and individuality at work and in play.[35] The admission of creativity at every level of the process of production, integrating art with technology, would replace the concept of technology as an instrument of domination with 'a post-technological rationality, in which technics is itself the instrumentality of pacification, organon of the "art of life"' and in which 'the function of Reason [...] converges with the function of Art' (Marcuse 1991: 238).

This 'one-dimensional' late-capitalist society on which Marcuse focuses appears only in Saramago's later fiction; notably in *A Caverna*, which explores the human experience of the clash of pre-modern and late-capitalist socio-economic modes.[36] *Memorial*'s account of Joanine Portugal, however, not only foregrounds how technology is geared towards warfare, and towards displays of State power (notably, the waste of engineering skill on the fatuous task of transporting the monstrous stone for the Mafra basilica façade), but also incipient forms of 'surplus repression'. Considered from a (psychoanalytic) Marxist viewpoint, state-sponsored pageants of sacrifice, violence, and death, which often blatantly enact the agonistic struggle of Christian 'good' against 'evil', serve to awaken and manipulate the erotic and destructive drives (*Memorial*: 98; 29). As Bartolomeu explains, the 'furor' [rage] stimulated by, for example, bullfights and autos-da-fé 'torna mais fechadas [...] as vontades [...] como na guerra' [makes the wills denser [...] like during battle] (*Memorial*: 144). In the procession of the *Corpo de Deus*, 'as almas e os corpos se debilitam [...] a ponto de não serem capazes, sequer, de segurar as vontades' [souls and bodies are weakened [...] to the point of being unable even to hold onto the wills] (ibid.).[37] Thus, official culture variously dissipates popular will, or channels it into the legitimation of the Church-State oligarchy. Independent and potentially liberating inventions must, meanwhile, either be appropriated — as Dom João hopes Bartolomeu's *passarola* may be (*Memorial*: 64; 160) — or denounced as diabolical or heretical. In the case of the *passarola*, however, this response comes too late to prevent Bartolomeu's friends from comprehending human *vontade* as a human creative and libidinal energy, or from re-directing their own and others' *vontades* into a mode of material production geared to the satisfaction of human needs material, spiritual, emotional, and sexual.

The contrast that Cecucci, amongst others, has noted (1993: 214) between work on the *passarola* in the utopia of A Pedreira, and work at the Mafra building site, serves to illustrate a Marxist theory of alienation, and indeed to echo Marcuse's observation of how an oppressive economic system can manipulate desire, or make it 'productive', by channelling it into socially policed cognitive and behavioural norms that reinforce the prevailing hegemony, while simultaneously reducing the 'pleasure principle' (Marcuse 1991: 75–84). While Baltasar and his co-workers at Mafra are pushed together into labour that 'não lhe alimenta [...] a alma' [does not nourish [...] the soul] (*Memorial*: 213), the trade in the sex and alcohol that offer them solace completes the formation of a 'società perversa e malvaggia' [perverse and villainous society] (Cecucci 1993: 214) with its own economy of brutality and domination governed by rapists, pimps, and syphilis (*Memorial*: 272–73). Moreover, as Lima (1990: 44) has noted, the Mafra project literally crushes genuinely free and loving desire when porter Francisco Marques, distracted by a longing to make love with his wife, falls under the giant mason's cart and dies with his abdomen and genitalia pulped under the cartwheel (*Memorial*: 259). At A Pedreira, however, the voluntary and creative collaboration on the *passarola*'s construction delivers an opportunity to 'viverem três pessoas um sonho' [for three individuals to live out a dream] (*Memorial*: 142). The substitution of a 'dream' for soul-starving alienation arises from Baltasar and Blimunda's spontaneous and experimental approach to the construction of the *passarola* (an approach that chimes with Bartolomeu's Kabbalistic view of God himself as a creator who learns from his own actions (*Memorial*: 163). Collaborating on equal terms, and eschewing sexist conventions of the division of labour, the lovers successfully integrate creativity, work, play, and lovemaking. When Domenico Scarlatti first visits the *quinta*, he encounters a seemingly prelapsarian idyll of bountiful gardens and orchards, from which Blimunda approaches the busy workshop 'sorrindo e oferecendo o cesto [de cerejas]' [smiling and proffering her basket of cherries] with 'brincos de cerejas nas orelhas' [cherries hung over her ears for earrings] for Baltasar's amusement (*Memorial*: 168). Later, interludes of lovemaking sustain Baltasar and Blimunda while they work on the *passarola* (*Memorial*: 270), as the couple live and sleep in a corner of the workshop (*Memorial*: 173). Marcuse's idea of an organon of desire, art, and work is most blatantly expressed when Domenico Scarlatti lends his artistry to the project, improvising at his harpsichord alongside the forge (*Memorial*: 177–78). His music's role in coaxing Blimunda back to health when the horrors of the Lisbon plague break her spirit (*Memorial*: 184–85) could even be considered a negation of the process of 'desublimation' that Marcuse decries in the contemporary convention of 'Bach as background music in the kitchen [...] [or] Plato and Hegel, Shelley and Baudelaire, Marx and Freud in the drugstore' (1991: 67).

A new mode of production is improvised pragmatically, taking advantage of perspectives and skills of both genders, rather of the woman's subjection. Blimunda takes charge of building a forge for the *passarola*'s metalwork, since she 'tinha mais rigor no olhar, mais precisão no traço' [had a more exacting gaze, more precision in tracing a line] (*Memorial*: 142). Later, when they renovate the hidden *passarola*, they pay no heed to the traditional division of labour regarding needlework (to women, if the cloth is for domestic use, but to men if for military use) (*Memorial*: 270), and '[m]ais por a terem cuidado homem e mulher do que por terem sido dois os cuidadores, a máquina parecia renovada' [more by virtue of a man and a woman having taken care of it than by there having been two caretakers, the machine appeared to be restored] (*Memorial*: 271). This non-sexist, pragmatic approach to work develops concomitantly with more loving and candid forms of social interaction, as when Bartolomeu, departing, blesses his friends, and all three instinctively break ecclesiastic protocol: 'eles beijaram-lhe a mão, mas no último momento se abraçaram os três, teve mais força o amor do que o respeito' [they kissed his hand, but at the last moment the three of them embraced, love proved stronger than deference] (*Memorial*: 96). The effacement of social hierarchy, the rehabilitation of corporeality and *eros*, and the emergence of a micropolitics of egalitarian love, rather than of domination, all inform a departure from Catholic theology, in the direction of an atheist spirituality. The three friends' rejection of conceptions of divinity as an authoritarian patriarch, and of humanity as innately sinful, emerges in their changing ideas about the sacrament of confession, which Blimunda consistently declines, saying she has nothing to confess (*Memorial*: 88–89, 354). Blimunda's refutation of the notions both of original sin, and of erotic desire as corruption, is progressively expanded by Bartolomeu, for example when he eases Baltasar's concern about 'pecados que, por se acumularem, vão esquecendo' [sins that, by mounting up, were being overlooked] (*Memorial*: 183).[38] The egalitarian principle, meanwhile, leads Bartolomeu to the (heretical) conclusions that God should not be above justice, and that priests have no special qualification to dispense divine justice. Ultimately, Bartolomeu refuses to impart blessings on the grounds that 'não sei em nome de que Deus [as] deitaria' [I do not know in which God's name to bestow them], advising his friends that blessing one another 'é quanto basta' [is sufficient] (*Memorial*: 187). The three friends' de-institutionalized and effectively humanist devotion is expressed in improvised rituals that not only emphasize the affectionate egalitarianism of their relationships, but also celebrate the life of the body. Bartolomeu presides over a 'wedding' ritual wherein he entreats Blimunda to eat from Baltasar's bowl and spoon, 'fazendo seu o que era teu, agora tornando a ser teu o que foi dele' [[after] making his what was yours, now making your own what was his] (*Memorial*: 56). This marriage appears still more revolutionary if Blimunda's repeated promise (*Memorial*: 56; 77) not to 'look into' Baltasar is read as her refusal to be possessive of her lover's mind or 'spirit', but rather to accept his status as an autonomous individual.[39] Later, after the couple first make love, Blimunda performs an unabashedly carnal act of blessing or 'baptism':

> Correu algum sangue sobre a esteira. Com as pontas dos dedos médio e indicador humedecidos nele, Blimunda persignou-se e fez uma cruz no peito de Baltasar, sobre o coração. (*Memorial*: 57)
>
> [A little blood trickled onto the straw mat. With the tips of her middle and index fingers, Blimunda crossed herself and traced a cross on Baltasar's chest, over his heart.]

Thus, with emphasis on the reciprocity and spontaneity that are also found in *Levantado*'s accounts of couples consummating loves unsanctioned by Church and patriarchy (but which are notably lacking from Dom João's relations with either his wife or his mistresses), *Memorial* overturns Christianity's banishment of the erotic from the realm of the sacred:

> Este casal, ilegítimo por sua própria vontade, não sacramentado na igreja, cuida pouco de regras e respeitos, e se a ele apeteceu, a ela apetecerá, e se ela quis,

quererá ele. Talvez ande por aqui obra de outro mais secreto sacramento, a cruz e o sinal feitos e traçados com o sangue da virgindade rasgada. (*Memorial*: 75)

[This couple, illegitimate by their own wish, their marriage not sanctified in church, has little concern for rules and expectations, and if he has become aroused, she too will be aroused, and if she has desired intimacy, he too will desire it. Perhaps what is at work here is a different, more secret, sacrament, the cross and sign first made then drawn with the blood of a rent virginity.]

The sanctity of physical love is re-emphasized by allusion to the Christian Holy Family when the couple bed down in a cowshed and make love on the 'palha remexida' [scattered straw] while 'os bois [...] ruminam na manjedoura' [the oxen chewed cud at the manger] (*Memorial*: 138): as the narrative voice claims, 'entre o amor dos que ali dormiram e a santa missa não há diferença nenhuma' [between the love of who have slept there and the holy mass there is no difference] (ibid.). The emphasis on reciprocity here neutralizes the conventional opposition of male agency to female passivity, intimating not simply sexual equality, but, further, the potential for the resurgence of 'feminine values' that Marcuse's late writings advocate:

Difícil é saber que parte há em cada parte, se está perdendo ou ganhando a alma quando Blimunda levanta as saias e Baltasar desláça as bragas, e está a vontade ganhando ou perdendo quando ambos suspiram e gemem, se ficou o corpo vencedor ou vencido quando Baltasar descansa em Blimunda e ela o descansa a ele, ambos se descansando. (*Memorial*: 138)

[It is hard to know which part lies within which, if the soul is losing or gaining when Blimunda lifts her skirts and Baltasar unlaces his breeches, and if the will is gaining or losing when the two of them sigh and moan, if the body has been victorious or vanquished when Baltasar rests inside Blimunda and she gives him rest, both of them resting.]

A later love scene (*Memorial*: 270) uses the same rhetorical tools to connote reciprocity: 'nus, sôfrego entrou ele nela, ela o recebeu ansiosa, depois a sofreguidão dela, a ânsia dele' [naked, hungrily, he entered her, she, yearning, received him, then the hunger was hers, and the yearning was his]. The contrast between Baltasar and Blimunda's frank yet tender sexual expression, and the tawdry and joyless eroticism produced by patriarchal laws and the Church's vilification of the flesh, is perhaps most touchingly depicted when Blimunda and Baltasar become 'o escândalo da vila de Mafra' [the scandal of Mafra] by habitually and unabashedly embracing in full public view (*Memorial*: 326).[40] However, the villagers' disapproval, or incomprehension of the couple's free spirits, reminds that the atheistic, egalitarian, and sexually liberated social order pioneered at A Pedreira is hopelessly anachronistic. As the narrative voice notes, 'tem cada coisa seu tempo' [everything has its proper time] (*Memorial*: 69). The attempts at aviation, and at the freedom and equality that Marcuse envisaged replacing mature capitalism, both depend on Blimunda's freakish powers of vision both technologically — from the collection of human wills, to the detection of faults in the metalwork of the *passarola* (*Memorial*: 90) — and ideologically, in providing critical insights into unsubstantiated religious dogma (as in the *Corpo de Deus* procession) and into evidence of human corporeality and a basic human equality.⁴¹ Yet, in a fearful society unwilling to receive these insights, the populace remains, in Marcuse's terms, immunized against political action, accepting the dominion of the Crown, the Church, and its *Santo Ofício* [Inquisition], which suppresses activities at A Pedreira. As Ornelas notes, the Church can even make the *passarola*'s flight contribute to its 'controlo da circulação de discursos' [control of the circulation of discourses] (1996: 123), by explaining its sighting over the Mafra monastery as the intercession of the Holy Spirit (*Memorial*: 207).

IV — Grounding Utopianism, Re-envisioning the Revolutionary Bloc

Thus the *passarola*, after alighting on the slopes of Monte do Barregudo, must be hidden until Baltasar and Blimunda return, years later, and attempt its renovation. Having restored the bodywork and sails of the 'triste ruína' [sorry ruin] that resembles 'os ossos de um pássaro morto' [the bones of a dead bird], the couple make love in the interior that now seems 'como o dentro de um ovo' [like the inside of an egg] (*Memorial*: 270), before debating what to do with the machine and its captured wills, 'coitadas delas, fechadas há tanto tempo, à espero de quê' [poor things, locked up for so long, and waiting for what] (ibid.). The changes rung by Saramago's metaphors here — from a living bird, to its skeleton, and to its egg — suggest that the 'sonho' realized at A Pedreira, while appearing dead, in fact survives, but survives only in embryo. The machine's womb-like interior provides a last redoubt for the couple's revolutionary relationship; outside, however, social conditions are not — yet — propitious for learning and technology to be employed as instruments of popular will. Stalled in this way, the *passarola* story becomes a parable of the limited — yet crucial — value of both ucronian imagining and utopian speculation. While the project has provided only a temporary refuge from the horrors of Joanine theocracy, it has offered an alternative vision of the potential triumph of popular will over a tyrannical god and his ministers, as well as of unalienated and non-hierarchized industrial and erotic economies, and of the instrumentality of female emancipation in achieving these. Saramago's fiction after *Memorial* presents increasingly sombre scenarios, wherein socialist transformation becomes an ever more remote prospect. However, *Memorial*'s model of 'visionary' popular intellectuals propagating socialist values of solidarity, compassion, and egalitarianism, while sustaining a 'dialectical' outlook, productively alternating empathy with a dissident, critical vision, remains the foundation of Saramago's literary and political project.

Baltasar's story ends tragically, however, because, as Frier argues, the *passarola* becomes the instrument of an obsessive pursuit of self-affirmation through an individual co-optation of popular will, rather than something that promotes collective emancipation through the free co-operation of *vontades* en masse. Frier (1994) shows how, in both *Memorial* and *Levantado*, subtly contrasted images of upward and horizontal movement indicate the need to pursue a 'gradual, collective' emergence from socio-economic oppression (*Memorial*: 128–33). As noted earlier, *Levantado*'s reworking of the neo-realist metaphors of wheat and harvest stresses the organic and collective logic of workers' liberation. Correspondingly, diverse images of upward movement collectively demonstrate that the rise which ultimately is successful here is a gradual, collective effort. All of the workers involved in it must keep their feet on the soil of the community [...]. (Frier 1994: 128)

In *Memorial*, Bartolomeu initially conceives of flight as the collective destiny of humankind: 'assim como o homem, bicho da terra, se fez marinheiro por necessidade, por necessidade se fará voador' [just like man, that earthworm, became a sailor through need, through need he will become an aviator] (*Memorial*: 64). By trapping *vontades* in a jar, however, Bartolomeu presumes to seek that destiny by co-opting collective will. This 'hybris', Frier argues (1994: 131), infects Baltasar, who is punished like Icarus for daring to venture 'perto do sol' [near to the sun] (*Memorial*: 236). Significantly, however, whereas Icarus is punished by the jealous Apollo, Baltasar's undoing is not any divine anger, but rather his misperception of his own powers and limitations. Unwilling to recognize that the *passarola*'s rise above the hegemonic powers can neither improve the lot of the general populace, nor end the enslavement of their *vontades*, Baltasar, effectively, is indulging a delusion of his own god-like status. Frier (1994: 132) points out how Bartolomeu's belief that his one-handed friend is God-like is disproved, since Baltasar's missing hand prevents him from controlling the machine's flight. Baltasar's attempts to rebuild the machine single-handedly recall the unitary, one-handed God whom Bartolomeu once claimed metamorphosed into a trinity, reinforcing the novel's message that the most successful creations are the result of pluralism and co-operation, and of trial and error. Subordinating two thousand wills to those of one — or three — is not a viable way to defy God's supposedly anointed on Earth, or to be raised from the ground.

With tragic irony, Baltasar's accident occurs just as, for the first time, he moves to thinking in terms of a collective project:

> lhe ocorria a ideia, desmontar a máquina peça por peça, transportá-la para Mafra, [...] se pudesse combinar com os amigos mais chegados, confiar-lhes metade do segredo[.] (*Memorial*: 334–35)

> [He had the idea of dismantling the machine piece by piece, [and] transporting it to Mafra, [...] if he could only hatch a plan with his closest friends, confide part of his secret in them.]

Alas, in Joanine Portugal, rural workers have few means of asserting their will against the authorities; fewer, indeed, than have the nuns who stage a sit-in protest against new restrictions on their social contact (*Memorial*: 93). Moreover, though, Baltasar fails to appreciate the *passarola*'s value merely as a utopian project, which contradicts hegemonic dogma and affirms the viability of change. Piero Cecucci's study of utopianism in Saramago notes the pertinence of Luigi Firpo's argument, in *L'utopia e le sue forme*, that the true utopian must understand his/her project as 'prematuro, avveniristico, estratemporale [...] un invito alla riflessione nel profondo della coscienza, gettando un seme che maturerà molto lentamente nei secoli futuri' [premature, speculative, anachronistic [...] an invitation to reflect in the depths of one's consciousness, sowing a seed that will reach maturity very slowly over future centuries].[42] Such an 'invito alla reflessione' is the purpose of *Memorial*'s utopian scenarios, and an attentive reader will spot the irony of Baltasar's complaint, when Blimunda suggests releasing the captive *vontades*, that '[se] as deixarmos ir, será o mesmo que se não tivesse acontecido nada' [if we release them, it will be just as if nothing had ever happened] (*Memorial*: 271). Just as it matters less whether or not the historical Bartolomeu de Gusmão's experiments succeeded than that they provided resistance to religious tyranny and obscurantism, so too the construction and flight of *Memorial*'s *passarola* are incidental to its value in affording Baltasar an alternative vision of his world. The presentation in each case of an alternative vision to the accepted account contributes to the education of the reader (in the first case) and protagonist (in the second) as potential 'organic intellectuals'.

Tragically, Baltasar does not recognize how his experiences equip him to 'gettare un seme' in the form of challenging ideas and progressive attitudes, even after his allusion to those experiences inadvertently triggers a daring theological discussion among his workmates (*Memorial*: 236). As Frier observes (1994: 133), however, Baltasar's vital contribution to the slow germination of a new consciousness is illustrated in the chance meeting of Baltasar's former workmates José Elvas and Julião Mau-Tempo in Montemor (near Julião's descendants' home of Monte Lavre), and their speculation about the clandestine achievement of human flight: 'Deve haver um segredo. Haverá' [There must be a secret. Could be] (*Memorial*: 311). Hence, while his attempts to restore the *passarola* are literally a step in the wrong direction, Baltasar is unwittingly 'contributing to what will one day be a successful change', just as Frier claims is true of João Elvas (1994: 133). In contrast, Blimunda recognizes from the outset her allotted role as precursor of *Levantado*'s Gramscian organic intellectuals. She gives an example of the value of (metaphorical and real) earthbound horizontal travel when she follows João Elvas in '[moving] across the surface of the country [...] raising new questions and questioning established hierarchies' (Frier 1994: 133–34).[43] Frier (2007a: 155–58) also explores the Gramscian resonances of the 'fermento de desassossego' that Blimunda leaves in her wake. While not belonging 'to any formalized structure of resistance' (2007a: 157), Blimunda, condemned to wander through dangerous terrain as the sole surviving architect of an over-ambitious *sonho*, cautiously disseminates to other women aspects of the heretical 'vision' afforded by her own, and her fellow aviators', enquiry into the nature of human will. Her status as an 'organic' thinker and agitator, who understands that her utopian vision can only come to fruition after many decades of increasing resistance to absolutist abuses, is indicated by one of the connotations of her sobriquet 'Sete-Luas'. In the oppositionist symbolic code of the Salazar era, moonlight was frequently deployed as a metaphor for resistance, and of hope during the 'night' of dictatorship (most memorably so in Luís de Sttau Monteiro's allegory of the failed Gomes Freire revolt of 1817, in his 1961 play *Felizmente há luar!*). Blimunda Sete-Luas is not only the embodiment of a resurgent feminine power, and the possessor of vision that can penetrate the dark; she is also the woman who reflects the 'enlightenment' of the socialist 'dawn' into the 'night' of tyranny, so as to provide guidance towards, and confidence in, a better future. It is thanks to her vision, and to her perseverance, that, in his dying moments, Baltasar can make a final gesture of solidarity in defiance of their oppressors, when '[d]esprendeu-se a vontade de Baltasar Sete-Sóis, mas não subiu para as estrelas, se à terra pertencia e a Blimunda' [Baltasar Seven-Suns' will broke free, but did not rise to the stars, for it belonged to the Earth, and to Blimunda] (*Memorial*: 357). His refusal to lend his will to the sustenance of God, plus the horizontal journey and earthly destiny of his *vontade*, successfully defy clerical power.[44] Baltasar's will, stored up on Earth in his wife's body, may yet become the first of many *vontades* that gather in solidarity, and 'rise from the ground' in defiance of gods and rulers.

Blimunda's story following Baltasar's disappearance makes a further contribution to *Memorial*'s refreshed vision of revolutionary agency, however, by referencing her not only to Gramsci's concept of organic intellectualism, but simultaneously to Marcuse's discussions of a 'new sensibility' that might reanimate a progressive consciousness under late-capitalist conditions, a 'new type of human being',

> free from the aggressive and repressive needs and aspirations and attitudes of class society, human beings created, in solidarity and on their own initiative, their own environment, their own *Lebenswelt*, their own property. (1969c: 24)[45]

Marcuse's analysis of how this 'new sensibility' and its concomitant 'post-technological rationality' could be instilled, given consumer society's immunization of the proletariat against political action, has notorious lacunae.[46] *An Essay on Liberation* and 'Liberation from the Affluent Society' do, however, explore how the 1960s radicalization of social constituencies contesting complex structures and forces of oppression (notably, women, black and other ethnic minority people, and LGBT&Q constituencies) was altering consciousness and values in ways that created new potential for socio-economic transformation, or, at least, for what Marcuse later termed an 'effectively organized radical Left, assuming the vast task of *political education*, dispelling the false and mutilated consciousness of the people' (1972: 28).

In addition to a clear consciousness of their position both as individuals and as a collective in relation to conditions of production, these humans would possess 'a different sensitivity' and would 'follow different impulses', having 'developed an instinctual barrier against cruelty, brutality, ugliness' (Marcuse, 1969b: 21). Specifically, this barrier would guarantee the rejection of the 'performance principle' that breeds aggressive behaviour. New systems of production would allow humans to '[rid themselves] of the aggressiveness and brutality that are inherent in the organization of established society, and in their hypocritical, puritan morality' (Marcuse, 1968: 197). With radically different socio-economic motivations, people would develop 'good conscience of joy and pleasure, and [...] work collectively and individually for a social and natural environment in which such an existence becomes possible' (ibid.).

When one takes account of Marcuse's connection of this 'new sensibility' to the growth of a socialist feminist movement, the precise political significance of Blimunda's anachronistic knowledge and of her compassionate, cooperative sensibility becomes clearer. While his later essays — especially 'Marxism and Feminism' (1974) — recognize the weight and particularity of women's continuing oppression under late capitalism, Marcuse claims that the patriarchy's demand for their domestication and pacification meant that women had been 'frequently freed from repression in the work sphere, brutality in the military sphere, and competition in the social public sphere' (Kellner 1984: 340). Men's socialization rewards aggression, competition, and domination in ways that galvanize the situational or indirect complicity of many men, across all social classes, with the hierarchical and coercive principles underpinning an exploitative socio-economic system. By contrast, women's socialization — in accordance with the norms of exemplary femininity — distances them from the 'Performance Principle'. Furthermore, Marcuse claims, 'advanced capitalism [has] gradually created the material conditions for translating the ideology of feminine characteristics into reality [...] and making feminism a political force in the struggle against capitalism, against the Performance Principle' (1974: 284). The commitment of a socialist movement to 'feminine' qualities of 'receptivity, sensitivity, non-violence [and] tenderness' could constitute 'the negation of the exploiting and repressive values of patriarchal civilization [...] of the values enforced and reproduced in [capitalist] society by male domination' (Marcuse 1974: 281; 283).[47] Marcuse stresses, however, that such a resurgence of values traditionally designated 'feminine' is not (yet) fully represented by Marxian socialism, and could become achievable only in tandem with the eradication of patriarchy's oppression of women.[48] As Kellner summarizes, the consequent 'emancipation of female and feminine energy, physical and intellectual, in the established society', and the dissemination of 'feminine' values into social and industrial spheres could 'subvert the dominant masculine values and the capitalist performance principle' (Kellner: 341).

Echoes of Marcuse's analysis are identifiable in *Levantado*, which depicts the continuing revolutionary potential of the working class as increasingly dependent on the establishment of a more equitable relationship between men and women in all areas of life. However, women's gradual occupation of physical and discursive locations previously denied them, and their claims to equal status as workers and activists, succeed only after 'visionary' men such as João Mau-Tempo and Manuel Espada forswear the 'performance principle' and recognize women's equality as partners and parents, deferring to their decision-making, and indeed risking humiliation by repudiating patriarchal privileges, rather than embracing them as compensation for their own subjugation by the State and *latifundium*. To a degree, such processes recall Marcuse's suggestion that 'we men have to pay for the sins of a patriarchal civilization and its tyranny of power' and his claim that women's struggle to 'determine their own life [...] as an individual human being' will be one 'permeated with bitter conflict, torment, and suffering (mental and physical)' (1974: 288). *Memorial*, however, presents clearer parallels, first in terms of the greater brutality that the dominant ideology inculcates in men. Army life, which leaves Baltasar desensitized to killing and to handling carcasses (*Memorial*: 69; 78), instils conformity to the 'performance principle' in an especially brutal manner. Even in civilian life, the legitimacy of the state's violent domination is affirmed performatively in autos-da-fé, processions, and bullfights wherein male protagonists are authorized to torment, kill, and (self-)chastise. Women's restriction to subservience and passivity, meanwhile, goes hand in hand with the religious cult of pornographically violent martyrdoms such as those of Saint Lucy (*Memorial*: 138), and the widespread toleration of domestic violence (*Memorial*: 189), rape (*Memorial*:

230; 337), and 'honour' murders such as that of a Lisbon woman (*Memorial*: 45–47), her mutilated body recovered with 'os seios, cortados como laranjas' [her breasts sliced off like oranges], like those of St Eulalia (*Memorial*: 46). Women, according to what Bartolomeu claims, nevertheless retain their *vontades* until death more often than men (*Memorial*: 143), suggesting their superior resilience and integrity. The narrative voice's assertion that 'é a grande, interminável conversa das mulheres [...] que segura o mundo na sua órbita' [it is the great, unending, dialogue of women [...] that holds the Earth in its orbit] (*Memorial*: 109) implies, moreover, that women possess not only greater aptitude for dialogue, empathy, and co-operation, but also, the humility and perception necessary to avoid Bartolomeu's egotistic failure of judgement: 'não fosse falarem as mulheres umas com as outras, já os homens teriam perdido o sentido da casa e do planeta' [were it not for women discussing amongst themselves, men would no longer know their way home or about the planet] (ibid.). Blimunda's remark to the village women that she meets on her travels, that they are all lumbered with the role of 'cordeiro que tirará o pecado do mundo' [lamb that takes away the sins of the world] (*Memorial*: 354), encapsulates Marcuse's observations about how women are distanced from the 'Performance Principle'; relegated to the role of supporting their male kin, and of redeeming the aggression and selfishness that is fostered in them so as to keep the wheels of an exploitative economic system turning.[49] As Saramago's subsequent novels make clearer, only where and when men concede to learn from women's repudiation of the 'performance principle', and to aid women's economic and intellectual emancipation, will the struggle for revolution and redemption move forward.

Memorial's focus on Baltasar's growing humility, compliance, and gentleness in relation to Blimunda expands on *Levantado*'s implicit message that working men must not only curtail their complicit or active role in women's oppression, but also cultivate more 'feminine' attitudes themselves. The lovers' complementary sobriquets — 'Sete-Sóis' and 'Sete-Luas' — may initially seem to reiterate the conventional gender binary that subordinates the female to an alleged male primacy. However, by the novel's close, these two characters and their relationship have come to represent a more complex, dynamic model of gender, and the significance of this in a revolutionary struggle. It is notable that Blimunda's association with the moon and moonlight — her superhuman clairvoyant powers that wax and wane with the lunar/menstrual cycle — links her with the lunar goddesses of pagan cults that, unlike Catholicism, did not denigrate women by distancing them from the divine principle. While committed to the 'feminine' values of affection and co-operation, Blimunda, like such pre-Christian figures, is not constrained by conventional 'feminine' ideals of self-sacrifice and passivity. Being always a 'mulher para dar o primeiro passo, para dizer a primeira palavra, para fazer o primeiro gesto' [a woman disposed to take the first step, say the first word, make the first gesture] (*Memorial*: 332), she assumes conventionally masculine virtues of initiative and innovation, so as to exemplify Marcuse's argument that 'feminine' values, 'far from fostering submissiveness and weakness, [could] activate aggressive energy against domination and exploitation' (1974: 286). She challenges women's designated role as passive 'vessels to be filled' by collecting human *vontades* in just such a 'vaso de receber'

(*Memorial*: 11). Furthermore, instead of taking marriage vows and devoting her life to a domineering husband and demanding children, she achieves a genuinely egalitarian relationship with Baltasar.

Her most 'masculine' attitude, of course, is the recourse to defensive violence, when she uses the missing Baltasar's prosthetic *espigão* [spike] to stab the Dominican friar who attempts to rape her (*Memorial*: 344–46). This episode at once furnishes a symbolic revenge against the agents of Blimunda's mother's ruin, and an equally symbolic triumph of Blimunda and Baltasar's unabashedly sexual, egalitarian union over the dehumanizing and perverse sexual and moral codes of a patriarchal Church.[50] This episode, which finds Blimunda at her loneliest and most vulnerable, is a crucial indicator of Saramago's thinking about ideals of community and collective agency. More precisely — and in keeping with Marcuse's claim that a feminist Marxism could transform the 'masculine–feminine antithesis [...] into a synthesis — the legendary idea of *androgynism*' (1974: 286) — it is crucial in suggesting the dissolution of an essentialist gender binary as the basis for a deeper, more egalitarian communion between men and women. The episode is particularly significant insofar as it invites analysis of Blimunda in relation not only to the Mau-Tempo women in *Levantado*, but also to the Doctor's Wife in the later *Ensaio sobre a Cegueira* [*Blindness*] (1995). The Doctor's Wife, the only character not afflicted by the contagious white blindness of the novel's title, kills the leader of the gangsters who have enslaved her and her fellow inmates quarantined in a hellish sanatorium, and who have repeatedly raped the females (*Cegueira*: 185). As Atkin has explored, Saramago's claim, in 1995, that the Doctor's Wife is the 'irmã gêmea' [twin sister] of Blimunda points to the later novel's development of a substantial dialogue with *Memorial*, achieved through the parallels between these characters and their agency and symbolic resonances.[51] As explored first in Sabine (2001: 140–41) and later by Atkin, in both cases, the significance of killing as not only defence against male sexual violence, but also an act of retribution for it, is emphasized by the phallic nature of the weapon employed.

In Blimunda's case, one might ask if — since the weapon belongs to Baltasar — she is following the model of the *mujer varonil* of Golden Age Iberian drama, whose defence of honour with her absent kinsmen's sword can be read less as an assertion of her own phallic credentials than as her metonymic protection by those of her menfolk.[52] Alternatively, the phallic agent here — a replacement for Baltasar's left hand that is tied on with leather straps — could be considered as less like a penis than like a strap-on dildo. Hence, the *espigão*'s transfer from Baltasar to Blimunda affirms the lovers' solidarity but, moreover, suggests how 'masculine' and 'feminine' behaviours might be tools at the disposal of men and women investing in egalitarian inter-dependence in love, in work, and in resistance to oppression. The establishment of the *espigão*'s metaphorical status as a replacement hand, prior to its role as a weapon with phallic connotations, reminds the reader that — as Blimunda tells Baltasar — 'tu e eu temos três mãos' [you and I have three hands] (*Memorial*: 100), and that while two hands are better than one, three hands are better still.

The implicit lesson of Blimunda's story, that society will remain *maneta* [one-handed] until women are allowed to make a free and full contribution, is both recalled and elaborated by the stabbing in *Cegueira*. Whereas Blimunda's *espigão* penetrates the friar just before he succeeds in penetrating her (*Memorial*: 345), the Doctor's Wife attacks the gangster with a pair of scissors *after* he has forced her to fellate him, and, in fact, while he is assaulting one of her companions (*Cegueira*: 177; 185). The differences of the weapon and the timing are both significant. As Atkin notes, the scissors 'while phallic, are not clearly gendered or marked as belonging to another person' (2012: 110). Hence, the Doctor's Wife's actions mark her clearly as a woman *independently* appropriating masculine credentials to 'activate aggressive energy against [patriarchal] domination and exploitation' (Marcuse 1974: 286). Moreover, as Atkin argues,

> in the asylum [...] personal belongings have little individual value, and personal identity loses its significance. The scissors thus come to have a universal quality: they serve to protect all women. Although a phallic object, they come to represent the taking back of power by a woman — by all of the women. (Atkin 2012: 111)

The importance of the principle of collectivity, and the *physical* enactment of solidarity, is also conveyed in the way that the doctor's wife's attack relies for its success on the cover that is provided by the other women's cries, which drown out the sounds of her footsteps and breathing (*Cegueira*: 185). If, as both Ornelas (2006) and Sabine and Martins have proposed, Saramago's work in general, and *Cegueira* in particular, set out to '[reconceive] "humanity" as the product of conscious attempts to combat universally endemic moral flaws' (Sabine and Martins 2006: 19), the Doctor's Wife and Blimunda are the figures who most consistently display such humanity, and guide others towards attaining it.[53] The Doctor's Wife's killing of the gang-leader and rapist, shocking though it might be, is an exemplary case. As Ornelas argues,

> she is not a rational murderer since she only kills to preserve a higher good, the mere survival of humanity. [...] Her action [...] is an act of humanity or an act of solidarity with other human beings to re-establish reason, the very fabric of dialogic human interaction, which is the only alternative to despair and impotence (2006: 135).

Notions of solidarity and collectivity, one could add, are essential to this reconception of humanity. As Atkin observes, the violated women, recognizing the Doctor's Wife's objective as being one of collective redemption, rather than personalized revenge, will, before the novel's conclusion, 'come to see themselves as a multi-faceted whole, bound together in solidarity due to their shared experiences' (2012: 111). As Atkin notes, Blimunda's use of Baltasar's *espigão* (which later seems to her like Baltasar's hand, as she washes the blood off it (*Memorial*: 347)) contributes to a pattern of bodily references in both novels that suggests collectivity and cooperation. In *Cegueira*, the bonding of individuals into a collective, co-operative body, which the Doctor's wife evokes by describing herself and her companions as a single 'mulher com dois olhos e seis mãos' [woman with two eyes and six hands] (*Cegueira*: 266), begins with the women's unwitting cooperation when she avenges their collective violation. The shared motif of stabbing the rapist, meanwhile, connects this process to Blimunda's (supernatural and ahistorical) embodiment of the ideal 'new humanity', and to the examples that Baltasar provides of the contrasting consequences of male pride and individualism, and of male humility and deference to 'feminine' values, respectively. While the disaster of Baltasar's solo flight stems from his impatience with the stalling of a project pursued by a collective possessed of only 'três mãos', it is the possession of a prosthetic 'third hand' that saves Blimunda. At the novel's end, the dying Baltasar has seemingly learned the lesson, permitting Blimunda to 'look inside' him, and agreeing to unite his *vontade* with hers within a single body, making her a 'vaso de receber' in an active, empowered sense that is the opposite of that intended by the tyrannical Church and State patriarchy (*Memorial*: 357). Saramago's fiction challenges his male readers to do better than the husbands in *Cegueira*, whose initial response when their wives submit to rape so as to feed their families is not solidarity, but suspicion (*Cegueira*: 165–66). That challenge is to forge solidarity with women as equals, and to accept that, even when they lack magic powers, women — and their distinct socialization, experiences, and priorities — are as essential as men to any worthwhile movement for progressive change.

Memorial's call to recognize the particularly enlightened perspective and agency of women, and the indispensability of their liberation to attempts to challenge oppression, or to mitigate its effects through love, solidarity, and the perpetuation of a critical vision, is of course just one of several ways in which it expands the literary and political project commenced in *Levantado*. It also fine-tunes the literary form of its predecessor. Negotiating more deftly between a Brechtian reconception of the 'documentary' historical novel, and a 'counter-factual' and fantastical mode, it broadens Saramago's speculation both on irrecoverable historical data that attests to subaltern agency, and on the unrealized potential of past — and present — situations. Further, *Memorial* expands *Levantado*'s critical revision of *História Pátria* and its interrogation of Catholic and nationalist mythology. This it achieves through a new project of creative 'de-/re-construction' of an apparently obsolete literary aesthetic: not neo-realism, but the Iberian baroque, here deployed to remarkably elaborate satirical and allegorical effect.

In the realm of ideology, meanwhile, *Memorial* goes further in identifying blind-spots in revolutionary socialist theory and praxis that must be addressed in order to consolidate (or advance beyond) the modest gains of the struggle against capitalist exploitation and inequality in April 1974. Despite its setting in a distant past, the novel's allegorical function effectively permits speculation on how to build a revolutionary counter-hegemony in conditions where — according to Marcuse — unprecedented obstacles to the radicalization of subaltern consciousness had developed. *Memorial* infuses the Gramscian model of political mobilization sketched in *Levantado* with a Marcusean emphasis on the role of desire, spirituality, and affect. Both novels illustrate the abnegation of the Self in deference to solidarity with the Other, as well as the work of the organic intellectual, and the operation of an unending dialectic between eccentric and established perspectives, and between empathy and independent critique. Yet *Memorial* puts more emphasis on the necessary negation of the aggressively 'masculine' values underpinning both capitalism's patriarchal hierarchy and its exploitative and oppressive economic logic.

The response to these concerns, and the pursuit of freedom and equality, demand that we think beyond the limits of what is immediately viable: to embrace the 'importância do erro', while acknowledging — and yet defying — the fact that not all of what we need to see is visible.

Notes to Chapter 2

1. Paulo Pereira interprets the novel's depiction of Joanine autocracy as at once 'um meio de alegorizar a história recente do país' [a means of allegorizing the country's recent history] and 'uma parábola sobre a grandeza e a miséria do passado histórico português' [a parable about the grandeur and poverty of the Portuguese historical past] (1991: 122). Elvira S. Presedo notes the 'singular óptica de que é perspectivada e posta em causa a guerra colonial' [distinctive optic through which the colonial war is viewed and called into question] (1984, p. 42).
2. The Mafra monastery complex has a total floor area of 38,000m^2, with over 1200 rooms, over 4700 doors and windows, and 156 staircases (source: Instituto dos Museus e da Conservação, at <http://www.ipmuseus.pt/pt-PT/museus_palacios/ContentDetail.aspx?id=1125> [accessed 13 December 2012].
3. On the construction of the Mafra complex, see Pereira (1994: 132–35).
4. On Saramago's use of early accounts of the life and works of Bartolomeu de Gusmão, see Frier (2003). On Saramago's use of accounts of clairvoyant individuals in seventeenth- and eighteenth-century Portugal to inform *Memorial*'s characterization of Blimunda, see Arnaut (1997: 62–67), Costa (1999), and Maia (1991: 62–63).
5. See *Memorial*, p. 64. This punning comparison of humankind to a 'bicho da terra' is borrowed from Camões's *Lusíadas*, canto 1, stanza 106 (1947: IV, 51).
6. Santos (2006) concurs that the novel's pervasive duality and tension between opposites is a 'traço fundamental do espírito barroco' [essential trait of the baroque spirit]. Aside from Costa (1997) and Kaufman (1991b: 129), curiously few later studies have elaborated directly upon Lopes's observations about *Memorial*'s typically baroque conceptualist rhetoric and use of paradox.
7. See pp. 102–03. For a full account of Sarduy's theory of the 'neo-baroque' and its relationship with mid-to-late twentieth-century Spanish American writing and aesthetics, see Zamora and Kaup (2010).
8. The formula by which Dom João is introduced in this opening sentence may allude to Monteiro (1749). Certainly, Monteiro's and other royalist panegyrics of the era perfectly exemplify the fulsome register that *Memorial* parodies. For further analysis of the opening chapter, see, amongst other studies, Reis (1986); Arnaut (1996: 37–41), and Mendes (1991: 14).
9. Further examples of irreverent, 'oral' conclusions to enunciations of an 'official' tone include the conclusion of the preparations for the royal couple's bedroom meeting with the phrase '[o] cântaro está à espera da fonte' [the bucket is ready for the pump] (*Memorial*: 13) and the account of the king's illness, serious enough for him to request confession (*Memorial*: 49–50) but in the end explained to have been provoked by 'só a tripa empedernida' [just bunged-up guts] (*Memorial*: 50).
10. Arnaut (1996: 97).
11. On the *Estado Novo*'s 'restoration' of the Castelo de S. Jorge and Lisbon's cathedral, and the subsequent demolition of much of the adjoining Mouraria district, see Dias (1997: 14–21), and Sapega (2002: 46–47). Saramago's depiction of Blimunda's lean-to arguably typifies the kind of 'counter-image' of even 'the most recognizable and enduring memory sites constructed by the Salazar regime' (2002: 48) that Sapega's study explores.
12. The phrase 'vã cobiça' is taken from Camões, *Os Lusíadas*, canto 4, stanza 95 (1947: IV, 239).
13. See, in particular, Benjamin (1985), and also Esther Leslie's assessment of this, the 'Convolute J' in Benjamin (1999), and other texts (2000: 199–200).
14. The use of the Ptolemaic cosmos as literary metaphor occurs most frequently in works celebrating prominent composers, wherein musical composition is presented as *imitatio*; the successful imitation of celestial harmony. For a full account, see Hollander (1961).

15. See Luis de León's poem for organist Francisco Salinas, 'El aire se serena' (1982: 207–08, at 208).
16. See Kirkpatrick (1953), and Joel Sheveloff's entry on Scarlatti in Sadie (1980: XVI, 568–78, esp. 570–72).
17. For a full account of the binary sonata form and Scarlatti's role in its development, see James Webster's 'Sonata form', in Sadie (1980: XVII, 497–508, esp. 497–99).
18. This description of Scarlatti's wondrous improvisation may be based on the famous testimony of composer Thomas Roseingrave, claiming that 'he thought ten thousand d****s had been at the instrument', quoted in Burney (1782: II, 704).
19. 'The dialectical image is one flashing up momentarily. It is thus, as an image flashing up in the *now* of its recognizability, that the past [...] can be captured' (Benjamin 1985: 49).
20. On the concept of *Veritas filia Temporis*, see Gordon (1980).
21. While Dom João took a number of lovers from the religious houses of his realm, for much of his reign his foremost mistress was Madre Paula Teresa da Silva, Prioress of the Convent of Dom Dinis in Odivelas, and mother of Dom José, one of the three of Dom João's natural sons known as the 'Meninos de Palhavã' who, as adults, exercised leading roles in the Portuguese Church hierarchy. For a full account of this matter, see Pimentel (2009).
22. As discussed below, Flor proceeds to question the presumption that this 'official' culture articulates a 'discurso hegemónico' [hegemonic discourse] resistant to individual artists' attempts at its subversion (ibid.).
23. *Memorial*'s description of the foundation ceremony draws very accurately on the contemporary accounts given by Prado (1751: 5–8) and Conceição (1818: VIII, 86–99).
24. Marques (1972a: I, 550–51). Disney, while claiming that Dom João V 'was not particularly autocratic [...] never an unmitigated despot' (2009: I 268) notes that the King's 'absolutism appears to have been at its most unambiguous in relation to the Church' (2009: I, 267).
25. See Hobbes (1651: title page).
26. See Saunders (2000: 54–56).
27. As Santos Alonso explains, Gracián's perspectivist rhetoric advances the belief that the world and humankind's destiny within it are not fixed in some immutably ideal state, but subject to the 'carácter cambiante y autodestructivo del mundo' [ever-changing and self-destructive character of the world] (Gracián 1980: 39).
28. Bartolomeu experiences a profound multiple identity crisis on p. 176, apparently provoked by his inability to reconcile to Catholic doctrine the observations of Blimunda and his own ruminations on the creation of the world. His confusion is compounded by his readings of the Torah and Kabbala (*Memorial*: 197); his conversations with heretics (*Memorial*: 60; 65); and his contact with pagan and satanic beliefs (suggested by a number of symbolic motifs including Bartolomeu's idea that Baltasar resembles God through the lack of a left hand). There are also significant points of contact between Bartolomeu's unorthodox theology and the seventeenth-century 'heresy' of Unitarianism, a faith that not only refutes the doctrine of the Trinity, but also, according to F. L. Cross, emphasizes 'belief in the abiding goodness of human nature', and that is 'critical of the orthodox doctrines of the Fall, the Atonement, and eternal punishment' (1983: 1408).
29. As Eduardo Lourenço puts it, '[n]ão há de um lado o reino de Deus e do outro o dos Homens; este último esforçando-se desesperadamente e em vão por reflectir a perfeição imóvel do primeiro. Há um só reino, como há menos um Deus que uma Unidade' [there is not the realm of God on one side and on the other the realm of Men, this latter striving desperately and in vain to reflect the fixed perfection of the former. There is but one realm, just as there is not so much a God as a Unity] (1990: 24).
30. Marcuse's ideas were presented in studies such as Reis (1973), and were debated in *Seara Nova* in March 1974 (17–22).
31. Lima (1990) supplies detailed textual evidence for *An Essay on Liberation*'s influence on *Memorial*, but is principally concerned with the question of 'o homem enquanto criador' [humankind as creator] (1990: 42). Lima interprets the *passarola* as metaphor for artistic creation and as a vehicle for a liberation which is essentially psychological rather than material: 'a máquina de voar [...] como exercício de libertação pode ser vista como uma imagem da produção artística' [the flying

machine [...] as the exercise of liberation can be seen as an image of artistic production] (1990: 46). Setting aside both Marcuse's and Saramago's preoccupation with revolutionary theory, she does not explore the revisions to Marxism's conception of socialist society which Marcuse argues are necessitated by the technological advances of the late twentieth century.

32. As Marcuse summarizes in *One-Dimensional Man*, 'the conflicts of the unhappy individual now seem much more amenable to cure than those that made for Freud's "discontent in civilization," and they seem more adequately defined in terms of the "neurotic personality of our time" than in terms of the eternal struggle between Eros and Thanatos' (1991: 80).

33. On this false ontological duality, see Marcuse (1970b: esp. 63). For a critical discussion of Marcuse's argument here, see Kellner (1984: 324–29).

34. This phrase from Marx is cited by Marcuse (1973a: 37). See Kellner (1984: 87–91) for a discussion of this essay. Marcuse returns to, and expands, this early essay's critique in (1969c), and briefly summarizes it in (1969b: 20–21).

35. See esp. Marcuse (1966).

36. On this theme in *A Caverna*, see Klobucka (2001: xv–xviii).

37. As Pereira notes, Dom João V dedicated unprecedented amounts of State revenue and attention to the annual Corpus Christi procession, a ritual that, through his patronage, 'proporcionou ainda uma alegórica representação do poder e do Estado' [also furnished an allegorical representation of power and of the State] (1994: 94).

38. In reply, Bartolomeu argues that 'Deus vê nos corações e não precisa de que alguém absolva em seu nome, e se os pecados forem tão graves que não devam passar sem castigo, este virá pelo caminho mais curto [...] ou serão julgados em lugar próprio [...] se, entretanto, as boas acções não compensarem por si mesmas as más, também podendo vir a acontecer que tudo acabe em geral perdão ou castigo universal, apenas está por saber quem há-de perdoar a Deus ou castigá-lo' [God looks into our hearts and does not require that anyone absolves in his name, and if the sins are so grave that they should not go without punishment, this will arrive in short order [...] or the sins will be judged in the appropriate place [...] if, in the meantime, good works do not of themselves compensate for the bad, it could also come to pass that everything will end with a general pardon or universal punishment, all that remains to be known is who should pardon or punish God] (*Memorial*: 183).

39. Óscar Lopes compares this motif to the Orpheus myth which similarly warns that 'amar alguém implica a impossibilidade de *ver* esse alguém, de o objectivar' [loving someone implies the impossibility of *looking* at that someone, of objectifying them] (Lopes 1986: 205). Blimunda apparently understands the necessity of the lover's retention of her/his independence of spirit, given her disagreement with Baltasar's speculation about the possibility of their *vontades* fusing during love-making (*Memorial*: 143).

40. The role of conditioning circumstances in these new sexual customs is indicated by the fact that, before meeting Bartolomeu and Blimunda, Baltasar's sexual behaviour and religious observance are as debased as anyone else's: he only visits church to pick up women (*Memorial*: 43).

41. On Blimunda's first demonstration of her powers (*Memorial*: 78–84), her description of human viscera, of colons bulging with excrement, and pudenda eroded by syphilis, bestows on Baltasar an awareness of the socially levelling factors that Montaigne highlighted with the reminder that 'les Roys et les philosophes fientent, et les dames aussi' [kings and philosophers shit, and so do ladies] (1979: 296).

42. Firpo (Bologna: Mulino, 1982), p. 12, quoted in Cecucci 1993, p. 211.

43. It is worth noting that the *passarola* is only of any practical use in that, having gained clearance of the ground, it can travel *horizontally* through the air, taking Bartolomeu away from death at the hands of the Inquisition.

44. The fact that Baltasar's *vontade* is still 'no centro do seu corpo' [in the centre of his body] (*Memorial*: 357) up to this point indicates that he is burned alive as an unrepentant heretic. As *Memorial* notes, the Inquisition, in the spirit of divine mercy, spared from the agony of the flames those heretics, heathens, and witches who had 'declarado que queria morrer na fé cristã' [declared their wish to die in the Christian faith] (*Memorial*: 54), by having them garrotted before incineration.

45. See also Marcuse (1968) and (1969b).

46. Kellner, for example, identifies a consistent failure in Marcuse's late writings to prove the connection between essentially reformist struggles and 'the radical change he envisages', to specify 'the sociological and political mediations that would make possible liberation and the construction of genuine socialism', or to analyse 'what sort of institutions and practices might help create the needs and struggles that he envisages' (1984: 346).
47. See also Marcuse (1973b).
48. As Marcuse warns, 'in Marxian socialism there are remnants, elements of the continuation of the Performance Principle and its values [...] the emphasis on the ever-more effective development of the productive forces, the ever-more productive exploitation of nature, the separation of the "realm of freedom" from the work world' (1974: 286).
49. In his interview with Beatriz Berrini, Saramago himself accounted for 'uma inegável reverência pela mulher' [an undeniable reverence for women] (Berrini 1998: 240) in his earlier fiction: 'Em criança e quando rapaz [...] encontrei [nas mulheres] um sentido crítico instintivo, como que uma risonha compaixão, uma benevolência paciente, cada vez que falavam dos homens. Talvez isto me tenha levado, depois, a não tomar demasiado a sério a autoridade e a suficiência masculinas, e, por contraste, a compreender melhor esse *ser outro* que é a mulher' [as an infant and as a boy [...] I encountered in women a critical instinct, like a kind of good-humoured compassion, a patient benevolence, whenever they talked about men. Perhaps this has led me, later, to avoid taking male authority and sufficiency too seriously, and, by contrast, to better understand that 'other being' that is womankind] (ibid.).
50. In this scene particularly, *Memorial* co-opts the symbolism and doctrines of pagan religion to attack the Church and its institutionalized misogyny. While the emphatic association of Blimunda throughout the scene evokes the figure of the moon goddess as embodiment of female wisdom and power, the phallic nature of the weapon with which Blimunda defends herself and the vows binding her to Baltasar recall the pagan exaltation of sexual intercourse as a religious ritual and means of communion with the divine.
51. See Atkin (2012: 107–18), and Alves (1995: 82).
52. For a full treatment of representations of women warriors, killers, and avengers in Spanish Golden Age drama, see McKendrick (1974: esp. 174–217; 261–75).
53. Ornelas, drawing attention to Saramago's 1996 claim that *Cegueira* allegorized a discussion of the human capacity to abandon rationality with murderous consequences, explores how the novel suggests that 'all human beings carry the infection [...] Thus, all individuals must learn how to manage to be constantly vigilant against all forms of epidemics' (2006: 124).

CHAPTER 3

O Ano da Morte de Ricardo Reis

Ricardo Reis, like its predecessors, is a story of dissidents living under a tyrannical state. However, while it builds on those predecessors' recuperation of national memory for an internationalist, socialist agenda, it focuses particularly on the notion of literary 'heritage', and on the political ramifications of writing, reading, and citing. When first published, the novel furnished an ambivalent response to the burgeoning cult of Fernando Pessoa (1888–1935), whose extraordinarily diverse *oeuvre*, anticipating key tenets of postmodernist thinking, was belatedly achieving recognition, as both the fiftieth anniversary of his death and the centenary of his birth approached. Saramago's conceit of a dead Fernando Pessoa conversing with a living incarnation of his literary alter ego, or 'heteronym', Ricardo Reis, capitalizes on an ingenious manipulation of historical coincidence. Pessoa's death on 30 November 1935 fell just before the military rising under Franco that precipitated Spain's Civil War of 1936–39, and that temporarily pulled Salazar's *Estado Novo* into closer alignment with Hitler and Mussolini's Axis. Saramago's novel resurrects the deceased Pessoa, and animates Reis, so as to interrogate the politics of their works in both their original and contemporary contexts. The historical backdrop of the rise of European fascism, the carnage in Spain, and, finally, the ill-fated Portuguese naval revolt of 8 September 1936 allows Saramago to throw into relief ethical and epistemological dilemmas that arise in Pessoa's writings, and whose examination complicates his latter-day status as national literary icon. The novel compels its reader to confront those writings' troubling conclusions regarding the limits of human comprehension, either of one's own consciousness and identity, or of the 'outside' world. And simultaneously, its plot forces the posthumous Pessoa and his heteronym to acknowledge the material, ideological, and social contexts from which they seek to abstract themselves in their introspective and elitist philosophy and writing.

As in *Levantado* and *Memorial*, the recuperation — and simultaneous interrogation — of suppressed subaltern histories is crucial in *Ricardo Reis*. However, this novel's most significant political observations are rather those deriving from analysis of the means by which culture, and intellectuals, might effectively challenge hegemonic powers — whether during dictatorship or its aftermath — when these co-opt literature and mythography to project their preferred image of reality. Through the character of Reis's indomitable lover, Lídia, *Ricardo Reis* updates Blimunda Sete-Luas's quasi-Gramscian stance of analytical and innovatory solidarity, in order to confront modern totalitarianism and its legacy. In contrast to Lídia, Saramago's Ricardo Reis repeatedly fails — or rather, refuses — to become a socially engaged intellectual. Through a brilliant exploration of the *Odes* that Pessoa ascribed to Reis, the novel manages to depict this refusal as a betrayal of the basic principles of Pessoa's thinking. Moreover, with a robustly materialist re-reading of Pessoa's best-known works, Saramago suggests how Marxism might take on board the Portuguese modernist's explosion of subjectivity. *Ricardo Reis* endorses Pessoa's reconception of selfhood not as *being*, but as a ceaseless, yet socio-economically contingent process of *becoming* a multiplicity of Others. This process — which Reis refuses to acknowledge — emerges in *História* and later novels as the basis from which utopian community — if not the 'revolutionary bloc' envisaged in *Levantado* — might arise, built by empathizing with, learning from, and loving the social Other. The self-centred and self-deceiving Ricardo Reis contributes much to making *Ricardo Reis* the gloomiest of Saramago's novels on Portuguese history. However, Reis is not so much its protagonist as an instructive foil to figures like Lídia, and, indeed, like *Historia*'s Raimundo Silva, through whom Saramago continues to explore the elaboration of a new and cautiously utopian socialist struggle in the postmodern, and post-structuralist, era.

The premise for *O Ano da Morte de Ricardo Reis*'s plot is the return of Pessoa's fictional doctor-poet to his native land from exile in Brazil, on receiving news of Pessoa's death.[1] Settling first in a hotel in between Lisbon's fashionable Chiado district and the Cais do Sodré waterfront, and later moving uphill to a flat in the Santa Catarina area, Reis plans to resume a life of lonely but sedate detachment. For the first eight months of 1936, as Salazar's *Estado Novo* deceives, intimidates, and brutally subjugates the Portuguese populace, and as still more virulent fascist tyrannies crush democratic freedoms and popular will in Spain, Italy, Germany and Abyssinia, Reis takes in the accounts of domestic and foreign affairs provided by the *Estado Novo*'s propagandist newsreels and by a heavily censored and acquiescent press. He meanwhile initiates two ill-considered affairs of a more amatory nature: one, with the hotel chambermaid, Lídia, that is vigorously consummated, and the other, with Marcenda — a lawyer's daughter with a mysteriously paralysed arm — preceded by a lengthy courtship, but barely sustained beyond a first kiss. Between his trysts and mealtimes, Reis wanders the rain-swept Lisbon streets like a failed flâneur, rarely inspired, and more often assailed both by the evident poverty and political oppression of its population, and by the ghosts of Portugal's literary and imperial past. A more literal ghostly presence in his new life is that of the newly dead Pessoa, who pays Reis a series of visits over what he explains are the nine months of posthumous existence that all humans are granted, and that is, 'salvo casos excepcionais, [...] quanto basta para o total olvido' [apart from exceptional cases [...] the time needed to achieve total oblivion] (*Ricardo Reis*: 80). Dispassionate and sardonic, Saramago's posthumous Pessoa questions the worth of the life and writings that he has just left behind, while teasing Reis about the gulf between his sordid and trivial daily life, and the pursuit of a dignified 'sad Epicureanism' extolled in his *Odes*. These dialogues form a counterpoint both to the government propaganda that Reis takes in from radio broadcasts and his daily newspaper reading, and to his conversations, of an increasingly political nature, with Lídia, whose brother Daniel is a sailor and Communist activist plotting the 9 September 1936 naval revolt. Reis's existential malaise — and the political malaise of the nation as a whole — come together when, having been spurned by Marcenda, Reis searches for her in vain at the pilgrimage site of Fátima. Eschewing sympathy with the wretched masses whom he encounters seeking their own miracles, Reis returns to Lídia, who is now pregnant with his child. Reis declines to acknowledge paternity or to marry Lídia, and withholds his solidarity even when, in the novel's finale, Daniel and his comrades are killed before his eyes as they launch their rebellion. No longer able to content himself with 'o espectáculo do mundo' [the spectacle of the world],[2] Reis abandons his lover and son, and accompanies Pessoa to the tomb.

I — Dead Authors, Living Texts, and the Politics of Literature

Ricardo Reis's focus on the writer, his/her works, and political conflict makes explicit the messages that are implicit throughout Saramago's earlier fiction. First, it exemplifies how all writing is inevitably an act of de-/re-constructive *re*writing. To a greater degree even than *Memorial*, *Ricardo Reis* creatively blends a plethora of literary reference with data carefully lifted from historical and journalistic sources, quoting verbatim and at length from national newspaper reportage of the period.[3] The protagonist's thoughts are as replete with literary allusion as are Pessoa/Reis's original *Odes*, and the novel quotes these extensively. Simultaneously, the novel demonstrates the inevitable political significance of all quotation, and all rewriting. Saramago makes this most obvious in Reis's musings on the *Estado Novo*'s cynical recontextualization, and ideological manipulation, of Luís de Camões and of his epic poem, *Os Lusíadas*. Yet if the novel exposes, and implicitly denounces, such manipulation of canonized literature, its own recontextualization of Ricardo Reis to a Lisbon blighted by poverty and injustice is itself an unmistakably political act, making the fatalistic abstraction of Reis's *Odes* ring hollow, and enabling an appropriation of aspects of Pessoa's thinking for socially engaged literature and socialist politics. Literature cannot impose its author's 'will', but can upset hegemonic regimes of representation, and invite the reader to devise alternatives — and, indeed, to *will* an alternative political praxis.

The novel's exploration of the politics of literary quotation is established immediately, when Reis disembarks where, in a paraphrase of Camões, 'o mar acaba e a terra principia' [the sea ends and the land begins], bringing ashore with him a detective novel, borrowed from the ship's library, which he will carry with him to the grave (*Ricardo Reis*: 11; 23).[4] This novel is *The God of the Labyrinth* by the Irish writer Herbert Quain; in other words, a non-existent text by another imagined author, this time the creation of Jorge Luis Borges.[5] As was first explored by Sabine and Martins, the presence here of Borges's fictional fiction alerts the reader to how, bearing in mind the inevitability of intertextual resonance, the practice of literary allusion transgresses in diverse ways the boundaries established between textual realms: boundaries between individual texts and the collective *oeuvres* of individual authors, between recognized literary genres possessing varied degrees of cultural capital, and between purportedly distinct literary traditions or canons (Sabine & Martins 2006: 1–2). The device, however, also implies the considerable political impact that such transgressions can achieve. Firstly, both Reis's absent-minded smuggling of an Irish writer's pulp fiction into Portugal, and Saramago's insinuation of Borges into a novel ostensibly about Pessoa, mock the attempted 'cultural policing' of national borders, whether literally, through censorship, or figuratively, through the strict delineation of a literary canon predicated on often blatantly ideological criteria ('native', not 'foreign'; 'noble', not 'popular', etc.) (Sabine & Martins 2006: 2). *Ricardo Reis*'s rebuff to cultural policing is, of course, primarily directed at the xenophobic, authoritarian, and hierarchical *Estado Novo*, and its efforts to prevent the ingress of subversive or degenerate 'foreign' ideas, representations, and customs.[6] However, it also addresses the increasingly jingoistic slant of 1980s celebrations of Pessoa, whose status as a 'national treasure', (mis)quoted by all comers seeking to demonstrate their patriotic credentials, was confirmed by his body's translation from Lisbon's Prazeres cemetery to the Hieronymite Monastery in Belém in 1985. By evoking an Argentine writer who develops fascinating responses to many of Pessoa's philosophical preoccupations, and who, in 1985, claimed, in a tribute to Pessoa, that 'nada te costó renunciar [...] al trabajoso empeño de representar a un país' [it cost you nothing to repudiate the arduous task of representing a country] (Borges 1984: 39), the novel undermines nationalist literary criticism's claims of Pessoa's 'uniquely' Portuguese qualities, demonstrating the global extent of the web of literary textuality.[7]

At the same time as the trafficking of Quain's book dissolves the national boundaries of culture, it also demonstrates that literary texts themselves have permeable borders, and that this permeability has serious political implications. Saramago can cherry-pick an element of Borges's original *ficción*, make it his own — by inventing plot details for Quain's detective thriller — and (as explored below) use it to subvert the ideal of philosophical detachment that Ricardo Reis's *Odes* extol. Beyond this, the title of Quain's novel becomes, in Saramago's hands, the starting point for a more troubling consideration of the high political stakes of literary quotation, in the light of post-structuralism's identification of how intertextual webs traverse all representation without ever encompassing a comprehensive truth. Borges looms large among the twentieth-century writers who have established the labyrinth as emblem of epistemic insecurity and deception.[8] Saramago repeatedly redeploys this metaphor from Reis's very arrival in Lisbon. Helena Kaufman (1991a: 169–70) and Rhian Atkin, amongst others, have noted how here, as also in *História do Cerco de Lisboa*, the Lisbon maze provides an apt backdrop for the 'protagonists' equally labyrinthine searches for a greater understanding of the self, and of political and/ or historical events' (Atkin 2012: 8). Atkin not only shows how these episodes anticipate the pervasive presence of labyrinthine images and preoccupations in *Ensaio sobre a Cegueira* and *Todos os Nomes*; she further argues, following Sabine and Martins (2006: 4), that they indicate the status of Saramago's entire *oeuvre* as — using the concept that Umberto Eco proposes in his 'Reflections on *The Name of the Rose*' — a 'rhizomatic' textual labyrinth, 'so constructed that every path can be connected with every other one. It has no centre, no periphery, no exit, because it is potentially infinite' (1985: 15). Like the protagonist of Eco's novel, William of Baskerville, both Ricardo Reis and Saramago's reader must eventually acknowledge that 'the world in which [...] he [*sic*] is living already has a rhizome structure: that is, it can be structured but is never structured definitively' (ibid.). Hence, all guiding threads are only of relative utility.

Saramago's clearest allegory of the political implications of this 'rhizomatic' nature of textuality appears in *Ensaio sobre a Cegueira*, with the conceit of the main characters escaping the deadly maze of the psychiatric hospital, only to find that the surrounding city has become a similarly hellish labyrinth, within which they must continue the struggle to establish their own haven of moral order. *Ricardo Reis*'s narrower focus on canonical 'national' literature as labyrinthine, and as indissociable from a larger, transnational, rhizomatic labyrinth, exposes and challenges the role of that national canon in corroborating a dominant narrative of history and shared values. At the same time, it exposes the consequent dilemma that faces the politically engaged literary writer. If the textual labyrinth of literature (or for that matter, of history or of nationhood) is rhizomatic, with no single centre to control, nor unique path to police, it can have no 'god' or transcendental order. This disquieting truth becomes evident as Ricardo Reis's daily perambulations of Lisbon both make him feel 'como se fosse dentro dum labirinto que o conduzisse sempre ao mesmo lugar' [as if he were inside a labyrinth that led him always to the same place] (*Ricardo Reis*: 70), and also apprise him of the political co-option of art and literature. Reis's perplexity peaks each time he finds himself back in Lisbon's Chiado district, epicentre of cultural and intellectual power in Portugal since the early nineteenth century. Populated both in 1935, and still today, with statues raised to the nation's most canonical authors, the Chiado is a palimpsestic space wherein succeeding generations have inscribed their own definitions of national identity and values. The Chiado's focal point is the *largo* [square] and statue dedicated to Camões. '[T]odos os caminhos portugueses vão dar a Camões' [all Portuguese roads lead to Camões] (*Ricardo Reis*: 181), and, the statue, erected in 1867, testifies to the nineteenth-century elevation of the epic poet to the status of a household god or sublime 'synthesis of the national character'.[9] Yet Camões's god-like status is predicated on the liberal humanist fallacy that the author is master or guarantor of his/her texts' meanings. As is manifest in the novel's conceit of a relocated Ricardo Reis reading Herbert Quain's novel, literary texts can escape their creator's intentions, but can equally be captured by critics, advertising agents, and political propagandists. As famously argued by Roland Barthes, the conception of the author as sage whose writings crystallize 'universal' truths or insights breaks down when one recognizes the text as 'a tissue of quotations' (Barthes 1977: 146), susceptible to being 'dismembered and rehashed in a subsequent act of quotation' (Sabine & Martins 2006: 3), and often for the most sinister of agendas. Hence, while Camões is lauded by the *Estado Novo*'s cultural mandarins in an annual ceremony as 'cantor sublime das virtudes da raça' [sublime bard of the virtues of our race], fragments of his *Lusíadas* are quoted or paraphrased out of context, in official speeches and reports made 'para que se entenda bem que não temos mais que ver com a apagada e vil tristeza de que padecemos no século dezasseis' [to make it clearly understood that we no longer have anything to do with the listless and mean-spirited sadness that afflicted us in the sixteenth century] (*Ricardo Reis*: 351).[10] Kaufman details how the 'leitura irónica que o narrador faz dos jornais da época' [ironic reading that [*Ricardo Reis*'s] narrator makes of newspapers of the period] emphasizes the 'evocação nacionalista' [nationalistic evocation] of Camões's poem's more affirmative treatment of myths of empire-building (1991b: 134). As the same narrative voice suggests, the epic poet's posthumous separation from his text, now so rarely read in full and in context — 'Veja Camões, onde estão as palavras dele' [here is Camões, where are his words] — reduces him to a 'boneco' [puppet] (*Ricardo Reis*: 358) of the regime. Moreover, such manipulation of canonical author and text is nothing new:

> este bronze afidalgado e espadachim, [...] se por estar morto não pode voltar a alistar-se, seria bom que soubesse que dele se servem, à vez ou em confusão, os principais, cardeais incluídos, assim lhes aproveite a conveniência. (*Ricardo Reis*: 70)
>
> [If this noble bronze swordsman, [...] being dead, cannot enlist for national service, it would be good for him to know that he is pressed into service by the powers that be, even the cardinals, whether in concert or willy-nilly, according to their convenience.]

This latest appropriation of Camões is central to the *Estado Novo*'s implantation of its ideology through a totalitarian transformation of culture, memory, and the built environment.[11] Everyday life was to be imbued with the beliefs and values of Salazarism, not only through legislation, prescriptive models of education, and corporatist organizations like the *Mocidade Portuguesa*, but also through literary and artistic censorship and canonization, and through the reconstruction and management of historic buildings and cityscapes. The 'restoration' of Lisbon's cathedral, completed in 1940, and of the Castelo de São Jorge focused less on conservation than on creating a monumental assemblage that directed collective memory towards Salazarism's preferred periods and initiatives in the national past.[12] As *Ricardo Reis*'s Reis and Pessoa note, Lisbon is also being purged of monuments to disfavoured writers and thinkers such as Pinheiro Chagas (1842–1895), and of sculptures that breach Salazarism's puritanical moral codes (*Ricardo Reis*: 358–59).

The appropriation of Camões as Salazarist 'boneco' apprises both Ricardo Reis, and the novel's reader, of an author's impotence: his/her supposed vatic status, and authority over his/her text, are relinquished once that text is in circulation and mined for quotations by others. The Barthesian argument that the writer enjoys authority only as another reader or critic of his/her work is implied by a recurrence of Saramago's favourite metaphorical trope of vision, deployed here in association with a trope of petrification that is adapted from the *Lusíadas*. Fernando Pessoa explains to Reis that, at his death, he lost the ability to read (*Ricardo Reis*: 80), and the narrative voice links the fact that 'já nem sequer é capaz de ler, coitado' [he can no longer even read, poor man] to the fact that 'não poderá acrescentar mais nada ao que foi e ao que fez, ao que viveu e escreveu' [he will not be able to add anything to what he was and what he did, to what he lived and wrote] (*Ricardo Reis*: 91). One scant consolation of this inability to read, perhaps, is Pessoa's ignorance of the obituarists who reductively label his esoteric and very ambivalently patriotic lyric sequence *Mensagem* a 'poema de exaltação nacionalista' [poem exalting the nation] (*Ricardo Reis*: 35), and who disregard his stated contempt for 'Christism'[13] when noting that he died 'num leito cristão do Hospital de S. Luís' [in a Christian bed in the Hospital of the Convento de S. Luís] (*Ricardo Reis*: 36). This conceit of blindness as symbol of the (both literal and metaphorical) death of the author is dramatically reiterated when it compels Reis to accept the reality of his own death. With consummate irony, Reis re-opens Quain's *God of the Labyrinth* to discern only 'uns sinais incompreensíveis, uns discos pretos, uma página suja' [incomprehensible symbols, some black figures, a blemished page] (*Ricardo Reis*: 415). Meanwhile, the author initially presented as the 'god' of the national literary 'labyrinth' is for his part equally clearly associated with visual impairment. Camões's statue depicts the poet as *zarolho* [one-eyed], subsequent to the loss of his right eye at the siege of Ceuta. But *Ricardo Reis* imagines Camões as wholly blind in posthumous effigy, his eyes allegedly pecked out by the pigeons and 'os olhares indiferentes de quem passa' [the indifferent gaze of those passing by] (*Ricardo Reis*: 257). This and further references to the poet's statue as a conscious but sightless and immobilized presence (e.g. *Ricardo Reis*: 351–52) connect Camões as 'dead' author to his fictional creation Adamastor, whose own nearby statue assumes increasing prominence in Reis's story. In Canto IV of the *Lusíadas*, Adamastor is the anthropomorphosis of the Cape of Good Hope, a titan seduced by the goddess Tethys and thereby tricked into imprisonment in the rock of Africa's southern tip, as punishment for his rebellion against the gods. As Sapega notes (2006: 33), Adamastor's statue in the Alto de Santa Catarina is instrumental in the gradual displacement of Camões and of his own statue respectively as the seeming 'god' and epicentre of the urban labyrinth. As Sapega, amongst others, has discussed, the novel's association of Adamastor with rage, tyranny, enslavement, and suffering, together with the irony of a titan, who was punished for attempting to usurp divinity, assuming centrality in the labyrinth, make his statue a potent symbol of the ultimate 'uncontrollability of representation' (2006: 32).

In this context, the statue's association with frustration and suffering indicates a bleak assessment of the politically engaged writer's dilemma. Under the *Estado Novo*'s harsh censorship, not even art can voice dissent or protest openly. And even where state hegemony is exercised less brutally, the writer can only make claims for the 'true' meaning of her/his texts, or assert her/his political philosophy, in his/her capacity as a public intellectual. In a manner that anticipates *Jangada*'s engagement with Jean Baudrillard's concept of simulation, *Ricardo Reis* illustrates the *Estado Novo*'s neutralization of the political loading of literary texts through their seamless incorporation into its day-to-day simulation of a fantasy ideal Portugal. In *Jangada*, state hegemony is shored up during the crisis of the Iberian Peninsula's displacement by the 'hyperreality' fabricated in TV and radio news bulletins, documentaries, and debates.[14] In *Ricardo Reis*, while the renovated 'historic' fabric of Lisbon serves as a day-to-day simulacrum of an imagined heroic national past, government agencies simulate a terrifying future through their public rehearsal of the response to an imagined air raid on Lisbon (*Ricardo Reis*: 337–41). The mock air raid blurs the boundary between 'real life' and spectacle, with a prominent role played by one of the country's biggest film and theatre stars, António Silva (*Ricardo Reis*: 337). Thus it enthrals the public to a dubious image of the present time in which the Republican government in Madrid poses an existential threat to Portugal. The same effect is pursued by propagandist cinema such as António Lopes Ribeiro's *A Revolução de Maio* (*Ricardo Reis*: 368; 378), which, as Luís de Pina explains, uses an 'história sentimental que transforma um revolucionário num bom patriota' [sentimental story that transforms a revolutionary into a good patriot] (1986: 81–82) to show that *Estado Novo* policies had positively transformed both a beleaguered nation and the outlook of its people.[15] The film's absorbing mishmash of (highly selective) recent history, a fictional 'personal drama', and upbeat enumerations of the *Estado Novo*'s achievements fosters acquiescence not only to authoritarian methods of maintaining public order, but equally to the state's monopoly on defining and depicting past and present reality. *Ricardo Reis* remarks the efficiency of this grim agenda in its account of a seeming PVDE raid that is revealed as a shoot for Lopes Ribeiro's film (*Ricardo Reis*: 365–68). The duplicitous verisimilitude of state media meshes with the theatricality of the state 'security' operations to stimulate not a sense of security, but one of fear.[16]

Even before the arrival of the mass-media technology that, according to Baudrillard, ushers in hyperreality, the *Estado Novo* can manipulate contexts for the reception of literature so as to determine what messages it transmits. This is evident in the performance that Reis attends of Alfredo Cortez's *Tá Mar* (1936), a Realist dramatization of the harsh and perilous existence of the fishing community of Nazaré, purportedly written in the local dialect (*Ricardo Reis*: 109), and drawing on an ethnographic observation of the town. In the context of the *Estado Novo*'s pervasive media control, however, such an attempt to distil the essence of daily life has the effect only of rendering life and art(ifice) hard to distinguish. This becomes apparent after the performance, when the actors are joined on stage by the real-life fisher folk of Nazaré, to be fêted in a ceremony contrived to illustrate how, under Salazarism, 'é fácil entenderem-se as classes e os ofícios' [it is easy for different classes and professions to understand each other] (*Ricardo Reis*: 113). The novel also follows Benjamin and Brecht's criticisms of realist theatre's enthralling affectivity: surrounded by 'mulheres lacrimosas e sorridentes' [tearful and smiling women] (*Ricardo Reis*: 112), Ricardo Reis can only think out his criticism of the play 'confusamente' [in a muddle] because 'afinal é difícil, ao mesmo tempo, pensar e bater palmas' [in the end it's difficult to think and applaud at the same time] (*Ricardo Reis*: 110). Cortez's drama of working-class suffering can be seamlessly 'reabsorbed' into the regime's hegemonic narrative of reality, because it does not challenge the orthodoxy that documentary representations of reality faithfully encapsulate a self-evident truth. The play's reabsorption is completed when the same fisher folk feature in newspaper and radio coverage of the event (ibid.), reportedly expressing their gratitude for the state's promise to build a safe harbour in Nazaré, and thus alleviate the dangers of earning a living in Europe's most turbulent and treacherous coastal waters. This promise, incidentally, remained unfulfilled when the regime fell in 1974.

Reis's observation of these various spectacles is used to illustrate first how, in every modern society, 'communal' or 'national' life past and present is perceived through the simulacra projected via radio, newspapers, popular film, and fiction, not to mention, in this case, historical pageants and folkloric spectacles. Under dictatorship, unilateral control of such simulacra suppresses any aspect of 'real life' that contradicts the dominant ideology, and fabricates any aspect of that ideology's vision that lived events fail to supply. While censorship ensures that writers and artists cannot project dissent or protest openly through their works, mediatic framing serves to contain or reconstrue even those works' more troublesome implications. What, then, can the politically engaged writer or artist do, either in times of dictatorship, or in its aftermath? *Ricardo Reis* invites condemnation of its protagonist, first and foremost, as a man who refuses to see the world around him as anything other than an *espectáculo*, who refutes the world's materiality and historicity, and, indeed, his own physical incorporation into that, and who thereupon eschews any responsibility or compassion for his fellow humans. Yet Saramago also criticizes Reis specifically as a writer who presumes to dominate, rather than dialogue with, his reader, and who refuses to think *politically* about the epistemological and aesthetic precepts and concerns of Pessoa's literary project. Saramago's fantasy of Reis in 1936 Lisbon contests this by both advocating, and exemplifying, modes of writing that demand an actively critical, and politically engaged, practice of reading. Under the *Estado Novo*'s efficient censorship, the narrative 'auto-interrogation' incorporated into texts like Redol's *Barranco de Cegos* featured among the few means by which literature could help to keep political critique and active dissent alive. In a fledgling liberal democracy like that of 1980s Portugal, however — and not ignoring Terry Eagleton's warning that presumptions of the reader's 'autonomy' are but a 'quasi-liberal humanist' fallacy (1976: 86) — Saramago's efforts to elicit such a reading practice can aim to combat the legacy of dictatorship, and to mitigate the continuing control of mass media by a coterie of commercial and governmental interests. They may also, however, attempt something more. His work uses poetic language and literary allusion to prompt the reader to a new analysis of socio-economic conditions, but it also warns that a renewed dialectical materialism and any radical transformation that it instigates will partake of conjecture and, inevitably, of errors of vision and judgement.

The seeds of a demand for writing that elicits not passive absorption, but active analysis and critique, are — ironically — found in Ricardo Reis's own objections to the Realist aesthetic of Cortez's play. Reis complains that

> o objecto da arte não é a imitação, [...] a realidade não suporta o seu reflexo, rejeita-o, só uma outra realidade, qual seja, pode ser colocada no lugar daquela que se quis expressar, e, sendo diferentes entre si, mutuamente se mostram, explicam e enumeram, a realidade como invenção que foi, a invenção como realidade que será. (*Ricardo Reis*: 109–10)
>
> [the objective of art is not imitation [...] reality does not tolerate its reflection, it rejects it, only some kind of other reality can be put in the place of that which one wishes to define, and being different to each other, they will expose, explain, and account for each other, the reality as the fabrication that it was, the fabrication as the reality that it will become.]

In each of Saramago's novels, of course, just such another reality, partaking of speculation, apocrypha, and fantasy, is put in the place of the hegemonic version of the past. Saramago's hedging of this juxtaposition with interruptions, disclaimers, and questions prompts the reader to scrutinize both, to pursue the insights, and utopian proposals, that emerge dialectically, and, thereupon, to re-imagine reality. Yet this passage, rather than simply offering a justification of Saramago's established practice, also matters for its relevance to *Ricardo Reis*'s manner of confronting, and seeking to 'reanimate', the multiple meanings of texts (and authors) that have been 'frozen' as national monuments. Such attempts at political reanimation of canonical literature — and, in particular, of the writings of Pessoa and his heteronyms — make conspicuous Reis's disregard for the political significance of his own distinction here between artistic mimesis as verisimilitude, and, alternatively, as what Elin Diamond terms 'a mode of reading that transforms an object into a *gestus* or dialectical image' (Diamond 1997: ii). In this latter understanding of the artistic or literary work, truths are not inherent to 'the model and its creative revisions' but rather 'produced in [the reader's] engaged interpretation' (ibid.). While Reis allows his *odes* to function as mere escapist alternative to life, Saramago incorporates numerous quotations from those poems, and from other Pessoan texts, into the 'other reality' of Reis's life in Lisbon. As this chapter's second section argues, this means that, when this imagined reality is juxtaposed with contemporary news reports and Saramago's own selection of historical data, the politically contentious — and in Saramago's own view, potentially obnoxious — meanings of texts safely subsumed under the label of 'national heritage' become apparent.

This is no more true of *Ricardo Reis*'s engagement with Camões and Pessoa, however, than of its distinctive and highly significant allusions to two nineteenth-century literary idols whose graven images are found in Lisbon's streets. Both are figures who famously commandeered the image of Camões for their own critiques of their nation's apparent decline under a decadent socio-political order, namely, the novelist and essayist José Maria Eça de Queirós (1845–1900), and the pioneering Symbolist poet Cesário Verde (1855–1886). Ellen W. Sapega has argued that *Ricardo Reis*'s narrative, like that of both Eça's *O Crime do Padre Amaro* (1880) and his later *Os Maias* (1890), 'aproveita a justaposição da estátua de [Camões] com cenas mesquinhas da vida quotidiana para chamar a atenção para a hipocrisia que caracteriza a sociedade narrada' [takes advantage of Camões's statue's juxtaposition with squalid scenes of everyday life so as to draw attention to the hypocrisy that characterized the depicted society] (1996: 105).[17] As Sapega also mentions (ibid.), *Ricardo Reis* makes three references to Eça's statue on the Rua de Alecrim, in between Reis's hotel and the Praça de Camões. Although Cesário Verde is not also evoked by name (possibly because his monument was erected only in 1955, situated two miles away in the Estefânia district), the same comparison can be made with his 1880 poem 'Sentimento de um Ocidental'. This celebrated account, by turns laconic and apocalyptic, of a sickly *flâneur*'s nocturnal perambulations was a seminal influence on Pessoa's poetic vision. Moreover, its format and imagery provide models for Ricardo Reis's wanderings through the 'sombra e humidade' [gloom and damp] (*Ricardo Reis*: 44) of fetid, shabby Lisbon streets, particularly when the lyric subject stumbles into

> [...] um recinto público e vulgar,
> Com bancos de namoro e exíguas pimenteiras,
>
> [[...] a common, public square
> With lovers' benches and lithe pepper trees]

where

> Brônzeo, monumental, de proporções guerreiras,
> Um épico doutrora ascende, num pilar!
>
> [A war-sized monument cast in bronze
> Stands, on a pillar, for an epic that was!]
> (Verde 1988: 154; trans. Verde 2011: 27).

Thus, *Ricardo Reis* alludes to a previous chapter in Camões's posthumous history as an icon serially appropriated as mascot for diverse political agendas: by the late 1870s, his statue had become a symbol of, and rallying point for, a Republican movement committed to democratization, secularization, and institutional reform. Such allusions are consistent with the novel's treatment of the national bard and his texts. *Ricardo Reis* never unequivocally co-opts either of these into the service of Saramago's ideology (although its focus on the persistence in the 1930s of the squalor that Eça and Verde decried points to the failure of the liberal Republican cause that they both espoused). Instead, the allusions draw attention to how many and diverse are the masters that Camões's image and words have served. Furthermore, they indicate how, instead of his images and words (and those of other, subsequently canonized writers) being co-opted, they might be cited not as accredited corroborators of a newly asserted image or argument, but rather as signifying systems in themselves, alive with potential meanings to be explored by the reader.

The potential consequences of *Ricardo Reis*'s evocation of Eça and Cesário's texts in particular are more fully illuminated by considering Jacques Rancière's essay on 'The Politics of Literature', and its definition of political discourse as

> a way of framing, among sensory data, a specific sphere of experience [...] a partition of the sensible, of the visible and sayable, which allows (or does not allow) some specific data to appear[.] (2010: 152)

By thus analysing politics in literary terms, Rancière shows how 'literature' is always political if it is conceived of as not simply a means of 'enabling words with the power of framing a common world' (2010: 155), but, additionally, as 'a specific regime of speaking whose effect is to upset any steady relationship between manners of speaking, manners of doing, and manners of being' (2010: 157). Discussing nineteenth-century French culture, Rancière credits an 'upset' in just such a 'steady relationship' to such writers as Gustave Flaubert and Charles Baudelaire. As Rui Miranda (2014) has argued, an analogous claim could be made, in the context of Portuguese culture, for Eça and Cesário, who both upset the 'old hierarchy' between 'high [and] low subject matters' (Rancière 2010: 156) with (amongst many other examples) their evocations of Camões's statue. The shock of the egalitarianism that is implied by such images may have been absorbed by a late twentieth-century western culture that admits of egalitarianism in principle, even if it fails to enact it. However, Saramago's frequently irreverent and incongruous quotation of others' writings, and his allusions to other writers' co-optation of their antecedents, create a fresh upset, flouting the rhetorical convention that canonized authors be invoked as household gods, and their works quoted as stable representations of established nostrums. Such obvious, and dubious, recontextualization has the effects of re-historicizing canonical writing, and of highlighting another radical impulse that Rancière attributes to such texts, namely the refutation of the 'connection between meaning and willing' (2010: 159). As Rancière argues,

> writing is not imposing one will on another, in the fashion of the orator, the priest or the general. It is displaying and deciphering the symptoms of a state of things, delving as the geologist does, into the seams and strata under the stage of the orators and the politicians. (2010: 161)

As Rui Miranda has suggested, it is to attempts such as Cesário's, in 'Sentimento', to '[buscar] e [conseguir] a perfeição das cousas!' [seek and attain the perfection of things] (Verde 1988: 155; trans. 2011: 33) through poetry that Rancière refers when he argues that literature enacts 'a kind of side-politics or meta-politics', when it reveals everyday, real 'social situations and characters' as 'a phantasmagoric fabric of poetic signs, which are historical symptoms as well' (2010: 163). When such literary 'dialectical images' task the reader with simultaneous semiotic and hermeneutic analysis, so as to illuminate the relationships between the powerful and the dispossessed, between labour and luxury goods, between past, present, and future, then political animation can replace mere political indoctrination.

Notwithstanding all this, it is hard to read *Ricardo Reis* without discerning, in its leitmotifs of rain, blindness, the labyrinth, and death, the melancholia of a postmodern distrust of all thought systems and all representations of reality. Yet the novel's account of Salazarism's cooption of literature and history stresses that simple resignation to the inadequacy of all ideologies ultimately risks surrender to tyranny exercised in the name of one, dominant, ideology. While only deconstructionist readings may avoid epistemological illegitimacy, pure deconstruction, sadly, remains ethically and politically insufficient, in a polity where ideologically loaded *reconstruction* is always, and inevitably, being undertaken. *Ricardo Reis* therefore provides space for Saramago, as 'orator and militant' (Rancière 2010: 163), to appropriate Pessoa's literary project, stressing the socio-economic contingency of subjective multiplicity and reinvention, and indicating ways in which these processes could contribute to a progressive politics. But the resulting vindication of a materialist socialism is presented neither as 'truth', nor as the 'true message' of Pessoa's work, but as the spoils of a self-evident literary theft.

II — Against Self-abstraction: A Materialist Appropriation of Pessoa

Pessoa's distinction in the canon of international modernism relates to his unique strategy of exploring the complexities of being-in-the-World in texts that he ascribed to dozens of alternative literary identities.[18] These 'heteronyms' were far more than mere pseudonyms. As Klobucka and Sabine summarize, they were

> fully developed *dramatis personae* who wrote poetry (and, to a lesser extent, prose) in their own highly distinctive styles [...]. The principal figures in what Pessoa called his *drama em gente* (drama in people) — Alberto Caeiro, Álvaro de Campos, and Ricardo Reis — were conceived as autonomous authors not just by virtue of the intrinsic distinctiveness of their writings: they were realized textually as existentially independent individuals, with biographic trajectories and interpersonal relationships of their own. (2007: 3–4)[19]

The acclamation of Pessoa's output, by luminaries as diverse as Giorgio Agamben, Octavio Paz, George Steiner, and Alain Badiou, as ranking among the defining artistic works of the twentieth century stems from a recognition of how this project of authorial multiplication and impersonation, or 'fingimento' ('feigning' or 'faking'), enabled Pessoa not only to engage with the aesthetic and philosophical dilemmas associated with the modernism(s) of his lifetime, but also to anticipate many of the key debates subsumed under the label of postmodernist thought.[20] Problematization of the concept of the unitary and sovereign human subject — initiated in Pessoa's youth in the new discourse of psychoanalysis — is of course foundational to the architecture of Pessoa's project. Pessoa was indeed among the tiny handful in Portugal reading Freud before the 1940s.[21] However, his radical dissolution and pluralization of subjectivity is much more consistent with post-Lacanian theories of language as the matrix of consciousness and identity, and explores many of the epistemological, existential, ethical, and political dilemmas that such theories imply.[22] José Gil, amongst others, has found in Pessoa a vision of identity, consciousness, and desire freed from the constraints of a coherent subjectivity, and likened this to Deleuze and Guattari's riposte to Lacan's conception of a universal, socializing, symbolic Law that is both inscribed in, and enforced by, language.[23] Other critics have compared Pessoa's conception of being — as a mercurial and linguistically constituted *fingimento* — to Judith Butler's notion of the 'performance' of gender and of other fields of identity.[24] The transformation — and global expansion — of critical discussion of Pessoa's work has derived in similar measure from its apparent anticipation of Jacques Derrida's assertion of the arbitrary, and only indirectly referential, nature of language, where meaning is constructed — but never fixed — by *différance* (Derrida 1982). Derrida's basic observation that lexical meaning is established by differentiation from other terms, yet ever vulnerable to deconstruction through the spectral presence of contradictory, 'deferred' connotations, and the anxiety arising from this observation, are expressed in many texts, and particularly in the *Livro do Desassossego*.[25] Pessoa's justly famous poem 'Autopsicografia' encapsulates the ideas of deferred meaning in language, when a writer does not 'express him/herself', but is inevitably a 'fingidor' [faker], who

> [...]
> Finge tão completamente
> Que chega a fingir que é dor
> A dor que deveras sente
>
> [[...] so good at his act
> He even fakes the pain
> Of pain he feels in fact.]
> (Pessoa 2006b: 241; trans. 2008: p. 247).

The readers' role in this process is, with equal inevitability, creative, feeling, in the 'pain' of which they read

> Não as duas que ele teve,
> Mas só a que eles não têm
>
> [Neither of the pains he has
> But just the one they don't.]
> (ibid.; trans. ibid.)

Saramago's novel thus resurrects what is, in Roland Barthes's terms, perhaps the most comprehensively 'dead' (and indeed suicidal) author in the Western canon. This strategy reflects the irony that 'the saturation of Portuguese and Lusophone cultural space with Pessoa-related discourse' (Klobucka and Sabine 2007: 4) in the 1980s had seen much of the critical exegesis focus on authorial intention. Refusing to bury the poet's corpse, such criticism instead pummelled it for definitive ethical, aesthetic, and ideological declarations, not infrequently also manipulating it as a political or cultural mascot. Such practices might seem misconceived when dealing with a poet whose texts frequently evoke a desire for a hermetic existence, freed from the constraints of the individual body and from interaction with the social mass. In the *Livro do Desassossego* particularly, Pessoa presents self-abstraction through writing, and the 'heteronymous' literary fabrication of emotion and identity, not just as a repudiation of fixed subjectivity, but also as an (imperfect, provisional) solution to a crisis of being-in-the-World.[26] The focus on authorial intention becomes more politically contentious, however, in the case of *Mensagem*, whose meditation on nationalist mythology is more critical and multi-layered than the *Estado Novo* cared to admit, or of Pessoa's less well-known, unswervingly elitist and individualist political writings.[27] *Ricardo Reis*, while acknowledging the ubiquitous possibility (or even the philosophical imperative) of deconstruction, nevertheless addresses the material reality of the textual effect and affect — pain — acknowledged in 'Autopsicografia'.

Saramago declared on several occasions that, having encountered Ricardo Reis's *odes* in his youth while unaware of Pessoa's authorship, he had simultaneously admired their limpid discipline yet been offended by the poet's disdain both for the social world, and for others' suffering.[28] In the confrontations that *Ricardo Reis* engineers between Reis and his texts, and the political and social contexts of the mid-1930s, Reis's philosophical stance is exposed as both morally questionable and physically unsustainable. Reis's cultivated indifference to others' suffering, and his pursuit of self-reliance, lead only to irrepressible feelings of loneliness and uselessness once he is possessed of a sentient, interactive body. Saramago presents this body not in the neo-Platonic or Augustinian conception of a mediator between the Self and the world, but rather as the Self *per se*. This presumption of the corporeal and material generation of human experience and consciousness underpins Saramago's incorporation of key elements of Pessoa's thought into the political philosophy of his fiction. The same presumption is the basis of *Ricardo Reis*'s suggestion that, in his attempts at self-abstraction, Reis falls short of Pessoa's own standards of authenticity.

When assessing Saramago's re-imagining of Reis, a useful point of reference and comparison is the description of the heteronym's philosophy of 'epicurismo triste' in an untitled text that Pessoa ascribed to Reis's brother, the literary critic Frederico Reis (2003: 280–81). According to Frederico,

> [c]ada qual de nós — opina o Poeta — deve viver a sua própria vida, isolando-se dos outros e procurando apenas, dentro de uma sobriedade individualista, o que lhe agrada e lhe apraz.

> [Each of us (contends the Poet) should live his own life, isolating himself from others and seeking, in an attitude of sober individualism, only what pleases and delights him.] (Pessoa 2003: 280; trans. 2001: 56)

Reis's modus vivendi does not suspend, transcend, or transform the experience of everyday phenomena through recourse to 'prazeres violentos' [violent pleasures] — as does, for example, the 'Sensacionismo' of Álvaro de Campos — nor does it 'fugir às sensações dolorosas que não sejam extremas' [flee from moderately painful sensations] (ibid.; trans. ibid.). Rather, Epicurean pleasure is tempered with a Stoic acceptance of the inevitable imperfections and frustrations of modern life. Reis advocates minimizing sadness by minimizing involvement, activity and responsibility, 'abstendo-se do esforço e da actividade útil' [abstaining from effort and useful activity] (ibid.). As Frederico explains, Reis's project is not a transcendental one:

> esta doutrina, dá-lo o poeta por temporária. É enquanto os bárbaros (os cristãos) dominam que a atitude dos pagãos deve ser esta. Uma vez desaparecido (se desaparecer) o império dos bárbaros, a atitude pode então ser outra. Por ora não pode ser senão esta.

> [the poet adheres to this as a temporary doctrine, as the right attitude for pagans as long as the barbarians (the Christians) reign supreme. If and when the barbarian empire crumbles, then this attitude may change, but for now it's the only one possible.] (ibid.; trans. Pessoa 2001: 56–57)

The conception of the world to which Frederico alludes is essentially a pagan one that 'se apoia num fenómeno psicológico interessante: numa crença real e verdadeira nos deuses da Grécia antiga, admitindo Cristo [...] como um deus a mais, mas mais nada' [is based on an interesting psychological phenomenon: a true and real belief in the gods of ancient Greece, with Christ [...] being admitted as one more god, but not more than that] (ibid.) (Pessoa 2003: 281; trans. Pessoa 2001: 57); Saramago's novel does not engage deeply with this phenomenon. The only significant reference in Saramago's text to Reis's pagan vision of the world is Reis's claim, in conversation with Pessoa, that 'Eu só aproveitei deles [os deuses] um resto, as palavras que os diziam' [I only made use of a trace of them, no more than the words that denoted them] (*Ricardo Reis*: 281). Reis's writing, then, features within this 'sad epicureanism' as something 'profundamente triste [...] um esforço lúcido e disciplinado para obter uma calma qualquer' [profoundly sad [...] a lucid and disciplined effort to obtain a measure of calm] (Pessoa 2003: 281; trans. Pessoa 2001: 57). Reis does not, in his verse, attempt to translate or communicate experiences or sentiments to a third party who might read his work: the futility of such attempts is, after all, demonstrated by the afore-mentioned 'Autopsicografia'.[29] Nor, according to a short preface seemingly written for a projected edition of Reis's odes, does Reis attempt to proselytize the pagan *Weltanschauung* in a Christianized world.[30] However, Frederico's text indicates that for Ricardo, writing assumes a therapeutic purpose, suspending a chaotic and imperfect reality, tragic to comprehend, in a crystalline and static image that can, by contrast, be contemplated without sorrow, and — by extension — that can console the poet by also suspending both his implication in the 'real' world, and the irruption within him of unruly appetites and identities.

Saramago's take on Reis questions not only his philosophy's moral and practical consistency, but also, whether or not the use of writing to pursue 'uma calma qualquer' [a measure of calm] has any existential (let alone ethical) value. Saramago suggests a 'real' human's inability to measure up against Reis's encomia to asceticism (and, indeed, an author's vulnerability to hostile recontextualization of his words) by setting up the doctor-poet's existence in Lisbon as an absurd parody of the scenario in the famous ode commencing 'Vem sentar-te comigo, Lídia, à beira do rio', wherein the poet proposes to the classical nymph:

> Vem sentar-te comigo Lídia, à beira do rio.
> Sossegadamente fitemos o seu curso e aprendamos
> Que a vida passa, e não estamos de mãos enlaçadas.
> (Enlacemos as mãos.)
>
> Depois pensemos, crianças adultas, que a vida
> Passa e não fica, nada deixa e nunca regressa,
> Vai para um mar muito longe, para ao pé do Fado,
> Mais longe que os deuses.
>
> Desenlacemos as mãos, porque não vale a pena cansarmo-nos.
> Quer gozemos, quer não gozemos, passamos como o rio.
> Mais vale saber passar silenciosamente
> E sem desassossegos grandes.
>
> [...]
>
> [Come and sit down with me, Lydia, on the bank of the river.
> Quietly let us watch it flowing and learn
> That life is passing, and we are not holding hands.
> (Let us hold hands.)
>
> Then let us think, as grown-up children, that life
> Passes and does not stay, nothing stops or ever turns back,
> It goes towards a sea very far away, towards where Fate is,
> Further away than the gods.

> Let us stop holding hands, for it is not worth tiring ourselves.
> Whether we enjoy it or not, we pass with the river.
> Better to know how to pass silently
> And without great disquiet.]
> (Pessoa 2007: 49; trans. by K. Bosley, in Pessoa 1995: 65)

Despite having made his way from the *Highland Brigade* straight to the Hotel Bragança, and insisted upon a room with a river view (*Ricardo Reis*: 19), Reis finds his 'calma qualquer' invaded by the political, economic, and sexual realities of his circumstances. Early in his stay, his contemplation of the river from Lisbon's Praça do Comércio is interrupted by the attentions of a passing police officer (*Ricardo Reis*: 115). This and Reis's subsequent surveillance by the malodorous PVDE agent Víctor (*Ricardo Reis*: 192–93 & *passim*) remind of the very material loss of freedom and 'calma' that was often the *Estado Novo*'s reward for independent thinking. Back at the Hotel, Reis discovers himself to be inherently ill-suited to asceticism, swiftly abandoning river views in favour of vigorous sex as soon as such is offered him by Lídia, the chambermaid. By day, committed to achieving contentment in the 'espectáculo do mundo', Reis passes hours in mostly aimless wandering or *flânerie* of the shabby streets, in idling over solitary meals in cheap *casas de pasto*, and staring out of his apartment window at the rain. Transferred from the riverbank of Arcadia to that of 1930s Lisbon, Reis has swapped an existence 'sem desassossegos grandes' for one more resembling that of the *Livro do Desassossego*'s Bernardo Soares, or of Pessoa 'ele-mesmo' in his more disconsolate mode. However, in contrast to Soares — whose *Livro* recalls the banality of rain-lashed cityscapes as a spur to intervals of self-abstraction and insight — Reis remains besieged by the surrounding ugliness of squalor, poverty, and human suffering.

The other 'gentle pleasure' that Reis allows himself is reading the newspaper daily: this is the key device by which Saramago integrates a detailed review of contemporary politics into his plot. Hereby, Reis not only accepts the flagrantly falsified image of the world offered by a press subordinated to Salazar. While justifying his reading as a 'questão de me pôr em dia com a pátria' [question of getting up to date with the life of the nation] (*Ricardo Reis*: 28), Reis consistently relies on the newspapers and their 'falar do mundo geral' [talk of the wider world] to serve 'de barreira contra este mundo próximo e sitiante' [as a barrier against this other, closer, and besieging world] (*Ricardo Reis*: 52), a barrier behind which he may hide in placid detachment. In a climactic scene of biting irony, however, it is this very 'barreira' that will force Reis to observe how writing (including his own writing, once it achieves a readership) is never simply a hermetically sealed refuge from the world, but is always capable of projecting images — and political and ethical ideas often unintended by the author — back into that world. An arresting instance of life colliding with the art through which Reis asserts his philosophy is provided by reports of the destruction of Addis Ababa by Badoglio's troops. Reading these, Reis involuntarily recalls lines from his longest — and perhaps most celebrated — ode, wherein a Persian city is sacked and its inhabitants massacred, while two chess players comply with Reis's 'sadly Epicurean' stance by calmly continuing their game:

> Ouvi dizer que outrora, quando a Pérsia
> Tinha não sei qual guerra,
> Quando a invasão ardia na Cidade
> E as mulheres gritavam,
> Dois jogadores de xadrez jogavam
> O seu jogo contínuo.
> [...]
>
> [I've heard that once, during I don't know
> What war of Persia,
> When invaders rampaged through the City
> And the women screamed,
> Two chess players kept on playing
> Their endless game.]
> (Pessoa 2007: 88; trans. Pessoa 2006a: 97)

Ensconced 'perto da cidade, | E longe do seu ruído' [Close to the city | And far from its clamor] (Pessoa 2007: 89; trans. 2006a: 97), the chess players will face death with resignation if it comes for them, but 'Inda que nas mensagens do ermo vento | Lhes viessem os gritos | [...] Inda que [...] | Uma sombra ligeira | Lhes passasse na fronte alheada e vaga' [Even if, in the bleak wind's messages, | They heard the screams | [...] Even if [...] | A fleeting shadow | Passed over their hazy, oblivious brows], they will neither stir to assist the 'mulheres | E as tenras filhas violadas [...] | Nessa vitória próxima' [women | And their tender daughters [...] raped | In the nearby victory] (2007: 89; trans. 2006a: 98 (adapted)). Nor will they allow an emotional response to disrupt their focus on the game:

> Ardiam casas, saqueadas eram
> As arcas e as paredes,
> Violadas, as mulheres eram postas
> Contra os muros caídos,
> Trespassadas de lanças, as crianças
> Eram sangue nas ruas...
> Mas onde estavam, perto da cidade,
> E longe do seu ruído,
> Os jogadores de xadrez jogavam
> O jogo de xadrez.
>
> [Houses were burning, walls were torn down
> And coffers plundered;
> Women were raped and propped against
> The crumbling walls;
> Children, pierced by spears, were so much
> Blood in the streets...
> But the two chess players stayed where they were,
> Close to the city
> And far from its clamor, and kept on playing
> Their game of chess.]
> (2007: 88–89; trans. 2006: 97)

It is noteworthy, first, how Saramago's narrative runs from the newspaper's account of the Abyssinian capital's fall directly into a quotation from this stanza of the ode:

> Addis-Abeba está em chamas, as ruas cobertas de mortos, os salteadores arrombam as casas, violam, saqueiam, degolam mulheres e crianças, enquanto as tropas de Badoglio se aproximam, Addis-Abeba está em chamas, ardiam casas, saqueadas eram as arcas e as paredes, violadas as mulheres eram postas contra os muros caídos, trespassadas de lanças, as crianças eram sangue nas ruas. Uma sombra passa na fronte alheada e imprecisa de Ricardo Reis, que é isto, donde veio a intromissão, o jornal apenas me informa que Addis-Abeba está em chamas, que os salteadores estão pilhando, violando, degolando, enquanto as tropas de Badoglio se aproximam. (*Ricardo Reis*: 301)

> [Addis Ababa is in flames, the streets strewn with corpses, the bandits smash their way into the houses, rape, loot, slit the throats of women and children, while Badoglio's troops approach, Addis Ababa is in flames, houses were burning, walls were torn down and coffers plundered, women were raped and propped against the crumbling walls, children, pierced by spears, were so much blood in the streets. A shadow passes over Ricardo Reis's abstracted and uncertain brow, what's this, from where did this intervention come, the newspaper merely tells me that Addis Ababa is in flames, that bandits are looting, raping, slitting throats as Badoglio's troops approach.]

This juxtaposition re-contextualizes the images of the chessboard and of the game played thereupon so as to question the nobility of surrendering responsibility to Fate. Quoting Reis's lines 'Quando o rei de marfim está em perigo | Que importa a carne e o osso | Das irmãs e das mães e das crianças?' [When the ivory king's in danger, who cares | About the flesh and bone | Of sisters and mothers and little children?] (2007: 89; 2006: 98 (adapted)), Saramago likens the chess players of the ode to Mussolini and the British Foreign Secretary, Anthony Eden, whose appeasement of Italian expansionism sacrifices the Ethiopian people (an estimated one million of whom fell victim to Badoglio's bombardments and mustard gas attacks) like pawns so as to keep the 'ivory king' of British East Africa out of danger.[31] The lesson here — that neither any game of chess, nor any literary act, takes place in a political or economic vacuum — is not directed solely at Ricardo Reis, who callously recovers his composure after the shock of mistaking what he has read for the text of his own ode. Rather, this scene brings home for the novel's reader the processes by which, both intentionally and otherwise, the meanings of Pessoa's now canonized texts have been repeatedly transformed by new, often highly politicized, contexts and associations.

For Reis, meanwhile, the re-contextualization of 'Ouvi dizer que outrora' entails a further irony, since it is at this juncture in the novel that his 'harmless pleasures' have resulted in the bonding of his own 'flesh and bone' with those of Lídia. The impending birth of a son that he refuses to acknowledge, followed by the 'spectacle' of Daniel's death on the river and Lídia's grief, brings to a head Reis's mounting crisis of identity and purpose, which can no longer be attenuated even in the purely literary expression of 'sad Epicureanism'. While Reis steadfastly refuses commitment to Lídia or anyone else, he increasingly finds it impossible to disregard either the irruptions of his corporeality, or his material interactions with his new habitat or fellow inhabitants. Reis's situation comes to resemble that of which Pessoa complains in 'Chove. Que fiz eu da vida?' [It's raining. What have I made of my life?]: 'Entre ódios pequenos | De mim, 'stou em mim dividido | Se ao menos chovesse menos!' [Amid petty hatreds | Of myself, I am separated from myself. | If only it would at least rain less!] (Pessoa 2006b: 246).

As will be explored below, Saramago's intricate allusions to a wide range of Pessoa's texts serve to present Reis's timid response to this dilemma as not just an abdication of civic responsibility (such as would scarcely have dismayed Pessoa), but equally as a lapse into existential and literary inauthenticity. Reis's anxiety about his identity manifests itself immediately on disembarkation in a city where, as in Álvaro de Campos's 'Lisbon Revisited (1926)', the poet questions whether it was he who was there 'em outros tempos, tão distantes' [in another, so distant, time], or alternatively 'alguém por mim, talvez com igual rosto e nome, mas outro' [someone on my behalf, perhaps with the same face and name, but someone other] (*Ricardo Reis*: 34).[32] Taunted by the undead Pessoa for leaving Brazil just as it was convulsed by the Prestes uprising and subsequent army reprisals, Reis protests that '[t]alvez que eu tenha voltado a Portugal para saber quem sou' [perhaps I've returned to Portugal to discover who I am] (*Ricardo Reis*: 119). Pessoa's mocking response articulates the accusation of a cowardly shirking of civic responsibility with observations on the facile and deceptive nature of Reis's claim. At this point, he has already ridiculed Reis for the gulf separating the identity represented in his *odes* from the reality of his existence in Lisbon:

> caríssimo Reis, vejo-o aí a ler um romance policial, com uma botija aos pés, à espera duma criada que lhe venha aquecer o resto [...] e quer que eu acredite que esse homem é aquele mesmo que escreveu Sereno e vendo a vida à distância a que está, é caso para perguntar-lhe onde é que estava quando viu a vida a essa distância (*Ricardo Reis*: 118)

> [my dear Reis, I see you there, reading a detective novel, with a hot water bottle at your feet, waiting for a chambermaid to come and warm up the rest of you [...] and you expect me to believe that the man in front of me is the very same who wrote Serene and watching life in the distance whereat it lies, it does beg the question of where you were when you watched life at that distance]

To Pessoa, the serious issue here is not the banality of Reis's real-life existence, but the fact that, whereas 'eu apenas fingi' [I merely faked] — faking, that is, rather than communicating, feeling in poetic language, as 'Autopsicografia' explores — Reis 'finge-se, é fingimento de si mesmo, e isso já nada tem que ver com o homem e com o poeta [...] você nem sabe quem seja' [faked yourself, you are a forgery of your own self, and that has nothing to do with the difference between the poet and the man [...] you don't know who you are] (*Ricardo Reis*: 118–19). If Pessoa's poetry insinuates the status of writing as an autonomous realm, wherein feelings and personalities may be fabricated so as to explore existential dilemmas and phenomenological uncertainty, Reis's odes, insofar as they assuredly extol a harmless *ars vitae* that their author does not, and cannot, live, are either pure fantasy, or represent a contemptibly smug false consciousness.

Reis's absurdly flattering literary self-portraits are, however, but the most overt instance of his reluctance to take full account of who he is. The novel's early chapters repeatedly depict Reis catching sight of his reflection in a mirror (*Ricardo Reis*: 27; 50; 52–53; 105; 132), the site in which — according to the psychoanalyst Jacques Lacan's (2010) seminal theory — the individual's false consciousness as a coherent unitary subject is created in infancy. Reis increasingly shares the narrator's insight into the mirror's deception (o espelho [...] está protegido contra o homem, diante dele não somos mais que estarmos, ou termos estado' [the mirror [...] is protected against man, before it we are no more than what we currently are, or have been] (*Ricardo Reis*: 52)). Yet he repeatedly proves unwilling to acknowledge either the face that it reflects — 'desviou os olhos, muda de lugar' [he has averted his gaze, he changes position] (*Ricardo Reis*: 53) — or the answers that the mirror implies to the question of who he is. Later in the novel, the trope of the mirror returns to emphasize Reis's failure to discover — or rather, to acknowledge — who and what he is when, while shaving in his bathroom, he is disturbed by an unrecognizable face confronting him in the mirror:

> Ricardo Reis olha-se perplexo, um tanto intrigado, inquieto, como se temesse que dali lhe pudesse vir algum mal. Observa minuciosamente o que o espelho lhe mostra, tenta descobrir as parecenças deste rosto com um outro rosto que terá deixado de ver há muito tempo [...] é como se tivesse passado muitos anos sem se olhar, num lugar sem espelhos, sequer os olhos de alguém, e hoje vê-se e não se reconhece. (*Ricardo Reis*: 345)
>
> [Ricardo Reis regards himself, puzzled, quite intrigued, uncomfortable, as if he feared that some harm might befall him here. He scrutinizes in great depth what the mirror shows him, attempting to uncover the similarities between this face and another face that he has perhaps not seen for a long time [...] it is as if he has passed many years without having regarded himself, in a place with no mirrors, only others' eyes, and today he sees, and does not recognize, himself.]

The great irony of Reis's failure to recognize himself is that the beginnings of an answer to his question are provided by one of Reis's best-known odes, 'Vivem em nós inúmeros'. In the first of a series of prominent allusions to this ode, Saramago's narrative voice notes that it is dated 13 November 1935, only a month and a half before Reis's arrival in Lisbon.[33] The ode's opening stanza is recalled by Reis as he unpacks in the Hotel Bragança:

> Vivem em nós inúmeros, se penso ou sinto, ignoro quem é que pensa ou sente, sou somente o lugar onde se pensa e sente, e, não acabando aqui, é como se acabasse, uma vez que para além de pensar e sentir não há mais nada. Se somente isto sou, pensa Ricardo Reis depois de ler, quem estará pensando agora o que eu penso, ou penso que estou pensando no lugar que sou de pensar, quem estará sentindo o que sinto, ou sinto que estou sentindo no lugar que sou de sentir, quem se serve de mim para sentir e pensar, e de quantos inúmeros que em mim vivem, eu sou qual, quem, Quain, que pensamentos e sensações serão os que não partilho por só me pertencerem, quem sou eu que outros não sejam ou tenham sido ou venham a ser. (*Ricardo Reis*: 24)
>
> [Innumerable people live within us, if I think or feel, I know not who is thinking or feeling, I am but the place where things are thought and felt, and, while not ending there, it is as though it has ended, since beyond thinking and

feeling there is nothing. If I am no more than this, Ricardo Reis thinks after having finished reading, who might now be thinking what I think, or do I think what I'm thinking in the thinking-place that is me, who might be feeling what I feel, or do I feel what I'm feeling in the feeling-place that is me, who is using me in order to feel and think, and among those innumerable people who live within me, which am I, who, *quem*, Quain, what thoughts and feelings might there be that I don't share because they belong to me alone, who am I that others are not, nor have been nor will come to be.]

Two aspects of this passage are especially noteworthy. First, the way that the reader is alerted to the fact that Reis's ode is not quoted in full ('não acabando aqui, é como se acabasse'). The second and final stanzas are thus a pregnant absence in the text:

> Tenho mais almas que uma.
> Há mais eus do que eu mesmo.
> Existo todavia
> Indiferente a todos.
> Faço-os calar: eu falo.
>
> Os impulsos cruzados
> Do que sinto ou não sinto
> Disputam em quem sou.
> Ignoro-os. Nada ditam
> A quem me sei: eu 'screvo.
>
> [I have more than just one soul.
> There are more I's than I myself.
> I exist, nevertheless,
> Indifferent to them all.
> I silence them: I speak.
>
> The crossing urges of what
> I feel or do not feel
> Struggle in who I am, but I
> Ignore them. They dictate nothing
> To the I I know. I write.]
>   (Pessoa 2007: 225; trans. Pessoa 1998: 137)

Secondly, it is important to note that the passage reveals how the conception of identity and consciousness that Saramago's Reis extrapolates from the lines of his ode takes up only one of two possible meanings of the sentence 'sou somente o lugar onde se pensa e sente'. While he characterizes the self as a hermetic forum for thought and sensation ('lugar que sou de pensar [e] [...] de sentir'), this line could equally well refer to identity and experience relating to the individual's situation in, and, hence, equation to, the social, historical, and discursive 'lugar onde se pensa e sente'. Saramago's Reis's interpretation of the stanza corresponds to his unwillingness to acknowledge that the surroundings that he wishes to be a mere spectacle or fiction are, in fact, implicating and exerting influence upon him: this is the unwillingness manifested when he uses the newspaper as a 'barreira' (*Ricardo Reis*, 52).[34] Using this newspaper barrier to split the world into two separate external *lugares* — 'o mundo geral' [the wider world] and 'este outro mundo próximo e sitiante' [this other, closer, and besieging world], Reis plays one off against the other, sheltering from the one that assails the 'lugar que sou de pensar' by receiving the news from 'aquele [mundo] de além' [that [world] beyond] as 'remotas e inconsequentes mensagens, em cuja eficácia não há muitos motivos para acreditar' [remote and inconsequential messages in whose utility there are but few reasons for believing] (ibid.). Reis's desire to abstract himself from a 'besieging' world is of course also evident in his attraction to sites of passage and impermanence: first the *Highland Brigade*, and then the Hotel Bragança, a 'lugar neutro, sem compromisso, de trânsito e vida suspensa' [neutral, non-committal place of transience and stilled life] (*Ricardo Reis*: 22). Even months after settling in his own nearby apartment, Reis hankers for the atmosphere of the Hotel and, according to the undead Pessoa, he 'anda a flutuar no meio do Atlântico, nem lá, nem cá' [keeps drifting in the mid-Atlantic, neither here, nor there] (*Ricardo Reis*: 361). As Pessoa also points out, '[é] esse o drama, meu caro Reis, ter de viver em algum lugar, compreender que não existe lugar que não seja lugar, que a vida não pode ser não vida' [that, my dear Reis, is the drama, the necessity of having to live somwhere, of understanding that there is nowhere that is not somewhere, that life cannot not be life] (*Ricardo Reis*: 154). And by the time that Reis comes to admit that 'a vida [...] está sempre perto' [life [...] is always close at hand] (*Ricardo Reis*: 183), it is clearer still that the Lisbon that he inhabits and the external life that surround him there are stimulating the emergence of a Reis, or Reises, different to the identity that his poetry affirms. Yet, reading the novel's allusions to Reis's awareness of 'mais eus do que eu mesmo', one notes his attempts to suppress irruptions of otherness within himself, aware no doubt that to admit such otherness means being called more frequently and insistently to live outside the odes' fantasy of non-situatedness. In particular, he spurns the otherness elicited by Lídia's emotional candour, generosity, and bold offer of companionship. One such 'outro eu' rears up when, a short while after they commence their affair, Reis returns to his hotel room to find Lídia has made his bed up with two pillows. Lying awake in bed longing for her appearance, he discerns the restlessness that she has inspired as being more than simply sexual:

> Deitou-se, apagou a luz, deixara ficar a segunda almofada, fechou os olhos com força, vem, sono, vem, mas o sono não vinha, na rua passou um eléctrico, talvez o último, quem será que não quer dormir em mim, o corpo inquieto, de quem, ou o que não sendo corpo com ele se inquieta, eu por inteiro, ou esta parte de mim que cresce, meu Deus, as coisas que podem acontecer a um homem. (*Ricardo Reis*: 99)

> [He lay down, switched off the light, leaving the second pillow where it was, closed his eyes firmly, come, sleep, come, but sleep would not come, a tram passed in the street, perhaps the last one, who might it be within me that does not wish to sleep, whose is this restless body, or who or what the incorporeal being that stirs with my body, all of me, or this part of me that's growing, dear God, the things that can happen to a man]

Here, Saramago's characteristically sly double-entendre — 'esta parte de mim que cresce' — heralds the emergence, concurrent with Reis's unsettling erection, of another consciousness or sensibility ('o que não sendo corpo com ele se inquieta'). As in both *Levantado* and *Memorial*, heterosexual erotic love that defies conventions of corporeal propriety and gendered behaviour, or transgresses class, racial and sexual hierarchies, becomes a catalyst for the transformation of consciousness and identity. Unusually amongst Saramago's male protagonists, however, Reis resists such a transformation. Opportunistically partaking of the body that Lídia offers him, he nevertheless repudiates both corporeal agency's impingement on his stance of non-engagement, and its impact on his subjectivity. When, later, Pessoa asks whether or not he loves Lídia, Reis betrays the distinction that he maintains between his 'self' and his body in his frigid response that '[a]té agora o corpo não se me negou' [so far my body has not denied me anything] (*Ricardo Reis*: 274).

Reis's infatuation with Marcenda is the one case in which he cedes emotionally to the desires elicited by another person. It turns out, however, to be the exception that proves the rule. When Marcenda visits his flat, Reis's flurry of deliberation about how he should interact with her is swiftly overridden by a determination to kiss her, precipitating an intense corporeal encounter where sensation, and the proximity of an Other, vanquish Reis's hermeticism and detachment (*Ricardo Reis*: 245–46). However, his desire for Marcenda is predicated on his recognition (or, more likely, misrecognition) of her as the Other whom he hopes will confirm his identity as that which is fixed in the *odes*. Her maidenhood, chaste passivity, and improbable air of frigidity recall the Lídia of the *odes* (as the undead Pessoa chides, 'essa impossível soma de passividade, silêncio sábio e puro espírito' [that impossible combination of passivity, sage reticence, and pure spirit] (*Ricardo Reis*: 118)) and equip her perfectly for the attitude of dispassionate companionship idealized in the *odes*. Meanwhile, her paralyzed arm, described by *Ricardo Reis*'s narrator as 'morte antecipada' [anticipated death] (*Ricardo Reis*: 168), precludes the clasping of hands that the poet eschews. Reis however repeatedly finds himself disinclined to let go of Marcenda's hand: first, when attempting a diagnosis of the cause of its paralysis (*Ricardo Reis*: 127), and again on the occasion of their final meeting ('[as] mãos de Ricardo Reis ainda apertam a mão de Marcenda' [Ricardo Reis's hands still clasp Marcenda's hand] (*Ricardo Reis*: 289).

Reis, as it transpires, would do well to heed the warning issued by the *Livro do Desassossego*'s Bernardo Soares, in his meditation on an ideal, sexless love:

> Se dentre as mulheres da terra eu vier um dia a colher esposa, que a tua prece por mim seja esta — que, de qualquer modo, ela esteja estéril. Mas pede também, se por mim rezares, que eu não venha nunca a obter essa esposa suposta. (Pessoa 2009: 324)

> [If from among the women of the Earth I should come one day to gather a wife, let your prayer for me be this: that, come what may, she be infertile. But ask further, if you should pray for me, that I may never come to obtain this imagined wife.]

Soares's insinuation is, of course, that the value of this ideal is that it sustains the fantasy of one's own ability to transcend the urgings of the body and the material world. When an apparently 'sterile' woman really turns up, Reis's inability to suppress libidinal drives and make himself sterile swiftly becomes manifest. It is significant that, in dramatizing Reis's discovery that he cannot match the asexuality that he fetishizes in others, Saramago plays on Soares's and Reis's common recourse to the time-honoured metaphor of Epicurean love as gathering roses, familiar to English speakers from the opening line of Robert Herrick's 'To the Virgins', 'Gather ye rose-buds while ye may' (1648: 93).[35] Soares's warning against the desire to *'colher* uma esposa' subtly intimates the folly not only of pursuing chaste Epicurean companionship, but equally of comparing either it, or its female object, to a flower. In Ricardo Reis's depiction of Reis's obsession with Marcenda, the floral imagery of Reis's *odes* is evoked in new and ironic contexts that reveal the contrasting aptness of flowers as symbols of the materiality, sexuality, interaction, and growth that Reis spurns. When Marcenda agrees to a tryst in his surgery, Reis deploys the imagery of the well-known ode 'A flor que és, não a que dás, eu quero' (I want the flower you are, not the one you give), and of 'Sábio é o que se contenta', to claim that he does not seek a physical relationship, and rather that

> Estamos a trocar vénias, ramalhetes de flores, é verdade que são bonitas, as flores, mas já vão cortadas, mortas, elas não o sabem e nós fingimos que não sabemos (*Ricardo Reis*: 291)
>
> [We are exchanging greetings [lit. 'bows'], posies of flowers, it is true that they're pretty, the flowers, but they're cut now, dead, they don't know this and we pretend that we don't know]

Reis's real 'pretence' here, however, is not to disregard that the flower 'that smiles today | Tomorrow will be dying' (Herrick 1648: 93), but to make believe in his own bodily disanimation, or suspension.[36] However, Reis's flowers, like his words, contain the seeds of more meanings than he can control. In reality, a flower's delightful scent, colour, and form all serve its purpose as the plant's sexual organ. Reis's words expose how, as a cod Epicurean, he fakes his ability to eschew lovemaking and gather rosebuds instead. Likewise, as a 'flower' himself, he struggles to control his seed:

> Ponho as minhas flores em água e fico a olhar para elas enquanto lhes durarem as cores, Não terá tempo de cansar os olhos, Agora estou a olhar para si, Não sou nenhuma flor, É um homem, sou capaz de perceber a diferença. (*Ricardo Reis*: 291)
>
> [I put my flowers in water and I sit looking at them for as long as the colours last, Then you won't have time for your eyes to get tired, Right now I'm looking at you, I am no flower, You're a man, I can tell the difference.]

Marcenda may or may not share Reis's desire for abstraction from the material world. The idea that she lacks the verve and fertility of a flower, and is averse to physical love, is however established by her name's connotation of wilting, and reinforced when she arrives for her first date with Reis walking between 'os canteiros sem flores' (*Ricardo Reis*: 183).[37] Either way, she breaks off relations after the two of them rub up against his manifest failure to match her real or illusory asexuality during the tryst in his surgery (*Ricardo Reis*: 291–92). As Marcenda is perhaps aware, Reis lacks the inclination of *Memorial*'s Baltasar to explore and learn from his lovers, or to become one half of an equal, cooperative, and revolutionary 'three-handed couple'.[38]

Reis's renewed dismay at the swelling in his loins, which mocks a self-image and ideals so ill-matched to body and environment, gains ironic power by being preceded by his experience of impotence during a visit from Lídia, significantly just after she has dropped a hint about steady relationships and marriage (*Ricardo Reis*: 285). Rather than simply offering comic relief, this episode illustrates afresh Reis's struggle against his internal Other(s), as if his flesh, driven by the other, suppressed 'parte de mim que cresce', finally rebels against his non-committal opportunism: 'era como se não lhe pertencesse, qual a qual, é ele meu, ou eu é que sou dele, e não procurava a resposta, perguntar já era angústia bastante' [it was as if it [he] didn't belong to him, which was the master, does it [he] belong to me, or do I belong to it [him], and he didn't seek the answer, asking in itself created anguish enough] (*Ricardo Reis*: 288). Reis, refusing the prompts to explore an 'other' self that is willing to join Lídia, instead collapses into the crisis described by Bernardo Soares on experiencing the impossibility of total abstraction from the social Other and the material world.[39] Unlike his fellow heteronym, however, Reis still resists the irruption of other selves — which for Soares can offer consolation — and clings to belief in himself as an embattled 'sad Epicurean': as he earlier wrote, '[e]xisto todavia | Indiferente a todos | Faço-os calar'.

As the undead Pessoa implies, one must question the value or use of Reis's poetry, if it offers neither truth nor lasting consolation, but only an illusion of the self that must trigger disillusion when it is reflected back into real existence. Pessoa complains that 'você afinal desilude-me, amador de criadas, cortejador de donzelas, estimava-o mais quando você via a vida à distância a que está' [you've turned out a disappointment to me, seducer of maids, flatterer of maidens, I had a higher regard for you when you contemplated life from the distance at which you find it] (ibid.), reiterating his earlier criticism that whereas 'eu apenas fingi' [I merely faked], Reis 'é fingimento de si mesmo' [is a forgery of his own self] (*Ricardo Reis*: 118–19). It is quite possible that despite Reis's intransigence relative to his surroundings, to Lídia, and to his silenced 'outros eus', Pessoa's earlier criticism hits home, since Reis apparently writes no poetry from their initial encounter until nearly five months later (*Ricardo Reis*: 331). Reis's odes meanwhile remain in a file locked away in a drawer, to be consulted only when he appears to read the lines of 'Ouvi que outrora...' interpolated into the accounts of Badoglio's bloody assault on Addis Ababa (*Ricardo Reis*: 302). Here, after rereading the ode's rhetorical query, 'que importa a carne e o osso das irmãs e das mães e das crianças' [of what consequence is the flesh and bone of sisters and mothers and children] (ibid.), Reis locks his poems away again and determines to maintain his stance of individualistic unconcern (*Ricardo Reis*: 302–03), a response that, as Frier argues, contrasts with that to 'news of such atrocities committed against priests and landowners [in Spain]', which exposes the anxiety underlying Reis's cultivated serenity 'once his own [class] interests are called into question' (2006: 47). Yet even when Reis next takes up his pen (*Ricardo Reis*: 331), Pessoa complains that 'já o tinha dito mil vezes' [you've already said it a thousand times] and Reis can only confess that '[n]ão tenho mais nada para dizer' [I have nothing more left to say] (*Ricardo Reis*: 332–33).

Meanwhile, the greater evidence for limitations of his ill-sustained philosophy is the loneliness of which Reis complains to Pessoa (*Ricardo Reis*: 227), which is also evoked by descriptions of Reis's chilly and echoing flat and the 'triste quarto' (sad bedroom) where he sleeps alone (*Ricardo Reis*: 222). Tragically, however, Reis comprehends neither Pessoa's diagnosis of the cause of his malaise, nor the implication it entails of the social purpose, shifting meaning, and political contexts both of literature and of its author:

> A solidão não é viver só, a solidão é não sermos capazes de fazer companhia a alguém ou a alguma coisa que está dentro de nós, a solidão não é uma árvore no meio duma planície onde só ela esteja, é a distância entre a seiva profunda e a casca, entre a folha e a raiz, [...] Deixemos a árvore, olhe para dentro de si e veja a solidão, Como disse o outro, solitário andar por entre a gente, Pior do que isso, solitário estar onde nem nós próprios estamos' (*Ricardo Reis*: 226–27)

> [Loneliness isn't living alone, loneliness is our not being able to keep company with someone or something which is inside us, loneliness isn't a tree in the middle of a deserted plain, it's the distance between the sap deep within and the bark, between the leaf and the root [...] Never mind the trees, look inside yourself and see the loneliness, As another [poet] put it, lonely wandering among other people, Worse than that, lonely being where even our own selves are not]

Here again, Reis dismisses the call to heed the unacknowledged 'outros eus' who 'disputam em que sou'. Misquoting Camões's description, in his sonnet, 'Amór é um fogo que arde sem se ver' [Love is a fire that burns unseen], of love as 'um andar solitário entre a gente' [a lonely walk amid other people] (Camões 1980: II, 83), Reis once again imagines himself as an exiled pagan forcibly turned *flâneur*; a visionary traversing a human crowd, from which he is distinguished by dint not simply of intellect but also, crucially, of *not* loving.[40] Pessoa's correction of this analogy — 'lonely being where even our own selves are not' — reiterates his challenge to Reis to forsake 'self-fakery', and examine the self — or selves — that he repudiates. At the same time, however, Saramago has his Pessoa raise doubts about the hermeticism of the search for 'alguém ou [...] alguma coisa dentro de nós' that is proposed in texts such as Pessoa's 'Notas para uma regra de vida', which advises the reader to 'aumentar a personalidade sem incluir nela nada alheio — nem pedindo aos outros, nem mandando nos outros, mas sendo outros quando outros são precisos' [augment your personality without including anything extraneous within it, neither asking anything of others, nor issuing orders to them, but being others when others are needed] (1990: I, 227).[41] The deceased Pessoa encourages the alternative 'life rule' of becoming other so as to reach out to other people, when he suggests a connection between loneliness and feelings of personal inutility:

> Pelo menos não me lembro de me ter sentido verdadeiramente útil, creio mesmo que é essa a primeira solidão, não nos sentirmos úteis, Ainda que os outros pensem ou nós os levemos a pensar o contrário, Os outros enganam-se muitas vezes, Também nós. (*Ricardo Reis*: 227)

> [At least, I can't remember having ever felt genuinely useful, I really think that that's the first type of loneliness, not feeling that we're useful, Even though other people might think — or we might induce them to think — to the contrary, Other people are often mistaken, So too are we.]

By thus positing the 'utility' of writing as an existential, as much as a purely ethical concern, Saramago drags 'his' Reis — but, by extension, Pessoa's whole literary project — into the heart of the novel's discussion of the politics of literature. Pessoa may not consider himself 'útil', and Reis may aspire to make poetry 'útil' only to himself, but just as Reis appropriates Camões's love lyric, so too António Ferro has appropriated his epic, and so too posterity will find new uses for the Pessoan canon. As the deceased poet wryly admits — mocking the critical studies that have missed Pessoa's work's point about literature as *fingimento* — 'não vai faltar quem dê de mim todas as explicações' [there'll be no shortage of people to provide every explanation of me] (*Ricardo Reis*: 119).

This reminder of the novel's wider critique of political appropriations of canonical literature, its authors, and their cultural capital adds urgency to Pessoa's question of how a writer might be 'useful', and further undermines Reis's literary pursuit of abstraction from the humanity that he disdains. The challenge to Reis to transcend a literary practice exposed as 'sub-Pessoan' wish-fulfilment is conveyed through further allusion to the statues of Camões and Adamastor, reactivating Saramago's tropes of blindness and petrification as metaphor for the author's inability to communicate or assert meaning through that which 'outlives' him, whether this be his own poetic creations (as in 'Autopsicografia') or metatextual intervention in the works of others. Pessoa's failing sight strikes Reis (who is himself already afflicted by poor vision (*Ricardo Reis*: 91)) as the most appalling aspect of his late friend's predicament: 'imagem de abandono, de última solidão, [...] a mais terrível das desgraças' [image of ruin, of the ultimate loneliness [...] the most dreadful of calamities] (*Ricardo Reis*: 228). At this juncture, Reis and Pessoa have been discussing the 'pobre criatura' [wretched creature] Adamastor, and, as Reis falls asleep he muses on Pessoa's presence in the room, motionless, expressionless, 'como uma estátua de olhos lisos' [like a statue with blank eyes] (ibid.), thus prompting the reader to reflect, in turn, on Reis's own impending fate.[42] Reis, whose literary objective is the achievement of 'uma calma qualquer' through the suspension of messy life into a decorous, dispassionate image, assumes the status of a kind of 'anti-Adamastor'. By refusing both Lídia's invitation to love, and Pessoa's suggestion that social utility might be the solution to loneliness, Reis eschews renewed animation; and, tiring of his futile existence as a morose Don Juan, he voluntarily embraces the oblivion revealed to him by a coterie of animated statues.

III — Philosophy and 'Usefulness': The Intellectual and the Emergence of a Revolutionary Community

The undead Pessoa's concession of the existential virtue of 'usefulness', of course, is the springboard for exploring the question of how writers, literature, and a literary process of becoming 'other' might be useful to a socialist politics, whether under a corporatist dictatorship, or neo-liberal late capitalism. Pessoa's use of writing to effect — or at least rehearse — his own abstraction from society may be fundamentally irreconcilable with such a concern. Saramago's novel nevertheless highlights the dubious political ramifications of this literary project. Ricardo Reis's reencounter with Lisbon evokes the projection of Pessoa's works into a polity that, through a combination of authoritarian coercion, rigid control of all mass media, and state incorporation of recreation and domestic labour, sought to fuse the population into the unthinking, and undifferentiated, incarnation of his Catholic and imperialist ideology. In such a context, Reis's crime and tragedy consist not only of his intellectual vanity and literary escapism, but moreover of indulging these even when presented with the evident critical acumen, compassion, and solidarity of his working-class mistress, Lídia. Consistently aggregating Lídia with what he considers an ignorant and passive, almost bovine, proletariat, Reis is consequently bemused by her deft political analysis and philosophical deductions. He fails to recognize how her defiance of the identity politics of Salazarism offers lessons not only for him, but also for the Communist Party for which her brother, Daniel, will sacrifice himself.

In all of this, Reis partakes of the same presumption of the bovine sub-rationality of a homogeneous 'plebe' that is exercised in Pessoa *ele-mesmo*'s writings, most picturesquely, and famously, so in the poem 'Ela canta, pobre ceifeira' [She sings, poor reaper].[43] In this reworking of Wordsworth's 'The Solitary Reaper', the poet, contemplating a farm labourer singing as she reaps in some timeless bucolic setting, compares her supposed blissful ignorance with his own existential anxiety, and laments

> Ah, poder ser tu, sendo eu!
> Ter a tua alegre inconsciência,
> E a consciência disso! Ó céu!
> Ó campo! Ó canção! A ciência
> Pesa tanto e a vida é tão breve!
>
> [Ah, to be you while being I!
> To have your glad unconsciousness
> And be conscious of it! O sky!
> O field! O song! Knowledge
> Is so heavy and life so brief!]
> (2006b: 172; trans. 2006a: 284)[44]

Reis's encounters with the working classes *en masse* and, more intimately, in the form of the extraordinary Lídia, contradict Pessoa's fond presumption of the 'alegre inconsciência' of the working classes, and demonstrate that individual freedom to observe Pessoa's self-fulfilling 'Regras de vida', or indulge in the 'jogo alado das teorias', has its material basis in social privilege. This privilege depends in turn upon the economic oppression of the same masses: people that Reis's *odes*, Pessoa's 'Regras de vida', and Soares's *Livro* often disregard, and that the Reis of Saramago's novel regards with fascinated disgust. Saramago's reinterpretation of Pessoa *ele-mesmo*'s use of rain as a symbol of existential despair, in poems such as 'Chove? Nenhuma chuva cai' [Is it raining? No rain is falling] (Pessoa 2006b: 77), effects a focus on how the deprivation suffered by a downtrodden populace, while palpably material, is equally a spiritual and intellectual one. Coming ashore in Lisbon, Reis witnesses a downpour assailing both the wretched 'passageir[os] da terceira classe' [passengers from Third Class] (*Ricardo Reis*: 14) returning home '[d]e ombros encurvados sob a chuva monótona' [with shoulders hunched under the monotonous rain] (*Ricardo Reis*: 13) and the porters, 'povo atrasado, de mão estendida, vende cada um o que tiver de sobejo, resignação, humildade, paciência' [backward people with outstretched hands, each one sells whatever he has to spare, resignation, humility, patience] (ibid.).⁴⁵ For both groups, who must remain 'indiferentes à grande molha' [indifferent to the great downpour] (ibid.), Stoicism is an economic necessity, and Pessoa's other existential philosophies but a remote aspiration. Later, Reis's first walk through the rain-swept city brings him to the 'nódoa parda, negra, de lodo mal cheiroso' [drab, black smear, (as) of foul-smelling mud] (*Ricardo Reis*: 70) of paupers awaiting the annual *bodo* [charity handout] of the pro-regime newspaper *O Século*. The most elderly and infirm are so despondent that 'dia de bodo é único em que se lhes não deseja a morte, por causa do prejuízo que seria [aos familiares]' [the day of the handout is the only one on which they don't long for death, on account of the loss that it would cause to their relatives] (ibid.). For these destitute souls, existentialist introspection could be fatal: '[s]e volta a chover, apanham-na toda, daqui ninguém arreda' [if the rain returns, they will suffer its worst, none will escape it] (ibid.).

As in *Memorial*, even the attempted celebration of Carnival week is confounded; here, by 'inundações que são as piores desde há quarenta anos' [floods that are the worst in forty years] (*Ricardo Reis*: 158). Once again, Carnival, rather than offering even temporary relief or redemption from the misery of the poor, exposes the physical, moral, and psycho-sexual debilitation and perversion engendered by an exploitative and hierarchical socio-economic order. The spectacle of the dreary state-regulated Carnival parades prompts an ironic echo of the concept of 'epicurismo triste', when the crowd's 'entusiasmo triste' [sad enthusiasm] (*Ricardo Reis*: 159) so depresses Reis that he suffers an attack of nausea (*Ricardo Reis*: 160). Description of the subsequent drunken revelry focuses on dysphoric images of the body, and on perverse, threatening, or humiliating pranks. Herein, Salazarism's oppressive and infantilizing deployment of the patriarchal family as standard building block and moral guarantee of a corporatist state is rendered grotesque, when a man in a nurse's dress and false breasts aggressively asserts his virility with obscene gestures, while another, dressed as an infant in a pram, drinks himself senseless with grog from a baby's bottle (*Ricardo Reis*: 160). The status of the *povo* as underdog is not temporarily overturned by Carnival, but rather confirmed, when a man walks by with the label 'Vende-se este animal' [this animal for sale] pinned to his back (*Ricardo Reis*: 161). As in *Memorial*, such images correlate to instances of bodily impairment that emphasize how the psychological violence and physical exploitation of elitist corporatism corrupt physically. While, for example, hotel porter Pimenta's crooked posture may have developed through years of 'esperando deferente e minucioso' [waiting, deferential and attentive] for clients, or may result from 'a continuação dos carregos' [the long execution of his duties] (*Ricardo Reis*: 45), either way, the root cause is his socio-economic subjugation. Elsewhere, while the cause of Marcenda's paralysis is never reliably ascertained, Marcenda's own conviction that it was a response to the death of her mother in December 1931 associates her disability with the constraints re-imposed on women by Salazarism, and with its cooption of women's energies, and of virtues traditionally considered 'feminine'.⁴⁶

Following these isolated examples of the socio-economic roots of physical and intellectual degeneracy, Reis's trip to the allegedly miraculous shrine at Fátima confronts him with the direst proof of how Salazarism seeks to dissemble these roots, and to manipulate the afflicted. Reis's medically trained gaze takes in a panoply of disabilities and chronic illnesses for which Church and State alike prescribe little more than obedience and supplication for divine intervention (*Ricardo Reis*: 308–18). The philosophies of the Pessoan coterie, with their various individualist and hermetic underpinnings, offer no substantive critique of the prevailing social and political systems, nor any recognition of their material foundations. Concerned only with identifying the conditions in which a 'neo-pagan' 'escol' or 'nata' could float on top of this undifferentiated human mass, Pessoa's political treatises also fail to interrogate how a disinclination to independent agency, and a lumpen devotion to Catholicism, are inculcated by Salazarism's increasingly pervasive monitoring and manipulation of popular culture and everyday activity. Salazar's determination to make the Portuguese 'live by habit'[47] was achieved not simply by pride in the imperialist and crusading past, obedience to Salazar as prudent father, and faith in the Virgin Mary as miracle-working, Communism-fighting mother, that are respectively propagated at Camões's statue, in Tomé Vieira's *Conspiração*, and at Fátima. In a manner inimical to Pessoa's conception of individual self-realization, the regime simultaneously exercised what Kimberley da Costa Holton terms a 'dialectical manoeuvring between fragmentation and unification' of the social mass, which dismembered autonomous organs of citizenship (political parties and trades unions, for example) (2005: 30) while constituting bodies such as the *Fundação Nacional para a Alegria no Trabalho* (FNAT), founded in 1935, and the more militaristic *Mocidade Portuguesa*, founded the following year, to corral the population during hours of leisure and co-opt its energies for the edification of the corporatist state.

The dehumanizing logic of the *Estado Novo*'s conception of the nation as a rigidly disciplined body, subservient to the head of state and his 'elite', is revealed when a Hitler Youth delegation visits an exhibition commemorating the tenth anniversary of Carmona's 1926 'National Revolution', and inscribes the slogan 'Nós não somos nada' [we are nothing] in the visitor's book. This gesture is lauded by a 'plumitivo de serviço' [servile scribbler] of the Salazarist press for its affirmation of how 'o povo nada vale se não for orientado por uma elite, ou nata, ou flor, ou escol' [the people will count for nothing if not guided by an elite, or cream, or flower, or chosen few] (*Ricardo Reis*: 363).[48] Yet while this explanation neatly paraphrases Pessoa's own assertion, published a decade earlier, that '[uma] nação vale o que vale o seu escol' [a nation is worth what its elite is worth], it now serves to justify the establishment of the very un-Pessoan *Mocidade Portuguesa*, from which, according to the same Salazarist hack, 'há de sair a elite que nos governará depois' [there should emerge the elite that will govern us in the future] (ibid.).[49] The inadvertent complicity of Pessoa & co. with corporatism's literal annihilation of popular autonomy and agency is made clearer by the irony that the slogan echoes the well-known opening of Álvaro de Campos's 'Tabacaria' [Tobacconist's Shop]:

> Não sou nada.
> Nunca serei nada.
> Não posso querer ser nada.
> À parte isso, tenho em mim todos os sonhos do mundo
>
> [I'm nothing.
> I never will be anything.
> I can't desire to be anything.
> That aside, I have within me all the dreams in the world.] (2002a: 320).

Campos's claim to contain 'todos os sonhos do mundo', and his defiant assertion of individual will and imagination over material circumstance, serve Saramago's purpose of exposing popular self-abnegation and ductility as ideologically inculcated, rather than eternally inherent. Unlike Campos, however, Saramago is concerned with how ideology dissuades the subaltern from exercising their will and creativity upon the material world: as *Ricardo Reis* claims, the slogan is

> aquilo mesmo que murmuraram, uns para os outros, os escravos que construíram as pirâmides, Nós não somos nada, os pedreiros e os boieiros de Mafra, Nós não somos nada, os alentejanos mordidos pelo gato raivoso, Nós não somos nada (*Ricardo Reis*: 374)
>
> [the very same thing muttered to one another by the slaves who built the pyramids, We are nothing, the masons and drovers of Mafra, We are nothing, the Alentejans bitten by the rabid cat, We are nothing]

Thus he links Campos's lines to a suggestion that the fascist slogan functions like a mantra, leading workers to perceive the products of their labour as the achievements of their rulers. The allusions to both *Levantado* and *Memorial* here recall those novels' respective explorations of collective consciousness and of the co-optation of will (*vontade*), suggesting that, if the builders of the *passarola* could 'viverem um sonho' anticipating the collectivization of revolutionary popular will by the Alentejan labourers, then why should the youth of 1930s Portugal abdicate 'todos os sonhos do mundo' to the Salazarist 'escol', and seek fulfilment only as mules in the corporatist treadmill?[50]

In these circumstances, a reader sympathetic to Saramago's agenda might consider the 'utility' of an intellectual like Reis to lie in re-animating the will of the oppressed, or, at least, in exposing the perfidy of the regime that co-opts that will. Yet in his only significant relationships with others, Reis dodges the opportunity to become 'useful' in this, or any other, way. In Marcenda's case, he fetishizes her passivity and vulnerability, mistaking them for the guarantors of his fantasy of self-abstraction. Reis is aware of how she detests her role in dissimulating her sanctimonious father's philandering (*Ricardo Reis*: 130), and her reluctant complicity contrasts ironically with the attitude of Marília, heroine of the thriller *Conspiração* (which Sampaio extols for its moral example), who denounces her Communist father to the authorities when he fails to 'repent' (*Ricardo Reis*: 142–43). Yet Reis gives Marcenda no encouragement to resist this abuse of her filial devotion. His attitude towards Lídia, meanwhile, is patronizing and ultimately callous, refusing to acknowledge the exceptional qualities by means of which this character mocks Pessoa and co.'s elitism. Reis's refusal to recognize her as his intellectual and social equal is encapsulated in his complaint that 'Lídia é a aia de Anna Karenine, serve para arrumar a casa e para certas faltas' [Lídia is Ana Karenina's nursemaid, she serves to keep house and to make good certain needs] (*Ricardo Reis*: 326). Yet by this juncture, the couple's conversations have demonstrated that, far from being 'nada', Lídia is a 'pessoa fora do comum' [extraordinary person] (p. 329) who typifies the suppressed or sequestered potential of the working classes. The characterization of Lídia first counters the intellectual condescension of 'Ela canta, pobre ceifeira', when she sings while, in a gesture of generosity and love, she spring-cleans the flat into which Reis has recently moved (*Ricardo Reis*: 252). This singing indicates no fatalistic or contented 'inconsciência', but rather Lídia's energy, initiative, and pragmatic relish of the 'prazer [...] de limpar, lavar e varrer' [pleasure [...] of cleaning, washing, and sweeping], by which she dispels Reis's melancholy long enough for him to exclaim that '[i]sto é como entrar no paraíso dos anjos' [[i]t's like entering paradise with all its angels] (*Ricardo Reis*: 252). Lídia also contradicts Reis's prescription of Catholic devotion as a consolation and moral compass for the masses ('pessoas de classe popular são próprias para terem tais devoções' [people of the working class are suited to keeping such observances]; *Ricardo Reis*: 304) with her statement that 'na minha família somos pouco de crenças' [we're not into religion in my family] (ibid.). Moreover, although she initially answers Reis's acquiescence to Salazarist orthodoxy with her brother Daniel's arguments, Lídia stands in solidarity with her brother but does not share his quasi-religious faith in Communism. Interrogating Reis's stubborn conviction that 'um jornal não pode mentir, seria o maior pecado do mundo' [a newspaper can't lie, it would be the greatest sin in the world] (*Ricardo Reis*: 388), Lídia sets out a deft summary of the dialectical method of analysis:

> eu sou quase uma analfabeta, mas uma coisa eu aprendi, é que as verdades são muitas e estão umas contra as outras, enquanto não lutarem não se saberá onde está a mentira (ibid.)
>
> [I'm almost illiterate, but there's one thing I've learned, and that's that the truths are many and some oppose the others, until they fight it out you can never tell where the falsehood lies]

If such insights make Lídia, as Frier suggests, 'one of the most striking instances of a figure comparable to Gramsci's organic intellectual' (2007: 158), Reis, however, will not see it. And far worse, as a contrastingly 'traditional intellectual' (2007: 156) who views himself as part of an 'escol', and who clings uncritically to bourgeois institutions when Marxist movements threaten his social class's interests, he compounds her disenfranchisement and obstructs her intellectual agency. His underestimation of Lídia is thrown into ironic relief when she answers his query regarding her views on the escalating conflict in Spain with the fascist youth movements' slogan: 'eu não sou nada, não tenho instrução, o senhor doutor é que deve saber' [I'm nothing, I've had no education, it's you who should know, Doctor] (*Ricardo Reis*: 375). Yet it is his refusal to accept her offer of egalitarian companionship, more than anything else, that leaves her 'a sentir-se nada' [feeling like nothing] (*Ricardo Reis*: 391) even before the death of Daniel.

When Lídia announces that she is carrying his child, Reis will neither flout the laws of bourgeois morality, nor grant her respectability through marriage (*Ricardo*

Reis: 355–56). While Lídia is initially heartbroken at Reis's lack of commitment, and prevaricates before ending their affair, her single-minded, and novel, response to her circumstances here can — as Ana Paula Ferreira argues (2001: 230) — be interpreted as an act of resistance to oppression, and one as radical and affirmative as any in Saramago's novels. Through her determination to keep her child (*Ricardo Reis*: 307), Lídia rejects being 'coopted for the moral support and sexual reproduction of the family-nation — as may be Marcenda's case' (Ferreira 2001: 227). Nevertheless, she ends the novel 'fulfilling an extension of the same functions in the horizon of the (all-male) movement of resistance against fascism and capitalist oppression' (ibid.) by 'performing a merely supportive, suffering maternal role vis-à-vis her brother's ultimately tragic activities' (Ferreira 2001: 230). Before this, however, she demonstrates how, even in the tragic and marginal circumstances to which she is increasingly confined, she can make small, everyday gestures of non-compliance with the ideology that legitimates her oppression. When cleaning Reis's apartment one last time after his refusal to acknowledge, or even support, his child, Lídia, according to Ferreira, sets 'a good example of how people-serfs can overturn not only the expectations of the fascist/paternalist reign but, along with it, the historical and cultural tradition feeding its myths' (2001: 228–29). Lídia 'foregoes the fiction of paternity [...] [and] performs mimically the quintessential act of ideal homebound femininity', while withdrawing the sexual favours that Reis has contrived to accept as a complimentary 'extra' to her paid labour as his housekeeper (Ferreira 2001: 229).

It is indeed significant that Lídia's unspoken complaint in this scene is that Reis has refused her the status not of a wife, but rather that of an 'amante' (lover): 'há igualdade nesta palavra, amante, amante, tanto faz macho como fêmea, e eles não são iguais' [there is equality in this word, lover, lover, whether male or female, and [yet] they are not equal] (*Ricardo Reis*: 391). The two characters' unequal status is manifest in their consistent addressing of each other as 'Lídia' and 'o senhor doutor', and only once — before their relationship has fully begun — is Lídia described in relation to Reis not as a 'criada' or 'rapariga', but as a 'mulher' (*Ricardo Reis*: 59). By thus signalling Lídia's awareness that no marriage to Reis (or to his like) would grant her equality, the novel reinforces the suggestion of her radical vision, and her attempts — akin to Blimunda's in *Memorial* — to live in accordance with it, on the social margin. This reading of Lídia's position is consolidated when one considers her earlier comment on the role of the *povo* in Spain's civil war. When Reis, questioning Daniel's claim that the Nationalists cannot win because 'vão ter todo o povo contra eles' [they will have the people united against them], asks Lídia how she defines the *povo*, she replies that 'o povo é o que sou eu, uma criada que tem um irmão comunista e que se deita com um médico em contra das revoluções' [the people are what I am, a chambermaid who has a Communist brother and who sleeps with a doctor who's opposed to revolutions] (*Ricardo Reis*: 375). This statement, acknowledging Reis's complaint that 'o povo nunca está de um lado só' [the people are never on just one side] (ibid.) illustrates neatly the entwined affective and financial ties that bind so many of the economically exploited to the imagined community affirmed, and regulated, by their exploiters. If Lídia, denied bourgeois prosperity, and having renounced the meagre comforts of concubinage, is to overcome the subsequent feeling of being 'nada' (*Ricardo Reis*: 391), it must be through investing in the idea of equality, and in the community of a family now bereaved of a patriarch three times over. In other words, she must embrace an identity wholly at odds with that to which Salazarist ideology summons her, and acknowledge — and resist — the reality of her own and her loved ones' oppression. Lídia is thus not simply the incubator of the (male) revolutionary subject who may witness the dictatorship's nemesis in Africa and protagonize the April Revolution: she is also, as Frier suggests, constitutive of the 'ferment' that — according to Gramsci — must survive during the revolutionary party's years of retreat. However, her significance — and the significance for Saramago of Gramsci's concept — lies in her manner of perpetuating analytical and innovative forms of resistance, learning to test, rather than slavishly repeat, Daniel's ideology in evolving socio-economic circumstances. In particular — and as with the heroines of *Levantado* and *Memorial* — Lídia's contributions as visionary and innovator affirm the indispensable role of female emancipation, and of a deterritorialization of (heterosexual) erotic desire, both in instigating individual renewal, and in building a revolutionary hegemony and social bloc.

If Lídia's story thus affirms the potential of the subaltern 'organic intellectual', Reis's story and its denouement also develop Saramago's critique of the established bourgeois intellectual, through the narrator's musings on 1930s Spain's most eminent man of letters, Miguel de Unamuno, and his famously bold equivocation at the outbreak of the Civil War. Whereas Reis might 'flutuar no meio do Atlântico' [float in the mid-Atlantic], Unamuno energetically asserted himself as the model of the modern Iberian public intellectual.[51] Hence, Unamuno's complaint in July 1936 that '[h]ay que salvar la civilización occidental, la civilización cristiana tan amenazada' [we must save Western civilization, the so greatly threatened Christian civilization] (*Ricardo Reis*: 378), set a stamp of respectability on Franco's nascent uprising against the Second Republic.[52] In a dramatic metafictional prolepsis, *Ricardo Reis*'s narrative looks forward to the events of 12 October (which Reis does not live to see), when Unamuno would change tack, deploring the brutality and intolerance of the Nationalist campaign, and denouncing the Falangist commander of the Spanish Legion, José Millán-Astray, as 'a cripple who lacks the spiritual greatness of a Cervantes [and] is wont to seek ominous relief in causing mutilation around him'.[53]

Ricardo Reis's quotation in full of Unamuno's philippic honours the courage of a figure who, according to Stephen Roberts, found himself, like Reis, 'perdido en una tierra de nadie, donde, [...] ya no se podía estar a salvo como espectador, y menos todavía como comentador' [lost in a no-man's-land, where [...] he could no longer safely remain a spectator, and still less a commentator] (2003: 233), yet who recognized that sometimes 'calar-se é mentir' [to remain silent is to lie] (*Ricardo Reis*, 384; trans. Thomas 1977: 503). However, the novel's juxtaposition of Unamuno with Reis implies that what was for Unamuno the tragic 'fracaso de la totalidad de su proyecto intelectual' [failure in its entirety of his intellectual project] (Roberts 2003: 233) is, for Saramago, the natural consequence of an elitist liberal humanism, which refuses to see either the socio-economic antagonisms and egotisms that sunder the communities that it affirms, or the agency of the disenfranchised masses. As Javier Alfaya has argued,

> que importa em *Ricardo Reis* não é tão somente o Unamuno contraditório e tópico que até há muito pouco tempo tinha um altar no coração de qualquer espanhol pensante, fosse ele da direita ou da esquerda. O que importa é ele como emblema e símbolo de uma atitude: a de uma determinada inteligência liberal que, enredada num conflito que já não é de ideias, que já não é sobre palavras ou sobre o seu espírito, retrocede assustada perante a eclosão de uma revolução que ele pensa ser uma ameaça para o seu eu e se filia, sem muitas hesitações, no partido da ordem. (1993: 25)

> [what matters in *Ricardo Reis* is not simply the contradictory and commonplace Unamuno, to whom, until very recently, every thinking Spaniard — whether of the political right or left wing — had raised an altar in his or her heart. What matters is rather Unamuno as emblem and symbol of an attitude: that of a certain liberal intelligence that, caught up in a conflict which is no longer about ideas, which is no longer about words or about their spirit, withdraws alarmed by the outbreak of a revolution that he believes is a threat to his ego and who, with little hesitation, throws his lot in with the party of law and order.]

Saramago's anachronistic interpolation of Unamuno's last stand, however, achieves more than an indictment of liberalism. By echoing the use earlier in *Ricardo Reis* (and in *Memorial*) of the trope of physical impairment, it enriches the exploration across Saramago's output of the intertwined problematics of epistemology, and of community with the socio-economically configured Other.[54] Unamuno's distinction between Millán-Astray (who lost his left arm and right eye in the Spanish–Moroccan Wars of the 1920s) and Cervantes (whose left arm was paralysed by a wound sustained at Lepanto) does not merely establish 'spiritual greatness' in place of physical ability or might as the measure of authority. It also harks back to Saramago's *manetas*, Baltasar and Marcenda, and to the possibility — realized only provisionally by the former, and not at all by the latter — that through intellectual and moral enquiry, selfless comradeship, and courage, they might rise above the socio-economic conditions that have 'crippled' them. However, the meaning of Unamuno's quip, and of the intra-textual allusions that it triggers, gains a further dimension or two in the wake of the undead Pessoa's enigmatic assertion to Reis that 'somos todos aleijados' [we are all crippled] (*Ricardo Reis*: 384). Particularly when reading *Ricardo Reis* relationally with *Levantado*, *Memorial*, and *Ensaio sobre a Cegueira*, it is tempting to connect this statement to the recurrent tropes of vision and of vision impairment, and particularly to *Cegueira*'s epigraph, from an apocryphal *Livro de Conselhos* [*Book of Advice*], '[se] podes olhar, vê. Se podes ver, repara' [if you can look, see. If you can see, observe] (*Cegueira*: back cover). The untrammelled vision of Blimunda and of *Levantado*'s kite metaphorically denote a superhuman perception of reality, thereby establishing more circumscribed vision as a cipher for the human failure to either comprehend or represent the world objectively or unequivocally. As *Cegueira*'s epigraph and allegory both assert, however, the greatest limitation on human vision is the lack of will to study, question, and reflect on what is looked at. If, in *Ricardo Reis*, the conceit of the dead poet's inability to read connotes an author's lack of ownership of, or control over, his/her texts' meaning and influence, then the living Ricardo Reis's metaphoric status as blind man suggests that his aloof, dispassionate contemplation makes him an individual who neither sees ('ver') nor pays attention to ('reparar') the political and affective ramifications of what he looks at ('olhar'). If Reis, besieged by evidence of his own status as intellectually *aleijado*, is to rise above seeking 'ominous relief in causing mutilation around him', then he should end his complicity with the socio-economic system that constrains, diminishes, and brutalizes so much of the population, and substitute solidarity and empathy with his two downtrodden girlfriends for his habitual elitism and condescension. Ironically, in attempting to separate his body from his spirit, and in accepting Lídia's sexual attentions while repudiating both her love and his own affective response, Reis ends up embodying the grotesque image of man that Pessoa attributes to 'o homen sem loucura' [man without madness], in the poem 'Dom Sebastião' in *Mensagem*, as a 'besta sadia | Cadáver adiado que procria' [healthy beast | A postponed corpse that breeds] (2004: 33; trans. 2006a: 376).

Redemption — as it is intimated in *Memorial*, and, later, more boldly posited in *Cegueira* — is predicated on a revised conception of ourselves as sovereign beings who choose to constitute parts of a collective social body (though, crucially, one very different to that conceived of by Salazarism). *Ricardo Reis* elaborates on this conception with its 'post-Pessoan' affirmation of the individual's capacity for plurality and growth. Yet personal regeneration cannot occur hermetically (as Pessoa's *regra de vida* asserts) but rather through acknowledgment of, and empathy with, the social Other. As in José Ornelas's reading of *Cegueira*, an endemic susceptibility to egotism is what blinds the individual to what — for Saramago at least — is the necessary precedence of human cooperation over competition. In this manner, the novel responds to the failure of Unamuno's liberal humanism with a socialist, or, more precisely, anarcho-syndicalist 'post-humanism' that, further to affirming human equality and universal entitlement to material security and freedom of conscience, also emphasizes both the diverse, protean nature of the human, and the definition of 'humanity' not as an innate characteristic but as an ethical ideal to be striven for.

What distinguishes *Ricardo Reis*, in terms of its contribution to the political agenda of Saramago's output, is its assessment of literary writing — and in particular the work of Fernando Pessoa — as an instrument that can variously dynamize or (in the wrong hands) retard the realization of this protean nature and the fulfilment of humankind's ethical capability. Saramago's creation of a tragicomically self-indulgent and self-deceiving Ricardo Reis enables not a simple rebuff to the aloof individualism of the original Reis *odes*, but a wider critique of the failure to recognize how those *odes*, like all poetic language, are susceptible to recontextualization and ideological cooptation. At the same time, amid the jamboree of anniversary celebrations threatening to 'petrify' Pessoa as an icon of national identity, Saramago's reanimation of the poet and his heteronym focuses attention on how Pessoa's writings demonstrate two things. It shows, first, that what we call subjectivity is infinitely more complex, varied, and mutable than is customarily presumed, and, secondly, that all readers contribute to the generation of literary meaning, and hence we should not passively accept, but critically appraise, the interpretations of canonical literature endorsed — or enforced — by powerful institutions. As to the cultural agent formerly known as 'the author', *Ricardo Reis*'s allegory of impaired vision and petrification intimates that a writer can only evade a figurative death, and enslavement as the ventriloquized puppet of the powerful, while he/she remains an engaged citizen, and while his/her writings remain engaged with a material, and political, world.

The undead Pessoa's role as Reis's mentor and critic helps to indicate how, while rejecting Pessoa's hermeticism, Saramago accommodates the poet's post-structuralist conception of identity and language into both his declared Marxist world-view, and his attempts to make literature — and himself as celebrated author — socially and politically 'useful'. First of all, Pessoa's exposure of the 'faker' Reis as an unwitting parody of figures as diverse as Don Juan, Adamastor, the Baudelairean flâneur, and the Dante of *Inferno*, not only mocks his clinging to a consistent Horatian ideal, but also helps illustrate how material and ideological circumstances (and, in particular, other people) trigger the performance by the same individual of diverse roles and identities. Secondly, the undead Pessoa's function of 'interrupting' the text's representational, narratological, and ideological consistency compounds the auto-interrogative character of Saramago's fiction. Just as, in Pessoa's oeuvre, heteronymity contributes to the deconstructive clash of the 'totalizing and interruptive impulses' that Irene Ramalho Santos labels 'Atlanticism' and 'Interruption' (2003: 19–22), in Saramago's novels, the interpenetration of fictional layers creates conditions that interrupt — or place quotation marks around — the component parts of Saramago's impassioned attack on Salazarism and its legacy. Of course, Saramago's conception of such literature's 'usefulness', in contrast to Pessoa's, stresses its capacity to alert the reader to the tyrannous hold that ideology seeks to take on language outside of the 'self-interruptive' text. For Saramago, if literature is to stimulate a practice of ideological critique and psycho-sociological and political analysis, then it must not present itself as a ready-made alternative to hegemonic representations of reality, but rather as the vehicle for 'dialectical images' to be held up against, and compared with, such hegemonic images and explanations of real-life phenomena.

A practice of writing that lends itself to such a dialectical 'perfeição das cousas', however, must also, *Ricardo Reis* suggests, find ways to engage those that Pessoa and his coterie dismiss as an undifferentiated and unthinking *plebe*, to challenge their marginalization in hegemonic representations of (purportedly) communal culture and history, and to explore how they have been, are, and might again become other to the identities and roles that the hegemonic ideology ascribes to them. *Ricardo Reis* admits of an increasing pessimism regarding the possibility of an effective mass mobilization of the subaltern classes. In contrast to *Levantado do Chão*, the only dialectical progression of politicization and socio-economic understanding that *Ricardo Reis* chronicles is that which Lídia initiates, only to be stymied by Reis's patronizing incomprehension. The novel's emphasis is instead on the stifling of the forms of educational dialogue, and of progressive communication, between the proletariat, other subaltern groups, and leftist and working-class elements within the military. This is made evident not simply through the failure of Daniel and his comrades' mutiny, but also through their evident failure to recognize either Lídia's intellectual and organizational talents, or the inadequacy of PCP orthodoxy in addressing the needs and aspirations of a woman in her social location. Both *Jangada* and *História* subsequently develop this critique of excessive 'democratic' centralism and of gender-blindness, while continuing in very different ways to explore the potential of Pessoa's ideas, in present-day scenarios wherein literature and myth, and their creative reinterpretation, are shown once more to contribute substantially to the difference between oppressive and progressive political projects.

Notes to Chapter 3

1. Here, Saramago draws on Fernando Pessoa's famous letter of 13 January 1935 to Adolfo Casais Monteiro, recounting the origins of Reis and his two other 'major' heteronyms: 'Ricardo Reis nasceu em 1889 [...] no Porto, é médico e está presentemente no Brasil' (1999: 344) [Ricardo Reis was born in 1887 [...] in Porto. He's a doctor and is presently living in Brazil (Pessoa 2001: 257)]. On this letter and Pessoa's alternative accounts of the 'birth' of his heteronyms, see Richard Zenith's introduction to this letter (Pessoa 2001: 250).
2. This phrase is taken from the opening line of one of the odes ascribed to Reis, which Saramago makes the novel's epigraph: 'Sábio é o que se contenta com o espectáculo do mundo' [Wise is he who contents himself with the spectacle of the world] (Pessoa 2007: 60).
3. On the novel's use of verbatim news reportage, see Grossegesse (2006: 61–67), Bertoquini (1999), and Matías (2007).
4. The novel's opening line is an ironic inversion of Camões's evocation of a heroic Portugal, 'quase cume da cabeça da Europa toda [...] Onde a terra se acaba e o mar começa' [foremost point of the head of all Europe [...] Where the land ends and the sea begins] in Canto III, stanza 20 of *Os Lusíadas* (Camões 1947: IV, 120).
5. Quain made his appearance in 'Examen de la obra de Herbert Quain' (Borges 1997: 77–85); the heteronym Reis was conceived, by Pessoa's own accounts, in 1912 or 1914 (1999: 342; 343).
6. On Salazar's development of a comprehensive system of prior censorship of all periodicals and all other texts touching on political and social matters, see Ó (1999), Rodríguez (2012), and Hignett (1988). For a discussion of the relationship between ideology and literary canon formation, see Gorak (1991) and Culler (1988).
7. Cited by Balderston (2006: 167).
8. See Faris (1988: 11–12; 88–120), and Barry (2002: 82).
9. See Santos (1930).
10. This passage quotes Camões's famous denunciation of 1570s Portugal's malaise in canto 10, stanza 145 of *Os Lusíadas* (1947: V, 258).
11. On the *Estado Novo*'s use of culture and cultural media, see, in particular, Torgal (2009: II, 119–216), Trindade (2008), and Ó (2008).
12. On the restoration of the Cathedral and Castle and its contribution to projecting the regime's image of the nation, see Sapega (2002: 46–47), and Vakil (2002: 29; 32).
13. See the 'Programa geral do Neo-Paganismo Português' [General Programme of Portuguese Neo-Paganism], (Pessoa 2003: 175–78).
14. See this volume's chapter on *Jangada*, pp. 164–66.
15. As Pina notes (ibid.), the stridently propagandist tone set by António Ferro's screenplay made the film something of an embarrassment to the *Estado Novo* leadership in the more subtly authoritarian post-war period.
16. On the PVDE's surveillance and torture operations, see Birmingham (2003: 167–68), and Caldeira et al. (2011: esp. 82–121).
17. Sapega here is referring to Queirós (1972: 500), and Queirós (1980: 565–89, esp. 573).
18. For just one influential vindication of Pessoa's distinction in the development of the culture and consciousness of modernity, see Bloom (1994: esp. 485–92).
19. For Pessoa's definition of his work as a 'drama em gente', see Pessoa (1928: 10).
20. See Agamben (2002: 117–19); Paz (1983); Steiner (1996), and Badiou (2005: 36–45).

21. On Pessoa's reading of Freud, see the former's letter of 11 December 1931 to João Gaspar Simões (Pessoa 1999: 248–58, esp. 250–53); see also Klobucka and Sabine (2007: 10–13) and Martinho (2003).
22. Amongst the vast critical bibliography on Pessoa's work, key English-language studies include Monteiro (ed.) (1982), McGuirk (ed.) (1988), Sadlier (1998), Monteiro (2000), Santos (2003), Klobucka and Sabine (eds) (2007), Jackson (2010), Frier (ed.) (2012), Castro (ed.) (2013), and Medeiros (2013). In Portuguese, essential readings of Pessoa's work include Coelho (1949), Lourenço (1973), Sena (1981), and Serrão (1981), Seabra (1985) and (1996), and Gil (1988) and (1999).
23. See Gil (1988) and (1999).
24. As Klobucka and Sabine suggest, '[l]ike the act of gender impersonation (as theorized by Judith Butler), the formation of the authorial egos of Pessoa's textual universe does not amount to an imitation of subjective identities; it is, rather, a dramatization of signifying gestures through which identity itself is established' (2007: 9).
25. The most ambitious and wide-ranging Derridian reading of Pessoa's work to date is Miranda (2010).
26. Now acclaimed as his prose masterpiece, the *Livro do Desassossego* occupied Pessoa intermittently from 1913, and remained incomplete at his death. The first attempt at a definitive edition of this most fragmentary of volumes (Pessoa 1982) caused a sensation on its publication. Although debate continues regarding the definitive corpus of texts that comprise the *Livro*, the eighth, revised edition of Richard Zenith's 2009 realization is widely considered the most authoritative to date.
27. The diverse lines along which *Mensagem* has subsequently been interpreted are represented in, amongst other studies, Cirurgião (1990), Ramalho Santos (2003: 40–57; 103–14), Freeman (1988), and Miranda (2010: 263–402). For a good selection of Pessoa's political writings, see Pessoa (1980: esp. 249–315), and Pessoa (1986b: vol. II, esp. 249–315). Pessoa's contempt for all forms of socialism and revolutionary syndicalism is summarized in an unpublished, untitled draft text, catalogued as MS 55-73/76 in Pessoa's archived papers, and published under the title 'O Preconceito Revolucionário' [Revolutionary Prejudice] (Pessoa 1980: 260–62). This text pointedly ignores Marxism's materialist thesis and insists upon the natural opposition between 'a plebe' [the masses] and the 'aristocracia e escol' [aristocracy and elite] so as to damn 'o bolchevismo' [bolshevism] as 'reaccionário e religioso' [reactionary and religious], since otherwise 'não o poderiam adoptar as plebes, incapazes de outra coisa que não a religião' [it could not be adopted by the masses, who are incapable of anything but religious conviction] (p. 260).
28. See Vale (1984: 2). Saramago also explained, in the same year, that '[a] minha intenção foi confrontar Ricardo Reis e a sua poesia com um tempo e uma realidade cultural que de fato não tem nada a ver com ele' [my intention was to confront Ricardo Reis and his poetry with a time and a cultural reality which in fact has nothing to do with him] (quoted in Campelo (1985: 43)).
29. On 'Autopsicografia', see, amongst other studies, McGuirk (1988), and Miranda (2010: 62–76).
30. As Reis claims in the 'Prefácio de Ricardo Reis ao seu livro *Odes*', '[o] que sentimos verdade dentro de nós, traduzimos para a palavra, escrevendo os nossos versos sem olhar àquilo a que se destinam. Uma reconstrução real do paganismo parece tarefa estulta em um mundo que de todo, até à medula dos seus ossos, se cristianizou e ruiu. Depunhamo-los [sic] como oferendas, tábuas votivas, no altar dos Deuses, gratos simplesmente porque eles nos hajam livrado, e posto a salvamento, daquele naufrágio universal que é o cristismo' [that which we feel to be true within ourselves, we have translated into words, writing our verses without regard to their destination. An actual reconstruction of paganism would seem a foolish task in a world wherein everything has been Christianized and corrupted to the marrow of its bones. Let us rather set them as gifts, votive offerings, upon the altar of the Gods, grateful simply for their having spared us and made us safe from that universal shipwreck that is Christism] (Pessoa 2003: 165).
31. On the history of the Italian–Ethiopian War of 1935–36, see Baer (1967), Zewde (2001: 150–60), Boca (1965), and Mallett (2003: 24–56). Saramago's attack on Eden, and his government's prior concern for British neutrality, for British East Africa, and its lucrative ivory trade, overlooks the

fact that it was Eden's predecessor as Foreign Secretary, Samuel Hoare, who first capitulated to Mussolini's invasion.

32. 'Mas sou eu o mesmo que aqui vivi, e aqui voltei, [...] Ou somos, todos os Eu que estive aqui ou estiveram | Uma série de contas-entes ligadas por um fio-memória | Uma série de sonhos de mim de alguém de fora de mim?' [But am I the same person who lived here once and returned, [...] Or are we, all the Is I was or were here | A string of bead-beings strung all together by a memory's strand | A string of dreams of myself which someone outside me dreamt up?] (Pessoa 2002a: 301; trans. Pessoa 1986c: 85).

33. The same ode is alluded to by the narrative voice (*Ricardo Reis*: 27), and again by Reis: 'Tenho um ode em que digo que vivem em nós inúmeros' [I wrote an ode in which I say that innumerable people live within us] (*Ricardo Reis*: 93).

34. This passage recalls Bernardo Soares's claim that '[a]chego-me à minha secretária como a um baluarte contra a vida' [I arrive at my desk as though at a bulwark against life] (Pessoa 2009: 57–58; trans. 2002b: 18).

35. This metaphor derives from the line 'Collige virgo rosas dum flos novus et nova pubes, | et memor esto aevum sic properare tuum' in the poem known as 'De rosis nascentibus', attributed to Ausonius (1991: 669–71, at 671), and formerly attributed to Virgil.

36. The ode 'Sábio é o que se contenta' depicts the 'wise man' using the pleasures of wine to make everything seem 'novo | E imarcesível sempre' [new | And forever imperishable] : 'Ele sabe que a vida | Passa por ele e tanto | Corta à flor como a ele | De Átropos a tesoura' [He knows that life | Is passing by him and that | The shears of Atropos cut | The flower and cut him] (Pessoa 2007: 60; trans. Pessoa 2006a: 89).

37. This passage alludes to Reis's ode 'Saudoso já de este verão que vejo' [Already wistful for this summer I behold], where the poet describes how

> [...] me anticipo a sombra
> Em que hei-de errar, sem flores,
> No abismo rumoroso.
>
> [[...] I await the shade
> In which I must wander, flowerless,
> In the murmuring abyss.]
> (Pessoa 2007: 35)

However, while Reis's ode no.18 looks forward melancholically from 'este verão que vejo' (line 1) to the winter of old age, in Saramago's novel, it is spring and yet the flowerbeds are empty.

38. See Chapter 2, pp. 111–13.

39. As Soares puts it, 'Pedi tão pouco à vida e esse mesmo pouco a vida me negou. [...] o não exigir nada dos outros nem exigirem eles de mim ... Isto mesmo me foi negado, como quem nega a esmola não por falta de boa alma, mas para não ter que desabotoar o casaco' [I have asked so little of life and life has denied me even that little. [...] to demand nothing of others, nor have them make demands of me ... Even this was refused me, in the manner of one who refuses a request for charity not out of a lack of good spirit, but so as not to have to unbutton his overcoat] (Pessoa 2009: 56). Reis, for his part, has earlier been dismayed to discover that 'a sua relação com o hotel, com o Salvador, é uma relação de dependência' [his relationship with the hotel, with Salvador, is one of dependency] (*Ricardo Reis*: p. 205).

40. Reis describes himself and his peers among Pessoa's 'neo-pagan' coterie as 'exilado[s] e casua[is] no meio de uma civilização inimiga' [exiled by happenstance amid a hostile civilization] in his 'Notas para um Prefácio a Alberto Caeiro', in Pessoa (2003), pp. 43–162 (p. 161).

41. On the allusion to this text, see also Sabine (2002: 41–42). NB this text is no longer universally considered a component of the *Livro do Desassossego*.

42. This notion of the dead Pessoa as statue-like is repeated when Reis 'tentou sentir-se morto, olhar com olhos de estátua o leito vazio' [tried to feel dead, to look upon the empty bed with the eyes of a statue] (*Ricardo Reis*: 233).

43. As Malcolm McNee argues, in a study that counters the reductive potential of *Ricardo Reis*'s incomplete introduction to Pessoa's political thinking, '[d]espite Pessoa's anti-Salazarist

sentiments and rejection of the notion of the *Estado Novo* as the awaited Fifth Empire, certain discernibly consistent aspects of his political philosophy closely paralleled those of the dictatorship, and there are at least two gestures of active collaboration, via his relationship with [António] Ferro, with the regime. [...] What Pessoa shared with the quasi-fascist ideology of the Salazar regime was the anti-democratic notion of the inability of the "common" people to govern themselves, to make rational political decisions' (1999: 63–64). However, McNee concludes, it is the Pessoa of 1935, 'disillusioned by an intertwining of the thematic of his own utopian/spiritual discourse with the increasingly repressive Salazarist ideological discourse' that is the model for Saramago's 'undead' poet (1999: 64). See also Pessoa (1978) and (1980).

44. On 'Ela canta, pobre ceifeira' and its reworking of Wordsworth's poem, see George Monteiro (2000: 20–28) and Klobucka (2013). On *Ricardo Reis*'s manipulation of Pessoa's use of rain as pathetic fallacy, see Sabine (2002: 42).
45. This scene pointedly alludes to at least one of the classic literary denunciations of the poverty and oppression enforced by Salazar's dictatorship, José Rodrigues Miguéis's 1936 story 'Gente da Terceira Classe' (1962: 9–31). I am deeply grateful to Dr Patricia Odber de Baubeta for kindly drawing my attention to this text.
46. Here we agree substantially with Ana Paula Ferreira (2002: 236, n.24) that 'Marcenda's losing the movement of her *left* hand [...] is suggestive of the crippling effect of Salazar's New State had on the (bourgeois) Republican Feminist women's movements', although Ferreira miscalculates the date of Marcenda's paralysis ('Fez quatro anos em Dezembro'; *Ricardo Reis*: 128) as 1933, the year of the *Estado Novo*'s promulgation.
47. Salazar, in conversation with Henry Massis, cited in Pinto and Rezola (2008: 154).
48. As Teresa Cristina Cerdeira da Silva notes, the slogan 'ilustra dois dos princípios básicos do fascismo que são o anti-individualismo e a crença na necessidade de uma elite dirigente da massa que tem por dever seguir os seus preconceitos' [illustrates two of the basic principles of Fascism, namely anti-individualism and the belief in the necessity of an elite guiding the masses, who in turn have the duty of following the dogmas of the elite] (1989: 112).
49. In an undated, unpublished text first published in Pessoa (1986a: III, pp. 577–78), Pessoa explains that '[o] escol não quer dizer uma classe, mas uma série de indivíduos' [elite doesn't mean a class, but a series of individuals] (1986a: 577).
50. On *Ricardo Reis*'s treatment of the phrase 'Nós não somos nada', and its intertextual relationship with *Jangada*, see also Frier (2007: 254–56).
51. On Unamuno's preeminent role in establishing the role and *modus operandi* of the 'public intellectual' in 1920s and 1930s Spain, see Roberts (2007: esp. 165–234).
52. An interview conducted by A. Boaventura in the last week of December 1936, and published in the *Diario de Noticias* of 3 January 1937, p. 1, and reproduced in Mezquita (2003: 413–15), attributes to Unamuno the reiteration that '[a]o movimento chefiado pelo general Franco importa salvar a civilização cristã [...] e a independência nacional, ameaçadas pela barbárie soviética' [what is important for the movement led by General Franco is to save Christian civilization [...] and national independence, both of which are under threat from Soviet barbarism] (Mezquita 2003: 414).
53. The comments that Saramago's text attributes to Unamuno are translated from the account given by Thomas (1977: 501–03), based on Luis Portillo's testimony. As Thomas notes, '[t]here will never be full agreement on what was said and the tone in which it was said' (503, n. 1). Mezquita claims that the account later given by Salcedo (1964: 409) (and acknowledged by Thomas) is 'la que más se ajusta a lo que de hecho ocurrió aquel día' [the one that sticks closest to that which really took place that day] (Mezquita 2003: 401, n. 34).
54. On Saramago's use of disability as a symbolic trope, see Ben-Moshe's (2006) critique of his 'exoticization' of blindness in 'an ableist discourse that constructs the blind as the ostensible other', and also Gallagher's (2006) response to Ben Moshe.

CHAPTER 4

A Jangada de Pedra

On New Year's Day 1986, Portugal and Spain were formally inducted into the European Economic Community after almost a decade of negotiations and planning. Later that year, Saramago's eagerly anticipated new novel offered a story set in the imminent future, wherein a deep crack opens up along the Pyrenees, and the Iberian Peninsula wrenches itself away from Europe and sails west across the Atlantic like a great stone raft. After several weeks, and as collision with the Azores archipelago is imminent, the Peninsula changes course several times, following a trajectory by turns rectilinear, then rotary, before coming to a halt somewhere between Central America and West Africa: very roughly, the centre of the post-colonial Spanish and Portuguese-speaking world. On one level, *Jangada* is a delightfully mischievous satire on the politics of EEC/EU integration, which Saramago would consistently denounce in numerous essays and interviews.[1] On a deeper and more philosophical level, meanwhile, the novel is a meditation on two more universal issues, one epistemological, the other political. First, it attempts to envisage what would happen if all current systems of knowledge, and all strategies for determining truth, suddenly failed in the face of an ineluctable mystery. While the novel's protagonists, political leaders, and scientists all vainly seek to establish the causes and consequences of the peninsula's movement, the reader — like most of the novel's critics — is repeatedly tempted to divine meaning in such central narrative tropes as Joana Carda's 'magical' elm wand and Maria Guavaira's infinite ball of yarn, interpreting these as allusions to familiar myths and histories, and thus to the teleologies that these enfabulate. Ultimately, however, *Jangada*'s devilishly ambiguous symbols only compound the epistemological uncertainty that underpins discussion of a second key issue, namely the possibility of reanimating socialist utopianism as a political project not only within Iberia, but also across an increasingly globalized wider world.

If Saramago's allegory of Iberia spurning a free-market European Union locates a socialist alternative in an attempted rapprochement with formerly colonized communities around the Atlantic basin, it offers no confident vision of this succeeding. As threats of natural disaster engender mass panic, political meltdown, and economic crisis, state authorities resort to coercion, deception, and nationalist jingoism. As in *Ricardo Reis* and earlier novels, Saramago explores the manipulation of history, literature, and culture by politicians, the state, and corporate mass media as perhaps the most pervasive of such strategies for the maintenance of hegemony. *Jangada* is different, however, not only in using a 'ucronian', rather than historical, setting, in order to critique present-day politics directly. It is also the first of Saramago's novels to explore mass-media simulation as an inescapable, and profoundly politicized, feature of contemporary life and communications. Saramago's narrative, parodying the discourses of state and corporate media, spotlights their cynical deployment of simulacra in representations of Iberia's movement and its consequences. Such fabrications, far from translating reality, merely corroborate the time-honoured metanarratives of national belonging and national destiny that are trotted out in order to bolster popular acquiescence to officialdom's projects and priorities. Meanwhile, a panicked political elite denounces and suppresses grass-roots social initiatives and mass demonstrations of popular will. With this imagined sequence of events, *Jangada* recalls the retrenchment that brought Portugal's socialist 'April Revolution' to a halt by the late 1970s.

Jangada's depiction of the mendacious power of mass media, and of the precarious nature of historical materialist analysis, evinces little optimism regarding orthodox Marxist revolutionary praxis. This is most likely why several studies have instead identified an optimistic message of specifically Iberian resurgence, presaged by supernatural phenomena and secured by reconciliation between erstwhile ethnic adversaries and by reinvigorated local traditions. Such readings arguably underplay *Jangada*'s deconstruction of the logic of nationalism, and its exploration of how a hierarchy based more on class and capital than on ethnicity underpins Iberia's subordination to a northern European elite. This chapter suggests an alternative reading of Saramago's 'trans-Iberianism' as a tactic deployed from an essentially internationalist position to contest his country's colonization by the EEC. *Jangada* shows Saramago attempting to accommodate popular desires for cultural rootedness and community within a renewed socialist utopianism. To the earlier novels' intimations that the socialist cause might yet be advanced through closer attention to human psychology, and a 'micropolitical' revolution in ethics, identities, and relationships as a precondition for social transformation he adds his proposal of what Klobucka, citing Mitchell Cohen (1992), terms a 'rooted cosmopolitanism' (Klobucka 2001: xviii) that reconciles ethnic belonging with openness to the Other.

By recounting not only Iberia's voyage across the Atlantic, but also the simultaneous journey of five strangers around their floating homeland, *Jangada* imagines just such a radical 'micropolitics' emerging on the margins of a society in turmoil. All five individuals have been caught up in bizarre occurrences simultaneous with the Peninsula's displacement. In Portugal, Joana Carda scratches an ineradicable line in the earth with a stick of elm wood; José Anaiço is followed everywhere by a vast flock of starlings, and Joaquim Sassa throws a large rock into the sea, only to watch it bounce away over the waves until it disappears from sight. Over the border in Galicia, meanwhile, Maria Guavaira unravels an infinite length of blue yarn from an old sock, and elderly Andalusian Pedro Orce becomes a human seismometer, able to feel the tremors of the moving peninsula under his feet. Suspecting that their actions may have precipitated the geological aberrations that have thrown their communities into turmoil, the five seek each other out. While the floating landmass assumes the properties both of an exploratory vessel and of the enchanted islands of Shakespeare, Camões, and others, these protagonists seek explanations for events in the seemingly exceptional objects and animals that they encounter; not least, in the fearsome-looking, yet benign, dog that leads them on much of their journey. These encounters, in circumstances fraught with uncertainty, precipitate experiences of personal renewal, as well as experiments with new customs of loving and living together. The novel's symbolism deploys a panoply of literary and mythological references to construe these characters' new socialist utopianism as a harmonious marriage of pluralist internationalism with local tradition. A majority of studies of *Jangada* have read it in an optimistic spirit, as Saramago's most affirmative reinscription of utopia. The travellers' innovations are, however, put to the test by unplanned pregnancies and a sudden bereavement, and the novel ends in a scene full of seeming symbolic portents and unanswered questions, which remind the reader that the material realization of utopia remains distant.

I — Fantasy Futures and the Re-viewing of Present Realities

In terms of its relationship with history and historiographical analysis, *Jangada*'s narrative is obviously a case apart from Saramago's earlier novels.[2] *Levantado*, *Memorial*, and *Ricardo Reis* challenge both a hegemonic national narrative, and the terms for discussion of the collective past, by means of simultaneously recuperative, revisionist, and auto-interrogative historical rewriting. *Jangada*'s narrative, meanwhile, developing within a wholly ucronian and fantastical sphere, challenges discussions of the *future* that function (in Elisabeth Wesseling's terms) as 'instruments of power in the present' (1991: 118). Far from indicating Saramago's abandonment of historicism, *Jangada* is the platform for a wider critique of faux-historicist discursive practices; a critique focused on how the projection of nationalist myths and teleologies into an unknowable future limits our capacity to conceive of that future as radically transformable.

Saramago sums up the case for making ucronian fantasy the vehicle of this critique in *Jangada*'s opening epigraph, quoting Alejo Carpentier's claim (1974: 77) that 'todo futuro es fabuloso' [all futures are fabulous].[3] In a 2010 interview, Saramago set out his interpretation of Carpentier's phrase as follows:

> Lo que yo quiero decir es que si al final de siglo XIX se reunieran unos cuantos científicos, filósofos y sociólogos para pensar, para reflexionar cómo sería el futuro, y luego se reunieran otra vez al final del siglo XX, a lo mejor no acertarían en nada o casi nada. Entonces, desde esta perspectiva, el futuro se presenta como una fábula. El futuro siempre está diciendo que hay algo más allá de lo que podemos imaginar. La situación social, política, económica y cultural concreta de alguna forma nos limita en nuestros juicios [...]. (Garza 2010)[4]

> [What I mean is that if at the end of the nineteenth century a number of scientists, philosophers, and sociologists had gathered to imagine and discuss what the future would be like, and then had gathered again at the end of the twentieth century, they would most likely be proven correct in nothing or almost nothing. Looked at from this perspective, the future is presented as a story. The future is always telling us that there exists something beyond what

we can imagine. Our social, political, economic, and cultural circumstances in some way limit our judgement[.]]

The tendency to package unsubstantiated 'stories' of the future as scientifically deduced and reliable predictions certainly had a profound influence on political debate in mid-1980s Portugal. As Helena Kaufman and José Ornelas summarize, an 'official discourse'

> was already preparing the road for a union with the EEC countries, processing and codifying images which would rationalize its objectives. Even the future of Portugal was called into question; without the union there would be no future. Thus, an impression was created that the raison d'être of Portugal, the identity of its people, depended entirely on the formalization of the union. (1997: 162)

It is easy to see how and why this alarmist and emotional discourse was being deployed to manufacture a pro-European consensus in Portugal. EEC membership had long been the goal of the centrist parties that formed governments after 1975. This goal, however, sat uneasily with established notions of national character and destiny, in a country long encouraged to view itself as a 'proudly alone' at the head of its global empire.[5] Anxiety about loosening ties with former colonies, and relinquishing national sovereignty to a community dominated by wealthier northern neighbours, was not confined to the political right. Many on the revolutionary left, who shared Saramago's opposition to an integrated free-market Europe, also advocated the reinvigoration of links with Spanish- and Portuguese-speaking America and Africa, and particularly with those regions (such as Cuba, Nicaragua, and Cabo Verde) where the struggle for revolutionary socialism continued unabated. In the increasingly lop-sided national debate about relations with the EEC, almost all contributions were predicated as much on cultural, mythological, and affective grounds as on economic, strategic, or sociological ones. Saramago's response was a literary intervention that would expose the 'official discourse''s affirmation of future 'certainties' as absurd. It would demonstrate that visions of the future cannot be articulated without being *enfabulated*, while it also fostered a discursive space for the consideration of genuinely alternative futures outside a European superstate.

Jangada's plot, of course, presents absurdities of its own, but with a deeply serious purpose. First, the fantasy of a world that confounds the will of rulers by changing its natural laws allows Saramago to expose how a dominant ideology seeks (and, for once, fails) to sustain control by means of its mass-media representations of that world.[6] Secondly, the absurdity of *Jangada*'s plot is a constant reminder that where the novel moves beyond satirical allegory, its vision is essentially speculative. Thirdly, the fantastical element allows such speculation to extend to consideration of how human societies might behave when all systems of knowledge are shown to be unreliable. The way in which *Jangada*'s 'fabulous future' serves all of these purposes is evident in a comic scene that recalls a genuine historical precedent for the failure of the dominant episteme to accommodate observed natural phenomena. The world's leading geologists and oceanographers have made exhaustive examinations of the seabed around the moving Iberian Peninsula. This, however, reveals no tectonic ruptures, nor indeed any other potential explanation for the landmass's rapid shift:

> Desesperado, um sábio norte-americano, e dos ilustres, foi ao extremo de proclamar [...] Declaro que é impossível que a península esteja a mover-se, mas um italiano, ainda que muito menos sábio, porém reforçado pelo precedente histórico e científico, murmurou, mas não tão baixo que o não ouvisse aquele providencial ser que tudo escuta, E pur si muove. (*Jangada*: 139)
>
> [In despair, a learned North American, one of the most renowned, went to the extreme of announcing [...] I declare that it is impossible for the Peninsula to be moving, but an Italian, much less learned, but supported by historical and scientific precedent, muttered, not so low as to be inaudible to that providential being who hears everything, E pur si muove.]

'E pur si muove' (and yet, it moves): the words that Galileo Galilei allegedly muttered under his breath after he was forced by the Inquisition to abjure his substantiation of Copernican heliocentrism.[7] In the 1940s, Bertolt Brecht used this story in his *Leben des Galilei* (1980) to explore the attempts of hegemonic powers to control and manipulate potentially epoch-making technology and discoveries. *Jangada* updates this message, to consider the responses in the late capitalist era to discoveries about the material world that challenged not only dominant epistemologies, but also the powers established upon them.

The recourse to ucronian fantasy is crucial here, for Saramago can dissect contemporary strategies to suppress and manipulate knowledge only by imagining a physical world turned sufficiently dynamic and untameable to repeatedly out-manoeuvre the dominant powers' attempts to control popular perception through mass-media simulation. This explains how, since the time of Brecht's play, communications technology has developed to serve power and capital by more subtly pervasive, but also more diffuse and deregulated means. The increasing power of media simulation to construe perceptions of real-life phenomena as 'common knowledge' is subtly conveyed through *Jangada*'s narrative form. Whereas *Ricardo Reis* uses Reis's newspaper reading as a pretext for its pastiches of regime-controlled media copy, *Jangada*'s narrative slips, without explicit signal, in and out of the discourse of newspapers and 'rolling' TV and radio accounts of the Peninsula's displacement, which the narrative voice regularly relays, and which the protagonists are repeatedly shown receiving. This is a society wherein many events of universal significance, and indeed even the most accessible components of reality, frequently are not directly accessed or experienced, but rather, as Steven Best and Douglas Kellner explore, 'artificially (re)produced as "real", hence becoming not unreal, or surreal', but — as Jean Baudrillard argues — 'realer-than-real, a real retouched and refurbished in "a hallucinatory resemblance" with themselves' (Best and Kellner 1991: 119, citing Baudrillard 1983b: 23). While, as a (self-styled) Marxist, Saramago might despise Baudrillard's enthusiasm for the resulting 'hyper-reality', he is not afraid to acknowledge the power of new forms of mediation of phenomena, or what Jacques Derrida more helpfully identifies as the problematic 'artifactuality' of 'current affairs' reportage (Derrida 2002: esp. 3–7; 20–21). As much in the news reportage from the Portuguese coast as in the staging of carefully rigged 'debates' about Iberia and Europe's futures (*Jangada*: 93; 164), *Jangada* shows how televisual images and signs simulate an external reality in a format that blends information, entertainment and state propaganda into a 'realistic' package that impacts upon, and threatens to determine, reality itself. Elsewhere, seemingly whimsical subplots — recounting the protagonists' unsuccessful attempts to witness the peninsula's voyage past Gibraltar (inaccessible because of traffic jams) or past the Azorean island of Corvo (out of bounds due to US and NATO monitoring of the phenomenon) — indicate the restrictions placed on individuals' contact with a 'real' that they are instructed to regard as important, but which is beamed into their living places in pre-packaged, mass-media form.

As reading *Jangada* alongside *Ricardo Reis* makes clear, Saramago acknowledges the phenomena of the 'hyperreal' and simulation not as unprecedented, but as an intensification of the existing mechanisms by which established metanarratives always threaten to become the matrix for our interpretation of new situations. His implicit recognition of what Baudrillard has discussed as the 'implosion' of the real does not, however, entail any complacency or surrender.[8] Rather, the 'fabulous future' that Saramago elaborates is precisely one in which improbable natural events contradict Baudrillard's conclusion that, as Best & Kellner summarize, 'computerization, information processing, media, cybernetic control systems, and the organization of society according to simulation, codes, and models [must] replace production as the organizing principle of society'.[9] *Jangada*'s inexplicable phenomena provoke a series of crises for the masters of production, such as endangered trade agreements and routes, disrupted production, financial panic, and restive workforces. They are most threatening, however, insofar as each new turn on the Peninsula's journey confounds *materially* the ruling elite's attempts to contain events within a revised and reassuring vision of the future, propagated through mass-media simulation.

It is noteworthy that, while all of the novel's protagonists except Maria Guavaira (the last of the five to enter the story) are initially distanced from processes of material production, the geographic, social, and economic transformations precipitated by the Peninsula's movement compel them to assume a more unmediated relationship with their world. Their voyage through Iberia's regions culminates in a journey to the precipitous escarpments where the Spanish Pyrenees have severed from Europe, an experience that provokes a 'jubilosa dor' [triumphant pang] of exaltation (*Jangada*: 295). This encounter's sublime nature, and the correspondingly ridiculous appraisal of the same phenomenon offered by Roque Lozano, who laments the wasted effort of his long journey 'à procura do que não existia' [in search of that which never existed] (*Jangada*: 307) remind the reader that the problem of comprehending the real is one to which — as yet — humankind has no answer. Nevertheless, we should not despair, or passively accept the dominant simulations and interpretations pumped out by mass media. While we may not be able to comprehend reality in full, our independent analysis of it, and our incredulity towards (and independent reinterpretation of) simulacra, enable us to *influence* reality, and to contest the power of oligarchies. In this sense, *Jangada* cautiously anticipates Arjun Appadurai's optimistic riposte to those Frankfurt School theorists who saw capitalism as an 'iron cage' for the imagination, and his claim that 'it is wrong to assume that the electronic media are the opium of the masses' since 'there is growing evidence that the consumption of the mass media throughout the world often provokes resistance, irony, selectivity, and, in general, *agency*' (1996: 6–7). Ironically, Saramago's use of ucronian fantasy seems strangely consistent with Baudrillard's later advice to '[be] more virtual than events themselves, do not seek to re-establish the truth, we do not have the means, but do not be duped' (1995: 66).

Jangada meets this need to be 'more virtual than events themselves' without 're-establishing the truth' by redoubling Saramago's usual efforts to render his own novelistic simulation incredible. Tableaux such as those of the latter-day Galileo use absurd humour and literary cliché to advertise the author's inability to 're-establish truth'. Meanwhile, rather than simply reprising his earlier novels' warnings about their accounts' inevitable selectivity, Saramago pulls out all of the stops to make his narrative voice confess its own inadequacies. The laundry-lists of data with which this voice interrupts its own storytelling get cut short 'por insuficiência do narrador e falta de tempo' [through the narrator's failings and lack of time] (*Jangada*: 34), and descriptions of events remain hazy because 'deles não houve testemunhas' [there were no witnesses to them] (*Jangada*: 258). Since 'a objectividade do narrador é uma invenção moderna' [the objectivity of the narrator is a modern invention] (*Jangada*: 215), Saramago even introduces a 'voz desconhecida' [unknown voice] or 'voz irónica' [ironic voice] that periodically interjects to disrupt or contradict the 'principal' narrative voice. This device splits the novel's enunciating authority, unsettling the cosy collusion between reader and 'narrator' that is encouraged by the latter's habit elsewhere of speaking in the first person plural.[10] The reader, consequently, must question the possibility, or benefit, of extrapolating any coherent interpretation of the plot.

This device also reinforces the intimations that the knowledge upon which humans predicate critical decisions frequently derives from 'vozes desconhecidas', ranging from folklore and 'old wives' tales', to the anonymous, remote 'sources' of mass-media news copy. Whereas Saramago's preceding novels feature characters — João Mau-Tempo, Blimunda, Lídia — invested with authority as witnesses to history, *Jangada* does not dignify its protagonists, or their experience of an imagined future, as sources of insight or wisdom for the reader's edification. Rather, the narrative, as it reports events, emphasizes the fragility of the explanations offered for them: '[s]abido é que todo o efeito tem sua causa, e esta é uma universal verdade, porém, não é possível evitar alguns erros de juízo, ou de simples identificação' [it is well known that every effect has its cause, and that this is a universal rule, however, it is not possible to avoid a few errors of judgement, or of simple identification] (*Jangada*: 14). The conclusion of the novel's plot stresses the protagonists' failure to establish the 'truth' of their present or future situations: 'que futuro, que tempo, que destino' [what future, what time, what destiny] (*Jangada*: 330). Repeatedly, the five travellers' experience of the phenomena that seem to direct their destinies is recounted with a degree of ironic detachment or burlesque hyperbole that suggests an 'erro de juízo, ou [...] identificação' [error of judgement, or identification] on their part. Such is the case of the arrival of Joaquim Sassa and his friends at Maria Guavaira's house (*Jangada*: 182–85), where their belief that destiny is fixed at pivotal historic 'moments' (*Jangada*: 149; 151) is bolstered by the seeming transfiguration of their surroundings. This 'moment' is heralded by an extravaganza of hackneyed symbolism and pathetic fallacy: as the sun bursts through the clouds to set in a blaze of glory, the grimy thread of Maria Guavaira's wool that the dog carries regains its original colour — a transcendental 'azul nem do céu nem do mar' [blue neither of the sky nor of the sea], the four friends become 'formosas criaturas' [beautiful creatures], the dog shines like a 'jóia cintilante' [glittering jewel], and even their car takes on renewed youth and vigour (*Jangada*: 183). Eventually, the narrator tips the wink to the reader, reminding that there are 'tantas razões para não acreditar' [so many reasons not to believe] in the hypothesis of destiny that is supported by so much aesthetic and rhetorical overdrive (*Jangada*: 184).

Here and elsewhere, the frequent intrusion of intertextual references, to genres as diverse as Hollywood melodrama and classical epic, not only disrupts the narrative's unity but lends cartoonish mock-heroic qualities to its protagonists. Maria Guavaira's account of the dog's appearance, 'assim como alguém que quisesse falar e não pudesse' [just like someone who wanted to speak and could not] (*Jangada*: 187), is the same trope straight out of the *Lassie* films that is earlier cited by the narrative (*Jangada*: 154).[11] Epic motifs are adapted to José and Joaquim's journey into Spain, to even more prosaic effect. For example, the chapter opening 'De pedras e estorninhos conversaram' [Of stones and starlings they conversed] (*Jangada*: 63), which mimics Virgil's much-imitated 'arma virumque cano', advertises the subsequent play on such Virgilian/ Camonian conventions as describing heroism by means of elaborate similes introduced by the formula 'qualis...' / 'tal como' employed to aggrandize the travellers' arrival at a customs checkpoint (*Jangada*: 69). This mock-heroic characterization — distinct from that of the earlier novels — ties in with the novel's simultaneously mock-epic and mock-disaster emplotment, the narrative being driven by a series of catastrophes, which, as Frier (1998: 713) notes, repeatedly threaten implausibly, only to be equally implausibly averted. Saramago ingeniously exploits ucronian fantasy's permission of this 'double' plot structure to undermine the visions of national apotheosis and of national eclipse presented (according to Kaufman and Ornelas) by the 'dominant discourse'. First, *Jangada*'s disaster motifs make a repeated mockery of European integrationists' apocalyptic warnings against Iberian isolation. Simultaneously, the mock-epic touches subvert the prophetic potential of Saramago's alternative vision of Iberia's future as a recuperation of the mid-1970s arrested revolution.

The manner in which *Jangada* undermines its own authority as much as that of the discourse of European integration that it opposes should alert us to the third discussion, of more universal significance, that the novel's 'fabulous' premises enable. Over and above asking what path Iberia should opt for, and how to contend with corporate news media's eclipsing of the real, *Jangada* uses the precedent of inexplicable geological and biological aberrations to ask what humankind does — and what it could, or should do — when all received knowledge and empirical observation is proven inadequate. Much ink has been spilled in attempts to make sense of the novel's seemingly supernatural occurrences and their potential symbolic significance, ever since the painstaking and ingenious excavation of references to classical and Portuguese sources in Mary L. Daniel's early reading. Such readings, however, must acknowledge the challenge posed by what most scholars acknowledge to be the consistently imprecise, and frequently over-determined, nature of such literary and cultural references. More problematic are attempts to answer the questions that Daniel poses of whether these are

> mere isolated symbols, or [...] part of a grand synchronic scheme? Is every human act a stone in the cosmic ocean which inevitably produces ripples in every other part of the ocean? (2005: 17)

Daniel suggests that one can trust the narrator's assertion that '(t)odas estas coisas, mesmo quando o não parecerem, estão ligadas entre si' [all of these things are interconnected, even when they do not appear to be] (*Jangada*: 19) and thereupon presume the existence of a law of the 'synchronicity of intentional coincidences' (2005: 20). The narrator suggests that 'a harmonia possível das coisas depende do seu equilíbrio e do tempo em que acontecem, não cedo de mais, não tarde de mais' [the potential harmony of things depends on their equilibrium, and on the time in which they occur, not too early, not too late] (*Jangada*: 185). Yet even if we believe this, we have little cause for optimism, given that the near certainty of misrecognition or misapprehension of the moment means that 'nos é tão difícil alcançar a perfeição' [it is so difficult for us to attain perfection] (ibid.).[12]

Moreover, the novel signals that the higher significance of 'intentional coincidences' cannot safely be divined through a search for historic, mythological, or literary precedents. As Frier points out (2007: 144), labyrinthine imagery recurs right up to the last chapter; here, the 'casas como paredes de labirinto' [houses like the walls of a labyrinth] (*Jangada*: 328) in the town of Orce forewarn of the lack of explanation or closure at the novel's end. Many of the novel's events and cultural references can be interpreted, as Frier puts it, 'tanto num sentido positivo como num sentido negativo' [as much with a positive meaning as with a negative meaning] (1998: 713–14). The imprecise and slippery nature of *Jangada*'s key tropes, and the semiotic and intertextual maze that this generates, cannot be accidental. As his earlier novels illustrate, Saramago is a writer as well-versed in popular folklore and visual culture as in canonical literature. Yet in *Jangada*, he chooses as his central motifs both a tree and a bird (the elm and the starling) of uncommonly limited significance in European folklore, in Christian and heraldic symbolism, or in literary texts. The elm has (infrequently) been emblematic of dignity in Christian iconography,[13] and in European lore dating back before Christianity, elm wood is said to have the power 'to attract love when carried'.[14] Both of these precedents fit with the significance Joana Carda attributes to her 'vara' [wand], but do not explain its supernatural agency or corroborate the regenerative powers that Rebelo, among other critics, attributes to it (see below). Rebelo links Joana Carda's wand to a plethora of precedents, from 'a significação emblemática do sofrimento da Humanidade' to the 'árvore da vida, bíblica vara de Jessé, símbolo da fertilidade e da renovação' [the emblematic symbol of the suffering of humanity [...] the tree of life, the Biblical rod of Jesse, symbol of fertility and renewal] (*Jangada*: 348). However, while the wand is distanced from 'símbolos de sofrimento' by the specific statement that it is *not* a cross on Pedro Orce's grave ('Não é cruz, como bem se vê' [it is not a cross, as can be clearly seen] (*Jangada*: 330), it also gives no proof of its potential as an 'árvore da vida', since the novel ends before it can take root (or not) and be reborn on Pedro Orce's grave. As for the starlings, while — as Frier notes (1999: 201–02; 205) — they may allude imprecisely to auguries of death and St Vincent's 'miraculous' ravens, it is equally significant that their flight through Seville transforms the statue of Faith atop the Giralda tower into a 'figura indefinível que tanto podia ser [...] o emblema da Descrença' [an indefinable figure that could as easily be [...] the emblem of Doubt] (*Jangada*: 77).

Moreover, Saramago frequently uses two closely related similes, with strikingly different symbolic connotations, to describe the same referent. The split in the Pyrenees, for example, is compared first to a sliced-open 'romã' [pomegranate] (*Jangada*: 33), a fruit whose association, variously, with fidelity, with Christ's passion, with ecclesiastical unity, and with the union of Catholic Spain post-1492, offers bewilderingly diverse 'clues' to the significance of Iberia's displacement. Soon afterwards the same rift is compared to a 'melancia' [watermelon] (*Jangada*: 71); again, a red, juicy, husked fruit, but one wholly lacking symbolic loadings.[15] Connecting *Jangada*'s symbolic motifs to pre-existing grand narratives requires a leap of faith, or a degree of fabrication or selectivity, and yet, as Frier argues, 'a ambiguidade deve ser vista como uma parte essencial e deliberada da concepção da obra' [ambiguity should be seen as an essential and intentional part of the work's conception] (1998: 715). Rather than offering an ingeniously encrypted key to a totalizing thesis of Iberian history, *Jangada*'s disparate fields of intertextual and mythological allusion combine to illustrate both the dangers and the opportunities arising from humanity's recourse to grand narratives when (or even before) empiricism fails to yield enlightenment. On the one hand, they offer examples of the folly of reading history in accordance with established narratives of communal identity, exceptionality, and/or 'destiny'. At the same time, they show the progressive potential arising from *creative* and *self-conscious* reinterpretations or reworkings of those grand narratives or of their constituent parts. First and most obviously, the allusion to Iberia's 'Golden Age' of maritime exploration and expansion, triggered when the peninsula 'sets sail' from Europe, allows Saramago to set a long-established narrative of national apotheosis at odds with the contemporary hegemonic narrative wherein the Iberian nations' future depends on their resignation to secondary and peripheral roles in a capitalist European union. The rupture that the novel thereby creates between the mantra of 'a Europa conosco' [Europe is with us], first popularized by the Portuguese Socialist Party in 1976, and the most treasured touchstones of Portuguese identity, simultaneously reveals how, as Frier has stressed, it is merely 'a auto-referencialidade do acto de *escrever* a história' [the self-referentiality of the act of *writing* history] that creates the 'o ar de ineluctabilidade que se pode atribuir à história' [history's air of ineluctability] (1998: 715). Frier's later readings have illuminated how imprecise, juxtaposed, or overlapping echoes of Camões with Homer and Virgil, with Cervantes's mock-heroic *Don Quixote* (whose opening sentence is paraphrased on p. 10 of the novel), and Celtic mythology both prevent a simple reiteration of the imperialist 'Golden Age' narrative, and attest to Iberia's age-old connections to other cultures along the North Atlantic and Mediterranean seaboards.[16] The lessons to be taken from this do not concern only the dangers of basing assessments of local identity and 'destiny' purely on current or recent political history. They also relate to the potential of shared narratives as a medium for inter-community dialogue, or as an inspiration for solidarity. When new or challenging circumstances require the assumption of new behaviour and habits, critical reinterpretation of such narratives can help to constitute new identities and — to borrow Appadurai's (1996) term — new 'imagined worlds' that may in turn abet initiatives for materially based social renewal.

II — From *Portugalidade* to Internationalism: 'Trans-Iberianism' as Inter-identity

The continuing lure of nationalism, in an ever-more globalized Europe, is starkly revealed by *Jangada*'s evocation of how grand narratives are reaffirmed in times of crisis. Yet the novel's depiction of Iberia fleeing from EEC expansionism by returning to former routes of imperialist expansion also risks reanimating some pernicious nationalist myths. The incongruities generated by the novel's overlapping intertextual allusions to epic and mock-epic genres, and to local and cosmopolitan narratives, should remind us of Saramago's fundamental observation that every historical event can be enfabulated (and every history interpreted) in many ways (*doutras maneiras*). Nevertheless, insofar as *Jangada* connects a vision of potential social regeneration to the consequences of the Peninsula's displacement, one must ask if — as Daniel, Rebelo, and many others have suggested — this betokens Saramago's faith in a benign Iberian separatism, and/or in the animation of a specific regional or national ethos. In a number of essays and interviews following the novel's publication, Saramago affirmed his concept of *'trans-ibericidade'* or trans-Iberianism, which recognized the Peninsular peoples' common historical and cultural inheritance and 'semi-peripheral' position within the globalized capitalist system, and argued for a federal union of the Iberian regions.[17] The following section of this chapter assesses *Jangada*'s success in conveying this call for a revolutionary *trans-ibericidade*, while avoiding a crude rehabilitation of ethnic essentialism or chauvinism. It considers first how the novel both exposes nationalism's effect in disguising the exploitative hierarchies of capitalism, and mocks presuppositions both of a unitary ethnic 'essence', and of naturally clear-cut geographic and cultural divisions between nations. Next, however, this section argues that, as an allegory of 'trans-Iberian' solidarity and independence, the flight of the Peninsula has limitations. The novel cannot resolve the internal contradictions even of the pluralist Iberianism that it suggests, nor does it eliminate the imperialist and neo-colonialist implications of Iberia's relocation to the epicentre of the Spanish and Portuguese-speaking Atlantic. Consequently, *Jangada*'s trans-Iberianism can be reconciled with Saramago's professed socialist internationalism only as an ideology deployed *tactically*, against both Eurocentrism and Spanish and Portuguese nationalisms. *Jangada* depicts state affirmations of ethnic specificity or exceptionality as relying on the abjection of problematic or disparaged traits and values onto an ethnic Other. Ethnocentric nationalism is thus inevitably exclusionary and chauvinistic. Moreover, for both individuals and communities, it is a self-defeating self-deception, whose insistence on a fixed psychic specificity, cultural homogeneity, and/or historical self-sufficiency hampers the self-reinvention, and accommodation of Others, that Saramago increasingly presents as fundamental to social renewal. Yet Saramago is alert to present-day populations' reluctance to abandon concepts of national identity, loyalty, and destiny. Hence, he proposes an alternative conception of community, referenced to local circumstances, culture, and heritage, but nevertheless pluralist, malleable, and open to the Other. An Iberian rapprochement is not an end in itself, even if — when founded on the critical rediscovery of a common, but often contested, history and a shared cultural inheritance — it stimulates enhanced self-knowledge and solidarity in addressing the region's problems. Rather, it is an opportunity for formerly antagonistic communities to learn how to co-exist in difference, as an essential preliminary to any socialist, and internationalist, transformation.

In the international crisis that *Jangada* imagines, as previously in *Ricardo Reis*, it is easy to spot an essentially Marxist critique of how modern nationalism — even in the era of globalization — serves capitalism. Nationalism reifies a false community of economically antagonistic social classes, while fostering division between subaltern populations with common economic grievances. It is to these ends that an embattled Portuguese Prime Minister seeks to make the Portuguese relish the envy of other Europeans, who 'vêem na aventura histórica em que nos achamos lançados a promessa de um futuro mais feliz e, para tudo dizer em poucas palavras, a esperança de um rejuvenescimento da humanidade' [see in this historic adventure into which we find ourselves launched the promise of a happier future, or, in a word, the hope of regenerating humanity] (*Jangada*: 169). In reality, however, this bombastic updating of the discourse on the 'historical adventure' of 'Discoveries' is an empty attempt to bolster disintegrating national solidarity: Portugal's property-controlling elite has just jumped ship for a 'futuro mais feliz' in Europe. The flight of the wealthy, and of the vast wealth in bank deposits, artworks, and moveable goods that they take with them (*Jangada*: 106), has a much more recent precedent in national history, namely the exodus of business and their capital following the 25 April coup and the proposed nationalization of key industries.[18] More importantly, such an exodus suggests that, in a deeply hierarchical class society, there are 'vários graus de pertença de cada um à pátria natural e administrativamente sua' [different degrees by which each individual belongs to his or her natural and administrative homeland], and they correspond directly to the economic freedom one has to bail out of a 'pátria' in crisis (ibid.). It is mostly members of the Iberian elite, who 'apesar dos apertados laços da tradição e cultura, da propriedade e do poder, tinham virado as costas ao desvario geológico' [despite their close ties of tradition and culture, of property and power, had turned their backs on the geological upset], that appear in the phoney televised debates, entreating their former compatriots to 'faça como eu, escolha a Europa' [do as I did, choose Europe] (*Jangada*: 164). For those with wealth to transfer from one country to another, *Jangada* suggests, patriotism serves essentially as a disincentive to their workforce to forge class-based, and international, solidarity. By imagining a future crisis that provokes a repeat of the mid-1970s flight of the captains of Portuguese industry, Saramago points to the cynicism and duplicity of the subsequent — and highly successful — mythologization of the April Revolution as a moment of national reconciliation and consensus in pursuit of a capitalist liberal democracy.

A second evil of nationalism is that the heroic archetypes by which it inspires a collective, 'national', subjectivity are sustained by complementary constructions of aberrant, exotic, or antagonistic ethnic Others. *Jangada* illustrates this by evoking how state discourses betray the animosity and mutual suspicion cultivated by the architects of modern Iberia's nation states. While the Portuguese Prime Minister resuscitates a smug self-image of pioneering 'Discoverers', Spanish state media deploy a contrastingly unheroic paradigm of *portugalidade* in a bid to soothe Spanish anxieties and humiliations. Television reports from the Portuguese coast paraphrase the image of the national character with which Miguel de Unamuno opens his *Por tierras de Portugal y de España* (1909):

> Represéntaseme Portugal como una hermosa y dulce muchacha campesina que de espaldas a Europa, sentida a orillas del mar, [...] los codos hincados en las rodillas y la cara entre las manos, mira cómo el sol se pone en las aguas infinitas. (1941: 10)
>
> [Portugal appears to me like a beautiful, gentle country girl sitting with her back to Europe at the brink of the ocean [...] resting her elbows on her knees and her head between her hands, as she contemplates the sun's descent into the infinite waters.]

For all his love of Portugal and its literature (which he read extensively), Unamuno here depicts his neighbour nation as effeminate, passive, and moribund or even suicidal, an anthropomorphism modelled after the *fin-de-siècle* fantasy of the *femme fragile*.[19] *Jangada*'s Spanish news broadcasters marry this romantic image of Portuguese decadence with footage of the coast, where

> estava muita gente a olhar o horizonte, com aquele trágico ademane de quem se preparou desde séculos para o ignoto [...] Agora ei-los ali, como Unamuno disse que estavam, la cara morena entre ambas palmas, clavas tus ojos donde el sol se acuesta solo en la mar inmensa, [...] Lírico, arrebatado, o locutor espanhol declama, Vejam-se os portugueses, ao longo das suas douradas praias, proa da Europa que foram e deixaram de ser (*Jangada*: 93)
>
> [there were lots of people watching the horizon, with that tragic expression of one who has for centuries readied himself for the unknown [...] See them there now, like Unamuno described them, your swarthy face between your hands, your eyes fixed on where the sun sleeps alone in the vast ocean [...] Lyrical, enraptured, the Spanish newscaster declaims, Look at the Portuguese, all along their golden beaches, once the prow of Europe, but now no longer]

Removed from the original context of Unamuno's examination of the anxious and decadent condition of both Iberian countries, this depiction functions for Spain in much the same way that Orientalist discourse, according to Edward Said, functioned for a Eurocentric West as the 'contrasting image, idea, personality, experience' (1995: 2) that defines and sustains a self-image as heroic, dynamic, and up-to-date or, essentially, superior (1995: 7).

Jangada's subsequent images of Portuguese responses to crisis confront Unamuno's 'orientalizing' inscription of *portugalidade* with very different paradigms. Furthermore, they suggest the need for conceptions of a shared identity to be non-essentialist, inclusive, and fluid. Before exploring this, however, it should be noted that *Jangada*'s critique of the logic of conventional nationalism goes beyond the observation that the nationalist affirmation of a stable, idealized collective self relies on its construction of an ethnic Other as negative or aberrant. The responses of Europe's political elites to the Peninsula's displacement show how affirmations of a unitary collective identity entail the policing of artificial geographic, linguistic, and cultural borders, and thus tend towards an authoritarian intolerance of dissident elements within the imagined community. In a 1993 essay extrapolating a thorough critique of the EEC/EU project from *Jangada*'s central allegory, Saramago directs his strongest condemnation towards this obnoxious impact of nationalism on domestic, as much as foreign, relations, denouncing 'aquele outro comportamento aberrante que consiste em ser a Europa eurocêntrica em relação a si mesma' [that other aberration that consists of Europe's taking a Eurocentric attitude towards itself] (1993: 86). Responding to Boaventura de Sousa Santos's discussion of Iberian 'semi-peripherality', he claims that throughout the modern era there have been 'duas Europas, uma central, outra periférica, com o consequente lastro de injustiças, discriminações e ressentimentos históricos cuja responsabilidade a nova Europa comunitária não parece disposta a assumir' [two Europes, one central, the other peripheral, with the consequent litany of injustices, discriminations, and historical grudges for which the new European community does not seem inclined to assume responsibility] (ibid.).[20] Just as the Spanish newscaster's pastiche of Unamuno dresses Portugal in *fin-de-siècle* decadentist drag, so too, 'para os Estados europeus ricos [...] o resto do continente continua a ser algo vago e confuso, um tanto exótico, um tanto pitoresco, merecedor, quando muito, do interesse de antropólogos e arqueólogos, mas onde, apesar de tudo, contando com adequadas colaborações locais, ainda se podem fazer alguns bons negócios' [for the wealthy European states [...] the remainder of the continent remains something vague and jumbled, a little bit exotic, a little picturesque, deserving, at best, of the attentions of anthropologists and archaeologists, but [somewhere] where in spite of everything, with sufficient local collaboration, one can still do a decent bit of business] (ibid.).

This logic, which enables the domination of a 'periphery' whose credentials as a component of a continental 'community' are endlessly called into question, but whose autonomy is never respected, is memorably satirized in *Jangada*'s account of the impact of the Peninsula's movement on the stationary rump Europe. A more paternalistic Eurocentrism assumes the role of a '[m]ãe amorosa' [loving mother] who 'afligiu-se com a sorte das suas terras extremas' [was distressed by the fate of her most far-flung lands] (*Jangada*: 33). A less indulgent lobby, however, asserts the trans-historical existence of a European ethnic purity defended by the natural boundary of the Pyrenees, 'indo ao ponto de insinuar que se a Península Ibérica se queria ir embora, então que fosse, o erro foi tê-la deixado entrar' [going so far as to insinuate that, if the Iberian Peninsula wished to leave, then let it leave, the mistake was to have let it enter in the first place] (*Jangada*: 44). Bidding good riddance to the 'parcelas espúrias' [spurious components] of the periphery, these latter Europeans look forward to the formation of a more exclusive EEC that would be 'um só país, quinta-essência do espírito europeu, sublimado perfeito simples, a Europa, isto é, a Suíça' [a single country, quintessence of the European spirit, a pure and perfect sublimate, Europe, that's to say, Switzerland] (ibid.). There is an obvious irony in comparing this European 'quintessence' to the state most consistently opposed to economic or political integration with its neighbours.[21] Moreover, this statement begs the question of what might be the particular merit of the Swiss model of European-ness, if not its respect for individual liberties, and the federal structures that have guaranteed the autonomy of its cantons and the prosperous co-existence of their diverse languages and customs.

Meanwhile, the intolerance of difference and of pluralism, shared by nationalisms and integralist models of European union, is evoked in the backlash against the elites' chauvinistic calls for the 'periphery' to conform to the values of the 'centre' or be damned. Idealist, self-styled young 'Iberianists' affirm an ideal of decentralization and cultural diversity. As a riposte to the EEC's agenda, they emblazon their slogan 'Nós também somos ibéricos' [We are Iberians too] all across Europe in every official state language (*Jangada*: 162–63). This slogan derives particular political and comic resonance from its echoes of a range of mottoes of mass movements for liberty, from J. F. Kennedy's assertion to Nikita Khrushchev and Walter Ulbricht that 'Ich bin ein Berliner', to the rebel slaves' claim that 'I am Spartacus' in Stanley Kubrick's 1960 epic *Spartacus*. Ultimately, the slogan provokes a horror-struck Pope into the attitude of a latter-day Belshazzar when it appears in Ecclesiastical Latin — 'Nos quoque iberi sumus' — daubed on the walls of the Vatican (*Jangada*: 163). Increasingly, however, the Iberianists realize that the right to an autonomous identity is served little better by the notion of a patchwork quilt of European nation states than it is by a centralized, homogenized European union. As their movement gains momentum, the Iberianists' slogan appears 'também nos dialectos locais, nas diferentes gírias, finalmente em esperanto, mas a este era difícil entendê-lo' [even in local dialects, in various forms of slang, finally, in Esperanto, though in this case it was difficult to understand] (*Jangada*: 164). En route to demonstrating the failure of Ludwik Zamenhof's dream of promoting peaceful ethnic co-existence by inventing a 'universal' language, the 'Iberianists' challenge the prevailing hegemony of what Benedict Anderson identifies as state-sponsored 'print languages'. As Anderson famously argues in *Imagined Communities* (1991: 67–82), the imposition of a standardized version of the vernacular as language-of-state first enabled early capitalism's expansion and state regulation of markets, and became increasingly instrumental in fostering the national consciousness that protected the state's integrity. The Iberianists reject the hegemony of print languages, returning to the dialects and 'minority' languages that nation-builders strove to eradicate, but that survive, straddling political borders and shading gradually into each other. By thus contesting official models of collective identity, 'tão laboriosamente formadas ao longo de séculos e séculos' [so laboriously created over hundreds of years] (*Jangada*: 160), the Iberianists end up exposing the myth of the nation state's organic ethnic uniformity, and reverse its delegitimization of diversity. The biased television 'debates' with which the establishment responds, to stay the centrifugal force of 'Iberianist' pluralism, meanwhile only constitute another fraudulent mass-media simulacrum. While these spectacles pay lip-service to the Enlightenment principles of liberty, fair play, and reason frequently cited as hallmarks of European culture, in reality they constitute a stage-managed refabrication of the EEC's artifice of a single European identity and destiny.

This deconstruction of the very concept of the nation sits awkwardly with the plot device upon which *Jangada*'s allegory of resistance to the EEC is founded. Iberia's severance from Europe not only legitimizes the drawing of a border between two states. It also bisects the catchment area of 'regional' languages increasingly boldly affirmed as print languages (and indeed as 'national' languages of state) by local populations: *Catalá* and *Euskera*. Indeed, scholars of Iberian regionalist politics and identity since the 1980s might argue that the most implausible thing about *A Jangada de Pedra* is not that the Peninsula sails away, but that Catalonia and the Basque Country do not split off and sail back to Europe.[22] Must one therefore conclude that *Jangada*'s allegory is irredeemably contradictory, or that it hypocritically denounces a homogenizing chauvinism of Eurocentrism and nationalism, only to admit of an Iberianism that is equally inclined to degenerate into the repudiation of perceived outsiders and dissidents? Frier's charge that *Jangada* posits 'a similar uniformity within the peninsula to that which it seeks to refute within Europe' (2007: 140) has some justification: certainly, the ready establishment of solidarity between the novel's Portuguese, Galician, and Andalusian protagonists effaces inter-regional tensions and preconceptions (such as might be harder to dismiss convincingly if the novel's Catalan protagonist were human and not a mute canine). Nevertheless, *Jangada* repeatedly celebrates the diverse cultures and histories of the Iberian regions. As its protagonists tour the peninsula's periphery — fleeing a Lisbon that becomes the seat of sinister state power, and by-passing Madrid altogether — the novel signals sympathy with Iberian regionalist agendas, by referring to the cities of Euskadi and Navarra by their Basque names ('Donostia' rather than 'San Sebastián, and 'Gasteiz' rather than 'Vitoria') (*Jangada*: 293; 284).

This acknowledgment of Iberian diversity, and of its potential as a foundation for linguistic and cultural pluralism, is what underpins Saramago's faith in 'trans-Iberianism' as a progressive, educational, and ultimately liberating initiative.[23] His vision of Iberia's separation from Europe as galvanizing its peoples into the harmonious pursuit of a common purpose only acquires real credibility, however, if one also recognizes how *Jangada* presents ethnicity neither as a fixed, all-subsuming essence, nor as a pernicious ideological chimera, but as an inchoate set of beliefs, behaviours, and allegiances that are firmly implanted through socialization from infancy. His championing of 'trans-iberismo' represents both an acknowledgment that his society cannot, or will not, easily abandon its sense of ethnic belonging and ethnic difference, and a recognition of the political opportunity afforded by Iberian peoples' shared historical experiences and common interpellation as 'marginal' or 'exotic' Europeans. A sense of cultural rootedness and distinction can only be purged of its xenophobic and fascist potential, however, if both collective and individual identities are recognized first as *discursive* (hence, as dynamic and situational), and secondly not as antagonistic, but as mutually enriching. Most importantly, as Saramago himself claimed,

> não haverá uma Europa realmente nova se esta que temos não se instituir como ser moral, e também não a haverá enquanto não tiver sido abolido, mais do que

os egoísmos nacionais ou regionais, reflexos defensivos quase sempre, enquanto não tiver sido abolido, repito, o preconceito duma suposta prevalência ou subordinação de umas culturas em relação a outras. (1993: 87)

[there will be no genuinely new Europe for as long as the one we currently have does not establish itself as a moral being, and unless we abolish, over and above national and regional selfishness, which is nearly always a defensive reaction, unless, I repeat, we abolish the presumption that some cultures may take precedence over, or be subordinated to, others.]

At the same time, however, *Jangada*'s playful treatment of Unamuno's and Camões's texts, and of how they have become tools of alternative, local 'egoismos', points to the danger for Iberians too of excluding or subordinating their ethnic neighbours, and of denigrating 'others' within their imagined national communities. The chauvinism extrapolated from such paradigms is repeatedly lampooned, as when Iberia's national governments reject European protests 'com másculo orgulho por banda dos espanhóis e feminina altivez pelo lado dos portugueses' [with macho pride on the part of the Spanish and feminine haughtiness on the Portuguese side] (*Jangada*: 167), a sardonic allusion back to Unamuno that ridicules any vision of Iberian union as one wherein Portugal, like a meek bride, should vow to honour and obey. However, if one infers from this that *Jangada*'s protagonists create the example of a more equal Iberian partnership, one must address Frier's aforementioned criticism (2007: 140). Does the novel's alternative to the subjection of populations by recourse to narrow preconceptions of cultural identity add up to more than a new, improved, Iberian specificity, as a 'reflexo defensivo' [defensive reflex] against a 'Eurocentralizing' agenda? The easy bonding of Spanish Pedro and Portuguese José and Joaquim dismisses the spectre of an endemic ethnic chauvinism or hostility, whereas the five travellers' unity is repeatedly threatened by divisions of gender and by sexual jealousy (*Jangada*: 127–30; 173–75; 286–93; 302–05; 324–26). At the same time, however, the solidarity between the protagonists is consistently connected to their fearful supernatural experiences, their flight from the authorities, and the subsequent crises that compel them to bond and cooperate. Moreover, several of the shared experiences to which those circumstances lead them do reveal the complexity and flexibility of ethnic collectivity, and ultimately suggest the need for a 'rooted cosmopolitanism' that respects and embraces the Other, rather than projecting on to her/him a negative image of the alleged and idealized characteristics of the self.

The discursive foundations of ethnic identity, and the reality of its renegotiation and modification in response to changing circumstances, emerge in the burlesque account of shantytown dwellers storming the empty Algarve hotels and setting up squatters' communes (*Jangada*: 97–105). Pedro Orce, Joaquim Sassa, and José Anaiço find themselves caught up in pitched battles between the squatters and police, prompting the narrative voice to reflect on Unamuno's distinction between Portuguese *meiguice* [gentleness] and Spanish aggression (1941: 11), when it jokes that Pedro Orce, 'apesar da idade, brigava como se esta fosse a sua terra, os outros faziam o melhor que podiam, talvez um tanto menos, por pertencerem à raça pacífica' [despite his age, fought as though this was his own land, the others did the best they could, perhaps a little less, belonging as they did to the gentle race] (*Jangada*: 103).[24]

However, on resuming its satire on both Unamuno's vision of the Portuguese as a spent force, and on Camões's claim for their innate heroism, the narrative voice sardonically concludes that

> Afinal [...] os portugueses são de duas espécies diferentes, há uns que vão para as praias e arribas contemplar melancólicos o horizonte, há outros que avançam intrépidos sobre as fortalezas hoteleiras defendidas pela polícia. (*Jangada*: 98)
>
> [In the end [...] there are two different types of Portuguese, some who go to the beaches and dunes to gaze melancholically at the horizon, and others who advance, intrepid, on the hotel-fortresses defended by the police.]

This cancelling-out of hegemonic models of national 'character' or 'values' reminds that while — like the national historical narratives discussed by Frier (1998: 719) — such models may inspire or influence agency, they should not determine or constrain agency. As Lough argues, '[t]here may even be a danger in any attempt to read into the novel a sense of identity which depends too much on the past and tradition' (2002: 155). In the case of the hotel occupations, the question of ethnic identity should not distract either the protagonists or the reader from how class and economic circumstance are factors in responses to the Iberian crisis. The aims and achievements of the hotel squatters are expressly socialist, and inspired by a common experience of grinding poverty (*Jangada*: 101). Rebelo, in one of the more sophisticated of many readings that hail the affirmation of a resurgent Portuguese 'autenticidade nacional' in *Jangada* (1986: 345), sees this as verifying the

> constância das principais determinantes do *ethos* lusitano: o lado contemplativo, o da expectativa messiânica daqueles que vão mirar o mar; e o lado pragmático daqueles que, pela actuação imediata, procuram acudir às prementes carências sociais da terra. (1986: 343)
>
> [constancy of the determinant principles of the Portuguese *ethos*: the contemplative aspect, that of the messianic conviction of those who go and gaze out to sea, and the pragmatic aspect of those who, through unhesitating action, seek to address the pressing social needs of their land.]

Lough retorts that Rebelo's definition of the Portuguese ethos 'is surely too general to be of any real meaning' (2002: 155). Even if Lough overlooks Rebelo's specific reference here to the inscription of Portuguese fatalism in the cult of Dom Sebastião, *Jangada* nowhere presents this attitude as something to be relied upon, much less celebrated.[25] Moreover, Lough's point about generality is borne out by the fact that, soon after the Algarve squatters' victory, precisely the same popular struggle erupts over the hotels of the Andalusian Costa del Sol (*Jangada*: 104). There is a notable overlap in Saramago's construction of proletarian and Portuguese identities here: the pragmatism and initiative of the hotel squatters (which Rebelo identifies with the Portuguese 'lado pragmático'), is, after all, consistent with Saramago's portrayal of the *povo* in *Levantado* and *Memorial*. However, insofar as this alternative national character, aligned with fraternity and pragmatism, informs further popular responses to successive crises in the novel, it coexists with intimations of a less idealized subjectivity. As the Peninsula's collision with the Azores islands threatens, accounts of the chaotic evacuation of the coastal regions detail not only the initiatives that many supposedly fatalistic Portuguese take while their leaders dither, but also widespread outbreaks of panic, irrationality, and a selfish violence that mocks the notion of national *brandos costumes* [gentle customs] (*Jangada*: 223–25; 235–37).[26]

Rebelo's reading of *Jangada* as imagining solutions to uniquely, or at least primarily, Portuguese dilemmas may be unnecessarily reductive. However, its inclusion as an afterword to Caminho's second, and subsequent, editions of the novel, and its many citations in later studies, attest to the wide recognition in Portugal of the novel's key tropes as relating to elements of national history and mythology. The first of two particular instances of this is the referencing of the seafaring peninsula to the voyages of 'Discovery'. Such references are already ideologically problematic, insofar as they invite a renewed celebration of national expansion that was based on imperialist aggression, colonial exploitation, and slavery. They become more problematic if one accepts Eduardo Lourenço's famous argument that the myth of the age of 'Discoveries' as a national 'momento solar' [moment of glory] is one that focuses collective self-belief and agency on an unrecoverable and unsurpassable past (1994: 10), and contributes to the fatalism and passivity in the present that José Gil (2004) characterizes as Portuguese 'non-inscription'.

A second instance, intimated by Rebelo's reference to 'os valores e as esperanças do 25 de Abril' [the values and the hopes of the 25 April Revolution] (1986: 345), is the parallel between the repercussions of the Peninsula's movement and the crises, conflicts, and vicissitudes of Portugal's April Revolution. The battle for the Algarve hotels — where, ultimately, soviet-style communes are established — is a case in point. This recalls both the housing collectives set up by shanty-town dwellers in occupied residential units in the Portuguese cities between 1974 and 1976, and the use of hotels deserted by foreign tourists as emergency accommodation not for homeless locals, but for some of the hundreds of thousands of penurious *retornados* fleeing Portugal's former 'overseas provinces' in Africa.[27] Similar echoes of the mid-1970s remind the (Portuguese) reader of the cynicism of the political elite, regrouping ineffectually into a 'Governo de Salvação Nacional' (*Jangada*: 212), and of the power of the US government, monitoring the upheaval in Iberia, ready to intervene with a heavy hand to protect its military and commercial interests. This latter development recalls the US State Department's domineering interventions in the aftermath of 25 de Abril, regarding Portuguese decolonization, the future of the US air base at Lajes, Azores, and Portugal's membership of NATO.[28] Such satirical re-imaginings of historical events convey more than Saramago's anger at the efforts of Portugal's elite and its NATO allies to suppress the revolutionary spirit of April 1974, and his hopes for a different outcome in the future. They also counter the widespread misinterpretation, identified by Eduardo Lourenço (2000: 47–62) amongst others, of the April Revolution as a new national apotheosis, furnishing a new narrative of Portuguese exceptionalism through the myth of the country's post-colonial 'exemplaridade democrática' [democratic exemplarity] (2000: 49).[29] Mainstream political discourse since the late 1970s has presented Portugal's revolution as a new 'gift' to the world whereby the Portuguese pioneered the managed transition from dictatorship to liberal democracy and EEC/EU accession that would be undertaken in turn by Spain, Turkey, and the former Warsaw Pact states of Central and Eastern Europe. It is significant that Pedro Orce contemplates events in Albufeira with 'certo despeito patriótico' [somewhat injured patriotic pride] (*Jangada*: 98). His sense of 'o pesar de não terem sido espanhóis os da iniciativa' [regret that it had not been Spaniards who took this initiative] (ibid.) connotes a distinction between the eruption of 'people power' during Portugal's 1974 revolution, and Spain's laboriously negotiated transition eighteen months later, which protected the interests and prestige of the *ancien régime* and perpetuated the enforced silence about egregious war crimes. While conceiving of the 'Discoveries' as a unique 'momento solar' undermines collective self-belief, by comparing agency in the present unfavourably with that in an irrecoupable and insurpassable past, a similar conception of the 25 April, construing it as the successful prosecution of unanimous national will, allows the present day — with all its social iniquities — to appear as an equally insurpassable 'end of history'. *Jangada* counters this by recalling the April Revolution not purely as a reaffirmation of time-honoured Portuguese *brandos costumes*, but also as a chaotic, and often dirty, class war.

The essential lesson of the battle for the hotels, and of its unsettling of the hegemonic narrative of 25th April, is that collective identity can never be unitary or even double-edged: the more it is scrutinized, the more polyvalent it appears. Moreover — as *Ricardo Reis*'s engagement with Pessoa's writings highlights, and as Saramago's subsequent work continues to suggest — identity is ever mutable in relation to material, economic, and social circumstances. It is this multiplicity and mutability that allows *Jangada* to envisage utopia built, as Rebelo effectively concedes (1986: 345), on the cooperation, negotiation, and love developing between three Portuguese subjects (Joaquim, José, and Joana) and their neighbours and nominal adversaries (Pedro and Maria). Saramago's fiction's consistent emphasis both on the human psyche's protean nature, and its development relative to social, economic, and historic circumstances, prompts a question about Orlando Grossegesse's statement that *Jangada* reclaims 'a common peninsular identity that has been buried by the anti-Hispanic definition since the seventeenth century' (2001: 168). Certainly, Grossegesse is correct in arguing that Saramago's vision 'stems from the *Iberismo* tradition cultivated by intellectuals and educated upper-class circles of the nineteenth century', which he 'transforms into a new cultural, social, and political concept of "trans-ibericidade"' (ibid.). This transformation, however, is more substantial than Grossegesse's reading makes clear. For a start, *Jangada* lampoons the tendencies of much *fin-de-siècle* Iberianism, particularly following the humiliations of the 1890 British Ultimatum and the 1898 Spanish-American war, towards both histrionic prophecies of doom, and messianic, essentially metaphysical, speculation about the region's eventual revival. Secondly, the novel rejects the ethnic essentialism that pervades much Iberianist thinking, and instead follows Antero de Quental's (1982) materialist, and socialist, focus on the historical determination of shared cultural traits. Furthermore — in a manner more reminiscent of the thinking of the Guinean-Cape Verdean revolutionary leader Amílcar Cabral — *Jangada* suggests the collective reinterpretation of cultural tradition. This might permit negotiation both between disparate communities pursuing a common objective, and between the weight of the past and the demands of the present. It is not the unitary qualities of Iberian customs and 'values' that matter: indeed, Saramago would agree with Antero's claim, in 1871, that many of the cultural commonalities linking Spain and Portugal — such as deference both to hereditary despots and to the Catholic hierarchy, and the messianic apologia for a decadent imperialism — have been the region's undoing (Quental 1982: esp. 269). Rather, Iberianism offers a valuable model to the present insofar as it may inspire the critical rediscovery of a shared history and of cultural common ground, both formerly assessed too exclusively through the narrow, and selective, optic of isolationist nationalism.

Numerous studies have, like Marisa Corrêa Silva, identified *Jangada* as affirming 'o iberismo autocentrado como via de resgate e afirmação de uma nacionalidade que supera desacordos históricos para se fundir em um todo harmonioso' [a self-interested Iberianism as a means of redemption and affirmation for a form of nationality that transcends historical disagreements so as to be dissolved in a harmonious whole] (2002: 67). Not all, however, have followed Marisa Corrêa Silva and Grossegesse in considering how the 'representação literária de uma "convivência harmoniosa" entre "diferentes regiões da Ibéria"' é [...] não apenas anti-convencional, mas absolutamente desconfortável para o leitor português' [literary representation of a 'harmonious coexistence' between 'different Iberian regions' [...] not only goes against convention, but is positively disconcerting for a Portuguese reader] (Silva 2002: 68).[30] In the mid-1980s, most Portuguese still viewed Spain as, at best, an erstwhile oppressor to be respected and feared in equal measure. Across the border, majority opinion returned the compliment in the form of continuing disdain for the smaller, poorer neighbour. *Jangada*'s model of Iberian solidarity is not only a riposte to the architects of the Single European Market, but equally what Silva terms 'uma provocação [...] polític[a] e ideológic[a]' [a political and ideological provocation] (ibid.), directed towards the Portuguese, and, to a lesser degree, towards both separatists in the 'marginal' Spanish regions, and Spanish 'integralists' advocating the dominance of Castile and Madrid. Saramago's vision is not simply one of an Iberianism revised to make greater concessions to pluralism. Rather, it is best understood as one of 'community in difference', which uses Iberianism tactically and dialectically, as a challenge to readers to learn to recognize and accept difference, to negotiate with and accommodate the Other, and even — as and where it is necessary or advantageous — to *become* other. This re-interpretation of Iberianism resolves the seemingly contradictory approach to the concept of national community that is implied by the allegory of the Peninsula's dislocation from Europe.

One might regret that 'trans-Iberianism''s potential as a staging post to an egalitarian 'rooted cosmopolitanism' or 'rooted internationalism' is not made more explicit. Greater clarity about this would dispel the nationalist myths that can be inferred from the Peninsula's relocation to the mid-Atlantic; the myths, that is, of the Iberian nations being both pre-eminent members of a global Spanish- and Portuguese-speaking community, and also uniquely empathetic intermediaries between Europe and the regions it colonized and evangelized. In several of his numerous commentaries on *Jangada* and on his own brand of Iberianism, Saramago appears sensitive to charges of a neo-colonialism implicit in the plot's conclusion, spelling out, in 1993, that

> se [...] descobrir o outro é sempre descobrir-se a si mesmo, o meu voto, ao escrever esse livro, foi que uma nova descoberta, um novo encontro, um diálogo novo com os povos iberoamericanos e iberoafricanos permitissem descobrir em nós capacidades e energias de sinal contrário àquelas que fizeram do nosso passado de colonizadores um terrível caso de consciência. (1993: 92)

> [If to discover the Other always involves discovering one's self, my hope, on writing this book, was that a new discovery, a new encounter, a new dialogue with the Spanish and Portuguese-speaking peoples of the Americas and Africa would permit the discovery within us of abilities and energies of an opposite stripe to those that have made our history as colonizers an appalling stain on our conscience.]

By re-encountering each other, and negotiating more egalitarian laws of engagement and community, the novel's protagonists make themselves fit to assume the role, long imagined for them by apologists for empire, of intercontinental mediators. Historically, they have failed to fulfil this role without violence and prejudice. However, it may be offered them when they re-encounter the formerly colonized peoples who await them (all too silently, as will be explored below) across the Atlantic basin.

In the meantime, as Grossegesse points out, *Jangada*, with its complex intertextual allusions to the Spanish canon, 'requires a Portuguese reader interested in Spanish literature and culture' (2001: 177). The novel's plot highlights how populations in the two newly liberalized Iberian states might benefit from the rediscovery of the neighbours and cultures on whom they have for centuries turned their backs, supporting Saramago's claim that different cultures 'valem-se umas às outras, e é pelo diálogo entre as suas diferenças, mais do que pelas suas semelhanças, que se acharão mutuamente justificadas' [are valuable to each other, and it's through the dialogue between their differences, more than through their similarities, that they find themselves justified by each other] (2003: 87). While officialdom persists in stimulating a chauvinistic consciousness of difference (*Jangada*: 203; 283), Saramago's protagonists, compelled to accept a common destiny and traverse each other's homelands, discover commonalities that dispel the binary model that opposes heroic 'self' to exotic, effeminate, or even dehumanized ethnic Other. They also learn how ideal collective self-images are sustained by historiography's suppression of aspects of their shared past that are inconvenient to the powers that be. Significantly, their journey leads them not via such sites of iconic Spanish–Portuguese conflicts as Aljubarrota, Toro, and Olivença (though the triumphs and grievances still nurtured by their respective victors and losers are noted (*Jangada*: 256; 276; 89).[31] Instead, it leads them to the site of the conveniently forgotten battle of Villalar (1521), where the Emperor Carlos V crushed widespread opposition from the Castilian communes to his assumption of the Spanish throne. His victory, as Pedro Orce recounts (*Jangada*: 277–80), came courtesy of the loan of fifty thousand *cruzados* from King Manuel I of Portugal, clearly not too great a patriot to assist the grandson of the Spanish monarchs who had bested his father and grandfather at Toro. Present-day notions of Spain and Portugal as consistently belligerent rivals are shown to disguise both the complication that 'o povo não é todo um [...] sem falar que os povos geralmente vivem enganados' [the common people are not all one [...] not to mention that the people are generally deceived] (*Jangada*: 278), and the historical prevalence of class antagonisms. As Joaquim Sassa puts it, 'as comunidades tinham de perder, os cruzados ganham sempre' [the communes were bound to lose, the cruzados always win out] (*Jangada*: 280). As Grossegesse suggests, the battle of Villalar 'prefigure[s] the basic idea of *The Stone Raft*: a desired revolt of the people against a Peninsula ruled by foreign economic powers with the consent of the Portuguese and Spanish governments' (2001: 181). The episode of the sojourn at Villalar does not, however, simply repeat Saramago's standard practice of uncovering nationalist historiography's suppression of data that contradicts its narrative of ethnic specificity, unity, and heroism. Beyond this, it offers one of the most powerful images of how inter-ethnic — or inter-regional — re-encounters on the itinerant peninsula can stimulate a challenging process of anamnesis with immense psychological and political potential: this process is, moreover, also available to the Portuguese (or Spanish) reader who embraces her/his Iberian neighbours' culture(s). In a ghoulish conclusion to the chapter, the dog Constante has a dream of Villalar that inexplicably translates into reality:

> Nesta noite o cão Constante sonhou que andava a desenterrar ossos no campo de batalha. Já tinha reunido cento e vinte e quatro crânios quando a lua se pôs e a terra escureceu. Então o cão voltou a adormecer. Dois dias depois, uns garotos que andavam no campo a brincar às guerras foram dizer ao alcaide que tinham encontrado um montão de caveiras num campo de trigo, nunca se chegou a saber como lá apareceram, tão juntinhas. (*Jangada*: 280)

> [That night, Constante dreamed that he was digging up bones on the battlefield. He had already collected one hundred and twenty-four skulls when the moon set and the earth fell dark. Then the dog dropped back off to sleep. Two days later, some boys who were playing war on the battlefield went to tell the Mayor that they had found a heap of skulls in a wheatfield, nobody ever discovered how they turned up there, gathered so close together.]

As an allegory of a history suppressed and excavated, this episode would have had a chilling resonance in the mid-1980s. For many Spanish readers, it would be impossible not to be reminded both of the thousands of mass graves of victims of Civil War executions and massacres lying unmarked across the country, and of the powerful taboo enforcing silence about Civil War atrocities, which was at this time starting to be challenged.[32] Portuguese readers, meanwhile, might more readily spot the connection that the tableau establishes between the history of Villalar and a later seeming conspiracy of Spanish and Portuguese autocrats, exposed in April 1965 when the remains of the murdered Portuguese opposition leader Humberto Delgado and his secretary, Arajaryr Moreira de Campos, were recovered from a ravine near Villanueva del Fresno, Badajoz.[33] Saramago's reference to Villalar thus reconstructs an historical context for (sometimes taboo) recent tragedies and atrocities that suggests that the common struggle of the Iberian peoples need be not only against EU centralists, but also against the often brutal connivance of their own overlords.

At the same time as it refutes nationalism's guarantee of harmonious solidarity between classes, the unearthing of Villalar's battle dead also, of course, develops a recurrent trope in *Jangada* of the exhumation of human remains from hidden, forgotten, or exiled graves. Collectively, these exhumations explicitly connect the recuperation of traces of the past — and their propensity to perturb, inspire, or simply mislead — to the question of societies' relationships to the land that they inhabit. On one hand, the trope debunks the notion of a stable, inescapable influence of place, race, and 'heritage' on individual and collective destinies. At the same time, however, it suggests that allegedly 'backward' or 'peripheral' societies can confront adversity, and construct their own alternative futures, so long as they are prepared to re-evaluate, reinterpret, and share their cultural and ideological inheritance, or to adopt a creative and critical attitude towards local tradition. The trope of exhumation is established in the fifth chapter, where José and Joaquim, en route to their encounter with Pedro Orce in Venta Micena, learn of the discovery there of skull fragments allegedly belonging to 'o europeu mais antigo de que há registo' [the oldest European known to have existed] (*Jangada*: 77). This 'Orce Man' motif suggests both the longevity of Iberian civilization, and a return to specifically local origins, when the five protagonists' progress around the peninsula concludes with the burial of a latter-day 'Orce man' — Pedro — outside Venta Micena. However, any association of the protagonists' journey with a redemptive retreat into the past is complicated (as will be discussed further below) by the intertwining of the Orce Man motif with that of the exhumation and burial of *generación del '98* poet Antonio Machado, whose grave in Collioure, France, has been plundered by

> um comando civil e literário de espanhóis que, pela calada da noite, sem medo ao pio da coruja e ao ectoplasma, assaltaram o cemitério [...] Acorreram os gendarmes, avisados por algum noctívago, e perseguiram os ladrões de cemitérios, mas não puderam alcançá-los. O saco de restos foi atirado para dentro da lancha que esperava na praia com o motor a trabalhar mansinho, e em cinco minutos punha-se o navio pirata ao largo (*Jangada*: 73)
>
> [Spanish literary and civilian commandos who, in the still of night, fearless of the crow's shriek and the shades of the dead, launched an attack on the cemetery. [...] The gendarmes came running, alerted by some passing night-owl, and chased after the grave robbers, but could not catch them. The bag of mortal remains was hurled into a launch waiting on the beach with its engine quietly turning over, and in five minutes the pirate vessel had put out to sea]

Significantly, however, some time before this daring act of piracy is reported with such comic hyperbole, Machado appears already to have stirred in his grave: 'um destes mortos, em Collioure, mexeu-se um pouco, como se estivesse a hesitar, irei, nao irei, [...] só ele sabe para onde, talvez nós o venhamos a saber também' [one of these dead, in Collioure, stirred a little, as if vacillating, shall I go, shan't I [...] only he knows whither, perhaps we too will come to learn of this] (*Jangada*: 30–31). In this passage, the trope of an undead poet and the paraphrase of the pregnant phrase from *Ricardo Reis*'s first chapter — 'acaso tornaremos a saber notícias dele' [perhaps we will hear news of him again] (*Ricardo Reis*: 16) — support Grossegesse's brilliantly developed insight that, in *Jangada*, Saramago aims 'to revitalize Antonio Machado as a poet and as a philosopher in a manner different than, yet quite complementary to, his revitalization of Fernando Pessoa [in *Ricardo Reis*]' (2001: 171). As Grossegesse argues, Saramago resurrects Machado's work 'within the narrative plot of an apocryphal "trans-ibericidade"' (Grossegesse 2001: 181) not simply on account of that work's critical analysis of Iberian culture and society at a time of regional crisis. Rather, Machado is most significant in *Jangada* for the 'home-grown' reflection on the relationship between time, perception, and historical conscience that he extrapolates from Unamuno's concept of *intrahistoria*. This is the contention, set out in the section of *En torno al casticismo* entitled 'La tradición eterna', that

> las olas de la Historia [...] ruedan sobre un mar continuo, hondo, inmensamente más hondo [...] la historia toda del 'presente momento histórico', no es sino la superficie del mar, una superficie que se hiela y cristaliza en los libros y registros, y una vez cristalizada así, una capa dura, no mayor con respecto a la vida intra-histórica que esta pobre corteza en que vivimos con relación al inmenso foco ardiente que lleva dentro. Los periódicos nada dicen de la vida silenciosa de los millones de hombres sin historia [...] Esa vida intra-histórica, silenciosa y continua como el fondo vivo del mar, es la sustancia del progreso, la verdadera tradición, la tradición eterna, no la tradición mentira que se suele ir a buscar al pasado enterrado en libros y papeles, y monumentos, y piedras. (Unamuno 2005: 144–45)

> [the waves of History [...] turn upon a sea that is prevailing and deep, enormously deeper [...] that history of the 'present historic moment' is only the surface of the sea, a surface that freezes and crystalizes in books and ledgers, and, once thus crystalized, [forms] a hard cortex no greater in relation to intrahistoric life than is this paltry tectonic crust that we inhabit in relation to the immense burning core that it encloses. The papers say nothing of the silent lives of the millions of humans without history [...] This intrahistorical life, tranquil and unending as the very depths of the sea, is the substance of progress, the genuine tradition, the eternal tradition, not the phoney tradition that is customarily sought in that past that lies buried in books and documents, monuments, and tablets.]

Machado's exploration, in *Campos de Castilla*, of the 'intra-historical' offers a precedent for Saramago's response to the question of Iberian 'destiny' and identity politics in several ways. Firstly, its contention that, as Arthur Terry summarizes, 'a history which is allowed to dominate the present must be rejected in the interests of the future' (2003: 23) anticipates the warning that Frier ascribes to *Jangada*, that the idea of a national destiny predicated on the past 'somente pode impedir os esforços de adaptação a um presente e um futuro que se mudam constantemente' [can only stymie attempts at adaptation to a constantly changing present and future] (Frier 1998: 720). Secondly, Machado's interrogation of an elitist 'official' history by means of a focus on the experience and agency of the 'hombres sin historia' [men without history], economically and socially bound to the Iberian soil that they work, supports Saramago's demonstration of the cynical and elitist construct of a 'parcial e parcelar' [partial and parcelled] narrative of *História Pátria*, and his insinuation that the common people, not the capitalist elites, are the 'true' Iberians, and therefore deserving of the power to determine the Peninsula's future. Finally, as Grossegesse illustrates, Saramago's utopian vision for Iberia, and his articulation of it through ucronian fiction, are well attuned to Machado's intimation, noted by

Terry, of 'a possibility that the future will make available the true nature of the past', and to the proposition, attributed by Machado to his heteronymic creation Juan de Mairena, of a practice of 'apocryphal history', intended to develop as a 'collective project [...] promoted by literature' (2003: 23).[34] Grossegesse (2001) cites José Luis Abellán's (1995: 103) identification in Machado's *Campos de Castilla* of a 'utopian meaning that the apocryphal acquires, as an attempt at inverting or critically reconstructing history' (Grossegesse 2001: 175), emphasizing the contribution of such reconstruction to a movement for social transformation. Saramago's fiction of the 1980s repeatedly demonstrates how such 'apocryphal history' can free events, mythology, identities, and cultural heritage from the grip of historically dominant ideologies, and allow them to be *self-consciously* re-used for a new political project. *Jangada*'s fantasy of Machado rising from the grave just before his bones are 'repatriated' from Collioure is a case in point, lampooning the dead poet's cultural capital as an icon of Republican patriotism before proposing more seriously to appraise the relevance of his ideas to present-day dilemmas.

Jangada's 'reanimation' of Machado also affects its representation of Iberian 'difference', of cultural tradition, and of the value or importance of both. Saramago could no doubt have used *Jangada* to develop his arguments about history and utopian politics without co-opting Machado. However, by excavating the precedent in Machado for his own literary and political challenge to *História Pátria*, Saramago simultaneously implants his project in the newly dug-over soil of local intellectual tradition, and disproves claims of Iberia's cultural lack, peripherality, or backwardness. Politically committed counter-factual or ucronian fiction, and the historiographical insights that it articulates, are not simple imports from a more enlightened global centre. The alleged 'periphery' need not deplore the obsolescence of its own intellectual and artistic heritage, since this may often contain the seeds of an effective response to new problems or challenges. As in the models devised by Amílcar Cabral and others for negotiating between hegemonic concepts of modernity and the indigenous epistemes of colonized 'peripheral' cultures, this productive 'return to the source', however, requires a conception of cultural tradition — in Unamuno's terms — not as an inert 'crystallization', but as organic, mutable, and never fully perceptible or reducible to a concise representation.[35] To return to Sousa Rebelo's concern for national 'authenticity', this is a conception of tradition that allows the national community to be plural, flexible, innovative, and even internationalist, 'sem diluir e perder a sua identidade' [without diluting or losing its identity] (1986: 345).

Saramago thus seeks to balance a desire for geographical and cultural rootedness and belonging with the recognition of plurality, mutability, and the need to re-examine the past from dissident perspectives that emerges, for example, in the work of Ernesto Laclau and Chantal Mouffe.[36] This is fundamental not simply to the reconciliation of 'trans-Iberianism' and socialist internationalism, but also to the imagination of any collectivism that will not degenerate into coercive conformity. It is curious — and regrettable — that this comes across with less consistent clarity in *Jangada* than in Saramago's subsequent (and often notably defensive) statements on the novel's vision of Iberia. This can, however, be attributed to the ambitious

— arguably, over-ambitious — construction of the novel as a political allegory whose meanings are at once satirical and utopian, local and global. The motif of the Peninsula's displacement permits a powerful (and very funny) attack on Iberia's subjection to disdainful Eurocentrism and chauvinist local nationalisms (and the capitalist agenda that benefits from them). Yet the same allegorical motif effaces the grass-roots of inter-regional tensions within Iberia; tensions that are also glossed over in *Jangada*'s vision of solidarity between five individuals united by exceptional experiences and circumstances. The same motif also makes it impossible to dispel altogether the spectres of ethnic essentialism and — as the Peninsula traverses the Atlantic — of imperialist historical narratives. Saramago, taking inspiration from Machado's search for the 'intrahistorical', uses his protagonists' story to sketch an agenda for Iberian regeneration clearer than the imprecise and mystical one offered in *Campos de Castilla*. The remainder of this chapter examines the essentially materialist programme for political emancipation into which Saramago fits Machado's thinking. As before, acts of acknowledging the Other, and even of *becoming* other — even while acknowledging the inevitability of sociological and historical *rootedness* — emerge here as a pre-requisite for the social and economic transformations that Marxism proposes. The novel remains, however, problematically incapable of stretching its central allegory far enough beyond a vindication of an Iberian localism to envision fully an egalitarian re-encounter between semi-periphery and periphery, between the former colonizers and colonized, or even between men and women.

III — Re-imagining Gender: The Micropolitics of Affect in a Fabulous Future

'Se não sais de ti, não chegas a saber quem és.'
[If you do not venture out of yourself, you will never discover who you are]

(SARAMAGO, *O Conto da Ilha Desconhecida*: 27)

As Klobucka has stressed, *Jangada* characterizes its plot 'contrapuntally', as 'on the macro level [...] predominantly dystopian [...] and on the micro level [...] predominantly utopian' (2001: xvii). Certainly, the radical agency of traditional mass movements is increasingly confined to the background, and, even then, such agency is presented in an ambivalent manner. While Saramago presents the communes established in the coastal beach resorts as ideal socialist polities emerging fully formed out of spontaneous working-class uprisings, he does not report to the reader on their long-term fortunes, or political impact. Indeed, what the five protagonists witness as they travel inland is that, while that crisis of a threatened collision subsides, 'as pessoas regressam aos hábitos e comportamentos normais, se é este o nome que devemos dar aos antigos hábitos e comportamentos' [people are returning to their normal habits and behaviour, if indeed that is the correct name for their former habits and behaviours] (*Jangada*, p. 308). As already discussed, the hotel occupations can evoke the course for Portugal's 1974 Revolution pursued by Saramago and other Communists, but curtailed by the accommodation reached between the NATO leadership, its supporters, and Mário Soares's Socialist Party.[37] However, Saramago offers no suggestion that, in *Jangada*'s counter-factual ucronia, such a different course would be any easier to steer. Meanwhile, the failure of revolutionary politics to galvanize and direct popular anger or dissent is suggested in the fruitless demonstrations of Europe's *iberistas*. Lacking a clear agenda for change, these demos degenerate into inchoate and violent clashes with police, and abate quickly when the collision crisis looms (*Jangada*: 213). This crisis also exemplifies how, on a global scale, events on the Peninsula are merely disruptive, rather than revolutionary. Business interests and world powers such as the USA continue to regulate international relations. The US government violates Portuguese sovereignty to assert control during the collision crisis (*Jangada*: 240), refusing Portugal representation in the scientific party monitoring the Peninsula's passage around the Azores. At the novel's conclusion, the US presidency is still weighing up whether Iberia's move towards the South Atlantic might 'trazer benefícios' [bring benefits], or simply 'agravar as indisciplinas da região' [worsen the region's unruliness] (*Jangada*: 322), a question that is — significantly — not answered by any reported reactions from South America or Africa. Meanwhile, unlike *Levantado*, *Jangada* makes no significant allusions to Communist Party activism in Iberia. Nor does it suggest that, fifty years after the discussions of *Ricardo Reis*'s protagonist and Lídia, left-wing politics is addressing the needs of women, or of other subaltern constituencies possessing distinct and under-acknowledged allegiances, desires, and experiences of oppression.

The confinement of progress to the microsociety of the five travellers thus suggests a deepened scepticism about the possibilities of a totalizing utopian ideology, and/or a universal revolutionary praxis. At the same time, however, it builds on *Levantado*'s and *Memorial*'s visions of how localized revolutions in everyday customs might prepare the ground for wider revolution in material and cultural conditions. It imagines the expurgation from customs of identifying and bonding, and from economic, political, and affective transactions, of patriarchal privilege and also — crucially — of ethnocentrism. Klobucka, drawing on Arjun Appadurai's *Modernity at Large*, considers *Jangada*'s microsociety as one of multiple 'experimental "ethnoscapes"' coalescing in the wake of Iberia's displacement and constructing new 'imagined worlds' out of their historically specific experiences (2001: xv). If, as Klobucka argues, quoting Appadurai (1996), the novel is an 'ethnographic parable [...] exploring [...] "the nature of locality as a lived experience in a globalized, deterritorialized world"' (ibid.), it can be added that the parabolic message is that a socialist and feminist micropolitics, cultivated precariously on the social margins, can be either strengthened or weakened by attitudes towards geographical and ethnic rootedness.

In *Memorial*, it is through 'os amores novos [...] a mais forte coisa que existe no mundo' [new loves, the strongest thing that exists in the world] (*Memorial*: 220) that individual men will aspire to advance the common good, and, as also in *Ricardo Reis*, it is through love that their commitment to collective aspirations will be tested. Micropolitical transformation gets underway when circumstance — and the urging of visionary and compassionate women — challenge ordinary men to become extraordinary. *Jangada*'s lovers, like their counterparts in *Levantado* and *Memorial*, in turn reject sexist conventions and presumptions in work, love, and family structures. Their stance is symbolically underpinned by their story's echoes of Greek, Celtic, and Iberian mythology, which generate revised archetypes of female agency and conjugal relations. One might question *Jangada*'s depiction of an all-powerful romantic love fostering such revolutionary initiatives: whether it is read as allegory, or as historical fiction inflected with fantasy, the five protagonists' story can seem to relapse into the biological regenerationism upon which earlier, discredited utopian visions have often depended. However, by reading this story in relation to Saramago's other historiographical fiction, and by exploring the ways in which its potential allegorical meanings are disrupted or undermined, one can identify a tentative 'materialist utopianism' that avoids empty optimism or messianism.

At the crux of this utopianism is the contingency of love's transformative power upon the courage to defy convention, and to change. Joana Carda tells her new companions 'Se fui a Lisboa procurá-los, não terá sido tanto por causa dos insólitos a que estão ligados, mas porque os vi como pessoas separadas da lógica aparente do mundo, e assim precisamente me sinto eu' [If I went to Lisbon to look for you, it was not because of the freak occurrences to which you were connected, but because I saw you as people cut off from the world's apparent logic, and that's precisely how I feel] (*Jangada*: 147). Joana stresses the value not of experiences comparable to her own, but of the three men's attitudes to these 'insólitos' and their consequences. Their individual responses to challenging circumstances bespeak a willingness to think and act beyond the boundaries of recognized 'logic', a willingness that is the distinguishing feature of Saramago's 'middle-of-the-road heroes'. Through responding similarly to the romantic encounters born of inexplicable experiences, José and Joaquim may both achieve personal fulfilment and facilitate the social renewal that those 'insólitos' [freak occurrences] may — or may not — foretell. If, for the love of strong-willed, independent women, they agree to disregard the sexist and hierarchical 'lógica aparente do mundo', a new model of heterosexual relations can emerge within a microsociety governed by compassion, affection, egalitarianism, and class solidarity. Overcoming fears of the Other, and allowing 'que a razão do outro pudesse prevalecer racionalmente sobre a nossa razão' [the other's reason to prevail rationally over our own reason] (Saramago 2003: 89), they take a step towards an egalitarian pluralism within their own community. The spread of such an attitude throughout a more mobile and globalized society would enable the redemptive reencounter of Iberia with Africa and the Americas that Saramago hopes for. As will be discussed below, however, *Jangada* does not — and perhaps could not — pursue this idea with full success.

As in the case of Baltasar and Blimunda in *Memorial*, these alternative customs are initiated by the couples' new rules of courtship and non-institutionalized rites of bonding. Joana Carda dispenses with the old-fashioned 'regras' [rules] of courtship that stipulate feminine modesty and passivity when she announces to her companions, in a 'voz clara' [clear voice] that startles even José, that she will share his bed on their first night together (*Jangada*: 172). The love scene that follows, like those in *Levantado* and *Memorial*, emphasizes a reciprocity of action and sentiment, and dissolution of contrasting, gendered behaviour:

> José Anaiço entrou em Joana Carda e ela o recebeu, sem outro movimento, duro ele, ela suavíssima, e assim ficaram, os dedos apertando os dedos, as bocas a sugarem-se em silêncio, enquanto a vaga violenta lhes sacode o centro do corpo, sem rumor, até à última vibração, ao último gotejar subtil (*Jangada*: 174)

> [José Anaiço entered Joana Carda and she received him, without any other movement, he rigid, she yielding, and so they remained, fingers clasping fingers, mouths suckling each other in silence, while the overpowering wave engulfs the core of their bodies, without a sound, until the last shudder, the last imperceptible drop]

Soon afterwards, Maria Guavaira and Joaquim Sassa advertise their instantaneous attachment to each other by binding his hand to her heart with the blue thread with which Maria 'catches' Joaquim on his arrival at her farm (*Jangada*, p. 189). This spur-of-the-moment rite of handfasting, of course, echoes *Memorial*'s association of dissident romantic unions with pre-Christian and pagan lore and ceremonies. As the protagonists subsequently travel inland to shelter from the Peninsula's threatened collision, they — like *Memorial*'s lovers — dispense (both by necessity and inclination) with the conventional sexist division of labour and authority. All five take turns at driving the wagon (*Jangada*: 221), and when they turn to peddling clothes for a living, each one contributes according to his or her talents and training, with the two women selecting stock, and Pedro Orce handling the sales patter, whilst Joaquim Sassa and José Anaiço stay back at the wagon, respectively taking accounts and preparing food (*Jangada*: 260–63).

As Frier (1999) and others have explored, the idea of a spontaneous reform of heterosexual matrimony is supported by the way that symbolic resonances of the 'insólitos' suggest feminist reworkings of familiar mythological narratives. Here, one must consider a significant risk run by *Jangada*'s allegorical strategy as a means of exploring recent political realities and alternatives. The intentionally two-dimensional, sketchy characterization of the novel's protagonists could make it easy to read them as mere reiterations of the character-ciphers of established, and patriarchal, redemption allegories. However, the imperfect analogues — and striking contrasts — with female figures in classic tales of heroes and their wives and lovers serve to transform, rather than reiterate, foundational narratives of patriarchal authority. As Frier (1999) has shown, *Jangada*'s ingenious double-referencing of Greco-Roman and Celtic-Iberian mythology not only reminds of the connections, prevailing across time and national borders, between Iberia and other cultures of the Mediterranean and Atlantic seaboards.[38] It also compounds the opportunities for referencing, and re-working, feminine archetypes. As was discussed earlier, from the outset *Jangada*'s narrative voice remarks echoes of mythological tropes, and simultaneously warns against accepting these as reliable analogies: 'Maria Guavaira não se chama Ariadne, com este fio não sairemos do labirinto' [Maria Guavaira is not called Ariadne, with this thread we will not find our way out of the labyrinth] (*Jangada*: 18). While the protagonists, as Iberians, must critically re-imagine their presupposed heritage as 'explorers' and 'mediators', so too, they must re-imagine their identity as members of heterosexual couples in ways that permit a more empowered female agency. This message is underpinned by re-deploying the time-honoured mythological trope of a journey into another realm, governed by women with esoteric powers, to construe the journeys both of Iberia and its peoples as a voyage towards radically revised gender politics.[39]

A key example of this emerges from the 'undeniable echo of Aeneas's descent into the underworld' that Mary L. Daniel first noted as uniting 'Joana Carda's *vara de negrilho*, José Anaiço's birds and the Cerberus-like guard dog' (2005: 17). Saramago's Anaiço is, of course, very much an Aeneas *manqué*: his journey of enlightenment is directed not by a golden bough, but by a stick of elm wood, to which he has been led not by two turtle doves and the prophecy of the Sibyl of Cumae, but by a flock of starlings. This mock-epic set-up encourages our scepticism regarding *Jangada*'s transformation of the character and agency of Virgil's female characters. In contrast to the ancillary role played by Virgil's asexual and otherworldly Sibyl, Joana Carda takes a primary, even heroic role. First, when she wields the elm wand to declare her freedom from an unloved husband, drawing 'um risco que me separava de Coimbra, do homem com quem vivi' [a line that would separate me from Coimbra, from the man with whom I lived] (*Jangada*: 148). It is this action that reveals the wand's only confirmed magical property, demarcating 'um risco que cortava o mundo em duas metades' [a line that cut the world into two halves] (ibid.) and setting the agenda for those who choose to stand 'do lado de cá do risco' [this side of the line]) (*Jangada*: 150).[40] Joana will actively pursue this agenda by travelling to Lisbon in search of those she identifies as belonging on 'her' side. She maintains this leading role in defiance of 'ladylike' convention, loitering in wait for José in a hotel notorious as a venue for Lisbon's sex trade, and rising to greet him with a forthright manner that contravenes the 'manual de etiqueta e boas maneiras' [book of etiquette and [ladylike] good manners] (*Jangada*: 119).[41] She then leads him and his companions on the next stage of their voyage, where enlightenment is sought from the earth itself, rather than from the ghost of a patriarch buried beneath it (such as Aeneas's father Anchises).[42] And while Joana swiftly becomes José Anaiço's partner, her fate will clearly not follow that of Aeneas's lover Dido, peremptorily abandoned when impatient destiny comes calling.[43]

As with *Memorial*'s characterization of Blimunda, *Jangada*'s allusions to archetypes of the wronged wife are superimposed on others of the sorceress or visionary. This highlights how Joana and Maria successfully defy patriarchal oppression, while eschewing any abuse of the powers they might wield over men.[44] Maria — whose uncanny wisdom, and understanding of animals and the natural world, make Joaquim consider her a 'minerva dos montes galaicos' [Minerva of the Galician mountains] (*Jangada*: 191) — is also referenced, through the motif of the unravelling of thread, to the Greek tales of Penelope and Ariadne. Subject, like Penelope, to predatory suitors, the widowed Maria Guavaira waits at home as 'instructed' by the dog (p. 188), who sets off carrying a wisp of the blue yarn to fetch her new husband Joaquim. Unlike Homer's Penelope, however, Maria does not unravel yarn so as to maintain uxorial fidelity: she can fend off her unwelcome suitors with her wit and the threat of 'um tição na cara' [a smouldering brand in the face]

(*Jangada*: 199).⁴⁵ Moreover, Saramago's reworking of the Homeric tale excises the theme of the restitution of the hero's patriarchal entitlements.⁴⁶ Instead, Maria's patient domestic vigil is, like Penelope's, rewarded with a husband's love. Yet, by subsequently leading the five friends' flight eastwards, she becomes — as Frier suggests — 'a modern, emancipated version of Penelope who engages in her own Odyssey' (1999: 205).

Maria's seemingly wondrous spool of thread also carries echoes both of the tragic Ariadne, and, as Frier (1999) explores, of Irish mythology's malevolent Queen of the Isle of Women who, with a ball of twine, reels in the mariner-hero Maele Duín to be her consort.⁴⁷ The contradiction implicit in this intertextual double-loading is, however, resolved by the manner in which Maria neither relinquishes her thread, as Ariadne does, to a hero who will love her and leave her, nor uses it to dupe and dominate her man, like the Irish queen (Oskamp 1970: 157). Rather, the fateful love betokened by the thread that Maria holds out, and that Joaquim catches, binds the two of them equally. Moreover, the love token is extended to their three companions, and indeed to the dog. When Maria weaves bracelets for them all out of the blue yarn (*Jangada*: 216), it binds them too into a new affective community or realm; one where female agency and leadership challenge patriarchal hierarchy and oppression. This accounts for Maria Guavaira's response to Joaquim Sassa's suggestion of breaking up, when she declares that she will row her own boat off the Iberian island:

> [E]u com um tição queimarei esta galera como quem queima um sonho, depois talvez consiga empurrar para o mar a barca de pedra e embarcar nela. (*Jangada*: 313)
>
> [With a smouldering brand I'll torch this wagon like someone burning a dream, and after that perhaps I'll manage to push that stone boat down to the sea and set sail in it.]

Here again, *Jangada*'s double-referencing of Classical and Celtic-Iberian mythology works to suggest Maria's unconventional determination to control her own destiny. Far from waiting, like Ariadne abandoned on Naxos by Theseus, to be 'rescued' afresh by a second adventurer (Ovid 1970: 7), Maria will if necessary seek out her other realm alone. As Frier suggests, 'Maria Guavaira [...] must be able to have her own say in the formation of her future, and be able to sail out on her own terms' (1999: 200) even if — given the 'commonplace' in cultures of the north Atlantic seaboard that 'the souls of the dead are transported to another world by boat' (1999: 194) — her destination is not the 'Tír na n-Óc' or Land of the Young' (1999: 200), but the realm of death.

This declaration signals Maria's refusal to resume the old way of living. She will as soon embrace isolation, or even death, as abandon the 'sonho' of cooperative, non-sexist romance and community that has been improvised on the five companions' journey through an unfamiliar and convulsed land. She also, however, makes evident how that community and its emancipatory customs remain unguaranteed for their two unborn children, not to mention for a 'new' Iberia. The surmisings of Piero Cecucci and others that these innovations prefigure the realization of socialist utopia are, in fact, premature. Cecucci stresses how *Jangada*'s women take the initiative 'nell' aprire la nuova età dell'oro, nella loro ostinata vitalità, rompendo la congiura del silenzio del ruolo secondario' [in opening up the new golden age, in their stubborn vitality, breaking the spell of silence of a secondary social role] (1993: 214). While the two principal female characters certainly attempt to work their way free from socio-economic entrapment, Cecucci's identification of the accomplishment of female liberation in a 'nuova età dell'oro' must be questioned, as this section will illustrate. Whereas *Levantado* presents the emergence of egalitarian matrimony and loyalty to class, not clan, as part of the progress of an irrepressible social and historic revolution, *Jangada*'s Joaquim Sassa compares the new lifestyle on which he embarks to that of 'ciganos' [gypsies] (*Jangada*: 256). Indeed, even as 'as pessoas regressam aos hábitos e comportamentos normais' [people return to their normal habits and behaviour] (*Jangada*: 308), the five companions move increasingly towards the margins, 'como nómadas nos modos e no trajar' [like nomads in their manners and their dress] (*Jangada*: 241) and out of step with the social and economic rhythms of modernity. When their nomadic lifestyle compels the five to steal a horse (*Jangada*: 247–48), the ambivalent claim that 'as pessoas têm de se habituar aos novos códigos morais' [people have to get used to new moral codes] (*Jangada*: 247) spotlights how the new *modus operandi* sets an example neither morally unimpeachable, nor practically viable on a wider scale. Such details challenge both the reading of the protagonists' adventures as anarcho-socialist collectivism in embryo, and as social and spiritual redemption through a return to earlier, and simpler, times, technology, and culture.[48] The seeming temporal regression is undoubtedly significant, not least in re-introducing the issue, implicit throughout *Levantado*, of the linear or cyclical logic of time.[49] Yet, as Klobucka suggests, the protagonists' evolution 'toward a distinctly premodern *modus vivendi* [...] is less a sign of a nostalgic escape from modernity than an acknowledgment of the heterogeneous makeup of contemporary Iberian societies [...] as semiperipheral, intermediate formations, whose distinguishing characteristics may be summarily qualified as "pre-postmodern"' (2001: xvii). The communities that *Jangada*'s protagonists encounter, and from which 'intrahistoric' insights can be gleaned, display 'elements of asynchronic stages of development and a corresponding variety of relationships between their social agents' (ibid.). Such developmental asynchrony ensures that their journey into the Iberian hinterland can lead — like *Memorial*'s retreat into the superficially Edenic space of the Quinta de São Sebastião — as much to innovation as to any return to first principles. In both cases, marginalization (voluntary or enforced) permits extrication from the economic, political, and libidinal 'lógica aparente do mundo'. Escape from the pervasive hyper-reality of capitalist mass-media does not, of course, provide *Jangada*'s protagonists with unmediated contact with the historical real in its totality, or suspend the influence of the dominant ideology on their psychology and libido. It does, however, encourage a more creative and critical practice of interpreting the world, and allow the protagonists to carve out a *provisional* space where alternative modes of being, desiring, and interacting — and what, following Klobucka's use of Appadurai's term, would be an experimental and revolutionary new 'ethnoscape' (2001: xiv) — may be improvised, in accordance with socialist and egalitarian principles.

It can be argued that this presages the emergence of the same 'dialectical concept of "rooted cosmopolitanism"' that Klobucka (2001: xviii) identifies in Saramago's later *A Caverna* (2000). However, the alternative identities, relations, and customs that the five protagonists improvise remain, to the novel's end, as precarious as is their livelihood as pedlars. The integrity of their microsociety is painfully challenged when Joana and Maria take the unilateral decision to sleep with '[c]oitado do Pedro Orce' [poor Pedro Orce] (*Jangada*: 286), apparently motivated by affection and compassion for the only single man in their community. This episode, as a vision of how young and attractive women might express love and solidarity, could well be considered implausible, clumsy, or politically insensitive. Nevertheless, as one of the devices whereby the novel reconciles allegory with examination of the day-to-day experience of real-life conditions of oppression and social conflict, it is crucial to the novel's political meaning. Joana and Maria's insistence that they need not offer explanations or feel guilt is underlined when Joana invokes both the elm wand that is the totem of her status as a free woman in search of a 'new realm', and the idea of a new division represented by 'outro risco aqui' [another line here] scratched in the earth (*Jangada*: 290). For Joana, respect for women's rights over their bodies and reproductive capacity (not to mention respect for their right to bestow affection) is what marks out 'quem fica de um lado e quem fica do outro, se não pudermos ficar juntos do mesmo lado' [who's going to stay on one side and who on the other, if we can't all stick together on the same side] (ibid.). Significantly, however, this critical point of negotiation regarding sexual morality, family structures, and affective relations in general is never fully resolved. While first José, and, less immediately, Joaquim, overcome their anger and resentment and agree to stay, it is on the unspoken condition that what has occurred will not be repeated: 'Joaquim Sassa [...] enfim disse, Ficarei, mas com uma condição. Não precisou de dizer qual' [Joaquim Sassa [...] finally said, I'll stay, but on one condition. He didn't need to say what it was] (*Jangada*: 290). The same passage suggests that, ultimately, it is humanity's physical and emotional needs, rather than a concordance of opinions, which effect a reconciliation, since,

> se a natureza humana continua a ser o que tem sido, é natural que por fadiga e desgosto, por compreensiva ternura e instante amor, mulher e homem se aproximem, troquem um primeiro beijo receoso, depois, bendito seja quem assim nos fez, o corpo acorda e pede o outro corpo (*Jangada*: 293)
>
> [if human nature remains what it has been, then it is only natural that, through exhaustion and upset, through overwhelming tenderness and instant love, man and woman should approach one another, exchange a first, apprehensive kiss, later, blessed be whoever made us this way, the body awakes and calls for the other body]

It is left to Maria Guavaira, when urging Pedro Orce not to take the blame and leave, to stress a continuing need to *understand* ('compreender') and empathize, without which the desires to love and be loved cannot be satisfied:

> Não parte, disse Maria Guavaira, e, se partir, o mais certo é que nos separemos todos, porque eles não serão capazes de ficar connosco nem nós com eles, e

não é porque não nos amemos, será por não sermos capazes de compreender. (*Jangada*: 290)

[Don't go, said Maria Guavaira, and, if you go, the greatest certainty is that we will all go our separate ways, because neither will they be able to stick with us nor we with them, and not because we don't love each other but because of not being capable of understanding one another.]

The episode thereby introduces a welcome grittiness, which recalls Marcuse's warning about 'bitter conflict, torment, and suffering (mental and physical)' (1974: 288) and complicates Saramago's vision of unconventional love transforming not just individual consciousness, but also social roles, values, and interactions. All the same, the appeal for understanding proves insufficient to resolve disagreements about uxorial responsibilities and paternal rights. This issue resurfaces when the two women reveal their pregnancies to their 'husbands' (so-called only *after* being cuckolded (*Jangada*: 291; 292; 307)), who respond with 'os gritos mais coléricos ou dilacerados [...] uma explosão de fúria, um esbracejar violento, uma pungente mágoa' [the most irate or lacerating cries [...] an explosion of fury, violent gesticulations, and intense misery] (*Jangada*: 304). The issue of paternity still threatens to dissolve the two couples even at the novel's end.[50]

At the same time as *Jangada* avoids pronouncing on radical changes to family structures, it is notable, and arguably regrettable, that it doesn't stray further from the heteronormative and family-oriented conventions of traditional fables and myths in ways that might have enhanced the depth and nuance of its vision of progressive micropolitical transformation. The scanty delineation of the central characters and their interactions (which contributes both to the reader's 'alienation' from the text, and to the plot's presentation as allegory) never allows for deep consideration of the potential of friendship, or, for that matter, of Platonic, inter-racial, or homoerotic relationships. Deep explorations of friendship between men are notably few in Saramago's novels, and references to homosexuality almost non-existent.[51] One must concede that, in 1980s Portugal, discussions of inter-racial and same-sex relationships, and equally of the presence of Luso-African '*retornados*', were constrained by powerful taboos, making difficult their integration into an allegorical framework. Nonetheless, the steadfastly heterosexual and reproductive matrix that *Jangada* imagines for a socialist new order threatens to reduce the novel's message to a new twist on the patriarchal cliché of regeneration through procreation. A further shortcoming is that, after Pedro Orce's death, *Jangada*'s protagonists can collectively be read as an allegory of the harmonious unity of a trans-national *lusofonia*. Miguel Vale de Almeida (2004: 61–63) and António Costa Pinto (2013) have both argued that the emergence of this concept in discussions of Portugal's place in the post-colonial world has simply supplanted the *Estado Novo*'s imperialist nationalism, without expunging all of its most chauvinistic and narcissistic presuppositions. Saramago might have pre-empted accusations that *Jangada* reiterates nationalist, Eurocentric, and colonialist grand narratives, if the human drama at its heart had candidly represented more of the diversity of identity, history, and aspirations that many champions of *lusofonia*, *iberismo*, *atlanticismo*, and related concepts have failed to acknowledge.

These problems of interpretation are, of course, magnified when Saramago brings his allegory of the stone raft to a climax, at the heart of the Atlantic world, with the simultaneous impregnation of 'todas ou quase todas as mulheres férteis [da península]' [all or almost all of the fertile women of the Peninsula] (*Jangada*: 318–19). Surprisingly, perhaps, most critics have viewed this mass pregnancy's significance as an unproblematic portent of Iberia's imagined future, and of its re-encounter with formerly colonized peoples. Piero Cecucci, for example, describes it as the 'compiuta redenzione attraverso l'amore' [total redemption through love] that predicates '[il] sorgere di una nuova umanità; di una nuova era sperata e sognata, ma anchè voluta e costruita' [the ascent of a new class of humanity; of a new epoch not merely hoped for and dreamed of, but also willed and constructed] (1993: 214). However, from both Marxist-feminist and anti-colonialist points of view, the episode's symbolic and literal implications are troubling, particularly given its echoes (almost unmistakeable for a Portuguese reader) of the *Ilha dos Amores* [Isle of Love]) episode that crowns the narrative of Camões's *Lusíadas*.[52] Given the number of satirical rewritings of the *Ilha dos Amores* episode that preceded *Jangada*, and the novel's echoes of sundry other 'enchanted island' myths that overdetermine the interpretation of the mass pregnancy, it is well worth asking if the text itself prompts the reader to be cautious about what he/she infers here. The episode is, after all, preceded by the narrator's questioning of 'o que seria de todos nós se não viesse a poesia ajudar-nos a compreender quão pouca claridade têm as coisas a que chamamos claras' [what would become of all of us were poetry not to help us to understand how little clarity there is in the things we describe as quite clear] (*Jangada*: 317). This commendation of poetry refers to the intervention of a certain 'poeta português que comparou a revolução e descida da península à criança que no ventre de sua mãe dá a primeira trambolha da sua vida' [Portuguese poet who compared the Peninsula's rotation and descent to a child in its mother's belly turning the first somersault of its life] (ibid). It is his 'feliz metáfora [...] glosada de todas as maneiras e repetidas por todas as bocas' [happy metaphor [...] glossed in all different ways and repeated by every mouth] (*Jangada*: 318) that appears subsequently to inspire a surge of procreation:

> Uma das mais interessantes consequências da inspirada comparação foi a ressurgência, se bem que mitigada pelas transformações que a modernidade transportou para a vida familiar, do espírito matricial, do influxo mátrio [...] As mulheres, decididamente, triunfavam. Os seus órgãos genitais, com perdão da crueza anatómica, eram afinal a expressão, simultaneamente reduzida e ampliada, da mecânica expulsória do universo. (ibid.)

> [One of the most intriguing consequences of this inspired comparison was the resurgence, albeit mitigated by the transformations that the modern world has brought to family life, of the motherly spirit, of the maternal instinct. [...] The women, resoundingly, were triumphant. Their reproductive organs, if you'll pardon the anatomical indelicacy, were in the end the simultaneously reduced and enlarged expression of the expulsory mechanism of the universe.]

This suspiciously hyperbolic account intimates that the mass pregnancy is not a wholly inexplicable miracle. Just as the narrative voice considers it necessary to censure the poet's 'cedência às tentações de antropomorfismo, que tudo vê e tudo julga em relação obrigatória com o homem' [surrender to the temptations of anthropomorphism, which sees and interprets everything in an obligatory relationship with mankind] (*Jangada*: 317), the reader must at least consider the possibility that the pregnancies that follow it are the fruit of a mass delusion, or at least of a collective will to interpret the peninsula's relocation as an auspicious new beginning.

The Portuguese poet's analogy appears strained, however, in view of the protagonists' conflicted reactions to the prospect of parenthood. Their differences, moreover, are not yet settled when the story concludes, leaving them — and the reader — in a state of expectation and uncertainty. The upbringing of Joana's and Maria's children will be the acid test of the new rules of partnership, paternity, and division of labour that they have negotiated with their husbands. Moreover, reading the episode in a literal, historicist vein, it remains difficult to accept unplanned pregnancy *en masse* as an unmitigated blessing. The enthusiasm for maternity is tempered by modernity's 'transformações' of family life, yet while Joana and Maria have blazed a feminist trail, such unspecified 'transformações' may still be in question in many families. Both *Levantado* and *Ricardo Reis* acknowledge how, under Iberian dictatorships that used the cult of traditionally large Catholic families to keep women out of public life and paid employment, maternity was frequently a site of oppression.[53] So it remained in 1980s Portugal or Spain, where, moreover, the Church still taught that contraception was a sin, and where abortion remained a criminal act in all but exceptional circumstances.[54] Pires de Lima draws attention to José Anaiço's mention of the legend of Dom João II and the 'ilha imaginária' and his confession that '[e]sta outra ilha, a ibérica, que era península e deixou de o ser, vejo-o eu como se, com humor igual, tivesse decidido meter-se ao mar à procura dos homens imaginários' [this other island, the Iberian one that was a peninsula and has ceased to be such, looks to me as though, with the same kind of humour, it had decided to set out to sea in search of imaginary people] (*Jangada*: 65). Even if, as Pires de Lima suggests (1988: 33), these 'homens imaginários' could be the twelve to fifteen million Iberian children gestating at the novel's close, it is hard to read the mass pregnancy as a seriously intended reiteration of the 'regeneration through procreation' trope. Until the infants are born, it is impossible to know whether they will be the creators of a new society, or whether they too will be governed by cynical opportunists such as those who rush to 'comparar esta fertilidade à esterilidade do resto do mundo ocidental' [compare this fertility to the sterility of the rest of the western world] (*Jangada*: 321). Such inquiries are already confounded by the ambiguities of the novel's symbolism. Equally, the uncertain paternity of Maria and Joana's unborn children makes it impossible to interpret them either as the symbolic offspring of a new order (represented by two young men who have in any case not definitively proven their feminist credentials), or, as Isabel Pires de Lima suggests (1988: 33–34), of a 'compromise' with the old, represented by Pedro. However, this interpretation overlooks both Pedro Orce's participation in most of the utopian innovations in the novel, and the fact that a 'utopia insular' [island utopia] (ibid.) remains far from fully constituted at the novel's end. Finally, since the novel does not indicate where and by whom these children will be raised, it is impossible to know whether or not their conception revises the *Ilha dos Amores* motif — long exploited as an allegory of Portugal's 'loving union' with its colonies — as a new allegory of 'miscegenation' between formerly antagonistic Spanish and Portuguese populations.

Whether by authorial intention or by accident, the plot's conclusion with the mass pregnancy, as the Peninsula comes to a halt in the mid-Atlantic, demonstrates both the dangers of the myth-making of nationalist historiography and literature, and the way in which such myths might — when recognized as fable rather than fact or prophecy — still serve as inspiration for new — and carefully cross-examined — utopian initiatives. On the one hand, presumptions of a national 'essence' and 'destiny' lead, with assuredly circular logic, to the interpretation of the mass pregnancy as the biological incarnation of national apotheosis, born of an endemic disposition to maritime adventure and *brandos costumes*. On the other, a critical appraisal of the Iberian states' shared history of colonizing the Atlantic world (and, more particularly, of colonizing women's wombs) encourages a view of the impending birth of a new generation, in a new location, as the opportunity for Iberians to recompense past animosities and offences, and even attempt to become the genuinely empathetic intermediaries of luso-tropicalist fantasy. With its focus on both mortality and new life, *Jangada*'s conclusion can be read as a hyperbolic reprisal of *Ricardo Reis*'s 'pregnant' ending. The inconclusive halt to the peninsula's movement at a pivotal moment in the protagonists' shared lives reiterates the point that 'o mar se acabou e a terra espera' [the sea ends and the land awaits] (*Ricardo Reis*: 415): after maritime adventures conclude, the land — or rather, lands — await the efforts of their inhabitants to rediscover, and redeem, themselves.

Despite the protagonists' conviction that they can recognize crucial moments, and despite Maria Guavaira's and Joana Carda's certainty that they know the best place to bury Pedro Orce (*Jangada*: 329; 327), no 'moment' — nor any cataclysmic change of destiny — arrives when the elm wand is planted on his grave. This last page's emphasis on bereavement, departures, and uncertainty, however, remains under-acknowledged even in many of the most impressive readings of the novel. Pedro Orce is laid to rest, but the urgent questions 'que futuro, que tempo, que destino' [what future, what time, what destiny] resonate in the chill, rainy dawn (*Jangada*: 330). Abandoned by the dog — here, significantly, named not 'Constante', but 'Ardente' — Pedro's four companions will continue on their way ('seguirão o seu caminho'; ibid.), still uncertain of whether or not to perpetuate their new lifestyle and values. Intimations of radical social change remain merely symbolic, and, moreover, ambivalent: to the image of the peninsula as an unborn child, and the millions of real gestating infants, is added the green but budless elm wand, which Joana Carda 'espetou [...] à altura da cabeça de Pedro Orce' [planted [...] above the resting place of Pedro Orce's head] (ibid.). This closing image effects a proliferation of the elm branch's already highly ambiguous connotations of a magic wand, a symbol of a wife's declaration of independence, and a lucky charm. Connecting the themes of love, death, and rebirth to the recurrent tropes of burial and disinterment, it reanimates discussion of the problematic relationship of identity to territory, and hence of the predication of social renewal on a specifically Iberian ethos or culture. Maria Guavaira's determination that Pedro should rest in his native soil recalls both her male companions' discussion of the repatriation of Antonio Machado's bones, and the distinction of Pedro's homeland as resting place of 'Orce Man', apparently Europe's earliest human inhabitant. As Grossegesse (2001: 179) has suggested, Pedro's burial is a gesture of 'compensation' for the burial that José Anaiço suggests befits Machado, 'em qualquer parte dos campos de Soria, debaixo de uma azinheira, que em castelhano se diz encina, sem cruz nem pedra tumular' [somewhere in the fields of Soria, under a holm oak, or *encina*, as it's called in Spanish, without either a cross or a tombstone] (*Jangada*: 74). This hypothetical burial is in turn inspired by that which Machado imagined for his friend and mentor Francisco Giner de los Ríos. Grossegesse's reading concludes that *Jangada*'s reworking of this tribute to Giner's dream of 'un nuevo florecer de España' (Machado 1989: I, 588) 'reclaims the spiritual heritage of the *Generación del '98* for the "new blossoming" of the whole Iberia' (Grossegesse 2001: 179). Grossegesse's meticulous scholarship, and judicious comparison with themes of regeneration and 'trans-Iberianist' affirmations elsewhere in Saramago's writings, make his argument persuasive; but equally, one must acknowledge how doubts regarding such a 'nuevo florecer' are simultaneously introduced by a second Machadian allusion, and by the recurrence of the Orce Man motif. Joana's planting of her elm wand as a grave marker creates a clear reference to a more wistful meditation on Iberian mortality in *Campos de Castilla*, in the poem 'A un olmo seco' [To a dying elm] (Machado 1989: I, 541–42). Here, the poet addresses a rotting, senile tree whose single green branch makes him long for 'otro milagro de la primavera' [another miracle of Spring] (1989: I, 542). Pedro is laid to rest not 'en tierra de tomillos, donde juegan | mariposas doradas' [in land where wild thyme grows and golden butterflies flit] (1989: I, 588) but in the barren 'terra ressequida' [parched earth] of Venta Micena (*Jangada*: 329). By association with this, the elm wand planted represents not the certain realization of utopia, but the precarious nature of human hopes and aspirations:

> Não é cruz, como bem se vê, não é sinal fúnebre, é só uma vara que perdeu a virtude que tinha, mas pode ainda ter esta simples serventia, ser relógio de sol num deserto calcinado, talvez árvore renascida, se um pau seco, espetado no chão, é capaz de milagres (*Jangada*: 330)
>
> [It is not a cross, as can well be seen, it is not a funerary marker, it is only a wand that has lost the value that it had, but that might still serve this humble purpose, of being a sundial in a petrified desert, perhaps a reborn tree, if a dry stick, stuck in the ground, is capable of miracles]

It was none other than Unamuno who suggested that the Portuguese have been ill-served by their faith in miracles, long before *Memorial* and *Ricardo Reis* dissected the serial abuse of that faith. *Jangada*'s closing sentence — 'A vara de negrilho está verde, talvez floresça no ano que vem' [the elm wand is green, perhaps it will bud next year] (*Jangada*: 330) — tempts the reader afresh with the notion of miracles while leaving the reassurances of physics, history, and ideology in ruins, and even those of love in doubt.

Moreover, while Pedro's burial echoes the 'apocryphal history' that Machado creates for Giner, with both figures imagined refertilizing the exhausted Iberian soil, its location near the Cueva de los Rosales, 'onde tinha sido encontrado o crânio do europeu mais antigo' [where the skull of the earliest European had been found] (*Jangada*: 329) advertises his status as a latter-day 'Orce Man'. Yet this association by no means unequivocally symbolizes Iberia's origins and continuity, or the eventual triumph of a 'materialist messianism' derived from Machado, as Grossegesse argues (2001: 179). Indeed, it reiterates the warning — issued earlier with specific reference to the (mis)naming of the 'Orce Man' — that '[e]ste mundo [...] é uma comédia de enganos' [this world is a comedy of errors] (*Jangada*: 79). Both apocrypha and recovered historical traces can also mislead, and neither prophecy nor science has successfully fathomed the mysteries of past or future: after all, *todo futuro es fabuloso*.[55] The unearthing of the Venta Micena skull fragment in 1982 overturned accepted archaeological knowledge. However, it also sparked an as-yet inconclusive debate amongst palaeontologists, some of whose number claimed in 1983 that the fossilized fragment belonged not to a hominid, but to a donkey.[56] Consequently, the 'Orce Man' find has become, for proponents of 'creationist' theory, a popular example of the alleged misapprehensions and fraudulent claims of evolutionists.[57]

Given the clandestine nature of the burial of Pedro Orce's remains, their hypothetical future discovery may — like that of the original Orce skull fragment — mystify, mislead, and divide future generations before it enlightens them.[58] Rediscovering Iberia, and Machado, in the spirit of a 'return to the source', can contribute to social renewal only when this return is undertaken in a questioning, creative, innovatory spirit. Even then, given the impossibility either of direct access to the past, or of objective verification of our less than empirical observations, the siren call of glib assumptions must be answered by critical interrogation, and the challenges of ambiguity must be calmly accepted.

Notes to Chapter 4

1. Saramago denied (Alves, Bélard and Seabra 1986: 32) that the novel's launch was timed to coincide with this event. His case against the EEC/EU's model of European integration is most clearly set out in Saramago (1989c), (1992b), and (1993: 87), and in Pontiero (1989).
2. On *Jangada*'s different relationship, see, amongst other studies, Lough (2002: 161).
3. On the significance of this quotation, see also Becker (1991: 129), Frier (1998: 720), and (2007: 149), and Ribeiro (2012).
4. Reading in the manner that Saramago suggests, it becomes necessary to question Frier's argument that the implication of the epigraph is 'utopian rather than pessimistic' (2007: 149). Saramago's interpretation of the epigraph vindicates both utopianism (in the sense that aspirational utopian visions of the future should not be ruled out) and pessimism (first in that there can be no reliable divination of the future, and secondly in that society is so frequently held to ransom by inauthoritative visions of future 'certainties').
5. See Lourenço (1978) for an influential critique of the *Estado Novo*'s depiction of Portugal as 'um herói isolado' [a lone hero] (1978: 20) and as *orgulhosamente só* [proudly alone]. See also Sapega (1997: 168–71). On the complicated history of the *Estado Novo*'s negotiations with the EEC, its membership of EFTA from 1959, and its attempts, from 1962, to create an alternative integrated free trade zone between Portugal and its African colonies, see Freire and Magalhães (1981), Magalhães (1987), and Rosas and Brandão de Brito (1996: I, 312–15).
6. Paulo Becker explores how *Jangada* presents a parallel universe set 'no futuro iminente' [the immediate future] where conditions equate to the mid-1980s to the degree that 'só projetamos

a história para o futuro porque a península ibérica ainda não se desprendeu da Europa' [we only project the story into the future because the Iberian Peninsula has not yet broken away from Europe] (1991: 129). The novel makes occasional tongue-in-cheek references to its recounting of a history of Iberia's future, as when the three male protagonists cross from Andalusia to the Algarve over the Guadiana bridge, 'que nestes dias de que vimos falando já se construiu' [which, in the days that we have been talking about, was already built] (*Jangada*: 97) but which was not completed and opened until five years after the novel's publication.

7. In standard modern Italian, this would be rendered as '*eppur* si muove'. According to both the *Oxford Dictionary of Quotations*, 7th edn (Oxford: Oxford University Press, 2009) (electronic edition) and Hall (1979: 383), the legend is first recorded by Giuseppe Baretti, in *Italian Library*, in 1757, and was made famous by its inclusion in Irailh (1761).
8. See, in particular, the essays 'In the Shadow of the Silent Majorities', and 'Implosion of Meaning in the Media', in Baudrillard (1983a: 1–61; 95–110).
9. Best and Kellner (1991: 118). According to these authors, '[t]he hyperreal for Baudrillard is a condition whereby models replace the real, as exemplified in such phenomena as the ideal home in women's or lifestyle magazines, ideal sex as portrayed in sex manuals or relationship books, ideal fashion as exemplified in ads or fashion shows, ideal computer skills as set forth in computer manuals, and so on. In these cases, the model becomes a determinant of the real, and the boundary between hyperreality and everyday life is erased' (1991: 119–20).
10. On the use of first person plural narration in Saramago's 1980s novels to establish solidarity with the reader and simultaneously with the protagonists, and to affirm 'a sua perspectiva contemporânea e a sua contextualização do passado à luz do presente' [the narrator's contemporary viewpoint and contextualization of the past in the light of the present], see, respectively, Lourenço (1991: 76), and Kaufman (1991: 160).
11. The motif of Lassie's struggle to tell her owners that someone is in need of help is a mainstay of MGM's *Lassie Come Home* (1943) and of eight subsequent feature films and sundry TV adaptations.
12. Pires de Lima considers that coincidence and 'the moment' in *Jangada* 'traz consigo a subversão da dimensão espacial e introduz uma espécie de filosofia do momento como instante da cintilação emocional e de clarividência' [bring with them the subversion of the spatial dimension and introduce a kind of philosophy of the moment as an instant of emotional illumination and of clairvoyance] (1988: 32–33). Arguably, however, as also in *História do Cerco de Lisboa*, such moments constitute epiphanies only in the sense of provoking an individual's emotional or intellectual consciousness, rather than in the sense of offering some transcendental revelation. While the meeting between Joaquim Sassa and Maria Guavaira is marked by abundant 'cintilação emocional', there is little evidence of any emergent 'clarividência'. Meanwhile, the need to make pronouncements on history and the danger of neglecting the past are highlighted both by the narrator (*Jangada*: 238) and by the patent absurdity of Roque Lozano's logic that 'se eu não a vir, é porque nunca existiu' [if I don't see it, it will be because it never existed] (*Jangada*: 71), which is questioned with the example of the moon, regularly present but invisible (*Jangada*: 308).
13. See Roig (1958: 69). On trees in general in Christian imagery, see Roig (1958: esp.173), and Speake (1994: 144).
14. See e.g. Cunningham (1987: 99).
15. See Roig (1958: 182), and Speake (1994: 114), on the Christian symbolism of pomegranates. The pomegranate, symbol of the Moorish city of Granada, was incorporated into the royal coat of arms by the 'Reyes Católicos' Fernando II and Isabel I to emphasize the completion of the Christian reconquest of Spain, as is noted at the internet site 'Flags of the World' at <http://www.crwflags.com/fotw/flags/es_r1700.html> and < http://www.crwflags.com/fotw/flags/es_15thc.html> [accessed 20 November 2014]. This site refers the user to Faustino Menéndez Pidal de Navascués's *Heráldica Medieval Española* (Madrid: Hidalguía, 1982) for further details.
16. See, in particular, Frier (1999) and (2007: 144–48; 150).
17. See, in particular, Alves, Bélard, and Seabra (1986), and Saramago (1988: 32).
18. As Kenneth Maxwell notes, referring primarily to the electrical, component assembly, and garment industries, 'once free collective bargaining became a possibility, much of the attraction of Portugal for these particular industries vanished [...] the temptation to strip assets was very

great. Those who moved did so quickly' (1995: 140). Martin Kayman discusses to what extent this 'reluctance to invest' was a 'political decision, part of a campaign of sabotage against the revolutionary regime' (1987: 190), and also notes the grave impact of the 'illegal export of capital' estimated at $120 million in 1975 alone (1987: 191).

19. Unamuno talks of two facets of the Portuguese *ethos* as represented in Guerra Junqueiro's poems *Os Simples* and *Pátria* : 'el Portugal campesino, resignado y sencillo [...] y [...] el Portugal heroico y noble' [the peasant Portugal, stoical and simple [...] and [...] the heroic, noble Portugal] (1941: 19). Yet Unamuno's observations on contemporary Portugal indicate that for him the former facet predominates (1941: 38–39) while the latter is largely lost in the Portuguese past. He compares the Portuguese to Ulysses who 'volvió a sus lares y ... cabe el hogar, contemplando el onduleo de las llamas de fuego que le recordaban el vaivén de las olas marinas, contaba a sus hijos y nietos los trances de la guerra y de sus errabundas navegaciones' [returned to his homeland and ensconced by the hearth, gazing at the undulations of the flames that called to his mind the ebb and flow of the waves, recounted to his children and grandchildren the escapades of war and of his far-flung seafaring] (1941: 21). Repeatedly, Unamuno evinces clear belief in the eventual, and possibly impending, 'death' of Portugal, venturing that Portugal is 'un pueblo de suicidas, tal vez un pueblo suicido' [a nation of suicides, perhaps a suicidal nation] (1941: 80).

20. On 'semi-peripherality', see, amongst other texts, Santos (1985).

21. Switzerland has maintained its neutrality through all foreign conflicts since 1815. In 1993, the Swiss government agreed to join the newly created European Economic Area only under considerable pressure from neighbouring states; in the same year the Swiss electorate rejected ratification of an agreement to enter the European Union. See 'Switzerland', in *Encyclopaedia Britannica: Online Academic Edition.* (Encyclopædia Britannica Inc., 2014). <http://academic.eb.com/EBchecked/topic/577225/Switzerland> [accessed 21 November 2014].

22. As Sabine (2001a: 226–28) explores in detail, the novel evades the problematics of regional identity politics in the Spanish state, particularly in its first fifty pages. The fate of the Catalan-speaking Balearic Islands is left open to question (*Jangada*: 29), although Saramago later confirmed that the Balearic and Canary archipelagos are left behind, 'agarradas ao fundo do mar, bem firmes' [clinging to the bottom of the sea, very securely] (1993: 85).

23. This focus on regional diversity is, after all, consistent with Saramago's claim that 'julgo ter começado a aprender melhor Espanha conforme ia reconhecendo e identificando [...] as diversidades nacionais que via emergir de unidade estatal' [I believe I started to learn more about Spain when I began to recognize and identify [...] the national variations that I saw emerge from the unity of the state] (1988c: 32).

24. Unamuno claims that, while the Portuguese, perhaps even more than the Spanish, cherish a 'culto al dolor' [cult of suffering], it does not, in the Portuguese, 'toma cierto carácter de ferocidad bravía que en nosotros tomó' [assume the degree of untamed ferocity that it did in us] (1941: 11). This ethnic paradigm informs Unamuno's appraisal of Portuguese literature: he classifies the 'más bravíos, más energéticos, más fuertes' [more impetuous, more energetic, more forceful] Camilo Castelo Branco and Guerra Junqueiro as 'más ibéricos, menos exclusivamente portugueses mas no por eso menos hondamente tales' [more Iberian, less exclusively Portuguese, but no less profoundly Portuguese for all that] (1941: 18).

25. On the contrary, as the Peninsula approaches collision with the Azores, the desperate efforts to decipher auguries and events in a 'súbita revivescência dos estudos ocultistas e esotéricos [...] a História do Futuro do Padre António Vieira e das Profécias do Bandarra, além da Mensagem de Fernando Pessoa' [sudden revival of occult and esoteric studies [...] Padre António Vieira's *The History of the Future*, the prophecies of Bandarra, as well as Fernando Pessoa's *Mensagem*] are unavailing (*Jangada*: 298).

26. For a recent, and polemical, critique of the commonplace notion of Portuguese 'brandos costumes', see Martins (2011). An earlier critical treatment is Alberto Seixas Santos's acclaimed 1976 film, *Brandos Costumes*.

27. For a fuller account of this, see Sabine (2001a: 239–40). The Portuguese tourist industry was severely hit by the unrest in 1974–75 (Maxwell 1995: 141). On the use of empty Algarvian hotels to accommodate *retornados*, see Morrison (1981: 51–52). Concern for the welfare of the *retornados* did not extend as far as allowing them to stay on in the hotels once tourists could be coaxed

back (Morrison, ibid.). For detailed contemporary accounts of the post-revolutionary housing struggles, see Downs (1979) and Ponte (1975).

28. Gomes and Sá confirm that the Nixon administration would not back Spínola's decolonization plan (2008: 53–54), and that, in the summer of 1975, Secretary of State Henry Kissinger pursued Portugal's subjection to full diplomatic and economic isolation as a means of warning the government of Vasco Gonçalves against a Portuguese realignment with the Warsaw Pact states (2008: 225–36).

29. A particularly egregious case of the manipulation, or ideological appropriation, of the 1974 revolution was the deployment in 2004 by the governing centre-right PSD-CDS coalition, of the slogan 'Abril é evolução' [April is evolution] and of the iconic carnation in its publicity campaigns. On this campaign and the public debate it generated, see Ribeiro (2013).

30. As Grossegesse summarizes, 'Knowledge about Spain [in Portugal] is limited to a few negative commonplaces that match the anti-Hispanic discourse of national identity present since the battle of Aljubarrota in 1385, still idealized as the affirmation of the country's eternal independence from Spain' (2001: 169).

31. The victory of the usurper Mestre João de Avis over the army of Juan I of Castile at Aljubarrota in 1385 secured his recognition as King João I of an independent Portugal. The victory of the allied 'Catholic Monarchs' Fernando II of Aragon and Isabela I of Castile at the battle of Toro in 1476, meanwhile, thwarted the aspirations of Dom Afonso V and his son, the Infante Dom João, to unite the throne of Castile with that of Portugal instead. The ceding to Spain of the Alentejan town of Olivença was the chief lasting consequence of the so-called War of the Oranges, the last major Spanish–Portuguese conflict, in 1801. Despite the undertaking to return Olivença to Portuguese sovereignty set out in the 1815 Treaty of Vienna, the town has remained part of the Spanish state.

32. For an overview of the estimated 200,000 extrajudicial and judicial murders of civilians committed during and after the Civil War, and of the official and popular practices of remembering, forgetting, and denying these atrocities, see Preston (2006: 301–07). Up to late 2011, approximately 2000 unmarked graves, the resting places of an estimated 120,000 people, had been identified, as is detailed on the Spanish government's Historical Memory website at <http://www.memoriahistorica.gob.es/> [accessed 5 December 2015]. See also Jerez-Ferrán and Arago (2010), and Renshaw (2011). Grossegesse makes a fascinating interpretation of this passage as reconfiguring Villalar as a kind of 'Golgota [sic] or Calvary of the Iberian man' (2001: 181).

33. In point of fact, the Spanish government's collusion in the plot appears to have been unpremeditated and unwilling: Filipe Ribeiro de Meneses's account of the affair stresses that, while the Spanish police had been monitoring Delgado's movements, they appear not to have been informed of the PIDE's assassination plan, and their investigation into his and Campos's deaths only concluded that Communist agents were the most likely culprits after an angry exchange with Lisbon (2010: 584–91, esp. 586–88). For brief accounts of Delgado's career as a figurehead of opposition to the Estado Novo, and of his murder, see Raby (1988: 159–218), Meneses (2010: 423–41), and Rosas and Brandão de Brito (1996: I, 253–54). For fuller accounts, see Garcia and Maurício (1977), and Humberto Delgado: O General sem medo, catalogue of exhibition at the Biblioteca-Museu República e Resistência, opened 10 February 1995 (Lisbon: Câmara Municipal de Lisboa, 1995).

34. As Terry asserts, this 'complex interlocking of time [...] less openly stated, appears in many of the best poems of Campos de Castilla' (ibid.). On Mairena's 'historia apócrifa', see Machado (1989: II, 2018), and Briosa (2007). On the comparison of Machado's creation of Mairena with Pessoa's practice of heteronymic writing, see Lourenço (1995) and Swiderski (2006).

35. See Cabral (1976a: 50–51) and (1976b: 59–63).

36. See, in particular, Laclau and Mouffe (1985).

37. On Saramago's bitter dispute with Soares and the Partido Socialista after Spring 1975, see Lopes (2010: 56–59), and Saramago's crónica in the Diário de Notícias of 18 July 1975 'A mão do imperialismo' in which he denounces 'as pressões nacionais e internacionais interessadas em fazer [Portugal] ingressar na jangada capitalista e hábil da social democracia' [the national and international forces interested in obliging Portugal to board the convenient and capitalist social-democratic raft] (Saramago 1990: 277–79 (p. 277)).

38. According to Frier (1999), this evocation of a trans-national 'Atlantic culture [...] is exploited by Saramago as a counterpoint to recent Iberian political debate, which has tended to look eastwards to what he regards as the stale, purely economic and political models provided by the European Union, offering instead a recognition of the importance of culture, popular and erudite, national and imported, in shaping any new society which is worthwhile' (1999: 205–06).
39. As Frier suggests, Joaquim and his companions are already 'on an unwitting journey towards the Blessed Islands of Celtic tradition' when they arrive at Maria Guavaira's homestead (1999: 203).
40. On the significance of Joana's challenge to José to 'cross the line', see Frier (2007: 140).
41. The fame of the Hotel Bragança of the 1980s as a 'casa de putas' (whorehouse) was confirmed by Pilar del Río, Saramago's second wife, in Ribeiro (2009).
42. See *Aeneid*, book VI, lines 679–892, in Virgil (2008: 515–44).
43. *Aeneid* book IV, lines 238–449, in Virgil (2008: 274–97).
44. This can be seen in Joana Carda's case when one considers the interplay between the sibylline and thaumaturgic connotations of her wielding of a magic wand and her connection, noted by Frier (1999: 205) and Sabine (2001: 250) to the princess Branwen in the medieval Welsh tale 'Branwen Ferch Llŷr' (*Y Mabinogion*: pp. 21–34). Having been unjustly banished by her husband, the King of Ireland, to work as a kitchen maid, Branwen uses a tame starling to send a plea for rescue to her brother Brân (*Y Mabinogion*: 27). Although starlings appear to be connected to her escape from an unhappy marriage, Joana Carda, unlike Branwen, does not, however, rely on any warmongering big brother to come and rescue her, laying waste to two islands in the process, and neither does she drop down dead of grief at the end of the enterprise (*Y Mabinogion*: 32).
45. See *The Odyssey*, book II, lines 85–110, in Homer (1991: 19–20).
46. Interestingly, a number of Portuguese texts contemporary with *Jangada* allude to, or parody, the story of Odysseus's homecoming with an emphasis on this theme, so as to represent the homecoming of *retornados* and war veterans from the ex-colonies, by analogy with or parody of the *Odyssey*. Such texts include Alegre (1971) and (1984), Antunes (1988), and the 1988 film 'Matar saudades', directed by Fernando Lopes. On this theme in Antunes (1988), see also Sabine (2009).
47. Frier notes how this allusion to the Queen of the Isle of Women underpins Maria's execution of 'a more active female role [...] than that of Ariadne' (1999: 202).
48. See, for example, Frier (1999: 196).
49. See Sabine (2001a: 245–47), for a fuller discussion of this issue, and particularly of how the mystery of Joaquim's bouncing stone allegorizes the question of whether human destiny follows a rectilinear trajectory (from cradle to grave, from barbarism to civilization, from capitalism to socialism) or a cyclical one (from paradise, through perdition and back again, or the cycle of birth and death of each generation). The question is also implicit in the novel's allusions to the 'Orce Man' fossil fragment, and the parallels subsequently suggested between this earliest Iberian and the modern 'Orce man', Pedro.
50. Readings of *Jangada* that see Pedro Orce as representative of the old social order and the others as representative of the new social order, such as Pires de Lima (1988: 33–34), or as symbolizing 'the authority and venerability of age' but also, at his death, 'the need for tradition and old ways to be questioned and renewed by the new' (Frier (1999: 202), make no mention of how conservative and patriarchal are the responses of the two younger men to the question of paternity.
51. One exception is the brief passage in *Cegueira* (166) that illustrates (and implicitly condemns) the correlation between sexism and homophobia.
52. On the relationship between Camões's allegory and the vindication of the sexual logic of Portuguese colonialism offered by Gilberto Freyre's *O Luso e o Trópico* and later writings, see Klobucka (2002).
53. On the *Estado Novo*'s Obra das Mães para a Educação Nacional (OMEN), and the annual 'Mothers' Weeks' that it organized, from 1938 until the 1960s, to encourage women's domestication and to reward mothers of large families with hand-outs of bed linen, baby's clothes, etc., see Rosas and Brandão de Brito (1996: II, p. 609; 676) and Pimentel (2002). On the essentially similar developments under the Franco regime in Spain, see Morcillo (2010) and Richmond (2003).

54. In Portugal in 1986 and up to a referendum of 2007, abortion was legal only in certain extenuating circumstances (see Manuel and Tollefsen (2008), and Magalhães and Tavares (2014)). Prior to 1984, it had been expressly banned in any circumstances. However, according to Salgado (1978: 8), in the period immediately prior to 25 de Abril, an estimated 200,000 illegal, and often very unprofessional, abortions were carried out annually, resulting each year in around 2000 *recorded* fatalities. In Spain, the laws criminalizing all abortions were relaxed in 1985 to permit termination in cases of rape, of physical damage to the foetus, or where the mother's health was gravely endangered. According to Ross (2002: 256), as late as 2001, an estimated 70% of abortions in Spain were carried out illegally. Abortion in all circumstances, up to the fourteenth week of pregnancy, was finally decriminalized in 2010.
55. According to Grossegesse, 'the idea of a coming history awaiting humankind in its process of political emancipation [...] implies a notion of human history as a paradoxical, predetermined possibility of overcoming capitalism: like a religion of salvation, but without any God from above. Thus, Saramago fuses Machado's notion with the historical materialism that employs theology in a sort of *materialist Messianism*' (2001: 172).
56. For an introduction to the ongoing debate about the nature of the Venta Micena skull fragment, see Gibert et al. (1989) and Cela-Conde (1999).
57. Examples of the citation of the 'Orce Man' debate in the popular dissemination of 'Creation' theory include the article on 'Evolution Fraud', at <www.nwcreation.net/evolutionfraud.html> and 'No Missing Links Here...', at <www.apologeticspress.org/apcontent.aspx?category=9&article=1353> [accessed 20 November 2014].
58. In this and its other imaginings of exhumation, *Jangada* arguably anticipates Saramago's later *Todos os Nomes*, where, as Bev Hogue argues, the tropes of the gravestone and exhumation serve to point out that 'monuments cannot preserve memory any more than archives can, for authentic memory exists only among the living, whose repertoire of knowledge is ephemeral, faulty, and incomplete' (2006: 136).

CHAPTER 5

História do Cerco de Lisboa

After *Jangada*'s journey into the fantastic in order to excavate Iberian mythology and outline new strategies for a radical micro-politics, *História do Cerco de Lisboa* pursues the same agenda through a plausible story. One should say, rather, a plausible story within a plausible story, since *História*'s re-imagining of Portuguese King Afonso Henriques's siege and capture of the Almoravid-ruled city of al-Ushbuna, in 1147, is presented as the creation of a fictitious figure, Raimundo Silva, living in late 1980s Lisbon. The successful assault on the city was critical in the emergence of the independent state of Portugal that Afonso Henriques had proclaimed in 1139. Hence, national historiography has consistently presented it as a foundational event, the climactic moment of the birth of a crusading, Christian nation.[1] Raimundo Silva's counter-factual rewriting of the siege upsets both the messianic and monarchist messages that *História Pátria* attributed to it; but his 'new' history is enclosed within the story of how his life is transformed by the act of deliberately falsifying history. Existing studies have explored how Raimundo's actions expose the subjectivity, selectivity, and uncertainty of historical accounts. This exposé adds up to Saramago's most direct and sustained critique both of narrative historiography, and of how such historiography's reception beyond academe shapes, but can also constrain, understanding of both past and present. Yet while *História* reiterates key concerns of Saramago's earlier fiction, it does so as an overture to the further development of his proposals for a renewed radical politics in postmodernity. While *História* shifts the focus to previously unexplored areas of past and present reality, it is easy to identify key concerns of the preceding novels. The proposals of recovering subaltern perspectives on past events, and of dismantling a nationalist and corporatist conception of 'community', are reiterated alongside those of embedding anti-racist, post-colonialist, and feminist critique in radical class politics, and of proposing a more innovative, plural conception of (inter-)identity. These themes are recalled through extensive intertextual allusion, and, in particular, through the recurrence of such symbolic tropes as vision, in new allegories built around the novel's central concept of besiegement.

The story of Raimundo Silva, a publishing house proofreader and life-long bachelor, begins when he is tasked with correcting the final proofs of an historian's new account of the Lisbon siege. As he reads, Raimundo finds in this history not merely a predictable number of factual and lexical inaccuracies; he also identifies the linguistic projection of an anachronistic patriotism, and a selective deployment of sources, that corral historical data into a well-worn nationalist narrative, wherein Portuguese heroism propagates Christian 'civilization' in the lands 'reconquered' from the 'infidel'. Provoked by this, Raimundo risks his professional reputation and his livelihood in an act of rebellion against the rules of populist narrative history. Further to his legitimate corrections to the proofs, he inscribes the word 'não' ('no', but, in this context, meaning 'did not') into a key sentence, altering the course of history to one in which Afonso Henriques *did not* secure the assistance of northern European warriors of the Second Crusade in laying siege to Lisbon. Only after the history book has gone to press is the costly, embarrassing, and self-evidently deliberate error discovered. The publishing house's directors call Raimundo to a meeting for disciplinary action. Here he meets the woman newly appointed as his line-manager, the mild-mannered but resolute Dra Maria Sara, and takes an instant dislike to her when she, while opposing the idea of firing Raimundo, presses him for an explanation of his act of sabotage. In a subsequent meeting, Maria Sara expresses her appreciation of what she identifies as Raimundo's questioning and imaginative intellectual disposition, and challenges him to write an alternative history of the siege, exploring what could have followed from the Crusader's refusal to help the Portuguese capture Lisbon. The task that Maria Sara proposes to Raimundo, and the love affair that ensues between them, force them both to reflect on more than the distant past and its representation. Raimundo reluctantly accepts Maria Sara's challenge, and hesitantly admits of the attraction between the two of them. In so doing, he not only ponders problems of history and language but also, in typical Saramago fashion, opens himself up to the kind of process of personal growth and change that *Ricardo Reis*'s protagonist resists, with significant political and affective consequences. Raimundo composes his 'alternative' history with scrupulous attention to the earliest sources, exploiting lacunae and incidental details therein as a starting point for historical conjecture. As he writes, his text becomes a laboratory for innovation in terms of imagining the past. He conjecturally reconstructs and foregrounds the formerly marginalized perspectives of history's underlings, and of a supposedly inimical ethnic Other. More importantly, he comes to conceive of historical investigation not as the accrual of certain knowledge, but as an approximation to *aletheia*, in the post-Heideggerian sense of 'disclosure', or 'unconcealedness'; a search wherein what is disclosed is often not facticity itself, but the irrecoverableness of any such facticity. Undertaking historical hypothecation as an avowedly creative or fictional act also prompts Raimundo to analyse, and reconceive of, his identity and social circumstances, and of his interaction with the social Other. Here, the novel invites comparisons with *Ricardo Reis*'s Ricardo Reis, as Raimundo's literary-historiographical experimentation enables him to 'heteronymize' himself — together with his hopes, anxieties, and moral values — in the figure of his history's protagonist, the foot soldier Mogueime. The imagining of Mogueime's role in the siege, and his attraction to his master's concubine, Ouruana, permits Raimundo's approximation to, and discovery of, the Other that is Maria Sara. She and Raimundo confess their love for each other, and seek to give up their single persons' habits in favour of a stable and egalitarian relationship. Thus, *História* advances Saramago's engagement with the Pessoan concepts explored in

Ricardo Reis, seeking to factor them into a materialist conception of humanity, and a socialist praxis of everyday life.

At a key juncture in their romance, when Maria Sara first visits the home on the site of Lisbon's medieval walls where Raimundo is writing his history, he professes that '[a]ndo a tentar dizer-lhe quem sou' [I'm trying to tell you who I am], and she replies '[e] eu a tentar descobrir como vamos viver' [and I'm trying to find out how we're going to live] (*História*: 261). The simplicity of this exchange is deceptive, since it can be interpreted as referring not solely to day-to-day living, but also to their shared exploration, through Raimundo's history, of how perceptions of the past can condition identities, behaviour, and decision-making in the present. *História*, by depicting its protagonists grappling directly with the epistemological and representational problems raised by the concept of history, foregrounds the question of how we might live from day to day with a different conception of the past. Unlike most of Saramago's previous novels, the novel makes little engagement with modern class-based politics, and offers no vision of a mass movement of subaltern groups as agent of socio-economic change. It focuses instead on two white-collar workers with no apparent aspiration to social transformation, and explores how a critical consciousness of the past might impact upon such individuals and their relations at the most basic and intimate level. In this way, *História* expands on *Memorial*'s and *Jangada*'s focus on the politics of day-to-day interpersonal relations, and suggests that a radical micropolitics of contemporary everyday life need not be mere fantasy. At the same time, it stresses — in its focus on historiography and on individuals' pursuit of love, understanding, and self-knowledge — that if such utopian aspirations are to retain a place in the politics of a postmodern era, then the architects of change must learn to work with uncertainty and conjecture; with — in a word — error. Such acknowledgment of the necessity of error, needless to say, goes hand in hand with the critique — or 'besiegement' — of errors in interpretations of the world that are commonly accepted as truthful.

I — Besieging History, Exploring Error

Besiegement serves as a multiple metaphor that is crucial to the development of both of *História*'s plot arcs. As Helena Kaufman first noted, the topic of the twelfth-century siege is reflected narratologically through the novel's composition in the form of concentric diegetic spheres, each of which is 'besieged' — analysed, appropriated, and recast, in different ways — by the author of the sphere outside it (Kaufman 1991a: 169). Adrián Huici (1996: 142–43) has argued that at least eight textual 'levels' or 'layers' are identifiable in the novel.[2] With more certainty one can talk of four principal concentric spheres, namely, from outermost to innermost, (i) the story of the life of Raimundo Silva in late 1980s Lisbon; (ii) the 'alternative' history of the siege that he authors as a riposte to; (iii) the draft *História do Cerco de Lisboa* whose final proofs he adulterates, and (iv) the pre-existing corpus of historical accounts from which this draft history draws its raw material, the key primary source for which is the eyewitness account 'De Expugnatione Lyxbonensi', conventionally attributed to one Osberne of Bawdsley.[3] The novel is narrated in the same inconsistently omnipotent voice that characterizes Saramago's preceding novels, vacillating between positions within and outside of the diegesis, questioning its own authority as processor and presenter of the disparate raw materials of the text, and assessing that material and its treatment with ironic detachment. The effect of this voicing in a text of concentric diegetic 'layers' is distinctive, however. The narrative voice's penetration of all but the innermost layer makes it simultaneously an intermediary between the author of each *história* and the reader of the text, and a conduit for the vision and thought processes of Raimundo Silva. Thus, as Maria Luísa Raimundo Mesquita suggests, it reconciles 'os múltiplos pontos de vista e a omnisciência' [multiple points of view with narrative omniscience] (1993: 5).[4]

This undifferentiated narrative mediation of concentric stories means that the reader who embarks on a reading of the novel is as much 'besieged' as are the authors and historical subjects of its different fictional layers. To a greater extent than its predecessors, *História* employs complexities of narrative structure to wrong-foot the reader. Rather as medieval siege warfare was waged partly through feigned attack and counter-attack, ambushes, and false or hidden castle entrances and escape routes, the novel's narrative tricks create false expectations, or otherwise disorient its reader regarding both the origins of blocks of narrative and their relationship to the novel as a whole. For a start, the novel opens with six pages of dialogue in which narrative mediation is restricted to the opening words 'Disse o revisor,' [The proof-reader said,] (*História*: 11). The reader can only guess at this conversation's context, or at the identities of this *revisor* and his interlocutor. The second chapter then makes what at first appears to be an abrupt, unannounced jump from the diegesis represented by that first chapter's conversation into another diegesis, which the reader naturally conjectures is that of the 'livro' [book] that was being discussed earlier (*História*: 14). This second narrative, however, is cut short with the statement that '[n]ão o tem descrito assim o historiador no seu livro' [the historian has not described it so in his book] (*História*: 19). The narrative is thereby revealed as an account simply of an image in the mind of the *revisor* Raimundo Silva, as he speculates about what details of the events of 1147 the historian might have omitted from his book (*História*: 22). It is also revealed (ibid.) that this conjecture of Raimundo's took place *before* the conversation in the first chapter. The reader is thus obliged to go back twelve pages to the novel's opening, and revise his/her understanding of the relationship between, and significance of, its component parts.

Such disorienting narratological tricks subject the reader to an experiential induction into Saramago's most thorough-going interrogation of semiotics, epistemology, and, in particular, the emplotment of narrative history. Where *Ricardo Reis* used the image of the labyrinth as a starting point for exploring both the rhizomatic nature of textuality, and the ethical dimension of the challenge arising from this, *História* uses the image of the siege to characterize modern humanity's textually mediated engagement with a vanished past, to whose traces we customarily look in search of justification, or explanation, of identities, attitudes, and actions in the present. While we are aware (or, at least, convinced) that a materially fixed past reality lies at the heart of our historical investigations, comprehension of that reality can only take place at second hand, through attempts at either interrogating, and/or 'capturing', textual sources. Part of the time, needless to say, the search for, or 'siege' of, past truths must be attempted indirectly, through the interrogation of a sequence of existing secondary sources. As was demonstrated some 400 years ago by Francis Bacon's 'estupenda lição [...] sobre os erros' [stupendous treatise on errors] (*História*: 28), these sources' diverse ideological interpretations of past events are encoded through shifting, polyvalent linguistic signs, and through tendentious rhetorical or narrative organization.[5]

As a consequence of this breach of textual boundaries, *História* exposes how, as previously explored in *Ricardo Reis*, the paradox of an author's demiurgic power imposes itself upon historiographical exegesis as well as upon, for example, lyric poetry, or Socratic dialogue. A writer can create a textual realm independent of any reality that he/she may claim it represents, but he/she does so by appropriating and refashioning existing writings. While the writer may rework such writings as suits his/her own agenda, taking possession of language, as it were, 'second-hand' means that his/her text is always alive with meanings that stray from, or even traduce, authorial intentions. The slipperiness of signification in language that accounts for what Bacon terms *idola fori* is repeatedly noted in *História*'s relating of Raimundo's interpretative and creative thought processes.[6] The narrative notes, for example, how 'a palavra, qualquer, tem essa facilidade ou virtude de conduzir sempre a quem a disse' [a word, any word, has that facility or virtue of leading always to the person who uttered it] (*História*: 65), whether this person be the modern Portuguese, Japanese, or American for whom, respectively, wildly different images are conjured by the words translated as 'dragon' (*História*: 67), or the twelfth-century Iberian Muslims and Christians for whom the word 'dog' has contrasting connotations (*História*: 70), or the ancient Greek and present-day European for whom 'cynicism' implies thoughtfulness or its opposite respectively (*História*: 79). As Saramago demonstrates with his own appropriation of an image from Goethe, if the writer is a demiurge or sorcerer, then 'a experiência nos [demonstra] diariamente que cada palavra é um perigoso aprendiz de feiticeiro' [experience shows us daily that every word is a dangerous sorcerer's apprentice] (*História*: 101).[7]

Moreover, Raimundo's reading of the original history outlines the critique, most famously set out by Hayden White's *Metahistory*, of the significance of an ideologically loaded narrative format for the data that the historian selects for evaluation (White 1973: ix–x). Raimundo's refutation of a distinction between history and fiction — 'tudo quanto não for vida, é literatura' [everything that is not life is literature] (*História*: 15) — serves not to condemn all scholarly practices of narrating the past. Rather, it addresses the myth that still underpins the popular reception of humanist historiography, that 'the difference between "history" and "fiction" resides in the fact that the historian "finds" his stories, whereas the fiction writer "invents" his' (White 1973: 6). As mentioned above, Saramago suggested that, of the two fundamental deceptions exercised by narrative history — those of being at once 'parcial' and 'parcelar' — the latter was the more pernicious (Reis 1998: 81).[8] His complaint is illustrated in *História* by the history book that Raimundo proofreads, which has such an 'abundância de pormenores realistas que chega a parecer obra de testemunha aqui presente, ou, pelo menos, hábil aproveitamento de qualquer documento coetâneo' [abundance of realist details, that it ends up seeming the work of a present witness, or at least, an intelligent use of some contemporary document] (*História*: 22). The discussion of such history's masquerade of completeness and incontestability can be related to White's interrogation of the *motific characterization*, or encoding, of a given event, process, or agent.[9] Casting events in terms of inaugural, transitional, or terminating motifs (White 1973: 5), the historian martials them into a '*completed* diachronic process, about which one can then ask questions as if he [*sic*] were dealing with a synchronic structure of relationships' (White 1973: 6), and from which one can extrapolate an unequivocal 'message' or 'lesson'. In the most basic instance, the propensity of terminating motifs to indicate 'the apparent end or resolution of a process or situation of tension' (White 1973: 6) presents such a diachronic process as confirmation of the post-Hegelian conception of human existence as a progression towards harmony and enlightenment. Long before Raimundo supplies a stubbornly inconclusive and ironic ending to both of *História*'s plot arcs, he notes the hazardous manner in which any such presumption of an overarching and determinant transhistorical *telos* conditions the purportedly empirical historian's conclusions in advance, inclining him/her towards construing historical 'evidence' in support of his/her conception of that *telos*. Raimundo observes that

> [c]ertos autores, quiçá por adquirida convicção ou compleição espiritual naturalmente pouco afeiçoada a indagações pacientes, aborrecem a evidência de não ser sempre linear e explícita a relação entre o que chamamos causa e o que, por vir depois, chamamos efeito. (*História*: 119)

> [some authors, perhaps on account of acquired convictions or a spiritual make-up naturally little disposed to patient enquiry, disdain the evident fact that the relation between that which we call the cause and that which, since it follows later, we call the effect is not always linear and self-evident.]

Raimundo comes to see the absurdity, and indeed the danger, of emplotment as a teleological device by means of which an historical narrative is presented as an authoritative 'explanation' of past events. By configuring everything as 'correntio, espontâneo, quase necessário' [fluent, spontaneous, almost imperative] (*História*: 130), narrative history fossilizes the traces of the past into incomplete, yet seductive, ideological representations of past events, like flies in amber jewellery. The history book that so offends Raimundo achieves 'a ardente expressão de um patriotismo fervoroso' [the ardent expression of impassioned patriotism] (*História*: 40) by plotting the siege of Lisbon in a carefully controlled blend of romantic and epic modes that characterizes the Portuguese as the forces of Good, pitted against Evil incarnated in an ethnically defined adversary.[10] The presentation of the past as a vindication both of nationalist ideology, and of its cartography of communal identities and prevailing socio-economic hierarchies, requires the omission, or marginalization, of such data — for example, the agency of women and children, or increasingly desperate supplications to an supposedly infidel religion (*História*: 19) — as might contradict the patriarchal and xenophobic ideology that emerges as divinely ordained and guaranteed by history. The absences and sutures in the resulting account are, moreover, airbrushed away by the fraudulent contrivance of a travelling, omniscient, narrative gaze. As AbdoolKarim Vakil has noted, Raimundo

> calls into question the historian's reliance on the eye-witness account of the event [...] and the fetishism of the document that would naively have us, in the quaint expression of one historian of the conquest of Lisbon, seeing through the eyes of the dead. To do so, after all, is to see only from the perspective of the victor. (2002: 32)

Together, selectivity, emplotment, and narratology minimize the reader's awareness of their historical and ideological location, and maximize their identification with figures from the past who are characterized as heroic subjects, around whom historical data is marshalled. This is especially so where the historian's concern for the shape and clarity of the narrative prompts the use of referents familiar in the present-day as metonyms for historical agents, events, or processes. Such is the case here with the pennants on the Portuguese coat of arms, and the crescent moon motif of the flags of Islamic nations. Raimundo longs to excise what he identifies as anachronistic references to these symbols, which had yet to come into use in 1147, but he recognizes that their removal would be 'como um terramoto na página' [like an earthquake on the page] (*História*: 42), emasculating the climax of the account of the siege and robbing it of an uplifting sense of closure.

It would be naïve to interpret Raimundo's encounter with this jingoistic and ill-researched account of the siege as a just indictment of contemporary academic historians' practice, or at least of the historiography that has responded to the interventions of Hayden White and his contemporaries. Rather, the story of Raimundo and his 'não' refers to the wider reception of history outside academe, through journalism, political discourse, and, especially, such 'info-tainment' as prime-time TV documentaries, or cinematic or novelistic blockbusters. It outlines how the target audience of such representations might — without having to take a degree in History — see through the deceptive presentation of the past as a 'cristalização predeterminada' [predetermined crystallization] (*História*: 130), and develop an approach to the past that acknowledges first that truth is never complete and that error is inevitable, and, secondly, that *exploring* error can often be instructive.

Both aspects of this alternative approach to the past motivate Saramago's treatment, once again, of the trope of vision. Here, the emphasis on vision and (in)visibility points to the significance not simply of seeing differently, but, equally, of envisioning that which is not, or was not, real, but that is, or could have been, possible. It is worth noting here that the Portuguese term for proofreader — *revisor* — derives from the Latin *revidēre*, which can mean to review, audit, or check, but also to correct or alter. The word attributes to Raimundo both the duty of *re-viewing*, or looking again, and also that of *revising*, or amending. Professionally trained to scrutinize and to revise, Raimundo proves himself psychologically inclined also to *re-envisage* what he reads. Significantly, the first instance of Raimundo's re-envisaging of the siege (in the novel's second chapter) comes when he notices that the original history's author has overlooked the fact that twelfth-century Lisbon's muezzins were almost invariably blind (*História*: 29). Raimundo's recuperation of this detail throws into ironic relief the manner in which the muezzin's perspective (or rather, the crucial fact of its irrecoverableness) is effaced by the history, which restricts its representation of the city's Muslim culture to 'um pouco de cor local e tinta histórica no arraial inimigo' [a touch of local colour and historical ink in the enemy camp] (*História*: 22). Vision is further associated with the pursuit of a less deceptive relationship with the past when, rather like Roque Lozano and the protagonists of *Jangada*, Raimundo sets out to search with his own eyes for evidence of the events about which he has just read. Having delivered the adulterated proofs of the history to his employer, and already fearful of the consequences of his actions, Raimundo takes a walk through 'os lugares da antiga cidade moura' [the location of the old Moorish city] (*História*: 60), following the route of the medieval city walls (*História*: 59–75). Here, as much as in his reading of that history, however, he notes first how what is commonly accepted therein as factual entails the accretion of myth and of dubious evidence, to the material traces of the past, and, secondly, how many data crucial to an understanding of the past are inaccessible to, or irretrievable for, the present. Twice during his walk, Raimundo encounters vestiges of the city's defensive wall: first 'um troço, se não da própria e incorruptível muralha, pelo menos um muro que ocupa o exacto lugar do outro' [a chunk, if not of the original, intact wall, then at least [of] a wall that occupies the precise location of the other one] (*História*: 68) and later 'um poderoso pano de muro, carcomido na base, estas são pedras vivas verdadeiramente, estão aqui há nove ou dez séculos, se não mais, do tempo dos bárbaros, e resistem' [a powerful expanse of wall, worn away at the bottom, these indeed are genuinely living stones, they've been here for nine or ten centuries, if not longer, from the time of the barbarians, and have withstood it all] (*História*: 74). These encounters attest to the complexity of the past, and to the propensity of its traces to furnish multiple narratives of origin, allegiance, and identity. The surviving walls incorporate the contributions of Phoenician, Roman, Celtic, Visigothic, Arab, and Portuguese settlers, who constructed walls reusing the materials and ground plans of their predecessors. What is left today is a mosaic, in which the contributions of different cultures and epochs could not reliably be distinguished, even if a comprehension of the totality of the city's past were to be attempted. What has more commonly been attempted, of course, is the imposition of a partial, ideological inscription of that past, falsely corroborated through the selective presentation of the city's most picturesque and evocative features — such as the city's iconic no. 28 tram (*História*: 71) — in films, advertising, and on the itineraries of coachloads of foreign tourists (*História*: 66–67), and through acts of ethnographic cleansing such as the 1930s rebuilding of the Castelo de S. Jorge, and the 1950s bulldozing of much of the multi-ethnic Mouraria district.[11] Raimundo Silva's explorations of old Lisbon reveal that the city can be 'read' only as a palimpsest; where the ineradicable traces not only of past constructions and events, but also of previous inscriptions of 'history', emerge to contradict the images that sustain currently dominant notions of a Portuguese national identity. Portugal's supposedly long-established ethnic homogeneity, for example, is questioned when Raimundo meets with a Roma girl — 'rapariguinha cigana, de uns doze anos' [a gypsy girl, about twelve years old] (*História*: 73) — begging at the door of the Alfama *casa de pasto* where he stops for lunch. This mute encounter makes evident the persistence, over nine centuries, of ethnic diversity, and often of ethnic antagonisms, in this purportedly Catholic city of *brandos costumes*. Neither the massacre of the captured city's inhabitants in 1147, nor the persecution and expulsions of 'infidels' and 'vagrants' in the centuries that followed, wholly eliminated Lisbon's minorities of Muslims, Jews, and, later, Roma and Protestants. When Raimundo momentarily imagines the Roma girl to be a twelfth-century 'moura, na hora da primeira necessidade' [Moorish girl, in the hour of direst need] (ibid.), *História* demonstrates that the multi-ethnic city is not a twentieth-century innovation. Here, Raimundo recognizes the persistence of ethnic prejudice and marginalization over the same period: 'o cerco não acabou, avisam os olhos da cigana' [the gypsy girl's eyes tell him, the siege has not ended] (ibid.). This encounter, together with Raimundo's later wandering first through the Mouraria (whose inhabitants today are 'acaso [...] descendentes directos dos mouros' [perhaps direct descendants of the Moors] (*História*: 160)), and then through São Cristóvão [the vibrant hub, since at least the nineteenth century, of the city's Luso-African community], also demonstrates that Lisbon's history is not reducible to a tale of two civilizations opposed like the armies of a chessboard, 'partes em litígio, as negras [e] as brancas, neste caso os mouros [e] os cristãos, segundo as cores' [conflicting parties, black and white, in this case, Moors and Christians, in accordance with their colours] (*História*: 233).

Both this encounter with the Roma girl, and Raimundo's similar reverie when he pauses for refreshments at a local milk-bar — *A Graciosa* — also home in on the issue of historiographical anachronism, and of *História Pátria*'s spurious attribution to its author (and, by implication, to its reader) of an innate empathy with the historical Other whom it presents as the ethnic self-same. Such affirmations of a trans-historically consistent national and religious community are challenged when Raimundo's 'notável talento de desdobrar-se' [remarkable talent for doubling up] (*História*: 22) — already manifested in his deliberation (*História*: 48–50) about whether or not to inscribe his fateful 'não' — leads him to imagine himself and his fellow customers in *A Graciosa* as inhabitants of the besieged Muslim city (*História*: 61–63). Raimundo's reverie reverses the polarity of the narcissistic projection encouraged by the omniscient gaze of conventional historical narrative; it attributes to those 'Moorish' inhabitants a horror at the atrocities perpetrated by the approaching Christian armies, a mortal fear, and the moral indignation for which they variously invoke divine vengeance, or question divine wisdom. This exercise compels Raimundo — and the novel's reader — to recognize the common humanity and unjust suffering of their historical 'enemy'. This radically changes the 'motific characterization' of Muslim Lisbon's inhabitants from that of an inimical Other, whose exoticism pegs the narrator's (and reader's) identity to an idealized false consciousness, to that of tragic heroes or of victims. It also, however, suggests the difficulties of recovering — and truly comprehending — anything of the historical Other's world-view, beyond their basic instincts towards compassion, community, and self-preservation.

Raimundo's experiences as he tours the site of the Muslim city animate a new 'consciência múltipla, caleidoscópica' [kaleidoscopic, multiple conscience] of this 'coincidência histórica e topográfica' [historical and topographic coincidence] (*História*: 60), with the image of the kaleidoscope here recalling Saramago's evocation, in his interviews with Carlos Reis, of a vision of the past as an 'arrumação caótica' where 'tudo está ao lado de tudo'.[12] Historical traces, and the raw material of potentially disparate historical narratives, survive even in such trivial everyday objects as the pastries in *A Graciosa*'s windows. *História* teasingly connects the milk-bar's croissants — 'com a forma que lhes deu o nome em francês, de crescente' [with the shape that gave them their French name, meaning crescent] (*História*: 62) — with the iconography and cosmology of Islam, but leaves it to the reader to recall the origins of the croissant (or, more precisely, of its Austrian counterpart, the *kipfel*) in the celebrations of the (Catholic) Austrian empire's resistance of the (Islamic) Ottoman empire's siege of Vienna in 1683.[13] Notwithstanding the loss to the present of masses of data pertaining to the past, the traces that survive exist in a mute and chaotic — or, to borrow Umberto Eco's metaphor, rhizomatic — relation to each other, and are made to 'speak' or 'make sense' only through the historian's decisions about which relationships and configurations to illuminate and explain.

The notion of such a rhizomatic 'chaosmos' that is comprehensible only 'kaleido-scopically' is also implied when Raimundo Silva compares the traces of the past to an uncountable mass of crumbs (*História*: 63). As he watches a 'mulher gorda' [fat lady] gobbling up a sweet pastry millefeuille, and attempting to gather the last delicious crumbs with a moistened finger, he imagines her as a burlesque allegory of the pseudo-Leibnizian notion of history as the amassing and analysis of unique and perfect cosmic particles, or monads, which, as a totality, offer a universal explanation:[14]

> [A] mulher [voltou] ao que resta do mil-folhas, daqui a pouco, disfarçadamente, por ser acto de má educação, catará com o dedo indicador molhado as migalhas do bolo, mas não conseguirá recolhê-las todas, sabemo-lo por experiência, são assim como uma poeira cósmica, incontáveis, gotículas de um nevoeiro infinito e sem remissão. (*História*: 63)
>
> [the woman has returned to what is left of the millefeuille, in a moment, discreetly, since it's a breach of good table manners, she will sweep up the pastry crumbs with a moistened index finger, but she will not manage to gather them all, as we know from experience, they are just like a cosmic dust storm, uncountable, tiny droplets of an infinite and unremitting fog.]

There is a comic irony in this allegory's situation in the city that Voltaire's *Candide* made emblematic of post-Leibnizian optimism's absurdity.[15] More importantly, however, the allegory also invites consideration of how *História*'s assault on *História Pátria* articulates further aspects of the critique of narrative historiography rehearsed by such works as White's *Metahistory*. As White argues, Leibniz's conception of the relationship between the constituent parts of the cosmos has underpinned a historiographical practice in which 'the processes of history [...] considered in their individual concrete reality and as moments of a total process [...] only *appear* to be dispersed in time and space' (1973: 61). This system legitimizes a synecdochic mode of comprehension of the past (such as is proposed, for example, in Lukács's theory of the historical novel).[16] The 'particular event' is conceived of as 'a microcosm of the macrocosm' and thus

> the representation of an event in its total context, the context itself being construed as a plenum of individual events that are *united in their difference* from one another, is [presented as] an adequate way of figuring that event's meaning and relation to the whole. (1973: 61)

In the absence of any divine grace that might (as Leibniz surmised) protect humankind from its own intellectual impotence in apprehending and analysing the 'particles' of history, Raimundo's musing on the pastry crumbs has simple but stark implications for any analysis of the past, including for dialectical materialism. Even if the materialist thesis is sound, the dialectical method cannot ever be applied so exhaustively to observable phenomena for the conclusions about an event's 'meaning and relation to the whole' to be unproblematically labelled truth.

Ultimately, Raimundo's *passeio* presents the development of human knowledge as the inverse of Hegel's ambitious, but ultimately comforting, conception of world history as a liberating journey towards total understanding, or as the 'development of the spirit's consciousness of its own freedom and of the consequent realisation of this freedom'.[17] Fresh knowledge inevitably exposes further areas of human ignorance, not least because it cannot be ascertained to be knowledge *in totality*. As Raimundo, recalling his reading of Seneca (*História*: 28), concludes,

> quando chegar ao fim do meu passeio saberei mais, mas também é certo que saberei menos. Precisamente por mais saber, por outras palavras, a ver se me explico, a consciência de saber mais conduz-me à consciência de saber pouco (*História*: 72)
>
> [when I get to the end of my walk, I will know more, but for certain I will also know less. And this precisely because of knowing more, in other words, let me see if I can explain it, the awareness of knowing more leads me to the awareness of knowing very little]

Raimundo's supposition here reconceives of historical enquiry, in terms not of the compilation or piecing together of a simulacrum of past reality, but more as a process of disclosure, and of the truth pursued thereby as *aletheia*. His thoughtful, sceptical reading of sources, and pursuit of primary evidence, identifies and sets aside history's false accretions, misleading omissions, and questionable characterizations. Yet what is uncovered and comprehended through this analytical work is not a whole, crystalline truth, but rather an image of the complexity of a given historical topic, and of the weight of 'unknowability' that attaches to it. This paradox of historical investigation as simultaneous enlightenment and revelation of doubt or uncertainty is explored through *História*'s metaphorical play on the tropes of light, vision, and clarification.

II — Seeing Differently: Disclosure, Empathy, and Error

When looking that this aspect of the text, it is instructive to compare Raimundo with Saramago's other protagonists who wander labyrinthine cityscapes in search of enlightenment. A first comparison would be with *Memorial*'s Baltasar, who, alerted by Blimunda to the bodies and circumstances of the people around him, gains awareness of their common biological constitution, and of the man-made origins of his society's socio-economic hierarchy. More significant, perhaps, is Raimundo's contrast with Ricardo Reis. Raimundo's walks in *História* lead him to the observation that '[o]lhar, ver, e reparar são maneiras distintas de usar o órgão da vista' [looking, seeing, and observing are three distinct modes of using the visual organ] (*História*: 166). Reis wanders the labyrinthine city and looks (*olha*), but rarely sees (*vê*) and does not observe (*repara*), or rather does not want to observe. And, as *História*'s narrative asserts, wanting to observe is part — but only part — of what brings vision, in its fullest sense, into being:

> Só o reparar pode chegar a ser visão plena, quando num ponto determinado ou sucessivamente a atenção se concentra, o que tanto sucederá por efeito duma deliberação da vontade quanto por uma espécie de estado sinestético involuntário em que o visto solicita ser visto novamente (ibid.)
>
> [Only observation can constitute full vision, when at a given moment or in rapid succession one's attention is concentrated, something that happens as much on account of a determination of the will as it does on account of a kind of involuntary synaesthetic state in which that which is seen demands to be seen afresh]

Observation, then, is a willed double vision, where the image is produced

> em dois lugares distintos do cérebro com diferença temporal de um centésimo de segundo, primeiro o sinal simplificado, depois o desenho rigoroso (ibid.)
>
> [in two distinct parts of the brain, with the difference in time of a split second, first, the simplified sign, then the painstaking depiction, in precise, commanding definition]

While the individual can never wholly step outside the episteme that determines what the eye recognizes, such a double-take entails the recognition of the subjectivity, or perspectival nature, of the initial act of looking, and prompts a 'revisionary' reflection. Developing such a faculty requires both practice and courage of Raimundo, who at this point remains 'ainda não de tudo preparado para ver, ele que de rever tem profissão, e que só ocasionalmente, por passageiro distúrbio psicológico, repara' [still not entirely prepared to see, he who has made a career of revising, and who only occasionally, on account of a fleeting psychological disturbance, observes] (*História*: 184–85). As Raimundo will eventually conclude,

> tenho-me divertido ou instruído, aos poucos, a descobrir a diferença entre olhar e ver e entre ver e reparar, [...] suponho até que o verdadeiro conhecimento estará na consciência que tivermos da mudança de um nível de percepção, para dizê-lo assim, a outro nível (*História*: 302)
>
> [I have been amusing, or educating, myself little by little, discovering the difference between seeing and looking and between looking and observing, [...] I might even suppose that true knowledge is found in our consciousness of the change from one level of perception, so to speak, to another]

História's exploration of this progression towards vision as the act of 'reparando' marshals its protagonists and plot-lines together with those of its predecessors, so as to anticipate *Ensaio sobre a Cegueira*'s epigraphic injunction, '[se] podes olhar, vê. Se podes ver, repara' [if you can look, see. If you can see, observe].[18] *Cegueira*'s protagonists must learn — through the harrowing experience of total physical blindness, and through the Doctor's Wife's exemplary actions — to observe, analyse, and question, rather than simply to take what they see as self-explanatory. Significantly, the Portuguese term *reparar* can also mean to amend, make good, or repair. Coming to terms with their own prior failure to examine their life and society, always in search of their political logic and of some kind of moral sense, they can ultimately reconceive of themselves and of their community, and thereby achieve a less wretched existence within an environment that is as labyrinthine and hostile in epistemological and ethical terms as it is in physical ones.

História's overlapping concerns with *Cegueira* are further signalled by the way that, as noted above, it connects the notion of vision with that of knowledge as *aletheia* by means of images of light and dark, day and night, clarity and obfuscation. This is introduced in *História*'s first discussion of symbolic and hermeneutic codes, their relationship to ideology, and their transformation over time and aesthetic fashion, when Raimundo takes issue with the historian's use of the cliché 'a noite dos tempos' [the night of ages] (*Historia*: 13). Significantly, while Raimundo considers the phrase inappropriate when discussing the history of writing (and of editing), he is unconcerned that it sounds hackneyed. Indeed, Raimundo claims that 'tudo pode aparecer como novidade, a questão está só em saber manejar adequadamente as palavras que estejam antes e depois' [anything can seem innovative, it's simply a question of knowing how to manipulate sufficiently the words that come before and afterwards] (ibid.). It is tempting to read this statement both as a justification of Saramago's recycling, in *Objecto Quase* and *Levantado*, of such metaphors as night, dawn, and other stock images used to encrypt the message of resistance in dictatorship-era writing, but also, and equally, as a signal to *História*'s reader that a further reworking of the same symbolic code will feature in this novel.[19] Maria Alzira Seixo (1999: 75) has noted the novel's association of light with the quest for truth, and of darkness with the prevalence of distortion. While not inaccurate, Seixo's characterization underplays the changes that the novel rings on the trope of contrasted darkness and light, night and dawn. Such changes serve both to superimpose, and unsettle, the trope's conventional connotations of clarity versus obscurity, truth versus falsehood, and good versus evil, plus, indeed, its associations with the supposed oppositions of Christian versus Muslim, Portuguese versus 'Moor', and self versus Other in general. As will be explored below, this reworked symbology also links the revelation of truth and falsehood, and of knowledge and ignorance, with a quest for love, personal growth, and interpersonal understanding. Yet the novel's nuanced manipulation of symbols consistently suggests that, in the pursuit of psychological or historical insight, 'clarification' equals not absolute truth, but rather the illumination of complexity and of the unknowable.

This 'illumination of complexity' is first intimated when Raimundo supplements his reading of historical tomes with his own scrutiny of Lisbon's medieval quarter. The day on which his objections to the history book's account lead him to adulterate the proof copy begins with his opening his bedroom window onto the city to find that

> uma neblina fria tapa o horizonte, aproxima-o quase ao alcance da mão, a cidade visível está reduzida a este lado, [...] o nevoeiro lhe deu na cara, denso, cerradíssimo, se no lugar das torres da Sé ainda estivesse a almádena da mesquita maior, decerto não a poderia ver. (*História*: 32; 36)

> [a cold mist is obscuring the horizon, and comes in so close that you could almost touch it, the visible city is restricted to this side of the river [...] the fog hit him in the face, dense, opaque, if the minaret of the main mosque were still standing in place of the cathedral towers, for certain he would not be able to see it.]

Raimundo's scepticism about the history book's reiteration of the dominant narrative, and his recourse to other sources of evidence and explanation, have dispelled the 'night' of Salazarist obscurantism. Daylight, however, brings not clarity, but instead an opaque whiteness, which evokes the historical investigator's uncertainty and ignorance, and recalls Raimundo's earlier pondering of Seneca's warning, in his essay 'De tranquilitate animi' [On Peace of Mind], that 'onerat discentem turba, non instruit' [a great collection [of books] confuses, rather than instructs, the scholar] (*História*: 28). For a reader familiar with Portuguese culture and history, of course, this blinding white fog will also recall an aspect of the messianic cult of King D. Sebastião (d.1578), who, according to a persistently influential myth, was destined to return one foggy morning, so as to inspire a Portuguese national revival founded on the Catholic, evangelist, and imperialist values for which he sacrificed his life (and those of thousands of his subjects) at the catastrophic battle of Ksar El-Kebir (in Portuguese, Alcácer Quibir).[20] This metaphor suggests that, even after the 'dawn' of democracy, epistemic uncertainty, and expectations born of either arcane knowledge or hearsay, continue to cloud the vision. As in Fernando Pessoa's well-known gloss on the Sebastianist myth in the concluding poem of his *Mensagem*, the 'nevoeiro' may portend a new golden age, but, equally, it may simply summarize the perception that '[t]udo é incerto e derradeiro. Tudo é disperso, nada é inteiro' [all is uncertain and waning | All is scattered, nothing is whole] (2004: 91).

Later, after Raimundo sabotages the history book, the lesson that 'clarification' and 'democracy' do not equal explanations and solutions, but merely illuminate the complexity of historical causation, discourse, and social relations is concluded, when Raimundo returns to his window at dusk so as to 'ver como está o céu' [take a look at the sky] (*História*: 52). With the earlier mist having cleared, what he beholds are not the stars of an 'abóbada celeste' [celestial vault] such as that which Bartolomeu de Gusmão contemplates in *Memorial* (*História*: 171), but the vast, manmade cosmos — or rather, 'chaosmos' — of the city's myriad lights:

> [o] nevoeiro desaparecera, não se acredita que tantas cintilações tivessem estado ocultas nele, as luzes pela encosta abaixo, as outras do outro lado, amarelas e brancas, projectadas sobre a água como trémulos lumes. (*História*: 52)

> [the fog had disappeared, one would not believe that so many sparkling lights could have been hidden within it, the lights running down the hill below, those others on the far side of the river, yellow and white, reflected over the water like tremulous flames.]

This message is fleshed out on the following day, when Raimundo takes advantage of clear skies and good weather (*História*: 62) to trace the material evidence by walking around the boundaries of the medieval city (*História*: 68–75). Later, as night falls, the fog returns (*História*: 75), and later that night his dreams of the city as 'uma muralha sem nada dentro' [a curtain wall with nothing inside] (*História*: 75) remind of his continuing lack of insight into either the 'Moorish' city that once lay within the walls he has studied, or the experiences of its (Muslim, Christian, and Jewish) inhabitants.

Even before the discussion of perception and error is conveyed through the dyad of mist and clarity, the trope of vision — or lack thereof — is introduced more literally in the imagined figure of the blind twelfth-century muezzin. Later, Raimundo will make the muezzin into a crucial character in his alternative history, or, in White's terms, the key to its inaugural and terminal motifs, as the account opens with the muezzin's calling the azan for *fajr* (dawn) prayers, and closes with his slaughter as the fallen city is invaded and plundered. The muezzin, prone to the objectifying gaze conjured by the history's narrative, recalls *Ricardo Reis*'s association of blindness with the posthumous inability to assert interpretations either of a written text, or indeed of a world comprehended textually. Yet a further layer of meaning, implying such narrative history's potential as an accessory to warfare and violence, is added when Raimundo's reverie in the *Leitaria a Graciosa* suggests that this muezzin lost his sight when his eyes were gouged out — 'vazados' — by the soon-to-be victorious Christian army (*História*: 62).[21]

Later, on the evening of the day when Raimundo's sabotage is discovered by his employers, images of luminosity and shadow serve to spotlight the problems of his reception of data about the past only as mediated by textual accounts and simulacra. As the vestigial 'luz suave, [...] afago luminoso' [soft light [...] luminous caresses] of the day fade, Raimundo sits in an unlit room watching TV with the sound turned down, surrounded by 'imagens luminosas que se movem, não apenas no ecrã mas também sobre os móveis, as paredes e sobre o [seu] rosto' [luminous images playing not only upon the TV screen, but also on the furniture, on the walls, and on his face] (*História*: 92). Configuring Raimundo's living room as a mock-up of Plato's cave, the novel emphasizes that Raimundo's quest for the 'truth' has done little more than throw the history book's artifice into relief, defining the outlines of its images and reminding us of their immateriality. It is tempting to relate this episode to Saramago's later *A Caverna* (2000), which recalls the original allegory so as to diagnose a contemporary society's enslavement to the 'spectacle' — or even, to turn to Baudrillard's concept, the simulacra — of late consumer capitalism.[22] *A Caverna* depicts a late capitalist dystopia that confines its working population to a retail panopticon. While the employees endure constant surveillance, the 'spectacle' of marketing not only ensures the obfuscation by commodity fetishism of the material conditions of production, but also confines the act of seeing to the stimulation of consumer desire. The discovery of a 'real life' Platonic cave under the gigantic and sinister *Centro* (shopping mall) is at first hushed up, then treated as one more marketing opportunity, with the cave thrown open to a paying public and touted as the *Centro*'s 'unique selling point'. The packaging of Plato's cave as 'spectacle' represents a disregard for observation, insight, and critical reflection, as well as a faith in a consumerist and neo-liberal late capitalism as the 'end of history', which reduces the postmodernist critique of empiricism and teleology to an ahistorical carnival of history and asserts the impossibility of future socio-economic progress or reform. Raimundo's contrasting acknowledgment of Plato's cave as allegory of the contingency of human experience and knowledge assumes still greater significance, however, when one considers how the impenetrable white *nevoeiro* that he confronted earlier creates for him a temporary experience of the white blindness that becomes so terrifyingly absolute in *Ensaio sobre a Cegueira*. This articulates the idea that the struggle to observe (*reparar*), rather than simply see (*ver*), will inevitably founder unless one can acknowledge — and somehow come to terms with — the imperfect conditions and potentialities of our vision, both in the context of historical enquiry and — as will be explored below — in that of individual and collective self–Other relations in the present day.

In the context of this comprehension of truth as 'unconcealedness', and of recurrent images of light or whiteness that blinds, or that exposes unknowing, it is well worth considering how *aletheia*, as a concept in modern philosophy, was first developed by Martin Heidegger through a critical reading of Plato's allegory of the cave.[23] By relating Raimundo's experiences of knowledge as revelation, but also as the recognition of unknowability, *História* skates over, without actually pronouncing upon, the debate, protagonized in particular by Marcuse and Althusser, regarding how Heideggerian phenomenology might or might not be reconciled with a materialist and (post-)Marxist analytical framework.[24] The tension between Raimundo and Maria Sara's recuperation of neglected traces of the materiality of past times, and their wariness of their own distorted perceptions of that past materiality, is fundamental to *História*'s proposals regarding the place of both literature, and popular understanding of history, in a reformed socialist politics. The parallels between Heidegger's reading of Plato's cave, and Raimundo's transformed understanding of perception, of truth, and of knowledge, attest to Saramago's sensitivity to the impossibility of definitively investigating, or closing, the gap between the material reality that he insists is 'out there', and the human perception of that reality as phenomena. As Maria Sara and Raimundo memorably conclude, near the novel's end,

> não há saída, vivemos num quarto fechado e pintamos o mundo e o universo nas paredes dele, Lembra-te de que já foram homens à lua, O seu quartinho fechado foi com eles (*História*: 300)
>
> [there's no way out, we live in a locked room and we paint the world and the universe on its walls, Remember that men have already travelled to the moon, Their locked room went with them]

The affirmation of truth as *aletheia*, rather than as correspondence, constitutes perhaps Saramago's most absolute interrogation of empiricism, and of any Marxist critical practice that maintains an unswerving faith in that empiricism. Since we cannot see 'through the eyes of the dead', and since, as *Jangada* claims, 'cada um de nós vê o mundo com os olhos que tem, e os olhos vêem o que querem' [each of us sees the world with the eyes that he or she possesses, and the eyes see what they want to see] (*Jangada*: 218), a closer approximation to past events as *aletheia* cannot be achieved without the dialectical counterposition of two or more perspectives, or, indeed, where possible, of two distinct or even conflicting epistemes. With this intimation, *História* harks back to *Levantado* and its depiction of the grass-roots elaboration of a dialectic of different subaltern perspectives, guided (but not policed) by the Party cadre as 'organic intellectual'. Yet *História* complicates *Levantado*'s vision. By expanding — as will be explored below — on *Ricardo Reis*'s exploration of the individual as 'o lugar onde se pense e sente', and of the human capacity for renewal and for 'becoming Other', *História* affirms the human potential to recognize, and negotiate critically between, different perspectives and perceptions. Less optimistically, it also suggests the enormity of the elementary task of securing recognition of the many and varied perspectives excluded from the hegemonic historical narratives, and from the hegemonic political discourse of the present.

While more pessimistic about the capacity of even a 'perpetual' dialectic of analysis to forge a substantially inclusive hegemony in history or politics, *História* hereupon presents Raimundo's alternative history as a vindication of counter-factual engagements with the past, at least as a means of contesting the retrograde identities, enmities, and agendas predicated on a monolithic account of that past. The case for counter-factual enfabulation is made after Raimundo has accepted Maria Sara's challenge to write an alternative history, and is consulting medieval accounts of Dom Afonso Henriques's negotiations with the Crusaders, in search of 'a causa indiscutível de terem-se ido embora os cruzados depois do seu rotundo Não' [the indisputable reason why the Crusaders would have left after their flat refusal] (*História*: 134). Venturing out to the Castelo de São Jorge in a vain search for 'uma impressão de tangibilidade visual' [a sense of visual tangibility] (ibid.) that would afford him insight into his topic, Raimundo is perched precariously on the highest ramparts when he experiences an undignified, but life-changing, epiphany:

> [n]um momento, o revisor experimenta uma sensação forte de ridículo, tem a consciência da sua postura cénica, melhor dizendo, cinematográfica, a gabardina é manto medieval, os cabelos soltos plumas, e o vento não é vento, mas sim corrente de ar produzida por uma máquina. E é nesse preciso instante, quando de uma certa maneira se tornou infenso e inocente pela ironia contra si próprio dirigida, que no seu espírito surgiu, finalmente claro e também ele irónico, o motivo tão procurado, a razão do Não, a justificação última e irrefutável do seu atentado contra as históricas verdades. (*História*: 135)

> [In an instant, the proof-reader experiences a strong sense of the ridiculous, he becomes aware of his theatrical, or rather, cinematic stance, his raincoat is a medieval cloak, his hair feathers, and the wind is not wind, but rather a jet of air produced by a wind machine. And it was at that precise moment, when he became somehow impervious to and innocent of the self-inflicted irony of the situation, that there appeared in his mind, crystal-clear and equally ironic, the long-sought motive, the reason for that Not, the ultimate and irrefutable justification for his assault on historical truths.]

'Visual tangibility' eludes Raimundo, but he achieves a different 'espécie de sinestesia involuntária'; a double vision of the castle at two moments in time, revealing the ridiculous fallacy of his comprehension of its past-time being. In this vision of his own stance as ridiculous, Raimundo turns upon himself the same destabilizing irony or mockery that he directed against the original history by inserting the 'não'. In picturing himself as a mocked-up Crusader or Arab defender, Raimundo recognizes that attempts to recreate their viewpoints are bogus. Meanwhile, the narrator's (or 'implied author''s) presentation of him, in his raincoat, and surveying the modern city from the rebuilt castle ramparts, could easily be read as a similarly comic parody of the 'narrative account to camera' format of televisual popular history, as pioneered in Portugal by the avuncular academician and apologist for Salazarism, José Hermano Saraiva.[25]

The imagined presence of the wind-machine and camera crew advertises Raimundo's musing on how to make self-evident the sutures of such slick and enthralling accounts of the past. One means of achieving this (as Maria Sara seems initially to understand better than does Raimundo) is an alternative history that uses self-evident falsehood to demonstrate the seduction of emplotment, and that attaches itself to the hegemonic account of the past in a dialectical relationship, exposing that hegemonic account as not an infallible *Livro de Conselhos*, but rather as an ideologically grounded thesis on the 'meaning' of past events.[26] Raimundo's alternative history will be written, then, not to replace the original, but to be read alongside it. It will not restore lost perspectives such as that of the muezzin, but, instead, advertise both their absence, and the implications of this for our understanding of our origins. His 'rebellion against historical truths' will oppose traditional delineations both of national identity or *portugalidade*, and of hierarchies of class, gender, and ethnicity, by imagining an alternative scenario that permits conjecture about how lower class and marginalized figures might achieve progressive agency and self-determination.

This paradox, of the need to understand the historical Other whose viewpoint has been lost or suppressed, and the impossibility of achieving this, is the starting point for what is perhaps *História*'s most significant innovation in the political agenda suggested by Saramago's preceding fiction. *História* foregrounds Saramago's insistence on the reform of self–Other relations at both collective and individual levels, and his observation of the potential contribution of reformed historical consciousness to this project. As Raimundo embarks on the *fingimento* of his history, he will reconceive both of himself, and of self–Other relations, in a manner that has far-reaching political implications.[27] This liberating subjective change will rely not only on his acceptance into his world-view and his affections of the Other that is Maria Sara, but also on his use of historiographical 'fingimento', and of the protagonist around whom he organizes this, to explore an 'other self', or revised individual and collective identity.

III — Being Differently: Ucronian Rewriting and/of the Self

From the outset, Raimundo's rebellion against *História Pátria* is commensurate with a burgeoning experience of himself as mutable. Raimundo's subjective multiplicity and mutability is first commented on — significantly, in terminology that Fernando Pessoa coined — in the novel's second chapter, when he imagines the muezzin calling the besieged city to prayer. As the narrative observes, Raimundo

> tem este notável talento de *desdobrar-se*, desenha um deleatur ou introduz uma vírgula indiscutível, e ao mesmo tempo, aceite-se o neologismo, *heteronimiza-se* (*História*: 22, my italics)
>
> [possesses this remarkable talent for doubling up, he inscribes a deleatur or inserts an indisputable comma, and at the same time, if the neologism may be permitted, he heteronymizes himself]

Yet until this juncture, both his imagination, and his capacity to assume distinct attitudes and perspectives, have been confined to 'pensamentos vagos' [idle thoughts] (ibid.). While the 'polifónicos edifícios verbais' [polyphonic verbal constructions] that Raimundo orchestrates may '[tornar] o seu pequeno escritório num espaço multiplicado por si mesmo' [turn his little study into a space multiplied by itself] (ibid.), neither those constructions nor his imagined Others venture beyond the study's walls. His *desdobramento* has been pure 'ponderação' [musing] (*História*: 59); a fantasy of alternative agency exemplified also in the 'fingimento' [make-believe] (another of Pessoa's key terms) of imagining himself as a medieval 'emissório' or messenger (ibid.).

His rebellion against the original history instigates a new attitude towards this 'ponderação', intimated when he compares himself to Fernando Pessoa, languorously gazing through his window onto the world outside:

> O nevoeiro desaparecera, [...] Raimundo Silva pensou, pessoanamente, Se eu fumasse, acenderia agora um cigarro, a olhar o rio, pensando como tudo é vago e vário (*História*: 52)[28]
>
> [the fog had disappeared, [...] Raimundo Silva thought, in Pessoan fashion, If I smoked, I would light up a cigarette now, contemplating the river, thinking about how everything is vague and variable]

Up to this point, not only does Raimundo not smoke, he has also maintained a strict and ascetic routine of living habits, expectations, and professional and personal relations.[29] His act of sabotage will be the first time that *desdobramento* changes from a sterile fantasy into agency that — with Maria Sara's inspiration and encouragement — will transform his existence.

Desdobramento first manifests itself in the context of the sabotage when Raimundo, biro poised to inscribe the fateful 'não', compares himself to Robert Louis Stevenson's (1886) Dr Jekyll morphing into Mr Hyde (*História*: 49). It is worth noting that Raimundo conceives of his psychic splitting in simple terms of an everyday 'good' self, and a newly irrupting 'bad' self, both here and also later, when his employers summon him to a disciplinary meeting. In that meeting, Raimundo's first attempt at the explanation that Maria Sara demands relies on the same image of himself: 'deve ter-se travado dentro de mim uma luta entre o lado bom, se o tenho realmente, e o lado mau, que esse temo-lo todos, entre um Dr. Jekill [*sic*] e um Mr. Hyde' [a battle must have broken out inside me between my good side, if indeed I have one, and my bad side, since we all have one of those, between a Doctor Jekyll and a Mr Hyde] (*História*: 88). His distrust or fear of subjective polyvalency or multiplicity is also comically intimated by his perception of Maria Sara's transformation from a 'frágil mulher' [delicate woman] into a 'leão [...] rugindo' [roaring lion] when she asks him to explain why he committed 'um abuso tão grave' [such serious misconduct] (*História*: 87). However, in his efforts to save face, Raimundo then offers Maria Sara a facetious analogy between this internal battle and Pessoa's psychic multiplication: 'às vezes pergunto-me que erros teria cometido Fernando Pessoa, de revisão e outros, com aquela confusão de heterónimos, uma briga dos diabos, suponho' [I sometimes ask myself what mistakes Fernando Pessoa might have made, in proof-reading and other pursuits, what with that riot of heteronyms, one hell of a ding-dong, I suppose] (*História*: 88). Her question in response — 'O senhor, além de Jekill e Hyde, é mais alguma coisa' [In addition to Jekyll and Hyde, are you anything else] (ibid.) — is arguably less facetious, but also suggestive of a deeper psychological insight. The proofreader now working under her direction claims, 'até agora' [up until now], to have 'conseguido ser Raimundo Silva' [managed to be Raimundo Silva] (ibid.). Following this, her recommendation — 'veja se consegue aguentar-se como tal, no interesse desta editora e da harmonia das nossas futuras relações' [see if you can put up with staying that way, in the interests of this publishing house and of the harmony of our future relationship] (*História*: 88) — subtly alludes to the moulding and constraint of the psyche, and of almost any personal interaction, by such socio-economic imperatives as holding down a job, and deferring to authorities. The scene points towards a careful negotiation between Marxist and post-psychoanalytic notions of subjectivity. If classical Marxism argues that subjectivity is rooted in socio-economic location, and is subsumable (to a greater or lesser degree) into a class identity, then *História*, while not contradicting a materialist world-view that stresses the importance of class configurations, embraces the idea of subjectivity as a false unity. It thereupon suggests that 'identity' and 'character' are not finite, fixed entities, but rather the effects of a more-or-less habitual un-self-conscious performance, scripted and prompted by ideology and memory from a material basis, and partly improvised in collaboration with others.[30]

It is Maria Sara who will perceive Raimundo's rebellion against both narrative history and his employers' commercial agenda as a reinterpretation, rather than a dereliction, of professional duties, and who will value his psychic 'something else', encouraging him to explore it through less destructive activities. From the very first, her intervention develops the theme of alterity in ways that recall *Ricardo Reis*. Raimundo, like Ricardo Reis, depends on the prompting of a (female) Other so as to recognize and respond to the 'other self' irrupting within him. Moreover, he will experience *becoming* something, or someone, 'além de Jekill e Hyde' as a process of difficult, but ultimately rewarding, personal renewal or rebirth. This process gets underway at the tête-à-tête to which Maria Sara calls him (*História*: 104–10), and in which, presenting him with a copy of 'his' sabotaged history book, she challenges him to write his own counter-factual account of the siege. Significantly, in defence of her suggestion, and of her wish to offer free rein to the 'espécie [...] de pensamento oblíquo bastante singular' [a quite distinct type [...] of lateral thinking] (*História*: 109) demonstrated in the act of sabotage, Maria Sara refers to the publishing house's archived collection of peer-reviews that Raimundo wrote. Raimundo, with what may or may not be conscious irony, dismisses his authorship of these texts as mere 'história antiga' [ancient history] (ibid.). To Maria Sara, however, the peer reviews confirm that, when inserting the 'não' in the history book, Raimundo was not 'mentalmente perturbado' [mentally disturbed] (*História*: 110), but was instead getting in touch with a long dormant 'alguém dentro de si' [someone inside him]; an author or critic that Maria Sara now proposes be reborn.

Maria Sara's proposal that Raimundo re-write the history in full precipitates a process of subjective transformation that, in an 'existência tão pouco dada a aventuras' [existence so averse to adventure] (*História*: 113) assumes a revolutionary magnitude or 'figura de revolução' (ibid.), an effect far greater than the momentary sense of estrangement that accompanied Raimundo's sabotage of the history book, and which 'não lhe [causou] efeito que de longe se parecesse' [caused him no effect that resembled this one even distantly] (ibid.). This change is heralded symbolically by Raimundo's mock 'baptism' or ritual cleansing, as he departs under heavy rain that soaks him to the skin (*História*: 112), and arrives home to experience

> uma curiosa impressão de estranheza, como se, experiência só imaginária, tivesse acabado de chegar de uma larga e demorada viagem por terras distantes e outras civilizações [...] a casa está como se fosse pertença doutra pessoa, e ele um estranho, até o cheiro é outro, e os móveis estão como deslocados ou deformados por uma perspectiva regida por leis diferentes. (*História*: 113)

> [a curious impression of estrangement, as if, and this is only an imaginary experience, he had just arrived at the end of a long and slow journey through distant lands and unfamiliar civilizations [...] the house appears as if it belonged to someone else, and he a stranger to it, even the smell is different, and the furniture seems to have been rearranged or skewed by a perspective governed by different laws.]

Heading out for lunch on the following day, Raimundo encounters his raincoat still sodden and feeling like 'a pele dum animal morto' [the pelt of a dead animal] (*História*: 131). This simile, while conveying the discomfort Raimundo feels on having to don the coat before braving further rain, also reiterates the connection that Orlando Grossegesse has noted, in *Manual de Pintura e Caligrafia* and others of Saramago's texts, of images of skin-shedding both to the act of writing, and to a kind of regeneration or rebirth of consciousness; a relationship that configures literary expression as a vehicle for 'an active ethics of self-liberation' (2006: 57–60).[31] As H, the protagonist of *Manual*, asserts,

> tal como a cobra, largamos a pele quando não cabemos, ou então vêm a faltar-nos as forças e atrofiamo-nos dentro dela, e isto só acontece aos humanos (*Manual*: 274)

> [just like a snake, we discard our skin when we no longer fit within it, or otherwise we end up losing our strength and waste away inside it, something that happens only to humans]

The raincoat–skin simile also signals *História*'s expansion of the concept of truth as *aletheia* into the realm of psychology. Although the full extent and complexity of consciousness can never be mapped, when Raimundo is prompted to apply his 'pensamento oblíquo' to his own self and his own existence, he perceives them anew, divested of the carapace of conventional (if not necessarily wholly 'false') consciousness.

The idea that a hitherto unsuspected truth of Raimundo's psychology is being uncovered is, moreover, first posited using the afore-mentioned association of the tropes of whiteness, light, vision, and clarification with the stripping away, or penetration, of deceptive façades, and the consequent disclosure of ungraspably complex truths. Earlier on the morning following his meeting with Maria Sara, Raimundo pours away the black hair dye with which for years he has (poorly) disguised his greying locks (*História*: 121). Thus he resolves a quandary that he has pondered since the morning when he issued his challenge to popular history's superficial falsifications, by handing the adulterated proofs to the company's typesetter, Costa. On that morning, Costa's early call to collect the proofs catches Raimundo still in bed and with 'um ar desamparado' [an abandoned look] (*História*: 54). Raimundo, greeting Costa in his 'roupão de falso escocês, a barba crescida, o cabelo grotescamente pintado a contrastar, triste, com as brancas da cara' [fake tartan dressing-gown, unshaven, his grotesquely tinted hair contrasting sadly with the white of his beard] (ibid.), is forced to acknowledge his own unconvincing falsification of history (or at least, of his personal, biological history). Initially too ashamed of his white hairs even to confront them in the mirror (*História*: 56), only after his meeting with Maria Sara and the experience of 'estranheza' does Raimundo let his dyed hair grow out, accepting that, even in personal matters, the incomplete deception of his raven locks and white roots is no worse than the consistently maintained yet obvious one of uniformly dyed hair, 'que lembra irresistivelmente uma peruca desbotada e roída de traças, esquecida e outra vez achada num sótão' [that irresistibly recalls a faded and moth-eaten wig, long forgotten and newly discovered in an attic] (*História*: 103). As Raimundo gains the strength of purpose to exhibit the character complexities that have remained long hidden under a cloak of respectability and servility, he also summons the courage to brave public ridicule of his half-black, half-white locks (*História*: 241).[32]

The reverie instigated by the discarded raincoat, whose clammy, deathly touch makes him shiver (*História*: 131), also leads Raimundo to recollections of Maria Sara wearing her own raincoat, and to an explicit connection of light and whiteness, of disclosure, and of the quest for truth with the two characters' budding relationship. His speculation on Maria Sara's blouse — 'branco-manhã' [morning white, or dawn white] (ibid.) in hue beneath her raincoat — recalls the time of day at which Raimundo both gave his adulterated proofs to Costa, and first pondered the idea that clarification is but the revelation of complexity and uncertainty. This conjunction of images suggests Raimundo's inability to dispel his curiosity regarding the as-yet undisclosed truth about his line-manager, as well as, obviously, his irrepressible erotic attraction to her. Examining this passage in the context of the novel's recurrent trope of vision, it is tempting to relate it to *Memorial*'s image of a clairvoyant woman 'looking into' her lover (or, in point of fact, promising never to do so) (*Memorial*: 56–57). Crucially, however, while Raimundo fantasizes about what Maria Sara's waterproof carapace may hide, he only succeeds in 'uncovering' the hidden truth about her after he has shed his own constraining 'pele'. Giving free rein to his 'pensamento oblíquo' enables Raimundo to 'reparar' both outwardly, onto his city's history, and inwardly, onto his own psyche. This dynamic of looking is evoked by the recurrent trope of the windows and balconies from which Raimundo is depicted gazing. As Seixo first observed (1991: 78–80), windows and Raimundo's balcony symbolize not only a subjective insight into external phenomena, but, equally, both the openness and vulnerability of the individual to outside intervention, as first when Raimundo compares the raindrops on the balcony roof above him to 'um rumor ainda longínquo de cavalgada' [a still distant murmur of cavalry [approaching]] (*História*: 116). Yet this journey of self-discovery and renewal is equally dependent on allowing Maria Sara to 'look into' him.

Thus, as is not quite spelled out by the deceased Pessoa in *Ricardo Reis*, the recognition of 'alguém dentro de nós' ultimately depends on — but also enables — approximation to, and empathy with, the Other.[33] The benefits of this empathy are experienced not simply in the vanquishing of loneliness and fear, but also in more perceptive and egalitarian forms of love. Maria Sara and Raimundo's agreement to progress from the search for 'external' truths to the discovery and expression of who they are, and of who they could become, leads to the blossoming of a more candid, trusting, romance. This is intimated both when Raimundo initiates an exchange of not red, but white roses (*História*: 245), and when he takes to writing the alternative history not in his windowless study, but 'às claras' in his bedroom, with its balcony overlooking the city (*História*: 181) and, one surmises, with the city glancing in on him. Here too, he and Maria Sara will finally consummate their love, not in a prudish nocturnal gloom, but in the intense glow of late afternoon sunlight (*História*: 295).

Raimundo's recognition of communion with the Other as both an ethical and an existential imperative thus makes him the antithesis of *Ricardo Reis*'s Ricardo Reis, who resigns himself to 'uselessness' and death. Moreover, though, he attempts this communion, and completes his joyous, enlightening, 'rebirth', through a reinterpretation of Pessoa's heteronymous creativity as a literary practice with potential political significance. In Raimundo's case at least, however, the act of 'heteronymizing' himself — pursuing the disclosure of another self through an imaginative act of writing — is shown to be fundamental to this progression towards existential satisfaction, communion, and what *Ricardo Reis*'s Pessoa posits as 'usefulness'. The transformative impact of Raimundo's alternative history on his life and happiness corresponds closely to his delineation of the life and loves of its protagonist, Mogueime. The history becomes a kind of textual laboratory or rehearsal room for experiments in new identity and behaviour. While Raimundo's spurious history creates a dialectic between itself and the original history, the alternation of *História*'s narrative thread between the two diegeses of its doubled plot-arc enables a similar dialectic between, on one hand, Raimundo's exploration of Mogueime's character and involvement with twelfth-century society and events, and, on the other, both Raimundo's and the narrative voice's reflections on his socio-economic circumstances and his relationship with Maria Sara. By re-writing history around Mogueime and his pursuit of the Galician concubine Ouroana, Raimundo can rehearse, in fiction, his real-life swerve from introverted sobriety to extrovert impetuousness, and his consequent romantic approximation to Maria Sara.

This process, with its implications for a holistic reading of Saramago's work, becomes all the more intriguing when one notices how Raimundo's relationship to Mogueime is not presented as that of a demiurgic author to that of his fictitious character. Mogueime's beginnings instead recall Pessoa's accounts of the 'emergence' of his heteronyms as autonomous other identities, rather than as fabricated literary devices. As the novel presents it, Raimundo does not invent his protagonist. Rather, in a metanarrative intervention that seems to force Raimundo's wary hand, the narrator demands the reader's complicity in the act of selecting a protagonist from among the figures that Raimundo encounters in the earliest accounts of the siege — 'busquemos-lhe alguém que [...] possa tomar o seu lugar no relato naturalmente' [let us find him someone who [...] can take his place naturally [unselfconsciously] in the story] (*História*: 185) — and selects the 'mancebo alto, chamado Moigema' noted by seventeenth-century chronicler António de Brandão as playing a pivotal role in the Santarém siege (Brandão 1945: 105). Even before Raimundo meekly accepts this choice — '[a]ceitou portanto [...] a Mogueime para sua personagem' [and so [he] accepted Mogueime as his character] (*História*: 190) — Mogueime's appearance in the text, to relate his participation in the earlier siege of Santarém (*História*: 186–89), reinforces the idea of him as an independent entity, who appears and speaks 'within' Raimundo, rather as Pessoa famously claimed that Alberto Caeiro did to him.[34] Having 'listened' to Mogueime's account of himself, Raimundo 'accepts' him as the new history's protagonist on the basis of the 'desenvoltura, se não mesmo o brilho' [nonchalance, if not indeed the élan] of his storytelling, and the strong humanitarian instinct that prompts him to question certain conventions of twelfth-century society and warfare: '[n]o moço Mogueime, atraiu-o [...] mais do que bondades literárias, aquele seu humanitário impulso' [in the young lad Mogueime, what attracted him [...] more than literary prowess was that humanitarian impulse of his] (*História*: 190). Through his relationship with his protagonist, Raimundo comes to terms with the convoluted nature of subjectivity, and with its implications for the pursuit of both historical truth, and communion with the Other. Raimundo is initially wary of Mogueime's weakness for embellishing the facts, but acknowledges how it compares with his own vice of 'fingimento', as, for example, in dyeing his hair (*História*: 194). As the narrator notes, these are but trivial instances of how 'a sinceridade, espontaneidade, a simplicidade, essas boníssimas e *luminosas* qualidades de carácter' [sincerity, spontaneity, simplicity, those most excellent and luminous character traits] (ibid., my italics) are inevitably compromised by humans' 'vaidade' [vanity] and 'vontade de parecer bem, tanto no físico quanto no moral' [desire to create a good impression, in physical terms as much as moral ones] (ibid.). However, while doubtful of humanity's capacity to 'viver a verdade' [live the truth] (ibid.), Raimundo, unlike Pessoa and co., will not desist from pursuing communion with another person who is likewise prone to 'fingimento': this is confirmed when Maria Sara confesses to having taken up colouring her hair in order to attract him (*História*: 260). Instead, Raimundo explores the interaction with Maria Sara that he both craves and fears through the romantic sub-plot uniting Mogueime with Ouroana.

Ouroana's 'appearance' to Raimundo Silva comes in the wake of a profound corporeal disturbance brought on by thinking about Maria Sara and her body. In a curious echo of the scene in *Ricardo Reis* wherein Reis's desire for Lídia prompts his awareness of the 'internal Other' simultaneously with a troublesome corporeal arousal,[35] Raimundo

> começou a sentir o seu próprio corpo, o que nele estava a acontecer, primeiro um movimento de sismo lento, quase imperceptível, depois a palpitação brusca, repetida, urgente. Raimundo Silva assiste, de olhos semicerrados segue o processo como se estivesse recordando mentalmente uma página conhecida (*História*: 225)
>
> [became conscious of his own body, what was going on within him, first, a slow, seismic shift, almost imperceptible, followed by a wrenching, repeated, insistent palpitation. Raimundo Silva looks on, eyes half closed, he follows the whole process as if he were mentally recalling an already familiar page]

This 'sismo' transports Raimundo to the riverbank where Mogueime first encounters his deceased master's paramour, left to fend for herself in the increasingly ill-disciplined Crusaders' camp. In an instructive counterpoint to Raimundo's current dilemma, Mogueime first muses on how the woman is out of his league socially (just as Raimundo still regards Maria Sara as unattainable). Next, quelling a profound physical agitation, he summons the courage to defy convention by introducing himself to her (*História*: 226–28). Raimundo agonizes similarly over whether or not to phone Maria Sara, though in this case she takes the initiative and phones him before he can follow Mogueime's example (*História*: 229). Raimundo's acceptance of Maria Sara's 'presumption' in phoning him shows how the fictional romance between Mogueime and Ouroana helps him not only to come to terms with desire itself, but also — as Atkin explores (2014: 37–38; 125) — to essay a new and non-hegemonic masculinity, compatible with his attraction to an independent 'mulher para resolutas acções' [resolute woman of action] (*História*: 184). The revelation of his suppressed self is simultaneously fitful — causing Raimundo surprise at the 'homem novo' [new man] reflected in the mirror (*História*: 241) — and as gradual as the re-emergence of his natural hair colour, 'talvez porque são vagarosos os progressos da verdade' [perhaps because the advances of truth are laggard] (*História*: 241). However, Raimundo, who formerly shrank from the disconcerting vision of his reflection (*História*: 56), is clearly making his own 'progresso vagaroso' in following Mogueime's example as 'alguma coisa diferente do comum' [something out of the ordinary] and disposed to 'a averiguação oblíqua dos seus motivos, [à] interrogação ingénua sobre a influência que cada um de nós tem em actos alheios sem o sabermos nós' [the oblique evaluation of his own motives, to the naïve interrogation of the influence that each one of us, without our being aware of it, exerts over the acts of others] (*História*: 227). The twin challenges of Maria Sara's overtures, and of his rewriting of history repeatedly threaten to overawe Raimundo. Yet he is reassured and emboldened by comparing his situation with that of Mogueime, as when he envisages Mogueime dreaming of Ouroana as he prepares for the assault on the city: '[p]ergunta-se agora Raimundo Silva que semelhanças há entre este imaginado quadro e a sua relação com Maria Sara' [now Raimundo Silva asks himself what resemblance there is between this imagined picture and his relationship with

Maria Sara] (*História*: 255). Only after having used Mogueime as a fictional proxy for examining his new circumstances does Raimundo summon the confidence to attempt the frank account of himself that Maria Sara's 'besieging' questions had solicited earlier (*História*: 259).

IV — *História*, Sex, Politics: The Utility of the Ucronian

Desdobramento rehearsed in fiction thus enables Raimundo to respond to Maria Sara's attraction to him as someone who understands that 'a distinção entre não e sim é o resultado duma operação mental que só tem em vista a sobrevivência' [the distinction between no and yes is the result of a mental operation that is concerned only with [personal] survival] (*História*: 299). What remains in question, of course, is whether or not their shared pursuit of fictional history can fulfil Maria Sara's claim that such an 'operação mental' might be 'socialmente útil' [socially useful], depending on 'quem forem os donos do sim e do não' [who are the proprietors of the yes and the no] (ibid.). 'Usefulness' can be claimed for Raimundo's alternative account in several ways. First, of course, it advertises the errors that — according to Bacon's description of *idola specus* and *idola tribus* — are inevitable in a history of conflict written by the victors, by counterposing the 'necessary error' of historicization of that which was not, but which might have been. *História* thereby reveals how the dominant narrative of Lisbon 1147 serves as the predicate for a partial and constraining conception of 1980s Portugal as a conservative society, devoutly Catholic, paternalistic, and hierarchical, and averse to either social or indeed technological innovation. The elaboration of an apocryphal, but not impossible, alternative history is a reminder that other values and characteristics are up for grabs.

It should be noted that, in imagining a concatenation of events that implies different conclusions about present-day identity, values, and political options, *História* stresses Raimundo's determination not to stray from the recorded facts up to the point of the 'não'. He is aware of the need to construct his spurious history on the basis of plausible patterns of causality.[36] From the outset, he recognizes the need to establish 'um motivo forte' (*História*: 127) for the Crusader's rejection of Afonso Henriques's request. Occasionally, he must back-track and revise his account when the longer-term consequences of the 'não' make details of his initial conception of the siege implausible. This occurs, for example, when his calculation that the king's diminished band of besiegers would have had to attack the city from the north makes a nonsense of the account, which he has attributed to the 'mulher gorda' in *A Graciosa*, of carnage at the southern Porta de Ferro (*História*: 220). The task of writing counter-factually yet plausibly — like working out the moves of a game of chess while 'conhecendo de antemão o resultado final' [knowing the final outcome in advance] (*História*: 233) — becomes a tussle between Raimundo's personal preferences and the history, ideology, and established powers that make up his world. While accepting the notion of the siege as an event that propelled a Portuguese nation into existence — and even attributing this understanding of it to Mogueime (*História*: 341) — Raimundo posits the possibility of a fairer, more progressive society emerging under a king who, in command of only a diminished, fractious army, is compelled to innovate and negotiate with his subordinates.

Raimundo's account of the Christians' advance on Lisbon, and of local Muslim reactions, attributes stupidity, greed, and hypocrisy to rulers on both sides. As noted earlier, his reverie in *A Graciosa* homes in on the savagery of Afonso Henriques's attacks on a society that held 'a vantagem em civilização' [the advantage in civilization] (*História*: 64). Murder, infanticide, and rape are considered a Crusader's prerogative (*História*: 187; 195–96), with inhabitants of outlying villages captured, mutilated, and driven south to Lisbon as 'o aviso que manda adiante o rei' [the advance warning sent by the king] (*História*: 61). While local potentates' alliances and conflicts emerge as motivated by economic and political calculations, the hostility between Arab and Portuguese subjects is fuelled by tribal divisions, not ethical or doctrinal ones. When Lisbon residents defect to the Portuguese camp, requesting baptism, they meet with 'o furor, a sanha dementada' [the fury, the deranged loathing] of the soldiers who curse, beat, and mutilate them rather than welcoming them into their faith (*História*: 344).

The manner in which Raimundo's history posits grounds for an alternative definition of 'Portugueseness' is noted by Kaufman, who focuses on how Raimundo's *História* depicts Afonso Henriques's technicians boldly overcoming both a shortage of military manpower, and their society's technological backwardness, by learning from their few remaining French and Norman allies how to build assault towers (*História*: 251), and by constructing their first such tower even faster than their mentors (*História*: 314). Kaufman suggests that with its 'valorização do engenho português que prevalece um pouco "apesar de tudo"' [celebration of a Portuguese ingenuity that prevails somewhat against the odds] (Kaufman 1991a: 178), *História* addresses a national inferiority complex relative to northern Europe, one that has arguably been aggravated by the reluctance of foreign historians, ever since the composition of 'De expugnatione', to grant due credit to the local army's role in the siege.[37] It is safer to say, however, that Raimundo's story of the 'Portuguese' tower echoes *Jangada*'s suggestion that 'os portugueses são de duas espécies diferentes' [the Portuguese are from two different species] (*Jangada*: 98). The tower's builders may indeed be resourceful and dynamic. Nevertheless, as Afonso Henriques warns, a large faction of his 'estado-maior' [estate] remains 'gente conservadora, agarrada ao artesanato' [conservative folk, wedded to homespun ways], who only sigh with self-righteous contempt when the first of the Portuguese army's 'engenhos estrangeiros' [foreign contraptions] is burned by Almoravid Lisbon's defenders (*História*: 316). The story demonstrates that enquiring minds and technological innovation, not an innate national *ethos*, are the motors of development. 'Progressive' change, however, is guaranteed only where a consensual, humanitarian ethics governs the application of such technology.

Further to this, both Raimundo's characterization of Afonso Henriques, and his re-imagining of the death of Mogueime's lord, the *cavaleiro* Henrique, dismantle that pillar of Salazarist inscriptions of *portugalidade* formerly attacked in *Memorial*, namely the notion of a country rich both in miracles and in charismatic leaders favoured by God. The hegemonic account of the Lisbon siege allots causative status to two such miracles: one, the apparition of Christ to Afonso Henriques before the battle of Ourique to assure him of victory over the Almoravids, and the other, the good deeds posthumously attributed to the Cavaleiro Henrique. Earlier, in Raimundo's reverie inspired by the original history (*História*: 17–25), the narrative voice questions the moral logic of Christ's intervention at Ourique: why urge the Christian king on into 'crudelíssima batalha' [battle most cruel], instead of appearing to the Muslims and thus effecting their 'conversão milagrosa' [miraculous conversion] instead (*História*: 20)? Raimundo will return to this question when research for his alternative history leads him to the sixteenth-century *Crónica de D. Afonso Henriques* of Frei António de Brandão, from which the novel quotes three full pages verbatim (*História*: 146–49).[38] Raimundo's collaging of passages from Brandão into his new account of the Crusaders' refusal and of its consequences transforms the characterization of Afonso Henriques, and, by extension, of the nation whose sovereignty he metonymically represents. In Brandão's account, Afonso Henriques himself questions Christ's claim that 'eu sou o fundador e destruidor dos Impérios do mundo, e em ti e tua geração quero fundar para mim um reino' [I am the founder and destroyer of the Empires of the world, and in you and your descendants I wish to found a kingdom for myself] (*História*: 148). Although the King suggests that '[m]elhor seria participarem os infiéis da grandeza desta maravilha, para que, abominando os seus erros, vos conhecessem' [it would be better for the unbelievers to be party to the greatness of this wonder, in order that they should know you and despise their errors] (ibid.), in Brandão's account, he is ultimately reconciled to this divine brutality and vainglory.[39] In *História*, however, where the quoted passage from Brandão breaks off it is followed by Raimundo's account of the King sleeping fitfully in his tent, attended not by divine apparitions, but by the demons of a troubled conscience (*História*: 151).

Prior to this, Raimundo finds the explanation that he sought for the Crusaders' refusal in the same scepticism regarding the Ourique 'miracle'. Imagining Afonso Henriques as an inexperienced diplomat and orator, who fails to endow his entreaty to the Crusaders with sufficient charisma, conviction, and flattery (*História*: 138–40), Raimundo concludes that the King failed to convince them of Christ's message that, after Ourique, 'ficará este reino santificado, amado de mim pela pureza da Fé e excelência da piedade' [this kingdom will be forever sanctified, loved by me for the purity of its faith and for its surpassing piety] (*História*: 148). The Crusaders do not refute Afonso Henriques's claims to have captured Ourique and Santarém by divine favour. They do, however, question his ability to gainsay the divine will that 'bem sabemos, só se manifesta onde e quando quer, não bastando pedir, rogar, suplicar, importunar' [only manifests when and where it wishes, as well we know, pleading, begging, praying, and pestering not being enough] (*História*: 141).

Raimundo's re-casting of the miracles of Cavaleiro Henrique, meanwhile, stresses not the glory of leaders invested with powers divine, but rather the sanctity of egalitarianism. From Brandão's account (1945: 121–22), Raimundo highlights the single miracle that vindicates the equality of all fallen soldiers, namely, Henrique's posthumous apparition to demand that the *escudeiro* [squire] who died alongside him also be buried alongside him, rather than in an unmarked grave pit (*História*: 332–33).[40] All the while, the verisimilitude of Raimundo's revisionist account — which also relates the imperfect outcomes of two further supposed miracles — is disrupted by the constant interjections of Maria Sara, reporting on the increasingly outlandish miracles that she finds attributed to St Anthony of Padua in an eighteenth-century panegyric in Raimundo's book collection (*História*: 332–35).

Well before this, Raimundo's retelling of Cavaleiro Henrique and his *escudeiro*'s deaths sets them on equal footing as individualized heroic subjects. Likewise, of course, Mogueime's and Ouroana's location at the epicentre of his history redresses the foot soldiers' marginalization in the original history's romantic-epic account. Mogueime is an unglamorous, imperfect, but honest and free-thinking *héros moyen* like *Levantado*'s João Mau-Tempo, or *Memorial*'s Baltasar. He displays humility, courage, and moral rectitude even amid the carnage of the siege, deferring respectfully to the will of the women he lusts after, and rejecting the temptation to cause the Cavaleiro Henrique's death so as to gain access to Ouroana (*História*: 314).[41] Yet Mogueime's greatest moment comes when he speaks up for the Portuguese vassals who seek to negotiate with the King for a 'parte justa no saque' [fair division of the spoils of victory] for all those who 'aqui veio dar o seu sangue, que, derramado, é igual na cor ao dos cruzados estrangeiros' [came here to give their blood, which, when it is spilled, is the same in colour as that of foreign Crusaders] (*História*: 342). Mogueime boldly rebuffs the King's complaint that the foot soldiers' insubordination suggests that '[e]ste país, pela amostra, começa mal' [this country, it appears, is making a bad start] (*História*: 341): punning on the word 'justo' (meaning both 'just' and 'straight'), Mogueime counters that the nascent country 'só começará mal se não começar justo [...], não queirais que torto nasça Portugal, [...] senhor' [will only make a bad start if it doesn't start out fair [...] do not wish that Portugal be born crooked, my Lord] (*História*: 342).[42] Raimundo's fiction of Afonso Henriques's increased reliance on his subjects' good will serves as the predicate for a story of feudal 'wage-bargaining', which places social justice on the agenda of the emerging nation, especially as it depicts the King as learning both humility and respect for his subordinates. This new narrative of progressive values and lower-class heroism is, however, undercut by Raimundo's emplotment of the siege, in what White would term a 'satirical' mode: the account ends only semi-conclusively, with a riot of bloodletting in the fallen city, and with the only humanitarian gestures confined to the social and geographical margin, where Mogueime encounters Ouroana.

Ouroana completes the new history's re-imagining of collective identity according to materialist, egalitarian, and pluralist principles. Raimundo's history examines her subaltern position, and the extreme vulnerability to which Cavaleiro Henrique's death reduces her. Yet in her determination to defend herself and to take her own decisions, Ouroana resembles Saramago's most visionary female characters. Like both *Memorial*'s Blimunda, and the Doctor's Wife in *Cegueira*, in the absence of her male lover's protection, Ouroana takes up a weapon to defend herself against would-be rapists (*História*: 318; 324–26). Arguably more remarkable is Ouroana's determination not simply to secure her freedom and choose a lover for herself, but to defy convention further by accepting Mogueime for his humility and courage, instead of the wealth and status that rival suitors offer.

The process by which Raimundo ponders Ouroana and Mogueime's courtship reveals their status as ciphers for the couple that Raimundo would like to form with Maria Sara. Imagining Mogueime falling for such an unconventional and resolute woman enables Raimundo to reconceive of his gender identity as well as his ethnicity, and to confront not only his fears about relationships, but also the sexist attitudes with which he has always lived. Raimundo imagines Mogueime's first encounter with Ouroana immediately after he has been speculating about whether or not he has a rival for Maria Sara's affections (*História*: 224–25). Raimundo notes that Mogueime is the lowliest of several men eyeing up Ouroana (*História*: 224), but also that he has already distinguished himself from his fellow men through his disapproval of the 'forçamento e degolação das mulheres mouras' [rape and beheading of Moorish women] at Santarém (*História*: 227). Thus, Mogueime's and Ouroana's status as the history's 'heroes' defies the prevailing socio-economic hierarchy, and particularly the convention of men's possession and domination of women. However, Raimundo's attitude towards such patriarchal 'rights' changes only gradually. This is evident from the mystery regarding Ouroana's two suitors, who, after threatening to take her by force, turn up stabbed to death a few days later (*História*: 226). Only at a later stage of writing the history does Raimundo decide — 'num relâmpago' [in a flash] (*História*: 318) — that Ouroana took up Cavaleiro Henrique's dagger in self-defence, and it is later still that he re-writes the account of the couple's first encounter, and rules out the idea that Mogueime might have eliminated his rivals, or rescued Ouroana (*História*: 326–27).

When Raimundo shares details of his narrative with Maria Sara, she intuits that its romantic sub-plot affords him a means of experimenting with an alternative identity. Her first question about the incomplete narrative — '[q]uem é esta Ouroana, este Mogueime quem é' [who is this Ouroana, and this Mogueime, who is he] — serves 'para indagar quem eles eram, estes, aqueles, outros quaisquer, em suma, nós' [to inquire as to who they are, these two, those two, and whichever others, that is, in the end, us] (*História*: 263). Later, Raimundo in turn imagines himself asking Ouroana '[c]omo te chamas [...] e ela respondeu, Maria Sara' [what's your name [...] and she replied, Maria Sara] (*História*: 290). By this means, the history remains a shared project: while Raimundo continues to write it, discussions with Maria Sara are essential to the moulding of Ouroana's character and destiny. That destiny, in turn, presages Raimundo's acceptance of Maria Sara as a genuine equal, regardless either of her superior professional status, or of his patriarchal privilege. Yet, even after they have consummated their love, Raimundo's mulling over the possible outcome of Mogueime's first meeting with Ouroana betrays his continuing anxieties regarding gender identity and social status. Raimundo's admission of a fear that Ouroana 'vire as costas a Mogueime quando descobrir que nunca será mulher de um capitão' [will turn her back on Mogueime once she discovers that she will never become a Captain's wife] (*História*: 329–30) prompts his and Maria Sara's most intense discussion of their future together. Rejecting Raimundo's suggestion that he should 'voltar à cadeira e à secretária do revisor, que é o que sou' [return to the chair and desk of a proof-reader, because that's what I am], Maria Sara challenges him to overcome his status anxiety, and to accept that she loves him for what he is ('gosto de ti pelo que és' (*História*: 330)). More importantly, she challenges him to disavow the 'macheza' that, she claims, prevents men from accepting any female lover as an equal:

> [o] mal está em vocês, homens, todos, a macheza, quando não é a profissão é a idade, quando não é a idade é a classe social, quando não é a classe social é o dinheiro (ibid.)
>
> [the problem lies with you, men, all of you, it's machismo, when it's not about careers it's about age, when it's not about age it's about class, when it's not about class it's about money]

Maria Sara's complaint here — which Raimundo tacitly accepts — is the crux of a more thorough and effective engagement than previously achieved in Saramago's fiction with the view of patriarchal privilege and misogyny as more than part of the ideological apparatus of capitalism. The relationship of Raimundo and Maria Sara suggests both how deeply ingrained is Raimundo's anxiety about his status as a man, and how he must both overcome his fear of a female equal, and repudiate a hegemonic, 'macho' identity, in order to transform romance from a state of siege into a love ('amor') that is 'o fim do cerco' [the end of the siege] (ibid.).

From Raimundo's first encounter with Maria Sara, the tropes of besiegement and invasion signal both Maria Sara's status as a self-possessed woman and Raimundo's initial fear and resentment of her usurpation of a 'masculine' role. Yet scenes that present Maria Sara in comic relation to clichéd paradigms of an invasive male lover signal her status as a beneficent invader, and the folly of Raimundo's fears. A key instance of this is when, in a parody of the stock image of the male seducer using his car as phallic symbol and means of entrapment, Maria Sara insists on giving Raimundo a lift home. Raimundo, irked by Maria Sara's presumptuous, forward manner, feels 'que a detestava como se detesta um invasor' [that he hated her as one hates an invader] (*História*: 173). He resists by reasserting his male prerogative in inviting Maria Sara indoors, an invitation she is obliged to decline (ibid.). Nonetheless, as Atkin (2014: 80) argues, this encounter is the catalyst for a step-change in Raimundo's composition of his history. Before long, Maria Sara will have penetrated not only his mind, and his house (*História*: 258), and also got into his bedroom, where it is she who first undresses and who initiates sexual intercourse (*História*: 293). The location of Raimundo's house on the side of the Alfofa Gate of the medieval city walls (*História*: 266) allows Maria Sara's eventual entry to parody both the chivalric narratives in which a male villain (or saviour) penetrates a woman's sanctuary (or prison), and the romantic narratives in which a Romeo-like lover ascends to his Juliet's balcony. The difference of Raimundo's case from this latter model involves not simply his gender, but also the fact that in the end, unlike the circumspect Juliet, Raimundo awaits Maria Sara 'mostrando-se sem disfarce, como quem, estando à espera, não se importa que se saiba e murmure' [undisguised, like one who, waiting, does not care if people know about it and gossip] (*História*: 291). As Atkin (2014) notes, Raimundo's growing willingness to assume a more 'feminine' identity vis-à-vis Maria Sara is also shown over the course of his two visits to the florist's to buy roses. While on the first occasion, he leaves 'um pouco envergonhado por levar uma flor na mão' [somewhat embarrassed about holding a flower in his hand] (*História*: 194), by the second visit (*História*: 241) 'he can bring himself to freely enter into conversation with the assistant, presenting himself as a kind of "new man" unafraid to show his feminine side' (Atkin 2014: 100). As Raimundo reconceives of gender relations, he and Maria Sara find themselves on the 'same side' in the siege. They compare themselves first to Afonso Henriques's troops (*História*: 246), and, later — as they stand on the balcony to contemplate the site of the siege, finally moving towards physical intimacy (*História*: 265) — to the defenders of Almoravid Lisbon (*História*: 267). Mutual respect and trust neutralize images of conquest when Raimundo Silva's 'mão [...] invasora' is met by Maria Sara's (*História*: 294) and, as in the love scenes of earlier novels, reciprocity and equality are emphasized by the dissemination of sexual agency to the various body parts — hands, mouths, tongues, and respiratory systems — of both lovers (ibid.).

The couple's relationship does much to bring Saramago's discussion of heterosexual romance as part of a revolutionary micropolitics of everyday life into a plausible present-day scenario, where Maria Sara takes initiatives, and dispenses wisdom, without the need for any superhuman vision. In contrast to what occurs in both *Memorial* and *Jangada*, here a man's 'enlightenment' thanks to the keener insights of a woman begins before sex, or even romance, is on the agenda. At the same time, one might well complain that the relative ease with which Raimundo sloughs off his macho chauvinism like a clammy raincoat smacks of the same facile optimism that compromises the radical gender politics of *Levantado* and *Memorial*. Raimundo's story pays scant attention either to the pervasive symbolic inscription of 'woman' as secondary and subordinate, or to the problem of extending the equal status that Maria Sara asserts for herself from a charmed circle of unmarried, middle-class, female professionals to women as parents and daughters, and/or in more straitened economic circumstances. Since children — and indeed also marriage — remain off the couple's agenda, Maria Sara is dissociated from the stereotype of woman in patriarchal utopian visions as regenerative guarantor of the future; yet, unlike *Memorial*'s Blimunda, she is never relegated to the status of a crone. This, however, also means that *História* provides no answers to the questions about parenthood and women's reproductive rights that are implicit in *Jangada*'s ambiguous ending.

The manner in which Raimundo must 'open up' to Maria Sara's 'invasion', while she is first attracted by his status as an 'invader' (i.e. of the author's history book), also places *História*'s take on gender relations centrally within a wider rethinking of self–Other relations, denouncing the human wish to 'deitar abaixo os muros do outro e continuar com [os seus]' [pull down the Other's defensive walls while keeping one's own standing] (*História*: 330). Raimundo may come to believe that love is 'provavelmente a última coisa em que o céptico ainda pode acreditar' [probably the last thing in which a sceptic may still believe] (ibid.); however, his own love story demonstrates that heterosexual romance, as it is commonly understood, requires reform, and only becomes a credible love through the courage to pull down one's own defences. In *História*, as more self-evidently in later novels such as *Todos os Nomes* and *O Homem Duplicado*, Saramago emphasizes the impossibility of really *knowing* the Other (or, indeed, of wholly knowing the self). Furthermore, he ponders what solution — if any — exists to the fear that this engenders: a fear that is, at the very least, self-defeating, and that, at worst, is externalized as hatred and fear of the Other. His focus on the malleability of ideologically configured identities and behaviours offers an inspiring, challenging model for the reconception of self–Other interactions more generally. The great innovation, relative to the earlier novels, lies in *História*'s focus on the need for humans to accept alterity in both others and ourselves, and to embed openness, egalitarianism, generosity, and compassion in the smallest everyday transactions, so as to hasten the integration — or 'organon' — of creativity, work, love, and politics envisaged by Marcuse.[43]

Yet the novel does not tackle the question (also largely side-stepped by Marcuse) of how revolutionary agency might move beyond this micropolitics of individual interactions towards the forging of more equal and more effective mass mobilizations for macropolitical transformation. A basic proposal that can be extrapolated, by reading *História* in relation to Saramago's preceding novels, is that of a dialogue between Marcuse's late writings — in particular, his emphasis on the radical conscience and agency of marginalized groups — and the revision of Gramsci's conceptions of hegemony and the revolutionary bloc that has been proposed by Ernesto Laclau and Chantal Mouffe (1985). *História*'s more nuanced imagining of strategies for breaking down patriarchal privilege and anxiety, and its critique of the ethnocentric prejudices and myopia prevailing in the mainstream discourse on Portuguese national identity, entail a recognition of the subversive power of (so-called) identity politics, and of the 'infusion' of new objectives, tactics, and perspectives into longer-established revolutionary left organizations. Moving beyond *Levantado*'s optimistic 'talking shop' model of the dialectical sublation of female, and other marginalized, perspectives into an unprecedentedly broad and united subaltern consciousness, *História* acknowledges the difficulties of comprehension of, and empathy with, the social Other, and the fear and division that they engender. Its emphasis on the multiplicity and malleability of identity, and on the need to challenge hierarchy and division in the minutiae of social and affective relations, urge closer attention to the under-explored, yet fertile, sociological territory of intersubjectivity. As such, *História* chimes with Steven Best and Douglas Kellner's criticism, in 1991, that radical left thinking after the 'postmodern turn' of the 1960s and 1970s had not adequately mediated the interrogation (or deconstruction) of theories of subjectivity (with all its implications for political agency) with 'theories of intersubjectivity which stress the ways that the subject is a social construct and the ways that sociality can constrict or enable individual subjectivity' (1991: 284).[44] Both Maria Sara and Raimundo demonstrate a capacity for intellectual inquiry and for self-renewal that increasingly enables them to coexist, cooperate, and even love in difference yet on equal terms. Yet to forge community or solidarity in difference multilaterally, across a wide social spectrum, would obviously be a challenge of a different order; and, moreover, the mutual suspicion of Raimundo and his fellow white-collar colleagues in *História* seems far removed from the comradeship of rural labourers in *Levantado*.

História's tender, humorous ending subtly reinforces the novel's message that the vision — and the personal liberation — its protagonists have achieved remains incomplete. At three in the morning, Raimundo creeps into bed with Maria Sara after ending his account of the siege in the thick of the battle for the city, as the blind muezzin is hacked down by the conquering Portuguese (*História*: 348). As the new history's 'terminating motif', signifying the 'apparent end or resolution of a process' (White), this image does not simply foreground the merciless violence of the victors, and but also reminds us of the limitations of the historian's subjective vision, and the inscrutability of the historical Other. By confining the reader's knowledge of events to the limits of perception that death and banishment impose upon the vanquished Muslims, this ending also acknowledges anew the effacement of the ethnic Other's historical perspective. While this bleakly satirical ending resolves Raimundo's worries about how to conclude his account of the siege (*História*: 298), it does not answer Maria Sara's insistence to Raimundo that 'tens de resolver as vidas daquele Mogueime e daquela Ouroana, o resto será menos importante' [you must sort out the lives of that Mogueime and Ouroana, the rest is less important] (*História*: 299). Raimundo, indeed, makes it clear to Maria Sara that the archetypically comedic terminating motif of his history's amorous sub-plot is not an unproblematically definitive ending, when he tells her that

> Na minha ideia, Ouroana vai voltar para a Galiza, e Mogueime irá com ela, e antes de partirem acharão em Lisboa um cão escondido, que os acompanhará na viagem. (*História*: 348)
>
> [As I imagine it, Ouroana is going to return to Galicia, and Mogueime will go with her, and before leaving they will find in Lisbon a dog hidden somewhere, which will accompany them on their journey.]

Here, as in *Jangada*'s tale of nomadic lovers and a dog, which Raimundo's reply parodies, the love engendered by an egalitarian, non-sexist ethics may provide the inspiration and courage for new departures and new alliances, but the fundamental political challenge deriving from epistemic uncertainty remains. It is no coincidence that images of light and shade impose themselves in the account of a bedroom 'que uma luz fraca apenas ilumina' [which a feeble light barely lit], where the narrative of Raimundo and Maria Sara's life together also ends inconclusively, with the couple lying awake while 'sob o alpendre da varanda respirava uma sombra' [under the roof of the balcony breathed a shade] (ibid.). At once figuring the darkness as a living entity, and evoking a ghostly presence (that of the Muslim historical subject whose legacy haunts posterity despite all efforts to efface it?), this enigmatic pun makes the *sombra* the symbolic vehicle of further and inescapable uncertainties that Raimundo, as historian, citizen, and lover, must contend with or accommodate even at this moment of seeming culmination and repose. The traces of the past, often yielding new insights when observed from fresh perspectives, are not source material to be configured with certainty or impunity into 'alternative narratives' of reality, and it is never enough to trust to the benign constancy of a transcendental design or teleology to dignify the ethics by which we aim to live. Wherever there are political ramifications to our encounters with historical narratives, we must, as readers and as citizens, unceasingly assume a critical distance from those narratives, seek out their flaws and omissions, and act upon our considered observations with due consideration for an ineradicable margin of error.

Notes to Chapter 5

1. As Vakil (2002) notes, the leading nineteenth-century historian Oliveira Martins described the conquest of Lisbon as 'the birth certificate of the nation'.
2. Huici considers the first chapter's dialogue as a separate narrative, and takes into account the narrative voice's metafictional asides to the reader.
3. On 'De expugnatione' and its authorship, see David's critical edition (2001), and Livermore (1990). A review of the three other, brief, first-hand accounts of the siege, and of the references to the siege in three late twelfth-century Portuguese chronicles, is offered in Villegas-Aristizábal (2007: 169–75). *História* (125) alludes to two of the shorter accounts, and to the twelfth-century chronicle 'Indiculum Fundationis Monasterii Sancti Vincentii'.
4. On the significance of this interventive and intermediary narrative voicing, see also, amongst other studies, Seixo (1999: 74), Fonseca (1994), Gobbi (1994: 73–90), and Finazzi-Agrò (2000).
5. See Bacon, Book 1, aphorisms 38–70 (1878: 207–56; trans. Johnston (ed.) (1965: 79–96).
6. On *idola fori*, or 'errors of the marketplace', see Bacon's aphorisms 43–44 and 59–60 (1878: 212–13; 229–32). As Bacon observes, '[c]redunt enim homines, rationem suam verbis imperare. Sed fit etiam ut verba vim suam super intellectum retorqueant et reflectant' [for men believe that their reason governs words; but it is also true that words react on the understanding] (1878: 229; trans. Johnston (ed.) 1965: 91).
7. This is an allusion to Goethe's poem *Die Zauberlehrling*.
8. See the Introduction chapter to this study, p. 6.
9. According to White, whereas a chronicle simply arranges events 'in the temporal order of their occurrence', a history turns this diachronic sequence into a story through 'arrangement of the events into the components of a "spectacle" or process of happening, which is thought to possess a discernible beginning, middle and end' (1973: 5).
10. See White (1973: 7–11), on his identification, informed by Frye's *Anatomy of Criticism* (1957), of 'at least four different modes of emplotment: Romance, Tragedy, Comedy, and Satire' (1973: 7). While different 'aspects or phases' of an historical account may be emplotted in different modes, White claims that 'a given historian is forced to emplot the whole set of stories making up his narrative in one comprehensive or archetypal story form' (1973: 8).
11. On the highly destructive 1950s 'redevelopment' of the Mouraria, see Sapega (2002: 46–47), Colvin (2008), and the exemplary photographs in Dias (1997: 14–21).
12. On this image of an 'arrumação caótica', see this study's chapter on *Levantado*, p. 65.
13. The custom of 'baking salted croissants, shaped like the Turkish [sic] half-moon' to celebrate the role of Vienna's bakers, who discovered preparations for a nocturnal assault by the besieging Ottoman forces, and thus facilitated the relief of the siege in September 1683, is noted in Macnicol (1978: xi).
14. See Leibniz (1898: 215–77). Leibniz conceives of the cosmos as a plenum of individual, perfect monads that, united, compose an autonomous and perfect transhistorical whole. *História* expressly alludes to Leibniz and his 'prova pela contingência do mundo' [proof of the contingency of the world] (119–20).
15. See Voltaire (1984). For a thorough account of Voltaire's attack on Leibnizian optimism in *Candide*, see Brooks (1964), and Mason (1992). The foundations of theistic optimism are set out in Leibniz (1951: esp. 128).
16. See this volume's Introduction chapter, pp. 7–8.
17. See Hegel (1975: 138). Hegel's conception here of 'freedom' as progress towards absolute knowledge is consistent with that developed in his earlier *The Phenomenology of Spirit*.
18. On this intertextual connection, see also this study's chapter on *Ricardo Reis*, pp. 153–54. On the tropes of vision and blindness in *Ensaio*, see, amongst other studies, Vieira (2009).
19. On Saramago's reworking of the symbolic encryption typical of oppositionist fiction, poetry, and song lyrics under the *Estado Novo*, see this work's chapter on *Levandado*, pp. 40–41 and pp. 50–51, p. 60, and p. 68 n. 19, and also Sabine (2010).
20. The link here to the cult of Dom Sebastião is more apparent to a reader who is familiar with *Ricardo Reis*, which makes a series of critical allusions to 'Sebastianism' (e.g. *Ricardo Reis*: 338),

and to Fernando Pessoa's reinterpretation of it. On the history of the Sebastianist cult in modern Portugal, see Miranda (2007).
21. In this passage, it is soon after the *mulher gorda* has reported seeing 'um pobre com os olhos vazados' [one poor soul with his eyes gouged out] among the survivors of Afonso Henriques's raids who are seeking refuge outside the Porta de Ferro that the muezzin interjects to lament that his eyes are 'como as pombas mortas que não voltarão aos ninhos' [like dead doves that will never return to their nests] (*História*: 62).
22. On *A Caverna* as a critique of consumerism as 'spectacle', and as an 'accusation against the cultural industry', see D'Angelo (2011). On the novel's treatment of Plato's allegory, see, in particular, Laird (2003).
23. See Plato (1994: 240–49) and Heidegger (1998).
24. See, in particular, Marcuse (2005: esp. 166–72), and Hemming (2013).
25. See Introduction chapter, p. 6 and p. 27 n. 17, on Saraiva's work for television and its profound influence on the popular reception of national history in post-dictatorship Portugal.
26. *História*'s epigraph, purportedly from the *Livro de Conselhos*, spells out the rationale of Saramago's counter-factual hypothecation in the aphorism '[e]nquanto não alcançares a verdade, não poderás corrigi-la. Porém, se a não corrigires, não a alcançarás. Entretanto, não te resignes' [Until you apprehend the truth, you will not be able to correct it. However, if you do not correct it, you will never apprehend it. In the meantime, don't give up] (*História*: cover).
27. On Saramago's reception of Pessoa's concept of *fingimento*, see Chapter 3, on *Ricardo Reis*, pp. 139–44.
28. Mesquita notes how all of the key 'marcas sémicas' [signifiers] of this passage 'remetem para os textos ortonímicos e heteronímicos [de Pessoa]' [allude to Pessoa's orthonymous and heteronymous texts] (1993: 142).
29. On this aspect of Raimundo's characterization, see also Atkin (2014: 70; 130; 136–37).
30. The reluctance of most schools of Marxist thought, other than that of the followers of Althusser, to entertain conceptions of subjectivity as non-unitary is both exemplified and defended in Eagleton (1985).
31. See also the *Levantado* chapter of this study, p. 67 n. 8, and Costa's account of *Manual*'s exploration of 'um segundo e verdadeiro nascimento propiciado pelo exercício da escrita, [uma] redenção através dela' [a second and true birth enabled by the exercise of writing, a redemption by means of writing], in Costa (1996: 281).
32. It is intriguing how Raimundo's repudiation of hair dye creates an ironic echo of Reis's brief dalliance, in *Ricardo Reis*, with the idea of disguising his grey hairs (*Ricardo Reis*: 103–04). Reis decides against this not because of any distaste for cosmetic falsification, but simply because he abhors being beholden to his physical body and to its maintenance: 'fatiga-o a simples ideia de ter de vigiar o cabelo todos os dias' [the mere idea of having to check on his hair every day exhausts him] (*Ricardo Reis*: 104).
33. See this study's chapter on *Ricardo Reis*, pp. 144–45.
34. Pessoa describes Caeiro's emergence as 'o aparecimento de alguém em mim [...] Desculpe-me o absurdo da frase: apareceu em mim o meu mestre' [This was the appearance in me of someone [...] Excuse the absurdity of this statement: my master had appeared in me] (1999: 343; trans. 2001: 256).
35. See this volume's chapter on *Ricardo Reis*, p. 140.
36. Gobbi (1994: 74–75) has demonstrated *História*'s 'concordância (supreendente?)' [(surprising?) correspondence] to the documented historical record. As she claims, the historical figures, military manoeuvres, geography, and technical innovations that feature in Raimundo's account all 'têm o seu "pé na História"' [have a firm basis in history] (1994: 74), being closely referenced to nineteenth-century Portuguese historian Alexandre Herculano's *História de Portugal*.
37. Herculano (1980: I, 509) stresses the contribution of Portuguese soldiers to the construction of the third tower used to assault the city in 1147. He also denounces foreign historians' failure to acknowledge the Portuguese contribution here, complaining that while the author of 'De expugnatione' was not so brazen as to deny that 'os seus tinham sido ajudados' [his own people had been assisted], he did '[deixar] no vago o facto' [leave this matter unclear] (ibid., footnote).
38. The quoted passage is taken, verbatim, from Chapter 2 of Brandão (1945: 7–9).

39. Although this passage demonstrates the basis for doubts about the unbiased veracity of Brandão's account, Brandão has, ironically, been extolled as a paragon of objectivity by comparison with his predecessor as the editor of the *Monarchia Lusitana* chronicles, Frei Bernardo de Brito. For this comparison, see A. de Magalhães Basto's 'Introducção' to Brandão (1944: vii–xxxix, at xvi–xviii).
40. As Brandão claims, the Cavalheiro Henrique's apparition asserted that 'não [era] justa a desigualdade do enterro em aqueles a quem a morte e merecimentos igualaram' [it was unjust for there to be inequality in the interment of those whom death and merit had made equal] (1945: 122).
41. Kaufman goes further in her estimation of Mogueime's virtues, asserting that with his 'esperteza [...] excepcional perceptibilidade e individualismo, Mogueime completa a galeria de personagens onde já colocamos Lídia e Blimunda' [intelligence, exceptional perception, and individuality, Mogueime completes the gallery of characters in which Lídia and Blimunda have already been installed] (1991a: 170).
42. Mogueime's comment refers to Afonso Henriques's own 'nascimento torto', i.e. the infantile atrophy of his legs, whose cure, through yet another purportedly miraculous intervention, is discussed earlier (*História*: 20–21).
43. On this, see this volume's chapter on *Memorial*, pp. 100–03.
44. Best and Kellner's stipulation that 'an adequate theory of subjectivity should stress the social construction of the subject, its production in discourses, practices and institutions' (1991: 284) is also consistent with *História*'s (and *Ricardo Reis*'s) riposte to Pessoa's conception of the triumph of a 'superior man''s will to become other over his material and ideological circumstances.

AFTERWORD

Much as *História*'s accounts of Mogueime and Orouana, and of Raimundo and Maria Sara, end not with any true closure, but with conjecture and deferral to future (hi)stories, so too these words in conclusion must admit of this study's incompletion, of the gaps in its coverage, and of the deferral of many discussions upon which it embarks to studies as yet unwritten. It is an admission that I make humbly, but also happily, in the hope that highlighting such gaps will prompt a constructively critical, and creative, response from readers. The contradiction of arguing for Saramago's entire *oeuvre* to be read as an integrated macrotext, while focusing almost exclusively on one decade of his literary career, is eased when one recognizes that no study can have the last word on the interpretation of a body of writing. As Saramago's narrative form so consistently — and insistently — goads us to acknowledge, there is no last word, either in the analysis of literature, or in that of socio-economic conditions and political options. Critical analysis should be a collective and dialogic activity; a debate that, when conducted in a spirit not of competition but of mutual respect and collaboration, not only enhances insight, but can also build a sense of community, or, at least, train individuals in the negotiation of difference and dissent.

In just such a collaborative spirit, and before summarizing my own current contribution to that debate, I should specify a few topics that are entertained too briefly or superficially in this study, and which I hope other readers and scholars of Saramago will continue to explore in more depth. Most obviously, there is more to be explored in the relationship of Saramago's 1980s novels to his works of the 1990s and 2000s. There is insufficient room in this study for a full response to the existing survey studies — including excellent book-length studies by Berrini (1998) and Frier — and to the expressly comparative close readings offered in, for example, Atkin, Amorim (2010), and the collections edited by Medeiros and Ornelas (2007, and forthcoming 2017), and Baltrusch (2014). Reading these 'historiographical' novels comparatively with the later, so-called 'allegorical' works (Martins 2006a: 111) could illuminate, in particular, the discussion of self–Other relations that emerges in *Ricardo Reis*, *Jangada*, and especially *História* in contexts of political contention and upheaval, and that proceeds with a view to forging empathy, solidarity, and genuinely equal love across divides of class, ethnicity, and gender. In *Todos os Nomes* and *As Intermitências da Morte* (2005), the issue of knowing, and accepting, the Other is both foregrounded and complicated. Parables not only of the fear of alterity, but also of attraction across social divisions, highlight problems beyond *História*'s intellectual challenge to recognize one's socio-economically configured identity and perspective, and its moral challenge to 'open oneself up' to an imperfectly known Other. *O Homem Duplicado* (2002) adds a disturbing twist to *Ricardo Reis*'s and *História*'s ideas of other selves, and of a politically inflected project of 'becoming other', with its radical recontextualization of the gothic horror trope of the doppelgänger.

This study follows — and has attempted to build upon — a substantial body of (mostly Portuguese and Brazilian) studies that explore how Saramago's conception both of the study of history, and of the political relevance of historical fiction, relate to Marxist precepts, and particularly to (post-)Marxist responses — and, indeed, anticipations — of the post-structuralist 'turn'. Nevertheless, there is still a need for a holistic study (ideally by scholars with expert knowledge of the German language and philosophical tradition) of how Saramago's conception of the political artwork, and of its allusion to historical realities, corresponds to that found in the work of Walter Benjamin. It is unlikely that Saramago was familiar, in the 1980s, with Benjamin's emphasis, in the *Arcades Project* texts, on the value of the allegorical mode as vehicle for, and/or stimulus to, the dialectical analysis of historical reality. Reading in the light of these texts helps to vindicate Saramago's penchant, especially in *Levantado* and *Memorial*, for elaborate neo-baroque conceits, and explain his more general use of allegorical frameworks, to mediate between historical documentation and hypothecation, and simultaneously to warn of the 'artifactuality' of its own representations and conclusions.

New Benjaminian readings could also profitably reassess Saramago's manipulation of the trope of vision, in the light of the *Arcades Project*'s analysis of looking, display, and spectacle in the modern city. Saramago's exhortation to 'observe' (*reparar*), rather than just 'see' (*ver*), aims at more than a simple critique of intellectual torpor and moral myopia. His characters' endeavours to 'look' and 'observe', and the consequences thereof, reveal how the act of seeing is conditioned by ideology, which constructs expectations and presumptions a priori, and places constraints on the imagining of possible realities. Benjamin's focus on visual phenomena, both as the projection of commodity fetishism, and the point of departure for socio-economic analysis, offers a precursory critique of Baudrillard's celebration of simulation. It could also contribute to a clearer definition of how Saramago's work advocates a return to Plato's allegory of the Cave, even as it insists on perpetuating — cautiously — a materialist (and inherently empiricist) analysis of history and politics. It follows that further exploration is also needed of the fault-line that shows up, most clearly in *História*, between dialectical materialism and Heideggerian phenomenology. Such analysis might also contribute to a clearer evaluation of the apparent correspondences between *Memorial*'s ucronian vision of a socially, economically, and affectively reformed micro-society with the later writings of Herbert Marcuse (even though Marcuse had by the 1960s disavowed much of his earlier use of Heideggerian constructs).

While such avenues remain to be explored, I hope that this study's application of Benjamin and Marcuse, while neither comprehensive nor seamlessly integrated, has demonstrated both the close relationship of Saramago's political outlook to Frankfurt School theorists, and the manner in which elements of their thinking are combined with both a post-Gramscian current of Marxism, and with ideas about culture, political consciousness, and social transformation from the Portuguese and Spanish-speaking worlds. It is a fundamental contention of this study that — however fascinating Saramago's narratological innovations and symbolic adaptations may be to literary historians — his work must continue to be read as politically engaged, and, indeed, agitational, literature. It is fiction that not merely invites reflection, but also incites the reader to act politically, rather than resigning him- or herself to the inaccessibility of historical truth, and hence the impossibility of progress. The question that inevitably follows such a demand for a 'political' reading is, of course, that of whether or not a consistent, clear, and complete political programme can indeed be extrapolated from this body of work by the reader(s) who accept(s) the challenge to respond to it.

Saramago himself disavowed attempts to identify cleavages or discontinuities in his output, and endorsed those readings that emphasized the unity within his writings.[1] There is an undeniable shift, in his output between *Levantado* and *História*, both in the conception of an 'interrogative' and politically agitatory text, and in the ideological proposals that are foregrounded. Such changes as this study has identified can, however, be considered not as an infirmity of belief or purpose, but rather as the pursuit of a more nuanced defence, in fast-changing socio-economic and discursive contexts, of the aspirations to social equality, fraternity, freedom from penury and persecution, acceptance of otherness, and compassion, and of the need for radical socio-economic reorganization in order to realize those aspirations.

This is true of Saramago's move away from Brechtian didacticism, commenced in *Levantado*. Here, the reader may be encouraged to infer Marxist conclusions from the depictions of wage bargaining, or of the introduction of the mechanized thresher. However, the most overt appeal for the reader's reflection and judgement — 'agora o que é preciso é pormo-nos nós a pensar' [what is necessary now is that we start doing some thinking] (*Levantado*: 168) — coincides with the novel's most self-evident (and self-conscious) use of fantasy and conjecture, in the 'ant's eye' account of Germano Santos Vidigal's murder. In his subsequent novels, Saramago expands the 'counter-factual' or ucronian spaces within which ideological 'lessons' are simultaneously imparted, and advertised as unreliably conjectural, 'partial', and 'parcelled'. *História*, with its fictional narrative within a fictional narrative, based upon an array of unreliable testimony to, and retelling of, past events, goes furthest in 'ironizing' the ucronian spaces within which a socialist reinterpretation of local history is foregrounded. Equally, it is the most explicit of these novels regarding the fundamental problems of epistemology and representation that undermine claims of the 'scientific' status of Marxist (or indeed any other) historiography or political analysis.

Yet even if historiography will always fail to deliver truth, it must nonetheless continue. The field of collective memory must not be left enthralled to the mythology and specious, selective journalism upon which mid-twentieth century dictatorships depended. Neither should it be handed over to more recent and more subtle practices of summoning the past to justify the present and all its iniquities, whether these practices partake of the convenient pessimism of a debased postmodernism — which sees the end of utopianism in the inaccessibility of objective truth — or of the Panglossian optimism with which Francis Fukuyama (1992) hailed 'the end of history' in the rise of neo-liberal parliamentarianism. As Fredric Jameson argues, for capitalism's discontents, 'there is no alternative to Utopia' in an era when 'late capitalism seems to have no natural enemies' and is 'tirelessly undoing all the social gains made since the inception of the socialist and communist movements' (2007: xii). Jameson's analysis of utopia points most clearly to the political 'usefulness' of Saramago's work when he asserts that

> [w]hat is crippling is not the presence of an enemy but rather the universal belief, not only that this tendency is irreversible, but that the historic alternatives to capitalism have been proven unviable and impossible, and that no other socio-economic system is conceivable, let alone practically available. [...] Utopian form is itself a representational meditation on radical difference, radical otherness, and on the systemic nature of the social totality, to the point where one cannot imagine any fundamental change in our social existence which has not first thrown off Utopian visions like so many sparks from a comet. (ibid.)

Saramago's output, while increasingly pessimistic in tone, holds fast to the fundamental utopian principle of the possibility of real social progress. While admitting the inevitability of historical consciousness being based on an 'ongoing struggle between different stories' (Korhonen 2006: 13), it encourages the reader to recognize not only the political agendas articulated in those stories, but also the discursive rules of engagement. This is a post-structuralist historiography that, as Korhonen puts it, seeks 'not to shut history into some structuralist "prison house of language"' but to help us 'free ourselves from those figures that, if we do not recognize them, predetermine our [historical] discourse' (ibid.). Hence, while those who struggle for social transformation may invest in Marxism's prioritization of matter and of human will, in its critique of capitalist economics, and in its dialectical analytic method; they must also recognize materialism's status as *hypothesis*, and the dialectical process's nature as always incomplete and provisional. And they must also consider the role of language and discourse, as they guard against the propensity of transformational political movements to follow the regimes that they seek to disestablish in becoming selectively myopic or ossified, or even in fostering totalitarian attitudes and practices.

In Saramago's fiction through the 1980s, one also encounters the expression of his dissent from certain key Marxist-Leninist theories of the construction of society and of radical political organization. Already in *Levantado*, Saramago's characterization of the labouring classes, and of the growth of their political consciousness and solidarity, owes much to theories of subalternity developed first by Gramsci and later by anti-colonialists across the 'global South'. Depicting the Communist-led struggle against Salazarism in the rural Alentejo with a clear emphasis on the pseudo-Gramscian insights and initiatives that were marginalized by the Party's 1950s turn to Stalinist orthodoxy, *Levantado* establishes Saramago's consideration of how a political movement might accommodate and represent the diversity of subaltern social constituencies, while also galvanizing them into a coherent and effective revolutionary bloc. His subsequent novels venture deeper, and with much less optimism, in charting the complexity of social divisions, and the obstacles to mass radicalization. In 1980s Portugal, his work served to challenge arguably narrow and ossified conceptions of subaltern subjectivity and political priorities.[2] Thirty years later it serves a different, more international, purpose, in asserting a need for emergent identity-based political movements to address the fundamentally exploitative and alienating nature of capitalist labour relations. *Memorial* develops the picture of how an idealized human nature is corrupted by the shortcomings and iniquities first of feudalism, and later of capitalism. The stories of João Mau-Tempo, Baltasar Sete-Sóis, and of numerous minor characters in *Ricardo Reis* indicate how malnutrition, excessive physical labour, and dangerous working conditions result in physical degeneracy or disability, while the alienating nature of labour exploitation — not to mention the subjection of women and their bodies to patriarchal imperatives — fosters moral as well as psycho-sexual perversions. The view of human behaviour in later novels — most obviously, in *Ensaio sobre a Cegueira* — is much more pessimistic than *Memorial*'s, suggesting, further to the direct psychological damage of alienation and of what Marcuse terms the 'performance principle', an endemic impulse to brutality and irrationality that can be excited and politically manipulated especially in periods of social upheaval, uncertainty, and material scarcity. The focus in *Ricardo Reis*, *Jangada*, and *História* on the Estado Novo's baleful legacy of jingoism and xenophobia, and its 'cleansing' of an racially and culturally hybridized heritage, exposes the function of modern nationalism in keeping an exploited populace fearful and divided along lines of race, ethnicity, and gender. In *Ricardo Reis*, the masses who are urged to proclaim that 'nós não somos nada' [we are nothing] direct their aggression against imagined 'foreign' foes, or against each other in gang warfare; frequently, like Lídia, they find themselves emotionally and economically complicit in the system that oppresses them. In *Jangada*, an unstable socio-economic scenario produces unpredictable, and only rarely sustained, subaltern solidarity with an aim of social transformation. The occupation of the Algarve hotels is depicted as a soviet-style success, and despite ironic elements in the narration of the battle with police, the occupiers' justification of their actions remains privileged over other discursive elements in the text. Thereafter, however, mass protest is depicted as confused and abortive. Intimations of a more equitable social order emerging are restricted to the presentation of the microsociety of the novel's protagonists, and even here, remain equivocal.

One might complain that Saramago's fiction is frustratingly imprecise about how, beyond *Levantado*'s endless dialogue punctuated by direct mass action, a new order of radical alliances might be built, and a broader array of subaltern perspectives and agendas synthesized. While in *Memorial* and later novels, Saramago no longer confidently depicts the organic growth of a revolutionary party, he instead focuses on the micropolitics of everyday life, and, in particular, on domestic and affective relations, as the origin of the growth of a revolutionary 'ferment'. Hence, these novels posit the revolutionization of gender relations, and the role of women as 'visionaries' leading a more fundamental critique of capitalist ideology, as the most important of initiatives towards social transformation. All five novels denounce patriarchal structures in public and private life, and mock male fears and prejudices about independent and intelligent women.

Judged by the criteria of socialist or post-Marxist feminist thinking of the last three decades, Saramago's characterization both of contemporary women and of the agenda and methodology of female emancipation presents significant problems. For a start, his fiction's ostensibly genderless narrative voice is generally more closely aligned to male characters' perspectives, leaving female characters not simply sidelined, but also often framed as the unknowable (and in Blimunda's case, exoticized) Other while the self-sameness of their male counterparts goes unquestioned. This disparity, of course, corresponds to a preponderant allocation of active, creative roles to male characters while females feature rather as instigators or facilitators. However, one might concede that by making such a distinction, one is ignoring the value of more subtle, and negotiated, initiatives that women take while laws and conventions deny them any right of leadership. A weightier problem is the ambiguous silence of so much of Saramago's fiction on the politics of procreation, parenting, and family dynamics. Although it laments working women's 'triple burden' and denounces the abusive paternalism behind the 'happy families' imagery of Salazarism, Saramago's fiction never offers a complete model of how such structural forms of women's (and children's) oppression might be eliminated. This absence means that Saramago's allegories of the struggle for liberation in an egalitarian society never fully exorcize from their representations of 'real' women the accompanying spectre of the 'eternal feminine' as useful or redemptive accessory to male endeavour. His emphasis on the contribution of individual affective relationships to a radical left politics corrects a tendency in left organizations to depreciate spousal relationships as a diversion from the formation of collective solidarity. But visions of social harmony that centre on love between equal, autonomous heterosexual couples veer perilously close to the hackneyed nostrum — so often fundamental to both left- and right-wing agendas in twentieth-century Portugal — of regeneration through procreation. Saramago seems unwilling, or unable, to accommodate within his allegories any fundamental challenge to the heteronormative matrix of gendered identity and family relations (much less any non-heterosexual characters). Consequently, readers are sometimes at liberty to read into his stories the patriarchal construction of the sign of 'woman' as secondary, passive, and supplementary.

Staying so firmly within an (admittedly much reformed) heterosexual matrix also restricts the potential of what are surely Saramago's most radical proposals for renewal in post-Marxist left politics. These are his increasing focus on interpersonal and affective micropolitics, and his depiction of the individual's moral and political 'growth' as a process of 'becoming other', which fosters not only empathy and, in time, solidarity, but also a practice of dialectical 'seeing', observation, and analysis. If the reconceptualization of the self, and of communities, is a prerequisite for revolutionary transformation, such a reconceptualization can be commenced, but by no means completed, by the contestation of established historical narratives that is these novels' ostensible subject. Accepting the multiple, and mutable, nature of one's being, as one analyses the material and ideological construction of one's subjectivity, strengthens attempts to conceive utopian aspirations, and to pursue them through consensual, collective action. Yet Saramago's 1980s novels focus almost exclusively on erotic, quasi-marital relationships as capable of catalysing individual's personal transformation: only in the chaotic hell of *Cegueira*'s psychiatric hospital, after romance and the nuclear family have become the focus of a despairing nostalgia, is the transformative potential of friendship (in particular, the solidarity of women around the figure of the Doctor's Wife) explored in any depth.

As *Ricardo Reis* explores at such length, literary texts achieve nothing politically in themselves; it is the creative work of readers that makes literature matter socially, or — while the author still lives — the creative dialogue that the text mediates between author and readers. Saramago, who was a prominent journalist and cultural and political activist before he achieved literary acclaim, was aware of this. But he was also alert to the contradiction, examined in Marcuse's essay 'The Affirmative Character of Culture' (1968a), that art and literature's establishment of an autonomous discursive realm from which a critique of social reality can be developed contributes to their own separation from their social context, and their relegation to a trivialized — and often commercialized — category of 'culture'. He was therefore wary of the literary institutionalization that, paradoxically, amplified his voice in the 1990s and 2000s, as an energetic blogger and campaigner, and as a wily manipulator of the commercial mass media. All 'grandes autores' [great authors], as he joked in 1998, 'vão a caminho da invisibilidade. O Camões transformou-se numa coroa de louros e num olho fechado; e o Fernando Pessoa é um chapéu, uns óculos e um bigode' [end up becoming invisible. Camões has turned into a laurel wreath and a lost eye, and Fernando Pessoa is a fedora, glasses, and a moustache] (Reis 1998: 70). One may surmise that, by that year's end, he was conscious of his own imminent reduction to a pair of horn-rimmed specs, a quizzical stare, and the Portuguese language's first Nobel Prize for Literature. Over the years since, Saramago has arguably become not quite the 'institution' that Jean-Paul Sartre claimed was the literary Nobel winner's fate, but rather, several institutions, which are frequently in partial or absolute contradiction to each other. While the Fundação José Saramago, which he himself established in 2007, continues to work for the promotion and study of his works, and to support cultural projects that (at least in theory) advance his political objectives, the prestigious José Saramago Prize for young Portuguese-language novelists is funded by corporate finance. Neither institution, meanwhile, can claim a monopoly of the image of a figure asserted as literary icon both of an often disparate and inchoate international left, and of the global Portuguese-speaking community, or *lusofonia*, whose purported leadership, the Community of Portuguese-Speaking Countries (CPLP), Saramago dismissed as 'esqueleto a que falta tudo para se tornar num ser vivo' [a skeleton lacking everything necessary to become a living being].[3] In such circumstances, and while his works circulate globally in an ever greater number of translations and adaptations, it is essential that we continue to read his works actively, and to discuss the responses that they elicit from us with consideration of their continuing relevance to changing political circumstances.

Notes to the Afterword

1. See Almeida (2001: 247).
2. See, for example, António Cascais's account of 1980s Portuguese left parties' hostility to LGBT rights campaigns, Cascais (2006: 113–16).
3. Saramago, entry for 2 February 1997, in Saramago (1998a: 31).

BIBLIOGRAPHY

Works of José Saramago

1977. *Manual de Pintura e Caligrafia* (Lisbon: Moraes)
1986. *Objecto Quase*, 3rd edn (Lisbon: Caminho)
1988A. *O Ano da Morte de Ricardo Reis*, 9th edn (Lisbon: Caminho)
1988B. *Levantado do Chão*, 8th edn (Lisbon: Caminho)
1988C. 'O (meu) iberismo', *Jornal de Letras*, 330 (31 October), 32
1989A. 'Europa sim, Europa não', *Jornal de Letras*, 340 (10 January), 32
1989B. *História do Cerco de Lisboa* (Lisbon: Caminho)
1989C. 'Sobre a invenção do presente', *Jornal de Letras*, 347 (28 February), 45
1990. *Os Apontamentos*, 2nd edn (Lisbon: Caminho)
1991. *O Evangelho segundo Jesus Cristo* (Lisbon: Caminho)
1992A. *Memorial do Convento*, 21st edn (Lisbon: Caminho)
1992B. 'A Península Ibérica entre a Europa e a América Latina', *Vértice*, 47 (March–April), 5–11
1993. 'Descobrir o outro, descobrir-se a si mesmo', *Espacio/ Espaço escrito*, 9–10 [special issue, *Juan Goytisolo / José Saramago*] (Winter 1993–94), 83–92
1994. *A Jangada de Pedra*, 6th edn (Lisbon: Caminho)
1995. *Ensaio sobre a Cegueira* (Lisbon: Caminho)
1997A. *Cadernos de Lanzarote III* (Lisbon: Caminho)
1997B. *Todos os Nomes* (Lisbon: Caminho)
1998A. *Cadernos de Lanzarote V* (Lisbon: Caminho)
1998B. *O Conto da Ilha Desconhecida* (Lisbon: Caminho)
2000. *A Caverna* (Lisbon: Caminho)
2002. *O Homem Duplicado* (Lisbon: Caminho)
2005. *As Intermitências da Morte* (Lisbon: Caminho)

Studies of José Saramago and his Work

ALDEAMIL, MARÍA JOSEFA POSTIGO. 2001. 'José Saramago y los proverbios', *Revista de Filología Románica*, 2, 267–99
ALFAYA, JAVIER. 1993. 'O compromisso moral e político na obra de José Saramago, ou um leitor espanhol perante Saramago', *Vértice*, 52, 23–27
ALMEIDA, ONÉSIMO TEOTÓNIO. 2001. Review of *Colóquio-Letras*, 151–52, *José Saramago: O Ano de 1998* (Jan–Jun 1999), *Portuguese Literary and Cultural Studies*, 6 [special issue, *On Saramago*] (Spring), 247–50
ALVES, CLARA FERREIRA. 1995. 'José Saramago: todos os pecados do mundo', *Expresso: Revista*, 28 October, pp. 81–86
ALVES, CLARA FERREIRA, FRANCISCO BÉLARD, and AUGUSTO M. SEABRA. 1986. 'A facilidade de ser ibérico: José Saramago', *Expresso: Revista*, 8 November, pp. 36–39
AMORIM, SÍLVIA. 2010. *José Saramago — art, théorie et éthique du roman* (Paris: L'Harmattan)
ARNAUT, ANA PAULA. 1996. *Memorial do Convento: história, ficção e ideologia* (Coimbra: Fora do Texto)

—— 1999. 'The Subversion of History in *Memorial do Convento*', *Portuguese Studies*, 15, 182–93
—— 2002A. '*Manual de Pintura e Caligrafia*: o novo realismo post-modernista', *Luso-Brazilian Review* 39.1 (Summer), 9–18
—— 2002B. *Post-modernismo no romance português contemporâneo: fios de Ariadne, máscaras de Proteu* (Coimbra: Almedina)
ATKIN, RHIAN. 2012. *Saramago's Labyrinths: A Journey through Form and Content in 'Blindness' and 'All the Names'*, Durham Modern Languages Series (Manchester and New York: Manchester University Press)
—— 2014. *Lisbon Revisited: Urban Masculinities in Twentieth-Century Portuguese Fiction* (Oxford: Legenda)
BALTRUSCH, BERGHARD (ed.). 2014. *'O que transforma o mundo é a necessidade e não a utopia': sobre utopia e ficção em José Saramago* (Berlin: Frank & Timme)
BECKER, PAULO. 1991. 'A Jangada de Pedra: navegando em busca de OUTRA humanidade', *Letras de Hoje* (Porto Alegre), 26.1 (March), 123–40
BEN MOSHE, LIAT. 2006. 'Infusing Disability in the Curriculum: The Case of Saramago's *Blindness*', *Disability Studies Quarterly* 26.2. Available online at <http://dsq-sds.org/article/view/688/865> [accessed 4 December 2015]
BERRINI, BEATRIZ. 1998. *Ler Saramago: o romance*, Estudos de Literatura Portuguesa (Lisbon: Caminho)
BERTOQUINI, MARIA INÊS PEIXOTO BRAGA. 1999. *Ricardo Reis e a história: morte, vida, e ressureição* (Porto: Universidade do Porto)
BESSE, MARIA GRACIETE. 2000. 'O mito do judeu errante em *Levantado do Chão* de José Saramago', *Latitudes: Cahiers Lusophones* 8 (May), 32–36
BLOOM, HAROLD. 2002A. 'José Saramago' in *El futur de la imaginació* (Barcelona: Empúrias), pp. 191–206
—— 2002B. *The Varieties of José Saramago* (Lisbon: FLAD)
CAMPELO, JURIL DE NASCIMENTO. 1985. 'A ficção da ficção em *O Ano da Morte de Ricardo Reis*', *Revista Letras* (Curitiba), 34, 39–43
CECUCCI, PIERO. 1993. 'L'Utopia Saramaghiana come progetto della storia umana', in *Il Girador: studi di letterature iberiche e ibero-americane offerti a Giuseppe Bellini*, ed. by G. B. de Cesare and Silvana Serafin (Rome: Bulzoni), pp. 209–15
COSTA, HORÁCIO. 1997. *José Saramago: o período formativo* (Lisbon: Caminho)
—— 1999. 'A construção da personagem de ficção em Saramago: da *Terra do Pecado* ao *Memorial do Convento*', *Colóquio-Letras*, 151 (July) [special issue, *José Saramago: O ano de 1998*], 205–16
D'Angelo, Biagio. 2011. 'A utopia do "centro" n'*A Caverna*, de José Saramago', *Ipotesi*, 15.1 (January–June), 39–46. Available online at <http://www.ufjf.br/revistaipotesi/files/2012/03/7-a-utopia.pdf> [accessed 20 November 2015]
DANIEL, MARY L. 2005. 'Symbolism and Synchronicity in José Saramago's *A Jangada de Pedra*', in *José Saramago*, ed. by Harold Bloom, Bloom's Modern Critical Views (Philadelphia, PA: Chelsea House), pp. 11–23; first pub. in *Hispania*, 74.3 (September 1991), 536–41
DUARTE, HELENA VAZ. 2006. *Provérbios segundo José Saramago* (Lisbon: Colibri-IELT)
DUARTE, LÉLIA PARREIRA. 1982. 'Nota do livro: *Levantado do Chão*', *Boletim do Centro de Estudos Portugueses*, 4.7, 85–89
FERREIRA, ANA PAULA. 2001. 'Cruising Gender in the 1980s (from *Levantado do Chão* to *The History of the Siege of Lisbon*)', *Portuguese Literary and Cultural Studies*, 6 [special issue, *On Saramago*], 221–38
FINAZZI-AGRÒ, ETTORE. 2000. '"Da capo": o texto como palimpsesto na *História do Cerco de Lisboa*', *Colóquio-Letras*, 151 (Spring) [special issue, *José Saramago: O ano de 1998*], 341–51

Fonseca, Maria Nazareth Soares. 1994. 'Jogos de encenação e de discurso em *História do Cerco de Lisboa*', *Boletim do CESP*, 14.17 (January–July), 7–15

Francès-Dumas, Marie. 2001. 'L'Animalisation de l'homme dans *Levantado do Chão* de José Saramago, ou une symbolique de l'être', *Quadrant*, 18, 199–229

Frier, David [G.]. 1998. 'Agouros e oportunidades: a *Jangada de Pedra* de José Saramago e o país desconhecido', in *Actas do Quinto Congresso da Associação Internacional de Lusitanistas*, ed. by T. F. Earle, 3 vols (Oxford and Coimbra: AIL), II, 713–20

—— 1999. 'José Saramago's Stone Boat: Celtic Analogues and Popular Culture', *Portuguese Studies*, 15, 194–206

—— 2003. 'Padre Bartolomeu Lourenço de Gusmão: Inspiration for *Memorial do Convento*?', *Romance Quarterly*, 50.1 (Winter), 56–68

—— 2007A. *The Novels of José Saramago: Echoes from the Past, Pathways into the Future* (Cardiff: University of Wales Press)

—— 2007B. 'Recuperar o passado, recuperar-se do passado em *Levantado do Chão* e "Cadeira", de José Saramago', in *Da possibilidade do impossível: leituras de Saramago*, ed. by Paulo de Medeiros and José Ornelas, Utrecht Portuguese Studies Series (Utrecht: Universiteit Utrecht), pp. 99–117

Gallagher, Deborah J. 'On Using Blindness as Metaphor and Difficult Questions: A Response to Ben-Moshe', *Disability Studies Quarterly*, 26.2. Available online at <http://dsq-sds.org/article/view/690/867> [accessed 4 December 2015]

Garza, Regina. 2010. 'Entrevista con José Saramago', *Cañasanta*, 14. Available online at <http://www.canasanta.com/entrevistas/entrevista-con-jose-saramago-000001.html> [accessed 3 January 2012]

Gobbi, Márcia V. Zamboni. 1994. 'A (Outra) História do Cerco de Lisboa: (Des)arranjos entre fato e ficção', *Revista de Letras* (São Paulo), 34, 73–90

Gomes, Renato Cordeiro. 1989. 'A alquimia do sangue e do resgate em *Levantado do Chão* de José Saramago', *Estudos Portugueses e Africanos*, 13 (January–June), 19–27

Grossegesse, Orlando. 1997. 'Messianismo telúrico em *Levantado do Chão* de José Saramago', in *'Sentido que a Vida Faz': estudos para Óscar Lopes*, ed. by A.M Brito, I. Pires de Lima, et al. (Porto: Campo das Letras), pp. 207–15

—— 2001. 'Journey to the Iberian God: Antonio Machado Revisited by Saramago', *Portuguese Literary and Cultural Studies*, 6 [special issue, *On Saramago*], 167–84

—— 2006. 'About Words, Tears, and Screams: Dante's *Commedia* Revisited by Borges and Saramago', in *In Dialogue with Saramago: Essays in Comparative Literature*, ed. by Adriana Alves de Paula Martins and Mark Sabine (Manchester: MSPS), 57–80

Hogue, Bev. 2006. 'Naming the Bones: Bodies of Knowledge in Contemporary Fiction', *Modern Fiction Studies*, 52.1 (Spring), 121–42

Huici, Adrián. 1996. 'Historia y ficción en *Historia del Cerco de Lisboa*', in *José Saramago: il bagaglio dello scrittore* (Roma: Bulzoni), pp. 137–61

Kaufman, Helena. 1991A. 'Ficção histórica portuguesa do pós-revolução' (unpublished doctoral dissertation, University of Wisconsin, Madison)

—— 1991B. 'A metaficção historiográfica de José Saramago', *Colóquio-Letras*, 120, 124–36

Kaufman, Helena, and José Ornelas. 1997. 'Challenging the Past/Theorizing History: Postrevolutionary Portuguese Fiction', in *After the Revolution: Twenty Years of Portuguese Literature*, ed. by Helena Kaufman and Anna Klobucka (Lewisburg, PA: Bucknell University Press), pp. 145–67

Klobucka, Anna. 2001. 'Saramago's Worlds', *Portuguese Literary & Cultural Studies*, 6 (Spring) [special issue, *On Saramago*], xi–xxi

Laird, Andrew. 2003. 'Death, Politics, Vision, and Fiction in Plato's Cave (After Saramago)', *Arion: A Journal of Humanities and the Classics*, 10.3 (Winter), 1–30

Lanciani, Giulia. 1993. 'Os universais irredutíveis de José Saramago', *Vértice*, 52 (January–February), 13–16

Lepecki, Maria Lúcia. 1988. 'Levantado do Chão: história e pedagogia', in Sobreimpressões (Lisbon: Caminho), pp. 83–95

Letízia, Marie-Eve. 1991. 'O lugar da mulher dentro do espaço e o processo da sua conscientização através da narrativa Levantado do Chão de José Saramago', Taíra, 3, 157–76

Lima, Isabel Pires de. 1988. 'Viagem e momento: espaço e tempo n'A Jangada de Pedra de José Saramago', Vértice, 6, 31–35

—— 1998. 'Saramago pós-moderno ou talvez não', in Actas do Quinto Congresso da Associação Internacional de Lusitanistas, ed. by T. F. Earle (Oxford and Coimbra: AIL), ii, pp. 933–41

Lima, Mirella Márcia Longo Vieira. 1990. 'Notas sobre José Saramago e sua máquina de fazer voar', Estudos Portugueses e Africanos, 16 (July–December), 39–56

Lopes, João Marques. 2010. Biografia — José Saramago (Lisbon: Guerra e Paz)

Lopes, Óscar. 1986. 'José Saramago', in Os sinais e os sentidos: literatura portuguesa do século XX, Colecção Universitária, 11 (Lisbon: Caminho), pp. 201–08

Lough, Francis. 2002. 'National Identity and Historiography in José Saramago's A Jangada de Pedra', Journal of Iberian and Latin American Studies, 8.2, 153–63

Lourenço, António Apolinário. 1991. 'História, ficção e ideologia: representação ideológica e pluridiscursividade em Memorial do Convento', Vértice, 42 (September), 69–78

Lourenço, Eduardo. 1990. 'Memorial, terrestre e divino', Jornal de Letras, 412 (29 May), 24

Maia, Armandina. 1991. 'Stregoneria e inquisizione nel Memorial: Una storia al femminile', in Viaggio intorno al Convento di Mafra, ed. by Piero Ceccucci (Milan: Guerini), pp. 53–64

Martins, Adriana. 2006a. A construção da memória da nação em José Saramago e Gore Vidal (Frankfurt-am-Main: Peter Lang)

—— 2006b. 'The Poetics of Correction in Gore Vidal's Burr and Saramago's História do Cerco de Lisboa', in In Dialogue with Saramago: Essays in Comparative Literature, ed. by Adriana Alves de Paula Martins and Mark Sabine (Manchester: MSPS), pp. 163–75

Matías, Felipe dos Santos. 2007. 'As notícias jornalísticas e o diálogo entre a literatura e a história em O Ano da Morte de Ricardo Reis de José Saramago', Mafuá, 7 (July). Available online at <http://www.mafua.ufsc.br/numero07/ensaios/matias.htm> [accessed 20 August 2013]

Mendes, Nancy Maria. 1991. 'José Saramago: poder e ironia em Memorial do Convento', Boletim do Centro de Estudos Portugueses, 13, 13–16

Mesquita, Maria Luísa Raimundo. 1993. 'Do estatuto polifónico do narrador em História do Cerco de Lisboa de José Saramago' (unpublished master's thesis, Universidade Nova de Lisboa)

Oliveira Filho, Odil de. 1993. Carnaval no convento: intertextualidade e parodia em José Saramago, Coleção Prismas (São Paulo: UNESP)

Ornelas, José N. 2006. 'Convergences and Divergences in Saramago's Ensaio sobre a Cegueira and Camus's The Plague', in In Dialogue with Saramago: Essays in Comparative Literature, ed. by Adriana Alves de Paula Martins and Mark Sabine (Manchester: MSPS), pp. 121–39

Neves, Margarida Braga. 1999. '"Nexos, temas e obsessões" na ficção breve de José Saramago', Colóquio-Letras, 151–52 (January–June) [special issue, José Saramago: O ano de 1998], 117–41

Pereira, Paulo. 1991. 'Inquisição: entre história e ficção na narrativa portuguesa', Colóquio-Letras, 120 (April–June), 117–23

Pontiero, Giovanni. 1989. 'Interview with José Saramago', Poetry News Review, 16.4, 38–42

Presedo, Elvira S. 1984. 'O Romance de intervençom nas literaturas portuguesa e galega actuais', Vértice, 44, 32–43

Rebelo, Luís de Sousa. 1986. 'A Jangada de Pedra ou os possíveis da História' (postface to the 2nd edn of Jangada) (Lisbon: Caminho), pp. 333–49

—— 1993. 'A consciência da História na ficção de José Saramago', Vértice, 52 (January–February), 29–38

Reis, Carlos. 1986. '*Memorial do Convento* ou a emergência da história', *Revista Crítica de Ciências Sociais*, 18–19–20, 91–103
—— 1998. *Diálogos com José Saramago* (Lisbon: Caminho)
Ribeiro, Raquel. 2012. 'Imaginary Atlantic Islands: José Saramago's Iberian Utopia and Maria Gabriel Llansol's European "Communities"', *Bulletin of Hispanic Studies*, 89.7 [special issue, *Beyond Slavery in the Iberian Atlantic*], 769–86
Sabine, Mark. 2001a. 'Form and Ideology in the Novels of José Saramago, 1980–1989' (unpublished doctoral dissertation, University of Manchester)
—— 2001b. '"Once but no Longer the Prow of Europe": National Identity and Portuguese Destiny in Jose Saramago's *The Stone Raft*', in *Portuguese Literary and Cultural Studies*, 6 (Spring) [special issue, *On Saramago*], 185–203
—— 2002. 'Re-incarnating the Poet: Pessoa, the Body and Society in José Saramago's *O Ano da Morte de Ricardo Reis*', *Journal of Romance Studies*, 2.2, 37–52
—— 2006. '*Raised from the Ground* after *One Hundred Years of Solitude*', in *In Dialogue with Saramago: Essays in Comparative Literature*, ed. by Adriana Alves de Paula Martins and Mark Sabine (Manchester: MSPS), pp. 141–61
—— 2011. 'Re-fitting the Lexicon of Resistance: Saramago, Symbolism and Dictatorship', in *Legacies of War and Dictatorship in Contemporary Spain and Portugal*, ed. by Alison Ribeiro de Meneses and Catherine O'Leary (Oxford and Bern: Peter Lang), pp. 39–65
—— 2012. 'Saramago's "other" Pessoas and "Pessoan" others: Heteronymic Creation and the Ethics of Alterity', in *Pessoa in an Intertextual Web: Influence and Innovation*, ed. by David G. Frier (Oxford: Legenda), pp. 148–71
Sabine, Mark, and Adriana Alves de Paula Martins. 2006. 'Introduction: Saramago and the Politics of Quotation', in *In Dialogue with Saramago: Essays in Comparative Literature*, ed. by Adriana Alves de Paula Martins and Mark Sabine (Manchester: MSPS), pp. 1–23
Santos, Rosemary Conceição dos. 2006. 'O mundo literário de José Saramago', *Literatura y Lingüística*, 17 (Santiago de Chile), 65–82. Available online at <http://www.scielo.cl/scielo.php?script=sci_arttext&pid=S0716-58112006000100005>_[accessed 22 November 2015]
Sapega, Ellen W. 1995. 'O papel da memória na construção de um novo sujeito nacional', *Luso-Brazilian Review*, 32.1, 31–40
—— 1996. 'Memória pública e discurso oficial: visões da época salazarista na obra de Irene Lisboa, José Saramago e Mário Cláudio', *Discursos: Estudos de língua e cultura portuguesa*, 14 (October), 99–113
—— 1997. 'No Longer Alone and Proud: Notes on the Rediscovery of the Nation in Contemporary Portuguese Fiction', in *After the Revolution: Twenty Years of Portuguese Literature*, ed. by Helena Kaufman and Anna Klobucka (Lewisburg, PA: Bucknell University Press), pp. 168–86
—— 2006. 'Saramago's "Genius": Camões, Adamastor, and Ricardo Reis', in *In Dialogue with Saramago: Essays in Comparative Literature*, ed. by Adriana Alves de Paula Martins and Mark Sabine (Manchester: MSPS), pp. 25–35
Seixo, Maria Alzira. 1999. '*História do Cerco de Lisboa* ou a respiração da sombra', in *Lugares de ficção em José Saramago: O Essencial e outros ensaios*, Temas Portugueses) (Lisbon: Imprensa Nacional — Casa da Moeda), pp. 73–82
Silva, Marisa Corrêa. 2002. 'José Saramago: o iberismo como utopia', *Acta Scientarum: Humanities & Social Sciences*, 24.1, 67–70
Silva, Teresa Cristina Cerdeira da. 1989. *José Saramago: uma saga de portugueses* (Lisbon: Dom Quixote)
—— 1996. 'Saramago e Redol: Referência e Reverência', in *José Saramago: il bagaglio dello scrittore*, ed. by Giulia Lanciani, Lusobrasilica: i protagonisti del racconto (Rome: Bulzoni), pp. 37–47

SIMÕES, MANUEL. 1996. 'Formas da cultura popular e irradiação semântica em *Levantado do Chão*', in *José Saramago: il bagaglio dello scrittore*, ed. by Giulia Lanciani (Rome: Bulzoni), pp. 73–82
VAKIL, ABDOOLKARIM. 2002. 'The Crusader Heritage: Portugal and Islam from Colonial to Post-Colonial Identities', in *Rethinking Heritage: Cultures and Politics in Europe*, ed. by Robert Shannon Peckham (London: I. B. Tauris), pp. 29–44
VALE, FRANCISCO. 1984. 'José Saramago sobre *O Ano da Morte de Ricardo Reis*: "Neste livro nada é verdade e nada é mentira"', *Jornal de Letras*, 121 (30 October), 2–3
VIÇOSO, VÍCTOR. 1999. '*Levantado do Chão* e o Romance Neo-Realista', *Colóquio-Letras*, 151–52 [special issue, *José Saramago: o ano de 1998*] (January–June), 239–48
VIEIRA, PATRÍCIA I. 2009. 'The Reason of Vision: Variations on Subjectivity in José Saramago's *Ensaio sobre a Cegueira*', *Luso-Brazilian Review*, 46.2 (December), 1–21
WITTMANN, LUZIA HELENA. 1997. 'Olhares sobre a natureza: José Saramago e o neo-realismo português', in *Nacionalismo e Regionalismo nas Literaturas Lusófonas*, ed. by F. Cristóvão, Maria de Lourdes Ferraz, and A. Carvalho (Lisbon: Cosmos), pp. 507–12

General Works

ANON. 1974. 'Herbert Marcuse', *Seara Nova*, 1542 (March), 17–22
ANON. 1980. *Y Mabinogion*, ed. by Dafydd Ifans and Rhiannon Ifans, with an intro. by Brynley F. Roberts (Llandysul: Gomer)
ANON. 1995. *Humberto Delgado: O General sem medo*, catalogue of exhibition at the Biblioteca-Museu República e Resistência, opened 10 February 1995 (Lisbon: Câmara Municipal de Lisboa, 1995)
ABELLÁN, JOSÉ LUIS. 1995. *El filósofo Antonio Machado* (Valencia: Pre-Textos)
ADORNO, THEODOR. 1998. *Beethoven: The Philosophy of Music*, ed. by Rolf Tiedemann, and trans. by Edmund Jephcott (Stanford, CA: Stanford University Press)
—— 2006. *Philosophy of the New Music*, trans. by Robert Hullot-Kentor (Minneapolis: Minnesota University Press)
AGAMBEN, GIORGIO. 2002. *Remnants of Auschwitz: The Witness and the Archive* (New York: Zone Books)
ALTHUSSER, LOUIS. 1969. 'The "Piccolo Teatro": Bertolazzi and Brecht', in *For Marx* (London and New York: Penguin), pp. 129–51
ALEGRE, MANUEL. 1971. *Um barco para Ítaca* (Lisbon: Sá de Costa, 1971)
—— 1984. 'Regresso a Ítaca', in *Chegar Aqui* (Lisbon: Sá de Costa), pp. 51–52
ALMEIDA, MIGUEL VALE DE. 2004. *An Earth-Colored Sea: 'Race', Culture and the Politics of Identity in the Post-Colonial Portuguese-speaking World* (New York and Oxford: Berghahn)
ANDERSON, BENEDICT. 1991. *Imagined Communities: Reflections on the Origin and Spread of Nationalism*, 2nd edn, revised and extended (London: Verso)
ANTUNES, ANTÓNIO LOBO. 1988. *As Naus* (Lisbon: Dom Quixote-Círculo de Leitores)
APPADURAI, ARJUN. 1996. *Modernity at Large: Cultural Dimensions of Globalization* (Minneapolis and London: University of Minnesota Press)
ARISTOTLE. 1925. *The Poetics of Aristotle*, ed. with notes and a translation by S. H. Butcher, 4th edn (London: Macmillan)
AUSONIUS, DECIMUS MAGNUS. 1991. *The Works of Ausonius*, ed. with an intro. and commentary by R. P. H. Green (Oxford: Clarendon)
BACON, FRANCIS. 1878. *Novum Organum*, ed. with an intro. by Thomas Fowler (Oxford: Clarendon Press)
BADIOU, ALAIN. 2005. *Handbook of Inaesthetics*, trans. by Alberto Toscano (Stanford, CA: Stanford University Press)
BAER, GEORGE W. 1967. *The Coming of the Italian–Ethiopian War* (Cambridge, MA: Harvard University Press)

BAKHTIN, MIKHAIL. 1973. *Problems of Dostoevsky's Poetics*, trans. by R. W. Rotsel (Ann Arbor, MI: Ardis)
—— 1981. 'Discourse in the Novel', in *The Dialogic Imagination: Four Essays*, ed. by Michael Holquist, trans. by Caryl Emerson and Michael Holquist (Austin: University of Texas Press), pp. 259–422
—— 1984. *Rabelais and his World*, trans. by Hélène Iswolsky (Bloomington: Indiana University Press)
BALDERSTON, DANIEL. 2006. 'Borges and Portuguese Literature', *Variaciones Borges*, 21, 157–73
BALL, GEORGE. 1982. *The Past Has Another Pattern* (New York and London: Norton)
BARATA, JOSÉ OLIVEIRA. 1997. 'The Historical Parable in Contemporary Portuguese Drama', in *After the Revolution: Twenty Years of Portuguese Literature*, ed. by Helena Kaufman and Anna Klobucka (Lewisburg, PA: Bucknell University Press), pp. 108–26
BARRY, PETER. 2002. *Beginning Theory: An Introduction to Literary and Cultural Theory*, 2nd edn (Manchester: Manchester University Press)
BARTHES, ROLAND. 1977. 'The Death of the Author', in *Image, Music, Text*, ed. and trans. by Stephen Heath (London: Fontana), pp. 142–48
BAUDRILLARD, JEAN. 1983A. *In the Shadow of the Silent Majorities, or, The End of the Social, and Other Essays* (New York: Semiotext(e))
—— 1983B. *Simulations* (New York, Semiotext(e))
—— 1995. *The Gulf War Did Not Take Place* (Bloomington: Indiana University Press)
BELSEY, *Critical Practice*, 2nd edn (London and New York: Routledge, 2002)
BENJAMIN, WALTER. 1973A. 'What is Epic Theatre?', in *Illuminations*, trans. by Harry Zohn, ed. with an intro. by Hannah Arendt (Glasgow: Fontana-Collins), pp. 149–56
—— 1973B. 'Theses on the Nature of History', in *Illuminations*, trans. by Harry Zohn, ed. with an intro. by Hannah Arendt (Glasgow: Fontana-Collins), pp. 255–66
—— 1985. 'Central Park', trans. by Lloyd Spencer and Mark Harrington, *New German Critique*, 34 (Winter), 32–58
—— 1999. *The Arcades Project*, ed. by Rolf Tiedemann, trans. by Howard Eiland and Kevin McLaughlin (Cambridge, MA, and London: Belknap Press–Harvard University Press)
BERNARD, J. P. A. 1972. *Le Parti Communiste et la question littéraire, 1921–1939* (Grenoble: Presses Universitaires de Grenoble)
BEST, STEVEN, and DOUGLAS KELLNER. 1991. *Postmodern Theory: Critical Interrogations* (New York: Guildford Press)
BIRMINGHAM, DAVID. 2003. *A Concise History of Modern Portugal*, 2nd edn (Cambridge: Cambridge University Press)
BLOOM, HAROLD. 1994. *The Western Canon: The Books and School of the Ages* (New York: Harcourt-Brace)
BOCA, ANGELO DEL. *The Ethiopian War, 1935–1941*, trans. by P. D. Cummins (Chicago, IL, and London: University of Chicago Press, 1965)
BORGES, JORGE LUIS. 1984. 'Carta a Fernando Pessoa', in *Boletim Bibliográfico*, 45.4, 39
—— 1997. 'La obra de Herbert Quain', in *Ficciones*, Biblioteca Borges (Madrid: Alianza)
BOURDON, ALBERT-ALAIN. 1986. 'L'Alentejo sous le regard de quelques romanciers néo-réalistes', in *L'Enseignement et l'expansion de la littérature portugaise en France: Actes du Colloque, Paris 21–23 Novembre 1985* (Paris: FCG, 1986), pp. 187–96
BRANDÃO, ANTÓNIO DE, FREI. 1944. *Crónica do Conde D. Henrique, D. Teresa e o Infante D. Afonso*, ed. with an intro. by A. de Magalhães Basto, Biblioteca Histórica — Série Régia (Porto: Livraria Civilização)
—— 1945. *Crónica de D. Afonso Henriques*, ed. with an intro. by A. de Magalhães Basto Biblioteca Histórica — Série Régia (Porto: Livraria Civilização)
BRECHT, BERTOLT. 1974. 'Against Georg Lukács', trans. by Stuart Hood, with an intro. by Terry Eagleton, *New Left Review*, 84 (March–April), 33–53

—— 1980. *The Life of Galileo*, ed. by John Willett and Ralph Manheim, trans. by John Willett, Bertolt Brecht Collected Plays (London: Eyre Methuen)

—— 1990. *A Short Organum for the Theatre*, in *Brecht on Theatre: The Development of an Aesthetic*, ed. and trans. by John Willett, 4th edn (London: Methuen Drama), pp. 179–205

BROOKS, RICHARD A. 1964. *Voltaire and Leibniz* (Geneva: Droz)

BRIOSA, JUAN. 2007. 'Antonio Machado y la tradición apócrifa', *Anales del Seminario de la Filosofía*, 24, 215–36

BURNEY, SIR CHARLES. 1782. *A General History of Music, from the Earliest Ages to the Present Day* (London: Robson & Robinson)

DAVID BUSHNELL, *The Making of Modern Colombia: A Nation in Spite of Itself* (Berkeley: California University Press)

CABRAL, AMÍLCAR. 1976A. 'National Liberation and Culture', in *The Return to the Source: Selected Speeches of Amílcar Cabral*, ed. by Africa Information Service (New York and London: Monthly Review Press), pp. 39–55

—— 1976B. 'The Return to the Source', in *The Return to the Source: Selected Speeches of Amílcar Cabral*, ed. by Africa Information Service (New York and London: Monthly Review Press), pp. 57–69

CALDEIRA, ALFREDO ET AL. 2011. *Aljube: a voz das vítimas* (Lisbon: Fundação Mário Soares)

CALDERÓN DE LA BARCA, PEDRO. 1959. *La vida es sueño*, in *Don Pedro Calderón de la Barca: Obras Completas*, ed. with a prologue and notes by Angel Valbuena Briones, 3 vols (Madrid: Aguilar), I: *Dramas*, pp. 357–98

CAMÕES, LUÍS VAZ DE. 1947. *Os Lusíadas*, in *Obras Completas*, ed. by Hernani Cidade, 5 vols (Lisbon: Sá de Costa, 1947), IV (Cantos 1–5)–V (Cantos 6–10)

—— 1980. *Lírica Completa*, ed., with a preface by Maria de Lurdes Saraiva, 2 vols (Lisbon: IN-CM)

CANN, JOHN P. 1997. *Counterinsurgency in Africa: The Portuguese Way of War, 1961–1974* (Westport, CT: Greenwood Press)

CARDOSO, JOÃO JOSÉ. 2012. 'A minha vida sexual com José Hermano Saraiva (com vídeo)'. Available online at <http://aventar.eu/2012/07/20/a-minha-vida-sexual-com-jose-hermano-saraiva-com-video/#more-1162395> [accessed 18 August 2015]

CARNARVON, JOHN HENRY GEORGE HERBERT, EARL OF. 1848. *Portugal and Gallicia* (London: Murray)

CARPENTIER, ALEJO. 1974. *Concierto barroco* (México DF: Siglo Veintiuno)

CASCAIS, ANTÓNIO FERNANDO. 2006. 'Diferentes como só nós: o associativismo GLBT português em três andamentos', *Revista Crítica de Ciências Sociais*, 76 [special issue, *Estudos queer: identidades, contextos e acção coletiva*], 109–26

CASTRO, MARIANA GRAY DE (ed.). 2013. *Fernando Pessoa's Modernity without Frontiers: Influences, Dialogues and Responses* (Woodbridge: Tamesis)

CELA-CONDE, C. 1999. 'Choosing between Two Conflicting Scientific Hypotheses: The Orce Dilemmas', *Human Evolution*, 14.1, 47–61

CHALMERS, JOHN. 1995. 'The Future Made Flesh: Swift and the Satiric Body', in *Jonathan Swift and the Burden of the Future* (Newark, NJ, and London: Associated University Presses), pp. 78–102

CIRURGIÃO, ANTÓNIO. 1990. *O 'Olhar esfíngico' da 'Mensagem' de Fernando Pessoa* (Lisbon: ICALP)

COELHO, JACINTO DO PRADO. 1949. *Diversidade e unidade em Fernando Pessoa* (Lisbon: Ed. da Revista *Occidente*)

COHEN, MITCHELL. 1992. 'Rooted Cosmopolitanism: Thoughts on the Left, Nationalism, and Multiculturalism', *Dissent*, 39.4 (Fall), 478–83

COLVIN, MICHAEL. 2008. *The Reconstruction of Lisbon: Severa's Legacy and the Rewriting of Urban History* (Lewisburg, PA: Bucknell University Press)
CONCEIÇÃO, CLÁUDIO DA, FREI. 1818. *Gabinete Histórico, que a Sua Magestade Fidelissima Sennhor Rei Dom João VI, no Felicissimo Dia dos seus Annos, offerece Cláudio da Conceição*, 8 vols (Lisbon: Imprensa Regia)
CONNELL, R. W. 1995. *Masculinities* (Cambridge: Polity)
CORTEZ, ALFREDO. 1936. *Tá Mar!* (Lisbon: Lucas)
CROSS, F. L., and E. A. LIVINGSTONE. 1983. *The Oxford Dictionary of the Christian Church*, 2nd rev'd edn (Oxford: Oxford University Press)
CULLER, JONATHAN. 1988. *Framing the Sign: Criticism and its Institutions* (Oxford: Basil Blackwell)
CUMMINS, J. S., and LUÍS DE SOUSA REBELO. 2001. 'The Controversy over Charles Boxer's Race Relations in the Portuguese Colonial Empire, 1415–1825', *Portuguese Studies*, 17 [special issue, *Homage to Charles Boxer*] (January), 233–46
CUNHA, CARLOS A. 1992. *The Portuguese Communist Party's Strategy for Power, 1921–1989* (New York and London: Garland)
CUNNINGHAM, SCOTT. 1987. *Encyclopedia of Magical Herbs* (St Paul, MN: Llewellyn)
DAVID, CHARLES W. (ed.). 2001. *The Conquest of Lisbon: De Expugnatione Lyxbonensi*, 2nd edn, with a translation by the editor, and a foreword by Jonathan Phillips (New York: University of Columbia Press)
DELILLE, MARIA MANUELA GOUVEIA. 1991. 'Bertolt Brecht em Portugal antes do 25 de Abril: um capítulo da história da resistência ao salazarismo', in *Do pobre B. B. em Portugal*, 2 vols (Aveiro: Estante), I, 27–58
DERRIDA, JACQUES. 1982. 'Différance', in *Margins of Philosophy*, trans. by Alan Bass (Chicago, IL: University of Chicago Press), pp. 3–27
—— 2002. 'Artifactualities', in Jacques Derrida and Bernard Steigler, *Echographies of Television*, trans. by Jennifer Bajorek (London: Polity), pp. 3–27
DIAMOND, ELIN. 1997. *Unmaking Mimesis* (London and New York: Routledge)
DIAS, MARINA TAVARES. 1997. *Lisboa nos Anos 40: Longe da Guerra* (Lisbon: Quimera)
DISNEY, A. R. 2009. *History of Portugal and the Portuguese Empire*, 2 vols (Cambridge and New York: Cambridge University Press, 2009)
DOWNS, CHARLES. 1979. '*Comissões de Moradores* and Urban Struggles in Revolutionary Portugal'. Unpublished and conjecturally dated, Arquivo do Centro de Documentação do 25 de Abril, Universidade de Coimbra, no. 220, 332.34 Dow
EAGLETON, TERRY. 1976. *Criticism and Ideology* (London: New Left Books)
—— 1981. 'Carnival and Comedy: Bakhtin and Brecht', in *Walter Benjamin, or Towards a Revolutionary Criticism* (London: New Left Books), pp. 143–72
—— 1985. 'Capitalism, Modernism and Postmodernism', *New Left Review*, 152, 60–73
ECO, UMBERTO. 1985. 'Reflections on *The Name of the Rose*', *Encounter*, 64 (April), 7–18
ENGELS, FREDERICK [Friedrich]. 2001. Letter to Margaret Harkness, early April 1888, in Karl Marx & Frederick Engels, *Collected Works*, 50 vols (London: Lawrence & Wishart), XLIX: *Frederick Engels: Letters, January 1887–July 1890*, pp. 166–69
ESSLIN, MARTIN. 1984. 'The Brechtian Theatre: Its Theory and Practice', in *Brecht: A Choice of Evils*, 4th edn (London and New York: Methuen), pp. 110–34
FAGUNDES, FRANCISCO COTA. 1980. 'Tese e Simbolismo em *Uma Abelha na Chuva*', *Colóquio-Letras*, 58, 20–28
FARIS, WENDY B. 1988. *Labyrinths of Language: Symbolic Landscape and Narrative Design in Modern Fiction* (Baltimore, MD: Johns Hopkins University Press)
FERREIRA, ANA PAULA. 1992. *Alves Redol e o Neo-Realismo Português* (Lisbon: Caminho)
—— 1996. 'Homeward Bound: The Construction of Femininity under the *Estado Novo*', *Portuguese Studies*, 12, 133–44

FERREIRA, VIRGÍNIA. 1998. 'Engendering Portugal: Social Change, State Politics and Women's Social Mobilization', in *Modern Portugal*, ed. by António Costa Pinto (Palo Alto, CA: Society for the Promotion of Science and Scholarship), pp. 162–88

FLOR, FERNANDO DE LA. 2002. *Barroco: representación e ideología en el mundo hispánico (1580–1680)* (Madrid: Cátedra)

FOLEY, BARBARA. 1986. *Telling the Truth: The Theory and Practice of Documentary Fiction* (Ithaca, NY, and London: Cornell University Press)

FORGACS, DAVID. 1986. 'Marxist Literary Theories', in *Modern Literary Theory: A Comparative Introduction*, ed. by Ann Jefferson and David Robey, 2nd edn (London: Batsford), pp. 166–203

FREIRE, A. SIQUEIRA, and J. CALVET DE MAGALHÃES. 1981. *Os movimentos de cooperação e integração europeia e a participação de Portugal nesses movimentos* (Oeiras: Instituto Nacional de Administração)

FREEMAN, MICHAEL. 1988. 'Portugal Past and Present: Aspects of Pessoa's Nationalism', in *Three Persons in One: A Centenary Tribute to Fernando Pessoa*, ed. by Bernard McGuirk (Nottingham: University of Nottingham), pp. 43–50

FRIER, DAVID (ed.). 2012. *Fernando Pessoa in an Intertextual Web: Influence and Innovation* (London: Legenda)

FRYE, NORTHROP. 1957. *Anatomy of Criticism* (Princeton, NJ: Princeton University Press)

FUKUYAMA, FRANCIS. 1992. *The End of History and the Last Man* (Harmondsworth: Penguin)

GALLAGHER, TOM. 1983. *Portugal: A Twentieth-century Interpretation* (Manchester: Manchester University Press)

GARCIA, MANUEL, and LOURDES MAURÍCIO, *O caso Delgado* (Lisbon: Expresso, 1977)

GIL, JOSÉ. 1988. *Fernando Pessoa ou la métaphysique des sensations* (Paris: Édition de la Différence)

—— 1999. *Diferença e negação na poesia de Fernando Pessoa* (Lisbon: Relógio d'Água)

—— 2004. *Portugal, hoje: o medo de existir* (Lisbon: Relógio d'Agua)

GIBERT, J., ET AL. 1989. 'Anatomical Study: Comparison of the Cranial Fragment from Venta Micena (Orce; Spain), with Fossil and Extant Mammals', *Human Evolution*, 4.4, 283–305

GOETHE, JOHANN WOLFGANG. 1988. 'Die Zauberlehrling', in *Johann Wolfgang Goethe: Sämtliche Werke nach Epochen seines Schaffens Münchner Ausgabe*, ed. by Karl Richter, 21 vols, IV: 'Wirkungen der Französischen Revolution 1791–1797: I', ed. by Reiner Wild (Munich and Vienna: Carl Hanser Verlag, 1988), pp. 874–77

GOMES, B., and TIAGO MOREIRA DE SÁ. 2008. *Carlucci v. Kissinger: os EUA e a revolução portuguesa* (Lisbon: Dom Quixote)

GORAK, JAN. 1991. *The Making of the Modern Canon: Genesis and Crisis of a Literary Idea* (London and Atlantic Highlands, NJ: Athlone)

GORDON, D. J. 1980. '"Veritas filia Temporis": Hadrianus Junius and Geoffrey Whitney', in *The Renaissance Imagination: Essays and Letters of D. J. Gordon*, ed. by Stephen Orgel (Berkeley: University of California Press), pp. 220–32

GRACIÁN, BALTASAR. 1980. *El criticón*, ed. with an intro. by Santos Alonso (Madrid: Cátedra)

GRAMSCI, ANTONIO. 1971A. 'On Bureaucracy', in *Selections from the Prison Notebooks of Antonio Gramsci*, ed. and trans. by Quintin Hoare and Geoffrey Nowell Smith (London: Lawrence & Wishart), pp. 185–90

—— 1971B. 'The Political Party', in *Selections from the Prison Notebooks*, pp. 147–57

—— 1971C. 'The Study of Philosophy: Some Preliminary Points of Reference', in *Selections from the Prison Notebooks*, pp. 323–43

HALBWACHS, MAURICE. 1992. *On Collective Memory*, ed. and trans. by Lewis Coser (Chicago, IL: University of Chicago Press)

HALL, A. RUPERT. 1979. 'Galileo nel XVIII secolo', *Rivista di filosofia*, 15, 375–78
HAMMOND, JOHN L. 1979. 'Electoral Behaviour and Political Militancy', in *Contemporary Portugal: The Revolution and its Antecedents*, ed. by Lawrence S. Graham and Harry M. Makler (Austin and London: University of Texas Press), pp. 257–80
HEGEL, GEORG WILHELM FRIEDRICH. 1975. *Lectures on the Philosophy of World History, Introduction: Reason in History*, ed. by James Hoffmeister, trans. by H. B. Nisbet, with an intro. by Duncan Forbes (Cambridge: Cambridge University Press)
—— 1977. *The Phenomenology of Spirit*, trans. with a commentary by A. V. Miller (Oxford: Clarendon)
HEIDEGGER, MARTIN. 1998. 'Plato's Doctrine of Truth', in *Pathmarks*, ed. by William McNeill (Cambridge: Cambridge University Press), pp. 155–82
HEMMING, LAURENCE PAUL. 2013. *Heidegger and Marx: A Productive Dialogue over the Language of Humanism* (Evanston, IL: Northwestern University Press)
HERCULANO, ALEXANDRE. 1980. *História de Portugal desde o começo da Monarquia até o fim do reinado de Afonso III*, ed. with a preface and notes by José Mattoso, 2 vols, Obras Completas de Alexandre Herculano (Amadora: Bertrand)
HERRICK, ROBERT. 1648. *Hesperides, or The Works both Humane and Divine of Robert Herrick, Esq.* (London: John Williams & Francis Eglesfield); facsimile edn published 1969 (Menston, West Yorkshire: Scolar Press)
HIGNETT, COLIN. 1988. 'The Censorship of Printed Books in Portugal, 1926–1974: A Select Bibliography', *Bulletin of Hispanic Studies*, 65.1 (January), 49–59
HOBBES, THOMAS. 1651. *Leviathan: or, The Matter, Form, and Power of a Common-wealth Ecclesiastical and Civil. By Thomas Hobbes of Malmesbury* (London: Andrew Crooke)
HOLLANDER, JOHN. 1961. *The Untuning of the Sky: Ideas of Music in English Poetry, 1500–1700* (Princeton, NJ, and London: Princeton University Press and Oxford University Press)
HOLTON, KIMBERLEY DA COSTA. 2005. *Performing Folklore: 'Ranchos Folclóricos' from Lisbon to Newark* (Bloomington: Indiana University Press)
HOMER. 1991. *The Odyssey*, trans. by E. V. Rieu, revised and ed. by D. C. H. Rieu with Peter V. Jones (Harmondsworth: Penguin)
HUTCHEON, LINDA. 1988. *A Poetics of Postmodernism: History, Theory, Fiction* (London and New York: Routledge)
INCLEDON, JOHN. 1986. 'Writing and Incest in *One Hundred Years of Solitude*', in *Critical Perspectives on Gabriel García Márquez*, ed. by Bradley A. Shaw and Nora Vera-Godwin (Lincoln, NE: University of Nebraska), pp. 51–64
IRAILH, AUGUSTIN SIMON. 1761. *Querelles Littéraires, ou Mémoires pour server à l'histoire des révolutions de la république des lettres* (Paris: Durand)
JACKSON, K. DAVID. 2010. *Adverse Genres in Fernando Pessoa* (Oxford and New York: Oxford University Press)
JAMESON, FREDRIC. 1991. *Post-Modernism, or The Cultural Logic Of Late Capitalism* (Durham, NC: Duke University Press)
—— 2007. *Archaeologies of the Future: The Desire called Utopia and Other Science Fictions*, 2nd edn (London and New York: Verso)
JELINSKI, JACK B. 1984. 'Memory and the Remembered Structure of *Cien Años de Soledad*', *Revista de Estudios Hispánicos*, 18.3, 323–33
JEREZ-FERRÁN, CARLOS, and SAMUEL ARAGO (eds). 2010. *Unearthing Franco's Legacy: Mass Graves and the Recovery of Historical Memory in Spain* (Notre Dame, IN: University of Notre Dame Press)
JOÃO, MARIA ISABEL. 2002. 'Public Memory and Power in Portugal, 1880–1960', *Portuguese Studies*, 18, 96–120
JOHNSTON, ARTHUR (ed.). 1965. *Francis Bacon* (London: Batsford)
KAUFMAN, HELENA, and ANNA KLOBUCKA. 1997. 'Politics and Culture in Postrevolutionary

Portugal', in *After the Revolution: Twenty Years of Portuguese Literature* (Lewisburg, PA: Bucknell University Press), pp. 13–30

KAYMAN, MARTIN. 1987. *Revolution and Counter-Revolution in Portugal* (London and Wolfeboro, NH: Merlin)

KELLNER, DOUGLAS. 1984. *Herbert Marcuse and the Crisis of Marxism*, Contemporary Social Theory (London: Macmillan)

KIRKPATRICK, RALPH. 1953. *Domenico Scarlatti* (Princeton, NJ: Princeton University Press)

KLOBUCKA, ANNA [M.]. 2002. 'Lusotropical Romance: Camões, Gilberto Freyre, and the Isle of Love', *Portuguese Literary & Cultural Studies*, 9 [special issue, *Post-Colonial Camões*] (Fall), 121–38

—— 2013. 'The Solitary Reaper between Men (and Some Women)', in *Fernando Pessoa's Modernity without Frontiers: Influences, Dialogues and Responses*, ed. by Mariana Gray de Castro (Woodbridge: Tamesis), pp. 101–12

KLOBUCKA, ANNA M., and MARK SABINE (eds). 2007. 'Introduction: Pessoa's Bodies', in *Embodying Pessoa: Corporeality, Gender, Sexuality*, ed. by Anna M. Klobucka and Mark Sabine (Toronto: Toronto University Press), pp. 3–36

KOLLONTAI, ALEXANDRA. 1977. 'Communism and the Family', in *Alexandra Kollontai: Selected Writings*, trans. and ed. with an intro. by Alix Holt (London: Allison and Busby), pp. 250–60

KORHONEN, KUISMA. 2006. 'General Introduction: The History/Literature Debate', in *Tropes for the Past: Hayden White and the History/Literature Debate* (Amsterdam and New York: Rodopi), pp. 9–20

LACAN, JACQUES. 2006. 'The Mirror Stage as Formative of the Function of the *I* as Revealed in Psychoanalytic Experience', in *Écrits*, trans. by Bruce Fink, with Héloïse Fink and Russell Grigg (New York and London: Norton), pp. 75–80

LACLAU, ERNESTO, and CHANTAL MOUFFE. 1985. *Hegemony and Socialist Strategy: Towards a Radical Democratic Politics* (London: Verso)

LE GOFF, JACQUES, and PIERRE NORA (eds). 1985. *Constructing the Past: Essays in Historical Methodology* (Cambridge: Cambridge University Press)

LEIBNIZ, GOTTFRIED WILHELM. 1898. *The Monadology and Other Philosophical Writings*, trans. with an intro. and notes by Robert Latta (Oxford: Clarendon Press)

—— 1951. *Theodicy*, trans. and ed. by A. Farrer (London: Routledge, 1951)

LESLIE, ESTHER. 2000. *Walter Benjamin: Overpowering Conformism* (London and Sterling, VA: Pluto)

LIVERMORE, HAROLD. 1990. 'The "Conquest of Lisbon" and Its Author', *Portuguese Studies*, 6, 1–16

LOURENÇO, ANTÓNIO APOLINÁRIO. 1995. *Identidade e alteridade em Fernando Pessoa e Antonio Machado* (Braga: Angelus Novus)

LOURENÇO, EDUARDO. 1973. *Fernando Pessoa revisitado: leitura estruturante do drama em gente* (Porto: Inova)

—— 1978. *O Labirinto da saudade: psicanálise mítica do destino português* (Lisbon: Dom Quixote)

—— 1994. 'Identidade e memória', in *Nós e a Europa*, Temas Portugueses (Lisbon: IN-CM), pp. 9–15

—— 2000. *O labirinto da saudade: psicanálise mística do destino português*, revised edn (Lisbon: Gradiva)

LOWENTHAL, DAVID. 1985. *The Past is a Foreign Country* (Cambridge: Cambridge University Press)

LUIS DE LEÓN, FRAY. 1982. *Fray Luis de León: Poesías*, ed. with an intro., notes and a bibliography by Oreste Macrí, 2nd edn (Barcelona: Editorial Crítica)

LUKÁCS, GEORG [György]. 1950. 'Balzac: *The Peasants*', in *Studies in European Realism*, trans. by Edith Bone, with a foreword by Roy Pascal (London: Hillway), pp. 21–46

—— 1962. *The Historical Novel*, trans. by Hannah and Stanley Mitchell (London: Merlin Press)
—— 1971. *The Theory of the Novel*, trans. by A. Bostock (London: Merlin)
LYOTARD, FRANÇOIS. 1984. *The Postmodern Condition: A Report on Knowledge* (Manchester: University of Manchester Press)
—— 1988. *The Differend: Phrases in Dispute*, trans. by Georges Van Den Abbeele, with a forward by Wlad Godzich (Manchester: Manchester University Press)
MACHADO, ANTONIO. 1989. *Obras Completas*, ed. by Oreste Macrí, with Gaetano Chiappini, 2 vols, Clásicos castellanos (Madrid: Espasa-Calpe, 1989)
MACNICOL, FRED. 1978. *Hungarian Cookery* (London: Penguin-Allen Lane)
MADUREIRA, N. L. 2007. 'Cartelization and Corporatism: Bureaucratic Rule in Authoritarian Portugal, 1926–1945', *Journal of Contemporary History*, 42.1, 79–96
MAGALHÃES, MARIA JOSÉ, 'Movimentos feministas em Portugal, 1970–2007', paper given at the conference 'As Faces de Eva: Perspectivas sobre a Mulher Portuguesa (1908–2007)', Vila Nova de Famalicão, 30 November. Available online at <https://www.researchgate.net/publication/259647794_Movimentos_feministas_em_Portugal_1970-2007> [accessed 1 December 2015]
MAGALHÃES, MARIA JOSÉ, MANUELA TAVARES and MARIA DO MAR PEREIRA. 2014. 'Three Decades to Legalize Abortion in Portugal', paper delivered at the international conference 'ABORTION: The Unfinished Revolution', University of Prince Edward Island, Charlottetown, 8 August. Available online at <https://www.researchgate.net/publication/266969264_THREE_DECADES_TO_LEGALIZE_ABORTION_IN_PORTUGAL> [accessed 12 December 2015]
MAGALHÃES, J. CALVET DE. 1987. 'Portugal e a integração europeia', *Estratégia*, 4 (Winter, 1987–88), 33–74
MALLETT, ROBERT. *Mussolini and the Origins of the Second World War, 1933–1940* (Basingstoke: Palgrave–Macmillan, 2003)
MANUEL, PAUL CHRISTOPHER, and MAURYA N. TOLLEFSEN. 2008. 'Roman Catholicism, Secularization, and the Recovery of Traditional Communal Values: The 1998 and 2007 Referenda on Abortion in Portugal', *South European Society and Politics*, 13.1, 117–219
MARAVALL, JOSÉ ANTONIO. 1975. *La cultura del Barroco: análisis de una estructura histórica*, Letras e ideas, 7 (Esplugues de Llobregat: Ariel)
MARCUSE, HERBERT. 1966. 'The Individual in the Great Society: Rhetoric and Reality' (part 1), *Alternatives*, 1.1 (March–April), 14–20
—— 1968A. 'The Affirmative Character of Culture', in *Negations: Essays in Critical Theory* (London: Allen Lane–Penguin)
—— 1968B. 'Liberation from the Affluent Society', in *To Free a Generation: The Dialectics of Liberation*, ed. by David Cooper (Baltimore, MD: Penguin), pp. 175–92
—— 1969A. *Eros and Civilisation: A Philosophical Inquiry into Freud*, new edn, Humanitas: Beacon Studies in Humanities (London: Allen Lane)
—— 1969B. *An Essay on Liberation* (Boston, MA: Beacon)
—— 1969C. 'The Realm of Freedom and the Realm of Necessity: A Reconsideration', *Praxis*, 5, 20–25
—— 1970A. 'The End of Utopia', *Ramparts*, 4 (April), 28–34. On-line edition available online at <http://www.marxists.org/reference/archive/marcuse/works/1967/end-utopia.htm> [accessed 1 August 2013]
—— 1970B. *Five Lectures* (Boston, MA: Beacon)
—— 1972. *Counterrevolution and Revolt* (Boston, MA: Beacon)
—— 1973A. 'On the Philosophical Foundation of the Concept of Labour in Economics' (trans. of the 1933 essay 'Über die philosophischen Grundlagen des wirtschaftswissenschaftlichen Arbeitsbegriffs'), *Telos*, 16 (Summer), 9–37

—— 1973B. 'A Revolution in Values', in *Political Ideologies*, ed. by James A. Gould and Willis Truitt (New York: Macmillan), pp. 331–36
—— 1974. 'Marxism and Feminism', *Women's Studies*, 2.3, 279–88
—— 1991. *One Dimensional Man: Studies in the Ideology of Advanced Industrial Society*, 2nd edn, with an intro. by Douglas Kellner (London and New York: Routledge)
—— 2005. *Heideggerian Marxism*, ed. by Richard Wolin and John Abromeit (Lincoln, NE and London: University of Nebraska Press)
MARQUES, OLIVEIRA. 1972A. *História de Portugal*, 2 vols (Lisbon: Ágora)
—— 1972B. *History of Portugal*, 2 vols (New York and London: Columbia University Press, 1972)
MÁRQUEZ, GABRIEL GARCÍA. 1967. *Cien años de soledad* (Buenos Aires: Sudamérica)
—— 1978. *One Hundred Years of Solitude*, trans. by Gregory Rabassa (London: Picador)
MARTIN, GERALD. 1987. 'On "Magical" and Social Realism in García Márquez', in *Gabriel García Márquez: New Readings*, ed. by Bernard McGuirk and Richard Cardwell (Cambridge: Cambridge University Press), pp. 95–116
MARTINHO, JOSÉ. 2003. 'Sobre a recepção de Freud em Portugal', *Metacrítica*, 3 (March), online at <http://revistas.ulusofona.pt/index.php/metacritica/article/view/2732/2086>
MARTINS, LUÍS ALMEIDA. 2011. 'As grandes mentiras da história portuguesa', *Visão*, 24 August. Available online at <http://visao.sapo.pt/actualidade/sociedade/as-grandes-mentiras-da-historia-de-portugal=f618163> [accessed 1 December 2015]
MASON, HAYDN. 1992. *Candide: Optimism Demolished* (New York: Twayne)
MAXWELL, KENNETH. 1995. *The Making of Portuguese Democracy* (Cambridge: Cambridge University Press)
MCGUIRK, BERNARD. 1988. 'Pessoa and the "Affective Fallacy"', in *Three Persons in One: A Centenary Tribute to Fernando Pessoa*, ed. by Bernard McGuirk (Nottingham: University of Nottingham), pp. 36–42
MCGUIRK, BERNARD (ed.). 1988. *Three Persons on One: A Centenary Tribute to Fernando Pessoa* (Nottingham: University of Nottingham)
MCKENDRICK, MELVEENA. 1974. *Woman and Society in the Spanish Drama of the Golden Age: A Study of the 'Mujer Varonil'* (Cambridge: Cambridge University Press)
MCNEE, MALCOLM. 1999. 'An Intertextual Intertwining of Mystic Nationalisms: Saramago's Post-Modern Challenge to the Pessoan and Salazarist Discourses in *O Ano da Morte de Ricardo Reis*', *Lucero*, 10, 57–66
MEDEIROS, PAULO DE. 2013. *Pessoa's Geometry of the Abyss: Modernity and the 'Book of Disquiet'* (Oxford: Legenda)
MENESES, FILIPE RIBEIRO DE. 2010. *Salazar: A Political Biography* (New York: Enigma)
MEZQUITA, EDUARDO PASCUAL. 2003. *La Política del Último Unamuno* (Salamanca: Anthema)
MIGUÉIS, JOSÉ RODRIGUES. 1962. *Gente da Terceira Classe: Contos e Novelas*, Colecção Latitude (Lisbon: Estúdios Cor)
MIRANDA, RUI GONÇALVES. 2007. 'Constructed Happiness: On the Seductions of Messianism — Portugal with or without Sebastian', in *Happiness and Post-Conflict*, ed. by Bernard McGuirk and Constance Goh (Nottingham: Critical, Cultural and Communications Press), pp.131–43
—— 2010. *A Casa por Fabricar: Aspects and Spectres of a Portuguesely I* (unpublished doctoral thesis, University of Nottingham)
—— 2014. 'Cesário Verde: *Sentimento* as a Radical Politics of Literature' (unpublished seminar paper, University of Nottingham)
MÓNICA, MARIA FILOMENA. 1978. *Educação e sociedade no Portugal de Salazar* (Lisbon: Presença-GIS)
MONTAIGNE, MICHEL DE. 1979. 'De l'experience', *Essais, Livre III*, ed. with an intro. by Alexandre Micha (Paris: Garnier-Flammarion), pp. 275–328

MONTEIRO, GEORGE. 2000. *Fernando Pessoa and Nineteenth-Century Anglo-American Literature* (Lexington: University Press of Kentucky)
GEORGE MONTEIRO (ed.). 1982. *The Man Who Never Was: Essays on Fernando Pessoa* (Providence, RI: Gávea-Brown)
MONTEIRO, PADRE MANUEL. 1749. *Elogios dos Reys de Portugal de nome de João* (Lisbon: Francisco da Silva)
MORCILLO, AURORA G. 2010. *The Seduction of Modern Spain: The Female Body and the Francoist Body Politic* (Lewisburg, PA: Bucknell University Press)
MORRISON, RODNEY J. 1981. *Portugal: Revolutionary Change in an Open Economy* (Boston, MA: Auburn House)
NAMORA, FERNANDO. N.D. [1963]. *O trigo e o joio*, 4th edn (Lisbon: Arcádia)
NAVASCUÉS, FAUSTINO MENÉNDEZ PIDAL DE. 1982. *Heráldica medieval española* (Madrid: Hidalguía)
NEWITT, MALYN. 1981. *Portugal in Africa: The Last Hundred Years* (London: Hurst)
NORA, PIERRE. 1996. 'The Era of Commemoration' in *Realms of Memory: The Construction of the French Past, Vol. III, 'Symbols'*, ed. by Lawrence Kritzman and trans. by Arthur Goldhammer (New York: Columbia University Press), pp. 609–37
Ó, JORGE RAMOS DO. 2008. *Os anos de Ferro: o dispositivo cultural durante a política do espírito, 1933–1949* (Lisbon: Estampa)
OLIVEIRA, CARLOS DE. 1987. *Uma abelha na chuva* (Lisbon: Sá de Costa)
OSKAMP, H. P. A. 1970. *The Voyage of Máel Dúin: A Study in Early Irish Voyage Literature Followed by an Edition of Immram Curaig Máele Dúin from the Yellow Book of Lecan in Trinity College, Dublin* (Groningen: Wolters-Noordhof)
OUSMANE, SEMBÈNE. 1966. *Les Bouts de bois de Dieu* (Paris: Presses Pocket)
OVID (Publius Ovidius Naso). 1970. *Metamorphoses: Book VIII*, ed. with an intro. and commentary by A. S. Hollis (Oxford: Clarendon)
PALACIOS, MARCO. 2006. *Between Legitimacy and Violence: A History of Colombia, 1875–2002* (Durham, NC, and London: Duke University Press)
PALMER, BRYAN. 1997. 'Critical Theory, Historical Materialism, and the Ostensible End of Marxism: The Poverty of Theory Revisited', in *The Postmodern Theory Reader*, ed. by Keith Jenkins (New York: Psychology Press), pp. 103–13
PATRÍCIO, MARIA TERESA, and ALAN STOLEROFF. 1993. 'The Portuguese Communist Party: Loyalty to the "Communist Ideal"', in *Western European Communists and the Collapse of Communism*, ed. by D. S. Bell (Oxford and Providence, RI: Berg), pp. 69–85
PAZ, OCTAVIO. 1983. 'El desconocido de si mismo', in *Los signos en rotación y otros ensayos* (Madrid: Alianza, 1983), pp. 105–28
PEREIRA, JOSÉ FERNANDES. 1994. *Arquitectura e escultura de Mafra: retórica da perfeição* (Lisbon: Presença)
PESSOA, FERNANDO [Nogueira]. 1928. 'Tábua bibliográfica', *presença*, 17 (December), 10
—— 1978. *Sobre Portugal: introdução ao problema nacional*, ed. with an intro. by Joel Serrão (Lisbon: Ática)
—— 1980. *'Ultimatum' e Páginas de sociologia política*, ed. by Joel Serrão (Lisbon: Ática)
—— 1982. *O Livro do desassossego por Bernardo Soares*, transcribed by Maria Aliete Galhoz and Teresa Sobral Cunha, and ed. by Jacinto do Prado Coelho (Lisbon: Ática)
—— 1986A. *Obra poética e em prosa*, ed. by António Quadros (Porto: Lello & Irmão)
—— 1986B. *Páginas de pensamento político*, ed. by António Quadros, 2 vols (Mem Martins: Europa-América)
—— 1986C. *Poems of Fernando Pessoa*, trans. and ed. by Edwin Honig and Susan M. Brown (New York: Ecco)
—— 1990. *Livro do desassossego por Vicente Guedes e Bernardo Soares*, transcribed and ed. by Teresa Sobral Cunha, 2 vols (Lisbon: Presença)

―― 1995. *A Centenary Pessoa*, ed. by Eugénio Lisboa, with A. C. Taylor (Manchester: Carcanet)
―― 1998. *Fernando Pessoa & Co.*, ed. and trans. by Richard Zenith (New York: Grove)
―― 1999. *Correspondência, 1923–1935*, ed. by Manuela Parreira da Silva (Lisbon: Assírio & Alvim)
―― 2001. *The Selected Prose of Fernando Pessoa*, ed. and trans. by Richard Zenith (New York: Grove)
―― 2002A. *Álvaro de Campos: Poesia*, ed. by Teresa Rita Lopes, Obras de Fernando Pessoa, 16 (Lisbon: Assírio & Alvim)
―― 2002B. *The Book of Disquiet*, ed. with an intro. by Richard Zenith (London and New York: Penguin)
―― 2004. *Mensagem*, ed. by Fernando Cabral Martins, 4th edn (Lisbon: Assírio & Alvim)
―― 2003. *Ricardo Reis: Prosa*, ed. by Manuela Parreira da Silva (Lisbon: Assírio & Alvim)
―― 2006A. *A Little Larger than the Entire Universe: Selected Poems*, ed. and trans. by Richard Zenith, Penguin Classics (London and New York: Penguin, 2006)
―― 2006B. *Poesia do Eu*, ed. by Richard Zenith (Lisbon: Assírio & Alvim)
―― 2007. *Ricardo Reis: Poesia*, ed. by Manuela Parreira da Silva, 2nd edn, Obras de Fernando Pessoa, 15 (Lisbon: Assírio & Alvim)
―― 2009. *O Livro do Desassossego, composto por Bernardo Soares, ajudante de guarda-livros na cidade de Lisboa*, ed. by Richard Zenith, 8th edn, Obras de Fernando Pessoa, 4 (Lisbon: Assírio & Alvim)
PIMENTEL, ALBERTO. 2009. *As amantes de D. João V* (Lisbon: Bonecos Rebeldes)
PIMENTEL, IRENE FLUNSER. 2002. 'Women's Organizations and Imperial Ideology under the Estado Novo', *Portuguese Studies*, 18, 121–31
PINA, LUÍS DE. 1986. *História do cinema português* (Mem Martins: Europa-América)
PINTO, ANTÓNIO COSTA. 1995. *Salazar's Dictatorship and European Fascism* (Boulder, CO: Social Science Monographs)
―― 2013. 'Para acabar de vez com a Lusofonia', published on-line in *Buala: Cultura contemporânea Africana* <www.buala.org/pt/a-ler/para-acabar-de-vez-com-a-lusofonia> [accessed 12 February 2013]
PINTO, ANTÓNIO COSTA (ed.). 1998. *Modern Portugal* (Palo Alto: Society for the Promotion of Science and Scholarship)
PINTO, ANTÓNIO COSTA, and MARIA INÁCIA REZOLA. 2008. 'Political Catholicism, Crisis of Democracy, and Salazar's New State in Portugal', in *Clerical Fascism in Interwar Europe*, ed. by Matthew Feldman and Marius Turda, with Turor Georgescu (Oxford and New York: Routledge), pp. 141–56
PIRES, JOSÉ CARDOSO. 1972. 'Changing a Nation's Way of Thinking', *Index on Censorship*, 1.1, 93–106
PITA, ANTÓNIO PEDRO. 1983. 'Neo-Realismo: ideologia e estética (A propósito de *O discurso ideológico do Neo-Realismo português* de Carlos Reis)', *Vértice*, 43 (July–August), 18–30
―― 1989. 'Conflito e unidade do neo-realismo português: a "polémica interna do neo-realismo" e a difusão do marxismo em Portugal', *Vértice*, 21 (December), 43–47
―― 2002. *Conflito e unidade no Neo-Realismo português: arqueologia de uma problemática* (Porto: Campo das Letras)
PLATO. 1994. *Republic*, trans. with an intro. by Robin Waterfield, 2nd edn (Oxford and New York: Oxford University Press)
PONTE, BRUNO DA, (attrib.). 1975. 'Housing Struggles in Portugal'. Unpublished and conjecturally dated, Arquivo do Centro de Documentação do 25 de Abril, Universidade de Coimbra, no. 167, 333.32 Pon
PRADO, JOÃO DE SÃO JOSÉ DO, FREI. 1751. *Monumento sacro da fabrica e solemnissima Sagração*

da Santa Basilica do Real Convento, que junto à villa de Mafra dedicou a N. Senhora e Santo António, a Majestade Augusta do Maximo Rey D. João V (Lisbon: Miguel Rodrigues)
PRAZ, MARIO. 1964. *Studies in Seventeenth-century Imagery*, 2nd edn (Roma: Edizioni di Storia e Letteratura)
PRESTON, PAUL. 2006. *The Spanish Civil War: Reaction, Revolution, and Revenge* (London and New York: Harper-Perennial)
QUEIRÓS, JOSÉ MARIA EÇA DE. 1972. *O crime do Padre Amaro*, ed. by Isabel dos Santos (Lisbon: Livros do Brasil)
—— 1980. *Os Maias* (Belo Horizonte: Itatiaia)
QUENTAL, ANTERO DE. 1982. 'Causas da decadência dos povos peninsulares nos últimos três séculos', in *Antero de Quental: Prosas sócio-políticas*, ed. by Joel Serrão, Colecção Pensamento Português (Lisbon: IN-CM), pp. 255–96
RABY, D. L. 1988. *Fascism and Resistance in Portugal: Communists, Liberals, and Military Dissidents in the Opposition to Salazar, 1941–1974* (Manchester: Manchester University Press)
RANCIÈRE, JACQUES. 2010. 'The Politics of Literature', in *Dissensus: On Politics and Aesthetics*, ed. and trans. by Steven Corcoran (London: Continuum), pp. 152–68
REDOL, ALVES. 1945. *Gaibéus*, 4th edn (Lisbon: Inquérito)
—— 1965. *Gaibéus*, 6th edn (Lisbon: Europa-América)
—— 1970. *Barranco de cegos*, 2nd edn (Lisbon: Portugália)
REIS, ANTÓNIO. 1973. *Marcuse e a teoria da revolução* (Coimbra: separatum from *Boletim de Ciências Económicas*, 16)
REIS, CARLOS. 1983. *O discurso ideológico do Neo-Realismo português* (Coimbra: Almedina)
RENSHAW, LAYLA. 2011. *Exhuming Loss: Memory, Materiality and Mass Graves of the Spanish Civil War* (Walnut Creek, CA: Left Coast Press)
RIBEIRO, ANABELA MOTA. 2009. 'A sorte de sermos os dois tão transgressores, tão rebeldes. Entrevista com Pilar del Rio', *Público*, 15 November 2009. Available online at <http://www.publico.pt/sup-publica/jornal/pilar-del-rio-a-sorte-e-sermos-os-dois-tao-transgressores--tao-rebeldes-18147924> [accessed 18 March 2014]
RIBEIRO, FILIPA PERDIGÃO. 2013. '"Uma revolução democrática é sempre uma revolução inacabada": Commemorating the Portuguese 1974 Revolution in Newspaper Opinion Texts'. Available online at <https://sapientia.ualg.pt/bitstream/10400.1/1412/1/A%20democratic%20revolution%20-%20F.%20Ribeiro.pdf> [accessed 18 March 2014]
RICHMOND, KATHLEEN. 2003. *Women and Spanish Fascism: The Women's Section of the Falange, 1934–1959* (London and New York: Routledge)
ROBERTS, STEPHEN. 2007. *Miguel de Unamuno o La creación del intelectual español moderno* (Salamanca: Universidad de Salamanca)
ROBINSON, R. A. H. 1979. *Contemporary Portugal: A History* (London: George Allen & Unwin)
RODRÍGUEZ, ALBERTO PENA. 2012. '"Tudo pela nação": Salazar, la creación del Secretariado de Propaganda Nacional y la censura', *Hispania: Revista Española de Historia*, 72 (January–April), 177–204
ROIG, J. FERNANDO. 1958. *Simbología Cristiana* (Barcelona: Juan Flors)
ROSAS, FERNANDO, ET AL. 1992. *Portugal e o Estado Novo*, Nova História de Portugal, XII, (Lisbon: Presença)
ROSAS, FERNANDO, and J. M. BRANDÃO DE BRITO (eds). 1996. *Dicionário da história do Estado Novo*, 2 vols (Venda Nova: Bertrand)
ROSS, CHRISTOPHER J. 2002. *Contemporary Spain: A Handbook*, 2nd edn (London: Arnold)
SABINE, MARK. 2009. 'Uma Penélope pós-colonial: des(a)fiando a odisseia lusa', in *António Lobo Antunes*, ed. by Ana Paula Arnaut, Cânone, 5 (Lisbon: Edições Setenta), pp. 170–74
SABINE, MARK, and CLAIRE WILLIAMS. 2010. 'Writing after the Dictatorship', in *A*

Companion to Portuguese Literature, ed. by Stephen Parkinson, Thomas F. Earle and Cláudia Pazos Alonso (Oxford: Tamesis), pp. 182–201

SADIE, STANLEY (ed.). 1980. *The New Grove Dictionary of Music*, 20 vols (London: Macmillan)

SADLIER, DARLENE. 1998. *An Introduction to Fernando Pessoa: Modernism and the Paradoxes of Authorship* (Gainesville: University Press of Florida)

SAID, EDWARD W. 2001. *Orientalism: Western Conceptions of the Orient*, new ed., with an Afterword (New Delhi: Penguin)

SALCEDO, EMILIO. 1964. *Vida de Don Miguel* (Salamanca: Anaya)

SALDÍVAR, JOSÉ DAVID. 1985. 'Ideology and Deconstruction in Macondo', *Latin American Literary Review*, 13.25, 29–43

SALGADO, ABÍLIO JOSÉ. 1993. *A situação da mulher na sociedade portuguesa actual: os preconceitos e a luta pela emancipação* (Lisbon: Iniciativas Editoriais)

SANTOS, BOAVENTURA DE SOUSA, 1985. 'Estado e sociedade na semiperiferia do sistema mundial: o caso português', *Análise Social*, 21.87–89, 869–901

SANTOS, F. REIS. 1930. 'O movimento republicano e a consciência nacional', in *História do regime republicano em Portugal*, ed. by Luís de Montalvor, 2 vols (Lisbon: Ática), I, 261–338

SANTOS, IRENE RAMALHO. 2003. *Atlantic Poets: Fernando Pessoa's Turn in Anglo-American Modernism* (Hanover, NH: University Press of New England)

SANTARENO, BERNARDO. 1984. *'O Judeu' e 'A Traição do Padre Martinho'*, in *Obras Completas de Bernardo Santareno*, ed. with an epilogue and notes by Luís Francisco Rebello, 4 vols (Lisbon: Caminho), III

SAPEGA, ELLEN W. 2002. 'Image and Counter-Image: The Place of Salazarist Images of National Identity in Contemporary Portuguese Visual Culture', *Luso-Brazilian Review*, 39.2, *Portuguese Cultural Studies* (Winter), 45–64

SARDUY, SEVERO. 1974. *Barroco* (Buenos Aires: Sudamericana)

SAUNDERS, ALISON. 2000. *The Seventeenth-Century Emblem: A Study in Diversity* (Geneva: Droz)

SEABRA, JOSÉ AUGUSTO. 1985. *O heterotexto pessoano* (Lisbon: Dinalivro)

—— 1996. *O coração do texto/ Le Cœur du texte: novos ensaios pessoanos* (Lisbon: Cosmos)

SENA, JORGE DE. 1981. *Fernando Pessoa & Ca. heterónima*, 2 vols (Lisbon: Edições 70)

SERRÃO, JOEL. *Fernando Pessoa: cidadão do imaginário* (Lisbon: Horizonte)

SILVA, GARCEZ DA. 1990. *Alves Redol e o grupo Neo-Realista de Vila Franca* (Lisbon: Caminho)

SOARES, ANTÓNIO GOUCHA. 2012. 'Portugal: An Incomplete Europeanization', in *Portugal in the Twenty-First Century: Politics, Society, and Economics*, ed. by Sebastián Royo (Lanham, MD: Lexington Books), pp. 121–43

SPEAKE, JENNIFER. 1994. *The Dent Dictionary of Symbols in Christian Art* (London: Dent)

SPIVAK, GAYATRI CHAKRABORTY. 1995. 'Can the Subaltern Speak?' (version abbreviated by the author), in *The Post-Colonial Studies Reader*, ed. by Bill Ashcroft et al. (London and New York: Routledge), pp. 28–37

STEINER, GEORGE. 1996. 'Foursome', *The New Yorker*, 8 January, pp. 76–79

STEVENSON, ROBERT LOUIS. 1886. *The Strange Case of Doctor Jekyll and Mr Hyde* (London: Longmans, Green, & Co.)

STTAU MONTEIRO, LUÍS DE. 1963. *Felizmente há luar!*, 5th edn (Lisbon: Ática)

SWIDERSKI, LILIANA NOEMÍ. 2006. *Antonio Machado e Fernando Pessoa: el gesto ambiguo — sobre apócrifos y heterónimos* (Mar de la Plata: Martín-Eudem)

TAVARES, MANUELA. 2000. *Movimentos de mulheres em Portugal: décadas de 70 e 80* (Lisbon: Horizonte)

TAVARES, MANUELA, MARIA JOSÉ MAGALHÃES, and DEIRDRÉE MATHEE. 2009. 'Feminismo(s)

e marxismo: um casamento "mal sucedido"? Os novos desafios para uma corrente política de esquerda dos feminismos', *Revista Virus*, 5 (January–February). Available online at <http://www.revistavirus.net/arquivo/8-virus-5-jan-fev-2009> [accessed 1 December 2015]

TERRY, ARTHUR. 2003. *Antonio Machado: Campos de Castilla*, Critical Guides to Spanish Texts (London: Grant & Cutler)

THOMAS, HUGH. *The Spanish Civil War*, 3rd edn (London: Hamish Hamilton, 1977)

TIERSKY, RONALD. 1985. *Ordinary Stalinism: Democratic Centralism and the Question of Communist Political Development* (Boston, MA, and London: Allen & Unwin)

TOLSTOY, LEO [Лев Николаевич Толстой]. 1972. *War and Peace*, trans. with an intro. by Rosemary Edmonds, 2 vols (London and Baltimore, MD: Penguin)

TORGAL, LUÍS REIS. 2009. *Estados Novos, Estado Novo: ensaios de história política e cultural*, 2nd edn, 2 vols (Coimbra: Universidade de Coimbra)

TRINDADE, LUÍS. 2008. *O estranho caso do nacionalismo português: o salazarismo entre a literatura e a política* (Lisbon: Imprensa de Ciências Sociais)

UNAMUNO, MIGUEL DE. 1941. *Por tierras de Portugal y de España (Austral)* (Madrid: Espasa-Calpe)

—— 2005. *En torno al casticismo*, ed. with an intro. by Jean-Claude Rabaté, Letras Hispánicas (Madrid: Cátedra)

VERDE, CESÁRIO. 1988. 'O sentimento dum ocidental', in *Obra completa de Cesário Verde*, ed. by Joel Serrão (Lisbon: Horizonte), pp. 151–58

—— 2011. *Cesário Verde: The Feeling of a Westerner*, trans. by Richard Zenith, ed. with an intro. by Anna M. Klobucka (Dartmouth: University of Massachusetts, Dartmouth)

VILLEGAS-ARISTIZÁBAL, LUCAS. 2007. 'Norman and Anglo-Norman Participation in the Iberian *Reconquista c.*1018 — *c.*1248' (unpublished doctoral thesis, University of Nottingham). Available online at <http://eprints.nottingham.ac.uk/10283/2/Norman_and_AngloNorman.pdf> [accessed 8 August 2015]

VIRGIL (Publius Vergilius Maro). 2008. *Aeneid: Books III–VI*, ed. by John Conyngton, with a general intro. by Philip Hardie and an intro. to the text by Anne Rogerson (Bristol: Phoenix)

VOLTAIRE [François-Marie Arouet]. 1984. *Candide, ou l'optimisme*, ed. with a commentary by Michel Char (Paris: Nathan)

WALLER, MICHAEL. 1988. 'Democratic Centralism: The Costs of Discipline', in *Communist Parties in Western Europe: Decline or Adaptation?*, ed. by Michael Waller and Meindert Fennema (Oxford: Basil Blackwell), pp. 7–25

WESSELING, ELISABETH. 1991. *Writing History as a Prophet: Postmodernist Innovations of the Historical Novel* (Amsterdam and Philadelphia, PA: John Benjamins)

WHEELER, DOUGLAS. 1978. *Republican Portugal* (Madison: University of Wisconsin Press)

WHITE, HAYDEN. 1973. *Metahistory: The Historical Imagination in Nineteenth-Century Europe* (Baltimore, MD, and London: Johns Hopkins University Press)

WILLIAMSON, EDWIN. 1987. 'Magical Realism and the Theme of Incest in *One Hundred Years of Solitude*' in *Gabriel García Márquez: New Readings*, ed. by Bernard McGuirk and Richard Cardwell (Cambridge: Cambridge University Press), pp. 45–63

ZAMORA, LOIS PARKINSON, and MONIKA KAUP. 2010. *Baroque New Worlds: Representation, Transculturation, Counterconquest* (Durham, NC, and London: Duke University Press)

ZEWDE, BAHRU. 2001. *A History of Modern Ethiopia, 1855–1991*, 2nd edn, revised and updated (Oxford: Currey)

ZOLA, ÉMILE. 1979. *Germinal*, ed. with an intro. by Coletter Becker (Paris: Garnier Frères)

—— 1993. *Germinal*, trans. by Peter Collier, with an intro. by Robert Lethbridge, Oxford World's Classics (Oxford and New York: Oxford University Press)

Filmography

Blindness, dir. by Fernando Meirelles (2008)
Brandos costumes, dir. by Alberto Seixas Santos (1975)
Enemy, dir. by Denis Villeneuve (2013)
A jangada de pedra, dir. by George Sluizer (2002)
Lassie Come Home, dir. by Fred M. Wilcox (1943)
Matar saudades, dir. by Fernando Lopes (1987)
A revolução de Maio, dir. by António Lopes Ribeiro (1936)

Broadcasts

O Tempo e a Alma, RTP, 1971–72
A Alma e a Gente, RTP2, 22 February 2003–17 December 2011

INDEX

A Caverna 101, 116 n. 36, 193, 119–20, 240 n. 22
Abelaira, Augusto 15
Abellán, José Luis 185
Adorno, Theodor 3, 21, 28 n. 39
Afonso I Henriques, King of Portugal 205, 206, 221, 230–33, 236, 240 n. 21, 241 n. 42
Agamben, Giorgio 130, 156 n. 20
Alfaya, Javier 153
Almeida, Miguel Vale de 194
Althusser, Louis 11, 17, 23, 61, 220, 240 n. 30
Anderson, Benedict:
  Imagined Communities 2, 27 n. 4
  print languages 174
Antunes, António Lobo 16, 203 n. 42
Appadurai, Arjun 165–66, 170, 192
  Modernity at Large 187
25 April Revolution 1974 2, 113, 152, 162, 171, 179, 202 n. 29
Arcimboldo, Guiseppe 94
Arnaut, Ana Paula 9, 12, 77, 79, 114 n. 4
As Intermitências da Morte 243–44
Asturias, Miguel Angel 45
Atkin, Rhian 111–12, 121, 229, 235–36, 240, 243
Ausonius, Decimus Magnus 158 n. 35

Bacon, Francis 209, 230, 239 n. 6
Badiou, Alain 130
Bakhtin, Mikhail M. 11–14, 30, 43, 74, 76–77
  carnival 12–13, 28 n. 33, 78–80, 86–88, 92–94
  dialogism 33, 35–36, 76
  heteroglossia 11, 28 n. 32
  polyphonic narrative 30, 67 n. 2
Ball, George 5
Balzac, Honoré de 7–8, 12, 27 n. 20
Barthes, Roland 122–23, 131
Baudrillard, Jean 2
  hyperreal 164–66, 200, n. 9
  simulation 124, 219, 244
Becker, Paulo 13, 199 n. 6
Beethoven, Ludwig van 21
Belsey, Catherine 17, 23
Ben-Moshe, Liat 159 n. 54
Benjamin, Walter 244
  on allegory 74, 81, 84–85
  Arcades Project 84–85, 244
  'Theses on the Nature of History' 64, 74, 85–86
  'What is Epic Theatre?' 9–10, 12–13, 37, 41, 125
Berrini, Beatriz 243
Besse, Maria Graciette 36, 37

Best, Steven, and Douglas Kellner 164, 200 n. 9, 237, 241 n. 44
Bloom, Harold 1, 26 n. 3
Borges, Jorge Luis 120–21
Bourdon, Albert Alain 39
Boxer, Charles 5
Brandão, Frei António 241 n. 39
  Crónica de D. Afonso Henriques 228, 232
brandos costumes 177–78, 179, 197, 201 n. 26, 213
Brecht, Bertolt 3, 113
  epic theatre 9–12, 13, 16–17, 23, 37, 39, 245
  on Lukács 9, 125
  The Life of Galileo 164
  Verfremdung (alienation) 13, 30, 41, 78
British Ultimatum, 1890 179
Butler, Judith:
  performance of gender 130, 157 n. 24

Cabral, Amílcar 3
  popular/ national culture 23, 42, 45
  'return to the source' 179, 185
Cadernos de Lanzarote 28 n. 36, 249
Calderón de la Barca, Pedro:
  La vida es sueño 63
Caminho Editora (press) 10, 28 n. 29, 45, 178
Camões, Luís Vaz de 15, 120, 122–24, 127–28, 249
  'Amor é um fogo' 144–45
  Os Lusíadas 15, 24, 80, 114 nn. 5 & 12, 123–24, 156 nn. 4 & 10, 167, 169, 176–77
  'Ilha dos Amores' sequence 162, 195, 203 n. 52
Carpentier, Alejo 78, 162
Catholic Church 4–5, 6, 29, 34, 71, 72–73, 74, 77–78, 79, 86–88, 89–91, 99, 101, 103–05, 111, 113, 115 nn. 21 &24, 117 n. 50, 148, 196
Catholicism 2, 5, 19, 37, 92, 97, 99, 103, 110, 113, 115 n. 28, 146, 148, 218
Cecucci, Piero 101–02, 106, 191–92, 195
Cervantes [Saavedra], Miguel de 12, 152
Chalmers, Alan D. 92–93
Chevalier, J., and A. Gheerbrandt 66
Cláudio, Mário 16
Cohen, Mitchell:
  rooted cosmopolitanism 25, 161
Community of Portuguese Language Countries (CPLP) 249
Conceição, Frei Cláudio da 89
corporeality 22, 71, 74, 77, 86–87, 92, 96, 103, 104–05, 108, 131–32, 136–37, 140–43, 154, 228–29, 240 n. 32

Index

Cortez, Alfredo:
   Tá mar! 125, 126
Costa, Horácio 12, 240 n. 31
counter-factual 17–18, 21–22, 23, 25, 50–51, 61, 71–74,
   75, 99–100, 113, 185, 205, 221, 230–31, 240 n. 26, 245
Cross, F.L. 115 n. 28
Cunhal, Álvaro 52, 69 n. 37

D'Angelo, Biagio 240, n. 22
Daniel, Mary L. 167–68, 170, 190
'De Expugnatione Lyxbonensi' 207, 231, 239 n. 3
Deleuze, Gilles, and Félix Guattari 130
Delgado, Humberto 54, 182, 202 n. 33
Derrida, Jacques 11
   artifactuality 164
   différance 130
Diamond, Elin 10, 127
Dionísio, Mário 8
'Discoveries', Portuguese Age of 5, 15, 27 n. 13, 169,
   171, 178–79
Disney, A.R. 115 n. 24
Duarte, Lélia Parreira 35, 37, 41, 57–58, 59
Duby, Georges 6

Eagleton, Terry 13, 77, 126, 240 n. 30
Eco, Umberto:
   rhizomatic labyrinth 121–22
Eden, Anthony 136, 157–58 n. 31
Engels, Friedrich 8
   see also Marx, Karl, *and* Friedrich Engels
Ensaio sobre a Cegueira 1, 26, 26 n. 3, 42, 111–13,
   117 n. 53, 121–22, 153–54, 203 n. 51, 216–17, 220,
   233, 247, 248–49
Estado Novo (Portugal) 3, 4–5, 27 nn. 10–14, 54, 66,
   68 nn. 18–19, 69 n. 40, 118, 194, 202 n. 33
   censorship 9, 10, 41, 119, 121, 124, 126, 1134
   colonial wars 24, 114 n. 1
   cultural policy 2, 80, 114, 121, 131, 156 n. 11
   FNAT 148
   historiography under 6, 19, 71–72, 79, 199 n. 5
   Mocidade Portuguesa 123, 148
   OMEN 203 n. 53
   PIDE/PVDE 34, 44–45, 68 n. 23, 202 n. 33
European Union/EEC 5, 25, 27 n. 16, 160–61, 163,
   167, 169, 171, 173–76, 178–79, 180, 182, 201 n. 21,
   203 n. 58

Fátima, cult of Our Lady of 80, 120, 148
feminism:
   feminist critique of Marxism 60–61
   Marxist feminism 3, 23, 30–31, 51, 55, 108–09, 111,
      195–96, 148
   radical feminism in Portugal 69 n. 38
   (Portuguese) Republican feminism 159 n. 46
Ferreira, Ana Paula 8, 9, 60–61, 151, 159 n. 46
Ferro, António 145, 156 n. 15, 159 n. 33
Firpo, Luigi 106

First Republic (Portugal) 34, 37, 68 n. 17, 128
First World War 38, 68 n. 16
Flor, Fernando de la 88, 115 n. 22
Fogaça, Júlio 52
Foley, Barbara 16
Francès-Dumas, Marie 42
Franco [Bahamonde], Francisco 118, 152, 159 n. 52
Freud, Sigmund 100, 102, 116 n. 32, 130
Freyre, Gilberto 203 n. 52
Frier, David 53–54, 97, 105–06, 107, 143, 150, 152, 167,
   168–69, 175–76, 177, 184, 189, 191, 199 n. 4
Fukuyama, Francis:
   The End of History 246

Galilei, Galileo 164, 166
García Márquez, Gabriel 45, 78
   Cien años de soledad 30, 46–48, 50, 63–66, 67 n. 3,
      69 n. 47
Gersão, Teolinda 16
Gheerbrandt, A., *see* Chevalier, J., and A. Gheerbrandt
Gil, José 178
globalization 22, 171
Gobbi, Márcia B. Zamboni 240 n. 36
Goethe, Johann Wolfgang von:
   'Die Zauberlehrling' 209
Gomes, Renato Cordeiro 35–36, 42
Gracián, Baltasar 92
   El criticón 94–95, 115 n. 27
Gramsci, Antonio 3, 244
   on democratic centralism 51–53, 68 n. 33, 69 n. 34
   hegemony 42–43, 45, 51, 54–55, 63, 66, 75, 86, 97,
      101, 113, 124, 152, 160, 221, 237
   historical/ revolutionary block 30, 42, 105–07, 119,
      152, 237, 246
   intellectuals 42, 52–53, 107–08, 113, 118–19, 150–52,
      221
Grossegesse, Orlando 67 n. 8, 179–80, 181, 182, 183–
   85, 198–99, 202 nn. 30 & 32, 204 n. 55, 225
Guattari, Félix, *see* Deleuze, Gilles, and Félix Guattari
Gusmão, Bartolomeu Lourenço de 19–20, 23, 72–73,
   81, 83, 107, 114 n. 4, 218

Halbwachs, Maurice 2
Hammond, John 39, 68 n. 23
Hegel, Georg Wilhelm Friedrich 98–99, 102, 210, 215,
   239 n. 17
Heidegger, Martin 210, 220–21, 244
Herculano, Alexandre 240 nn. 36 & 37
Herrick, Robert:
   'To the Virgins' 142
História do Cerco de Lisboa 1, 7, 25–26, 119, 121, 156,
   200 n. 12, 205–41, 243–44, 245, 248
   aletheia 206, 215, 217, 220–21, 225
   alter-ego/heteronym 25–26
      Mogueime 206, 227–28, 229–30, 233–34, 238
      Ouroana 227, 228–29, 233–34, 238
   balcony 227, 235–36, 238

desdobramento/self-doubling 26, 213, 221, 222–24, 230
Islam 211, 214, 212–13
light v. darkness 215, 217, 218, 219–20, 238
mist/fog 218–19, 220, 223
muezzin 211–12, 219, 222, 238, 240 n. 21
Platonic cave 26, 219–20
'reconquest' of Portugal 206
siege/besiegement (as symbol) 205, 207–09, 213, 235–36
windows 217–18, 223, 227
historical novel 5–9, 15–16, 31–32, 113
historiography 2–3, 15–16, 18, 21, 26, 64, 73–74, 82, 181–82, 205, 209–11, 214, 245–46
 história pátria 6, 11, 25, 71, 74, 77, 113, 184–85, 205, 213–14, 222
 historical materialism 14, 18, 22–23, 26, 66, 73, 86, 204 n. 55, 215, 246
 new historicism 2
 nouvelle histoire 2, 6
Hitler, Adolf 62–63, 118
Hobbes, Thomas:
 Leviathan 91, 93
 sovereignty 86
Hogue, Bev 204 n. 58
Holton, Kimberley da Costa 148
Homer 65, 169
 The Odyssey 190–91, 203 nn. 45 & 46
Huici, Adrián 207, 239 n. 2
Hutcheon, Linda 10
 historiographical metafiction 16–17
 A Poetics of Postmodernism 17–18

Italian-Ethiopian War 134–36, 157–58 n. 31

Jameson, Fredric:
 Archaeology of the Future 246
 Postmodernism, or the Cultural Logic of Late Capitalism 16, 23
Jangada de Pedra 1, 22, 25, 61, 124, 156, 160–204, 205, 207, 212, 220–21, 231, 236, 243, 247
 25 Abril 171, 178–79
 Azores 165, 177
 Balearic Islands 201 n. 22
 Canary Islands 201 n. 22
 Celtic myths 169–70, 188, 189, 191, 203 n. 39
  Branwen 203 n. 44
  Maele Duìn 191
 coincidence 167–68, 200 n. 12
 disaster narrative genre 160, 167
 exhumation 182–83, 197–98, 202 n. 32, 204 n. 58
 Greco-Roman myths:
  Aeneas 190
  Ariadne 189–91, 203 n. 47
  Dido 190
  Odysseus 203 n. 46
  Penelope 190–91
  Sibyl of Cumae 190, 203 n. 44

Iberianism 203 n. 38
 'Iberianist' protests 174
 late 19th/early 20th century Iberianism 25, 179–80, 184
 'trans-Iberianism' 161, 170–71, 175–76, 179–81, 182–83, 185–86, 197–98
 islands, magical/ mythical 161–62, 195–97, 203 n. 39
 luso-tropicalism 197, 203 n. 52
 mass media 25, 160–61, 163–66, 174–75, 192
 mass pregnancy 195–97, 204 n. 54
 mock-epic genre 167, 169
 movement of Iberian Peninsula 124
 narrative voice, *see* narrative voicing, in Jangada
 Orce Man 183, 198–99, 203 n. 49, 204 n. 57
 regional politics in Iberia:
  Basque Country 175
  Catalonia 175, 201 n. 22
 supernatural events (*insólitos*) 160, 161–62, 168–69, 176, 188–89
Jelinkski, Jack B. 47–48
João V, King of Portugal 3, 19, 21, 71–72, 77, 78–79, 86–91, 93, 101, 114 nn. 8 & 9, 115 nn. 21 & 24, 116 n. 37
Jorge, Lídia 16
Junqueiro, Abílio Manuel Guerra 201 nn. 19 & 24

Kabbala 115 n. 28
Kaufman, Helena 121, 123, 200 n. 10, 207, 231, 241 n. 41
 and Anna Klobucka 11
 and José Ornelas 15, 163, 167
Kayman, Martin 201 n. 18
Kellner, Douglas 100, 108–09, 117 n. 46
 see also Best, Steven, and Douglas Kellner
Kennedy, John F. 5, 174
Klobucka, Anna [M.] 161, 186, 187, 192–93
 and Mark Sabine 130, 131, 157 n. 24
 see also Kaufman, Helena, and Anna Klobucka
Kollontai, Alexandra 31, 55, 56–57, 69 n. 39
Korhonen, Kuisma 15, 246
Ksar El-Kebir, Battle of, 1578 218
Kubrick, Stanley:
 Spartacus 174

Lacan, Jacques 130, 138
Laclau, Ernesto, and Chantal Mouffe 185, 237
Le Goff, Jacques 2, 6
Leibniz, Gottfried Wilhelm 214–25, 239 nn. 14 & 15
León, Fray Luis de:
 'El aire se serena' 82
Lepecki, Maria Lúcia 29, 41
Leslie, Esther 74, 84, 86
Letízia, Marie-Eve 60, 69 nn. 42 & 43
Levantado do Chão 1, 22–23, 24, 26, 29–70, 71, 73–74, 75, 76, 77, 80–81, 84, 90, 97, 100, 103, 105, 107, 109, 110, 113, 118, 119, 140–41, 149, 152, 153, 155, 162, 177, 187–88, 189, 192, 196, 217, 221, 233, 236, 237, 244, 245, 246, 247

25 Abril Revolution, depiction of 29, 54, 59–60
ants 23, 49–50
biblical parody 35
  flight into Egypt 36
  Genesis 33, 56
  nativity 50–51, 59
  parables 34, 36, 67 n. 9
  passion of Christ 40
  resurrection 35, 66, 80
Constante the dog 44–45, 50, 54
  see also Jangada de Pedra, Dog
Estado Novo, depiction of 34–35, 39, 50, 52, 56, 62–63
First Republic, depiction of 37–39
folklore 36, 42–45, 68 n. 14
hares 44, 54
kite (*milhano*) 23, 66, 73, 153
Montemor riots 1958 54, 69 n. 37
narrative voicing 14, 24, 30, 33–34, 35–38, 39, 41–42, 49, 50, 69 n. 42
perception of time, depictions of 29, 46, 48–49, 64–65
Portuguese Communist Party, depiction of 30, 34, 42, 49–50, 51–54, 68 nn. 27 & 31, 69 n. 37, 221
rape, at Fonte do Ameeiro 49, 55, 58–59, 69 n. 43
strikes 34–35, 38, 39–41, 48, 49–50, 52, 54, 68 nn. 20 & 27
threshing machine (*debulhador*) 40, 245
women/ women's emancipation 37, 51, 55–61, 111
Lima, Isabel Pires de 196–97, 200 n. 12, 203 n. 50
Lima, Mirella Márcia Longo Vieira 102, 115–16 n. 31
Lisbon:
  Alfama 212
  Castelo de S. Jorge 79–80, 114 n. 11, 123, 156 n. 12, 212, 221–22
  cathedral (*Sé*) 114 n. 11, 123, 156 n. 12, 218
  Hieronymite monastery 121
  Mouraria 114 n. 11, 212–13
  Prazeres cemetery 121
  São Cristóvão 213
Lopes, Óscar 78, 96, 116 n. 39
Lough, Francis 177
Lourenço, António Apolinário 12, 200 n. 10
Lourenço, Eduardo 99, 115 n. 29
  'Identidade e memória' 178
  Labirinto da saudade 15, 199
Lowenthal, David 2
Lukács, György [Georg] 7, 9, 11–12, 30, 64, 214
  The Historical Novel 7, 51
  Studies in European Realism 7–8, 27 n. 20
Lyotard, Jacques François 2, 11
  The Differend 18
Mabinogion, Y 203 n. 44
Machado, Antonio 183–86, 196
  'A Don Francisco Giner de los Ríos' 198
  apocryphal history 185, 198–99
  Campos de Castilla 185–86
    'A un olmo seco' 198

  Juan de Mairena 185
magical realism 45–47
Manual de Pintura e Caligrafia 9, 225, 240 n. 31
Maravall, José Antonio 88, 92, 95–96
Marcuse, Herbert 3, 23, 61, 75, 97, 100–05, 108–13, 115 n. 30, 116 n. 34, 117 n. 46, 220, 237, 244
  'The Affirmative Character of Culture' 249
  Eros and Civilization 100
  An Essay on Liberation 100, 108, 115–16 n. 31
  on feminism 104, 108–09, 110–11, 194
  'Liberation from the Affluent Society' 108
  'Marxism and Feminism' 108
  One-Dimensional Man 100–02, 116 n. 32
  performance principle 108–10, 117 n. 48, 247
  surplus repression 100–01
  on technology 100–01, 105
Maria Ana Josefa, Archduchess of Austria and Queen of Portugal 78–79, 93
Maria Bárbara, Infanta of Portugal and Queen of Spain 77
Martin, Gerald 45–46, 47, 48, 64
Martins, Adriana [Alves de Paula] 243
  see also Sabine, Mark, and Adriana Alves de Paula Martins
Marx, Karl 67, 100–01, 102, 116 n. 34
  Capital 100–01
  Grundrisse 101
Marx, Karl, & Friedrich Engels:
  The German Ideology 18
  The Holy Family 28 n. 34
Marxism 3–4, 7, 11, 22–23, 30–31, 45, 46, 52, 73–75, 97, 116 n. 31, 157 n. 27, 161, 171, 186, 244, 245–46
  class consciousness 7–8, 23, 25, 26, 30, 34–36, 39–42, 44, 48–50, 51, 56, 63–64, 67, 74–75, 97, 113, 149, 155, 192, 237, 245 democratic centralism 30, 51–52, 156
  Leninism 3, 11, 28 n. 31, 246
  phenomenological Marxism 220, 244
  psychoanalytical Marxism 11, 111, 119, 224, 240 n. 30
  Stalinism 19, 27 n. 19. 30, 246
Maxwell, Kenneth 67 n. 12, 200–01 n. 18
McNee, Malcolm 158–59 n. 43
Memorial do Convento 1, 19–21, 22, 23–24, 25, 53, 60, 67, 71–117, 118, 120, 140–41, 142, 149, 151, 152, 153, 154, 162, 177, 187–88, 189, 190, 207, 218, 231, 233, 236, 241 n. 41, 247, 248
  baroque style 78, 85, 88, 92, 96, 113
  see also neo-baroque
  carnival (*entrudo*) 147
  emblems 85, 94
  Franciscan order 77, 79
  grotesque imagery 77, 86–87, 90–95
  Inquisition 72, 81, 82, 85, 91, 97, 105, 116 nn. 43 & 44
  lunar imagery 72, 107, 110, 117 n. 50
  Mafra palace-monastery 19, 71–72, 75, 78, 80, 88–90, 91, 101, 02, 105, 114 n. 2, 149

memorialism 76–77
music 19–21, 74, 81–85, 86, 102, 114 n. 14
passarola/ flying machine 23, 72–75, 78, 82, 83,
    84–85, 86, 91, 96–98, 99–100, 101–03, 104–07,
    115–16 n. 31, 116 n. 43, 149
phallic imagery 75, 88–89, 90, 93, 111–12, 117 n. 50
São Sebastião da Pedreira 24, 82, 85, 93, 97, 101–02,
    104–05, 192
technology 23–24, 75, 97, 100–01, 105
vision 163, 215–16, 226
    see also Saramago, José
vontades/ wills 23, 71, 72, 73–74, 90–91, 96–101,
    104–06, 107–08, 110, 113, 116 nn. 39 & 44, 149
Meneses, Filipe Ribeiro de 202 n. 33
Mesquita, Maria Luísa Raimundo 208, 240 n. 28
Miguéis, José Rodrigues:
    Gente da Terceira Classe 159 n. 45
Millán-Astray, José 152–53
Miranda, Rui Gonçalves 128–29
Montaigne, Michel de 116 n. 41
Monteiro, Luís de Sttau:
    Felizmente há luar! 9, 107
Monteiro, Padre Manuel 114 n. 8
Mouffe, Chantal, *see* Laclau, Ernesto *and* Mouffe,
    Chantal
Mussolini, Benito 118, 136, 157–58 n. 31

Namora, Fernando:
    O trigo e o joio 36
national identity 2, 6, 15–16, 25, 74, 81, 122–23, 152,
    154, 163, 169–77, 184–85, 194, 202 n. 30, 205–06,
    212–13, 222, 237
NATO 5, 29, 165, 178, 186–87
neo-realism 3–4, 7–9, 11, 27 n. 19, 29–32, 36–37,
    39–40, 67 n. 4, 113
    symbolic encryption in 30, 34, 40–41, 50–51, 66,
    67 n. 9, 105
Nora, Pierre 2

O Conto da Ilha Desconhecida 186
O Homem Duplicado 26 n. 3, 236–37, 244
Objecto Quase 12, 28 nn. 34 & 35, 33, 217
Oliveira Filho, Odil de 12, 79–80, 94
Oliveira Marques, António Henrique de 90–91
Oliveira Martins, Joaquim Pedro 239
Oliveira, Carlos de 9
    Uma abelha na chuva 50
Ornelas, José [N.] 105, 112, 117 n. 53, 154
    see also Kaufman, Helena, and José Ornelas
Orpheus 116 n. 39
Os Apontamentos 202 n. 37
Ousmane, Sembène 10, 28
    Les Bouts de bois de Dieu 45
Ovid (Publius Ovidius Naso):
    Metamorphoses 191

palimpsest 121, 212

Palmer, Bryan 18
Paz, Octavio 130
Pereira, José Fernandes 89, 116 n. 37
Pereira, Paulo 114 n. 1
Pessoa, Fernando 24, 25, 118–21, 126, 127, 128, 129–33,
    136, 145–46, 148, 154–55, 156 nn. 1, 5, 18, & 19,
    157 n. 26 &27, 179, 222–24, 228, 240 nn. 20, 28,
    & 34, 241 n. 44, 249
    Alberto Caeiro (heteronym) 228, 240 n. 34
    Álvaro de Campos (heteronym)
        'Lisbon Revisited 1926' 137, 158 n. 32
        'Tabacaria' 148–49
    Bernardo Soares ('semi-'heteronym)
        Livro do desassossego 130, 131, 134, 141–42,
        157 n. 26, 158 n. 34 & 39
    Fernando Pessoa '*ele-mesmo*'
        'Autopsicografia' 130–31, 133, 137, 145, 157 n. 29
        'Chove? Nenhuma chuva cai' 136–37, 146
        'Chove. Que fiz eu da vida?' 136–37
        'Ela canta, pobre ceifeira' 146, 150, 159 n. 44
        fingimento 130–31, 137, 143–45, 222–25
    Frederico Reis (heteronym), on Ricardo Reis
        132–33, 157 n. 30
    heteronymity 25–26, 130, 131, 155, 156 n. 1, 5, & 19,
        157 n. 24, 202 n. 34, 227–28
    Mensagem 124, 131, 154, 157 n. 27, 201 n. 25, 218
    neo-paganism 132–33, 148, 156 n. 13, 158 n. 40
    'Notas para uma regra de vida' 144, 146, 156,
        158 n. 41, 158–59 n. 43
    political writings 148–49, 157 n. 27, 159 n. 49
    Ricardo Reis (heteronym)
        'A flor que és, não a que dás, eu quero' 142
        'Ouvi dizer que outrora' 134–36, 143
        'Sábio ele que se contenta com o espectáculo do
        mundo' 154, 156 n. 2, 158 n. 36
        'Saudoso já deste verão que vejo' 158 n. 37
        'Vem-te sentar comigo Lídia' 133–34
        'Vivem em nós inúmeros' 138–39, 158 n. 33,
        227–28, 240 n. 27
Pina, Luís de 125, 156 n. 15
Pinto, António Costa 194
Pires, José Cardoso 9, 15
    O Delfim 9
Pita, António Pedro 8–9
Plato 26, 102, 132, 219–20, 240 n. 22, 244
Portuguese Communist Party (PCP) 3, 11, 27 n. 8,
    28 n. 31, 146, 187, 202 n. 33
    see also Levantado do Chão
Portuguese Socialist Party (PS) 15, 169, 187, 202 n. 37
post-structuralism 2–4, 11, 15, 18, 73, 119, 121, 155,
    242, 244
postmodernism:
    in literature 4, 9, 16–18
    in philosophy 23–24, 27 n. 9, 118–19, 130, 220,
        245–46
postmodernity 3–5, 14, 15, 21, 25, 26, 27 n. 7,
    28 n. 38, 129, 205, 207, 237, 245, 246

Praz, Mario 78
Presedo, Elvira S. 114 n. 1

Queirós, José Maria Eça de 127–28
　O Crime do Padre Amaro 127
　Os Maias 127
Quental, Antero de 179–80

Rabelais, François 12, 92
Raby, D. L. 52, 54, 69 nn. 35 & 37
Rancière, Jacques:
　politics of literature 128–29
Rebelo, Luís de Sousa 168–69, 170, 177–78, 179, 185
Redol, Alves 7, 9
　Barranco de cegos 9, 126
　Gaibéus 31–32, 40, 41, 67 n. 4
Reis, Carlos 2, 4, 77
Ribeiro, António Lopes:
　A revolução de Maio 125
Ricardo Reis 1, 24–25, 61, 63, 80, 118–59, 160, 162, 165, 171, 179, 183–84, 187, 196, 197, 198, 206–07, 208–09, 216, 219, 221, 224, 227, 229, 239–40 n. 20, 240 n. 32, 241 n. 44, 243–44, 247, 249
　canon, literary 24, 120–21, 122–23, 127–29, 131, 136, 145, 154–55, 156 n. 6
　Don Juan legend 145, 155
　Estado Novo (depiction of) 119–20, 122–25, 148, 247
　Fernando Pessoa ('undead' Pessoa) 123–24, 137, 140–41, 143–44, 145, 153, 155, 184, 227
　flâneur/ flânerie 119, 127–28, 134, 144, 155
　Herbert Quain, *The God of the Labyrinth* 120–21, 122, 124, 137, 156 n. 5
　Hotel Bragança 119, 127, 134, 138, 140, 158 n. 39, 203 n. 41
　mirrors 138
　naval revolt 1936 118, 120, 155
　newspapers 120, 122–23, 125–26, 134–36, 139–40, 147, 148, 150, 164
　'sad Epicurianism' 119–20, 132–33, 134, 136, 142–43
　statues 122, 145, 158 n. 42
　　Adamastor 124, 145, 155
　　Camões 122, 124, 127–28, 145, 148
　　Eça de Queirós 127
　　Pinheiro Chagas 123
Roberts, Stephen 152, 159 n. 51
Roseingrave, Thomas 115 n. 18

Sabine, Mark 67 n. 2, 68 n. 15, 111, 158 n. 41, 159 n. 44, 201 nn. 22 & 27, 203 nn. 44 & 49, 239 n. 19
　and Adriana Alves de Paula Martins 4, 112, 120–22
　and Claire Williams 6–7, 15, 28 n. 28
　see also Klobucka, Anna M., and Mark Sabine
Said, Edward:
　Orientalism 172
Salazar, António de Oliveira 4–5, 6, 24, 27 nn. 10–12, 34, 41, 42, 61–62, 118–19, 134, 148, 156 n. 6

Salazarism 5, 7, 71, 80–81, 85, 123, 124–25, 146, 147–48, 155, 218, 231, 248
　see also Estado Novo
Saldívar, José David 47
Salinas, Francisco 82
Santareno, Bernardo:
　O Judeu 9
　A Traição do Padre Martinho 9
Santos Alonso 95, 115 n. 27
Santos, [Maria] Irene Ramalho 155
Santos, Boaventura de Sousa:
　semiperipherality 173
Santos, José Adelino dos 54
Santos, Rosemary Conceição de 114 n. 6
Sapega, Ellen 15, 71, 114 n. 11, 124, 127, 156, 199, 239
Saraiva, José Hermano 6, 15, 27 n. 17, 222, 240
Saramago, José:
　see also entries for individual works
　allegory, use of 1, 12, 19, 243, 244, 248
　　in *A Caverna* 219
　　in *Cegueira* 26, 117 n. 53, 122, 153
　　in *História* 205, 214
　　in *Jangada* 160, 163, 170, 175, 182, 185–86, 188–89, 193–95, 197, 203 n. 49
　　in *Levantado* 23, 44–45, 50–51, 61
　　in *Memorial* 24, 71, 73–74, 75, 81, 84–87, 91, 94, 113, 114 n. 1
　　in *Ricardo Reis* 155
　anachronism, use of 22, 23, 39, 74, 104–08, 205–06, 211, 213
　apocrypha, in 'historical' novels 21, 23–24, 68 n. 20, 72–73, 127, 153, 184–85, 198–99, 230
　Biblical allusion & parody 80, 168
　　see also Levantado do Chão
　blindness, as symbol 66, 111, 123–24, 129, 145, 153–54, 159 n. 54, 211–12, 217, 219, 220, 238, 239 n. 18, 240 n. 2
　characters, construction of 32, 36, 68 n. 20, 111, 166, 167, 190, 233
　corporeal imagery 48–49, 74–75, 78–79, 86–89, 90–95, 112–13, 147–48, 236
　de-/re-construction of language 12, 33–34, 113, 120, 129
　disability 153–54, 147–48, 152–54, 159 n. 54, 247
　　see also blindness
　excoriation (as metaphor) 33–34, 67 n. 8
　on the family 48–49, 55–58, 61–63, 147, 149, 150–52, 188, 191, 193–96, 148–49
　fantasy, in novels 21–22, 23–24, 127, 245
　　in *Jangada* 162–64, 166, 167–68, 185, 188
　　in *Levantado* 30, 35, 41, 44, 49–50, 51, 65–66
　　in *Memorial* 71, 73–75, 78, 96, 99–100, 113
　　in *Ricardo Reis* 126
　film adaptations of works 1, 26 n. 3
　Fundação José Saramago 27 n. 8, 249
　gender 22, 55–57, 61, 67, 95–96, 120–22, 130,

140–41, 156, 157 n. 24, 176, 189–90, 222, 236, 243, 247
masculinity 109–13, 117 n. 49, 229, 234–35
femininity 61, 97, 104 107, 108–11, 113, 117 n. 49, 147, 151, 176, 188–89, 247–48
hands, as symbol:
  in *Memorial* 84, 97, 106, 111–13, 115 n. 28
  in *Ricardo Reis* 141–42, 159 n. 46
inter-identity 26, 100, 173, 175–76, 205
journalism 249
labyrinth 4, 121, 217
  in *História* 215–16
  in *Jangada* 189
  in *Ricardo Reis* 121–22, 124, 129, 208
literary awards and prizes 1, 26 n. 2, 27 n. 8, 249
on *lusofonia* 194, 249
micropolitics 26, 31, 60–61, 66–67, 75, 103–04, 161–62, 187–89, 194, 205, 207, 236–37, 247, 248–49
miracles 19, 72, 79, 80, 81, 119–20, 148, 169, 195–96, 198, 231–33, 241 n. 42
narrative voicing 8, 9, 13–14, 20, 22, 248
  in *Jangada* 164, 166, 176–77, 189, 195–96
  in *Levantado* 32, 34, 35–36, 41, 48, 50–51, 55, 57, 66, 67 n. 2
  in *Ricardo Reis* 123
neo-baroque 9, 12, 24, 74–75, 78–79, 84, 86, 91–92, 94–95, 114 nn. 6 & 7, 224
the Other:
  becoming other 25, 119, 140–41, 145, 180, 181*6*, 221–27, 229
  self-Other relations 25–26, 35, 75, 96, 112, 131, 144, 153, 154, 161, 171–73, 176, 180–81, 187–88, 206, 213, 217, 220, 222, 227–28, 236–38, 243–44
parody 13
  in *História* 222, 235
  in *Jangada* 161, 163–64, 167, 169, 174, 176, 203 n. 46, 222
  in *Levantado* 31–32, 36–37, 39–40, 41, 49–51
  in *Memorial* 78, 80, 87
  in *Ricardo Reis* 133–34, 155
and Portuguese Communist Party 3, 7, 11, 27 n. 8, 52
and Portuguese Writers' Association 10
Prémio José Saramago 249
punctuation 12–13, 20, 32
sexuality:
  asexuality 93, 141–42, 190
  heteronormative romance 56–57, 61, 140–41, 152, 191, 194, 236, 248–49
  homosexuality, *see* non-heteronormative sexuality
  marriage/matrimony 56–58, 77–78, 103–04, 143, 150–51, 189–91, 196, 236
  micropolitics of desire 60–61, 87, 100–04, 113, 151–52, 247, 248
  non-heteronormative sexuality 194, 248
  reciprocity in sexual intercourse 58, 103–04, 188–89, 236

Sado-Masochism 95–96
sexual violence 49, 87, 93, 109–12, 231, 234
skin shedding, as metaphor 225–26, 240 n. 31
statements on Marxism 3–4
subjectivity 1, 26, 31, 36, 67, 119, 129–30, 131–32, 136–41, 154–55, 172, 177–78, 222–26, 228, 237, 241 n. 44, 247, 248–49
translations of works 1, 26 n. 2, 67 n. 1, 249
work as translator 10–11, 45
on 'usefulness' 24, 144–45, 149, 155–56, 227, 230, 246
vision, as symbol 244
  in *História* 205, 208, 211–12, 213- 14, 215–17, 218–22, 226–27, 236, 239 n. 1
  in *Levantado* 23, 31, 63, 66
  in *Memorial* 22, 23, 73–74, 91, 99, 104, 105, 107–08
  in *Ricardo Reis* 123, 126, 153–55
  see also blindness
visionary characters 23, 51, 61, 104–05, 109, 112, 151–52, 153–54, 166, 187–88, 190–91, 215–16, 224–27, 233, 236, 241 n. 41
Sarduy, Severo:
  Barroco 78, 114 n. 7
Scarlatti, Domenico 19–21, 72, 74, 75, 81–85, 102, 115 nn. 17 & 18
Schoenberg, Arnold 21
Seara nova (journal) 7, 40, 67 n. 9, 115 n. 30
Sebastianism 218, 239–40 n. 20
Second World War 5, 35, 47
Seixo, Maria Alzira 217, 227
Seneca, Lucius Annaeus 215, 218
Shakespeare, William 162
Siege of Vienna, 1683 214, 239 n. 13
Silva, António 125
Silva, Maria Corrêa 180
Silva, Prioress Paula Teresa da, 115 n. 21
Silva, Teresa Cristina Cerdeira da 2, 9, 24, 28 n. 37, 40, 44, 67 n. 4, 68 nn. 14, 15, & 20, 98, 159 n. 48
Simões, Manuel 32, 43, 67 n. 6, 68 n. 14
Soares, Mário 15, 187, 202 n. 37
socialist realism 7, 29–30, 46
Spanish Civil War 41, 116, 151, 152, 179, 182
Spanish Succession, War of 72
Spanish-American War, 1898 179
Spivak, Gayatri Chakravorty 36
Steiner, George 130
Stevenson, Robert Louis:
  Dr Jekyll and Mr Hyde 223–24
Swift, Jonathan 91–93
  Gulliver's Travels 86, 90, 92

Terry, Arthur 184–85, 202 n. 34
Thomas, Hugh 159 n. 53
Tiersky, Ronald 52, 68 n. 33
Todos os Nomes 121–22, 204 n. 58, 236–37, 243–44
Tolstoy, Leo:
  War and Peace 68 n. 27

Torah 115 n. 28

Unamuno, Miguel de 152–54, 159 n. 51, 184–85
　En torno al casticismo 184
　on Franco 152, 159 n. 52
　on Millán-Astray 152, 153, 159 n. 53
　Por tierras de Portugal y de España 1172–73, 176–77, 198, 201 n. 19
Unitarianism 115 n. 28
utopia 4, 14, 23–26, 245–46, 248
　in Fernando Pessoa's works 159 n. 43
　in *História* 26, 207, 236
　in *Jangada* 25, 160–62, 179, 184–85, 186–88, 191–92, 196–98, 199 n. 4
　in *Levantado* 51, 61
　in *Memorial* 22–23, 71–72, 74, 75, 81, 93, 96, 100–08
　in postmodernist fiction 17–18, 28 n. 38
　in *Ricardo Reis* 119, 127

Vakil, AbdoolKarim 156 n. 12, 211, 239 n. 1
Verde, Cesário 127
　'Sentimento dum Ocidental' 127–28, 129
Viçoso, Víctor 9, 67 n. 4

Vidigal, Germano Santos 34, 41, 49–50, 245
Vieira, Padre António 201 n. 25
Vieira, Tomé:
　Conspiração 148, 149
Villalar, Battle of, 1521 181–82
Virgil (Virgilius Publius Maro) 158 n. 35
　Aeneid 167, 169, 190
Voltaire (François-Marie Arouet)
　Candide 214, 239 n. 15

Wesseling, Elisabeth 17–18, 21–22, 28 n. 38, 162
　ucronian fiction 17–18, 21
White, Hayden 2, 211, 233
　Metahistory 15, 214, 239 nn. 9 & 10
　motific characterization 21, 209–10, 219, 238
Williams, Claire, *see* Sabine, Mark *and* Williams, Claire
Williamson, Edwin 46–47, 63–64, 68 n. 25, 69 n. 47
Wordsworth, William 159

Zenith, Richard 156 n. 1, 157 n. 26
Zola, Émile 8
　Germinal 35, 66

www.ingramcontent.com/pod-product-compliance
Lightning Source LLC
LaVergne TN
LVHW061249060426
835507LV00017B/1984